D0916433

The Age of Reformation

Feb 23 Ryrie Preface, Chronology
pp xiii - xiv; xvii - xx

Religion, Politics and Society in Britain
Series editor: Keith Robbins

The Age of Reformation

The Tudor and Stewart Realms 1485–1603

Alec Ryrie

Routledge
Taylor & Francis Group

LONDON AND NEW YORK

First published 2009 by Pearson Education Limited

Published 2013 by Routledge
2 Park Square, Milton Park, Abingdon, Oxon OX14 4RN
711 Third Avenue, New York, NY 10017, USA

Routledge is an imprint of the Taylor & Francis Group, an informa business

Copyright © 2009, Taylor & Francis.

The right of Alec Ryrie to be identified as author of this work has been asserted
by him in accordance with the Copyright, Designs and Patents Act 1988.

All rights reserved. No part of this book may be reprinted or reproduced or utilised in any form or
by any electronic, mechanical, or other means, now known or hereafter invented, including
photocopying and recording, or in any information storage or retrieval system, without permission
in writing from the publishers.

Notices
Knowledge and best practice in this field are constantly changing. As new research and experience
broaden our understanding, changes in research methods, professional practices, or medical
treatment may become necessary.

Practitioners and researchers must always rely on their own experience and knowledge in
evaluating and using any information, methods, compounds, or experiments described herein. In
using such information or methods they should be mindful of their own safety and the safety of
others, including parties for whom they have a professional responsibility.

To the fullest extent of the law, neither the Publisher nor the authors, contributors, or editors,
assume any liability for any injury and/or damage to persons or property as a matter of products
liability, negligence or otherwise, or from any use or operation of any methods, products,
instructions, or ideas contained in the material herein.

ISBN: 978-1-4058-3557-2 (pbk)

British Library Cataloguing in Publication Data
A CIP catalogue record for this book can be obtained from the British Library

Library of Congress Cataloging in Publication Data
Ryrie, Alec.
    The age of Reformation : the Tudor and Stewart realms, 1485–1603 / Alec Ryrie, – 1st ed.
        p. cm.
    Includes bibliographical references and index.
    ISBN 978-1-4058-3557-2 (pbk.)
    1. Reformation. 2. Great Britain–Church history. 3. Great Britain–Church history–
16th century. I. Title.
    BR375.R97 2009
    274.1′06–dc22
                                                                                        2008054671

Set by 35 in 10/13.5pt Sabon

For my students

Contents

Series Editor's Preface

No understanding of British history is possible without grappling with the relationship between religion, politics and society. How that should be done, however, is another matter. Historians of religion, who have frequently thought of themselves as ecclesiastical historians, have had one set of preoccupations. Political historians have had another. They have acknowledged, however, that both religion and politics can only be understood, in any given period, in a social context. This series makes the interplay between religion, politics and society its preoccupation. Even so, it does not assume that what is entailed by religion and politics remains the same throughout, to be considered as a constant in separate volumes merely because of the passage of time.

In its completed form the series will have probed the nature of these links from *c.*600 to the present day and offered a perspective, over such a long period, that has not before been attempted in a systematic fashion. There is, however, no straitjacket that requires individual authors to adhere to a common understanding of what such an undertaking involves. Even if there could be a general agreement about concepts, that is to say about what religion is or how politics can be identified, the social context of such categorisations is not static. The spheres notionally allocated to the one or to the other alter with circumstances. Sometimes it might appear that they cannot be separated. Sometimes it might appear that they sharply conflict. Each period under review will have its defining characteristics in this regard.

It is the Christian religion, in its manifold institutional manifestations, with which authors are overwhelmingly concerned since it is with conversion that the series begins. It ends, however, with a volume in which Christianity exists alongside other world religions but in a society frequently perceived to be secular. Yet, what de-Christianisation is taken to be depends upon what Christianisation has been taken to be. There is, therefore, a relationship between topics that are tackled in the first volume, and those considered in the last, which might at first sight seem unlikely. In between, of course are the 'Christian Centuries' which, despite their label, are no less full of 'boundary disputes', both before and after the Reformation. The perspective of the series, additionally, is broadly pan-insular. The Britain of 600 is plainly not the Britain of the early twenty-first century. However, the current political structures of Britain-Ireland have arguably owed as much to religion as to politics. Christendom has been inherently ambiguous.

It would be surprising if readers, not to mention authors, understood the totality of the picture that is presented in the same way. What is common, however, is a realisation that the narrative of religion, politics and society in Britain is not a simple tale that points in a single direction but rather one of enduring and by no means exhausted complexity.

Keith Robbins, November 2005

Preface

The sixteenth century was an age of reformation in the British Isles – in several senses. Most obviously, this was the century of the Protestant Reformation, which touched every part of British society, culture and politics. It was also the century when 'Britain' – the name of an ancient Roman province – began to be on people's lips again. This book ends in 1603, when for the first time ever, the whole of Britain and Ireland came under the effective rule of a single sovereign. The relationships between the peoples of the islands, and between their political institutions, had been radically reshaped over the previous century, and like the religious Reformation, the consequences of this political re-formation are still with us. Nor was this simply a matter of English imperialism, for the English state itself had been reformed – indeed, transformed – during the century. The Tudor monarchs had set out to rebuild a stable, dynastic monarchy, following the ruinous wars of the later fifteenth century. They ended up creating something rather different: an immensely powerful monarchy, to be sure, but one which operated according to new, shifting and uncertain rules. A series of crises, most of which ultimately derived from religious change, had permanently altered the nature of English, and British, politics. This was, as the historians' jargon has it, an 'early modern' age: no longer medieval, not yet modern, an age with flavours, possibilities and perils all of its own. A century, then, of breakneck, switchback, multifaceted Reformations, thick with unintended – and enduring – consequences.

In surveying this fascinating and confusing period, this book has two main aims. One is to provide a clear narrative and explanation of events, for the sake of readers who have little or no background familiarity with the period. I have tried to avoid swamping the book with detail, so that it does not become a parade of names and dates. Sometimes, however, I have gone into a particular incident or example in some depth, if I think it is particularly important or that it illustrates a wider point particularly well.

Inevitably, too much has been left out. In particular, readers should note that 'Britain' here principally means Great Britain: Ireland is only tackled at length in the final chapter, and then mostly from the perspective of English policy towards the island. There is much more to be said on that and on every other subject discussed here; but the book has to fit between its covers. I hope those who want to know more will find the bibliography useful.

The book's other aim is to provide a fresh interpretative synthesis of the period, drawing together some of the best recent research and assembling it in a way which seems to me illuminating. Some of the themes this interpretation covers are the international religious context of the British Reformations; the stubborn persistence of *de facto* elective monarchy in England; and the way violence (whether judicial prosecution, mass protest, or warfare) tied religion and politics together, often in unexpected ways.

If the book has a single theme, it is contingency. The Tudor century makes a mockery of historical determinism. Chance determined the course of events at every turn – who happened to live and die, and when; coincidences and synchronicities; obvious roads not taken, and perverse choices persisted in. Against the enduring historical belief that whatever has happened was always inevitable, I try here to expose the fragility and contingency of events. The century is full of much-predicted events which did not happen. The chaos following Henry VII's death; Henry VIII's papally sanctioned divorce; Mary, queen of Scots' death in infancy, or her marriage to King Edward VI; Mary Tudor's children; the French victory in Scotland in 1560; any of a legion of catastrophes which might have befallen Elizabethan England – these events did not happen in reality, but they happened again and again in the imaginations of the people we are studying, and so we need to take them seriously. The true course of events was predicted by no-one, and if we understand what contemporaries *did* expect we will be better able to make sense of the world they lived in.

Acknowledgements

To call this book a 'synthesis' is a polite way of admitting that few of the ideas are my own. I have drawn heavily on other scholars' work, and to make matters worse, I have rarely acknowledged them directly: for this is a work of history, not historiography, and I have tried to avoid giving accounts of the debates between historians. I have particular debts to Pat Collinson, Catharine Davies, Sue Doran, Eamon Duffy, Liz Evenden, David Gehring, Tadhg Ó hAnnráchain, Eric Ives, Paulina Kewes, Peter Lake, David Loades, Diarmaid MacCulloch, Graeme Murdock, Michael Questier and Ethan Shagan. I am especially grateful to Eric Carlson, Jane Dawson, Tom Freeman and Natalie Mears, each of whom read draft chapters for me as well as allowing me to plunder their work. Highest honours go to Peter Marshall, who read more than half of the text amongst many, many other services. Keith Robbins, the series editor, and the anonymous readers for Longman, were kind about the book while making some invaluable suggestions and pointing out some egregious mistakes. I am confident, however, that I have still managed to smuggle some errors and misjudgements past these scholars' eagle eyes. Finally, writing this book has made plain to me how much I owe to my students, in particular those I taught at the University of Birmingham from 1999 to 2006. I am conscious, specifically, of debts to Louise Campbell, Anna French, Sylvia Gill, Bethan Palmer, Andy Poppleton, Sarah Spencer and Neil Younger, many of whom will recognise echoes of their work here. I hope I taught them a fraction as much as they have taught me, and I dedicate this book to them collectively in gratitude.

Chronology

1547	**Death of Henry VIII. Accession of Edward VI**
1547–50	Renewed Anglo-Scottish war ('Rough Wooing')
1549	Rebellions across much of England. Protector Somerset falls
	First reforming church council in Scotland
1553	**Death of Edward VI. Accession of Mary I**
1554	Mary of Guise becomes Queen Regent of Scotland
	England reconciled to Rome: Cardinal Pole returns
1555–58	Heresy executions in England
1558	**Death of Mary I and Cardinal Pole. Accession of Elizabeth I**
1559	'Elizabethan Settlement' in England
1559–60	Reformation–rebellion in Scotland
1560	'Elizabethan Settlement' in Ireland
1561	Mary, queen of Scots returns to Scotland from France
1567	**Deposition of Mary, queen of Scots. Accession of James VI**
1568–73	Civil war in Scotland
1568–87	Mary, Queen of Scots a prisoner in England
1569	Rebellion of the northern earls
1570	Papal excommunication of Elizabeth I
1572	St Bartholomew's Day Massacre in France
	Admonition against the Parliament
1577	Archbishop Grindal sequestered over the prophesyings
1578–82	Anjou marriage negotiations
1581	First presbyteries created in Scotland
1584	'Black Acts' in Scotland: James VI's personal rule begins
1585	Act of Association in England
1585–1604	England at war with Spain
1587	**Mary, Queen of Scots executed**
1588	Spanish Armada
1588–89	Martin Mar-Prelate tracts: crackdown against Puritanism
1595–1603	Nine Years' War in Ireland against Hugh O'Neill, earl of Tyrone
1599	Earl of Essex's failed expedition to Ireland
1601	Essex's rebellion and execution
1603	**Death of Elizabeth I. James VI succeeds to the English throne**

MAP x i x

Map 1 The Tudor and Stewart realms, 1485–1603

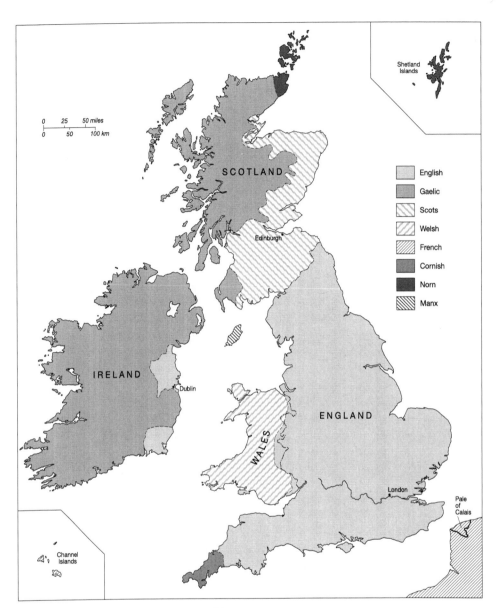

Map 2 Principal language zones in c.1500

CHAPTER 1

The World of the Parish

Living in early modern Britain

A lost world

The men and women who lived in Britain and Ireland five hundred years ago lived in a world which is lost to us. The difference is a matter not only of the material circumstances of their lives, but of their mental worlds and their imaginations. This is fundamental to any understanding of the religion, politics and society of the sixteenth century.

Imagine an English Rip van Winkle: a peasant who dozed off in the year 1500, overslept, and woke up in the modern United Kingdom. He would find himself in an exceptionally strange world. It would be a world filled with giants: the average height of an adult male in the sixteenth century was scarcely over five feet. It would be (as he would notice very quickly) a world filled with food, food in unimaginable quantity and variety. In his own century, our peasant would have derived some 80% of his calorie intake from a single foodstuff, bread. It would be a world filled with light: he would have grown up with nights that were pitch black, and with artificial light that was dim, often prohibitively expensive, and which stank. Indeed, the modern world would generally seem strangely devoid of smell – but filled with noise. Our sleeper's home country was normally quiet. Only thunderstorms, bells and those rare things, crowds, could make truly loud noises. Above all, the sheer numbers of people in the modern world would astonish him. Sixteenth-century England had a population density like that of Highland Scotland today. It was a country of scattered settlements and subsistence farmers. Agricultural productivity was low; a peasant family might need to farm a dozen acres simply to feed themselves. There was almost nothing that we would nowadays call a town. In 1500, London was the only settlement in Britain or Ireland with a population of more than 10,000 people.

The makeup of modern crowds might unsettle him most of all. The numbers of elderly people (over forty) would be surprising. The lack of the visibly sick, crippled and deranged would be more remarkable. Positively disturbing would be the lack of children. He would be familiar with a country where perhaps a third of the whole population was under the age of fifteen, and where babies and children were ever-present. To his eyes, the modern British would look like the survivors of a dreadful child-specific plague.

His world was both smaller and larger than ours. Smaller, for he lived – like some nine-tenths of England's population – in a community of a hundred or fewer households, often many fewer. In other words, he knew all his neighbours and they all knew him. Strangers were instantly recognised as such and treated with some suspicion. Anonymity was rare except in the towns. Even there, privacy in the modern sense scarcely existed, for most houses had more inhabitants than rooms, and their walls could rarely exclude prying eyes, let alone wagging ears. News from the outside world was, in rural areas, occasional and unreliable, although this was beginning to change. Government was distant: a face on a coin, quarter-sessions held by the county magistrates. More important were the parish priest, the churchwardens, and the local lords or gentry. Roads existed, but were ill-maintained and hazardous. Water transport, the only practical means of moving heavy goods, was slow, and there were few navigable rivers. Travel of all kinds was arduous and dangerous.

And yet it was a larger world than our own, because its vast emptiness could not be shut out. Britain and Ireland in 1500 were populated by around three million people, compared to some sixty-five million in the early twenty-first century. Wolves, bears and boars were long extinct, and the wild woods had mostly been tamed or chopped down, commemorated only in the towering forests of columns in the great Gothic cathedrals. Yet the natural world remained a place of fear. The modern conviction that wild is beautiful is a very new idea, the product of an age when nature can be kept out by well-insulated walls. The long nights of winter, and the pervasive cold and enforced idleness that went with them, were annually marked by peaks in the death rate. And if there were no wild animals outside, there were wild men. Violent crime was ever-present, and policing flimsy and informal. And there were worse threats, too, out in the dark: fairies, witches, the Devil himself.

We might smile at such credulity, but the truth was that early modern life was by any standards dangerous and insecure. Life expectancy at birth was somewhere in the thirties, but this is misleading, since comparatively few people actually died at that age. The one significant group who did were mothers, for some 6–7% of women died from complications of pregnancy or childbirth. Maternal mortality, however, was a fraction of infant and child mortality, and it is that universal tragedy which skews the statistics. In some times and places, as many as half of children born alive died before the age of fifteen. Those who survived this appalling cull and made it into their teens might, on average, expect to live into their late fifties. But this, too, is a deceptive figure. Old age was not especially uncommon: the tough and the lucky survived into their seventies or eighties. But death rates were high at every age. War and civil unrest regularly claimed civilian lives. By European standards, England escaped lightly, but in Scotland and especially in Ireland the toll of both large-scale and small-scale violence was appalling. War often also aggravated the ever-present problem of food shortages. England, at least, was free of real famine until the very end of our period, the hungry 1590s, but malnutrition was a constant possibility at the bottom of the social scale.

Other hazards were more universal. Simple accidents were a significant cause of death: in an age when water had to be fetched and carried daily, and when bridges were rickety and guardrails non-existent, accidental drowning claimed a great many lives. Those too grand to fetch water risked falling from horses. Housefires killed frequently, and also, proverbially, reduced the prosperous to penury within minutes. Perhaps nothing would seem more alien to our sleeping peasant than the modern culture of 'health and safety'. But most of the worst hazards were simply unavoidable by early modern means. Endemic disease and injuries of all kinds took a regular toll: everything from the new disease of syphilis, through the constant and often fatal problem of dental infections, to the biggest killer of them all, plague.

Plague and its aftermath

Bubonic plague and a series of related diseases had arrived in Europe in the mid-fourteenth century without warning, nearly eight centuries after the last major pandemic. Between 1345 and 1352, the 'Black Death' killed a third or more of the population across an arc of territory stretching from India to Iceland. This was the first of a series of outbreaks of plague, some local, some international, which persisted until the seventeenth century. Plague roughly halved the population of Britain and Ireland between 1345 and 1400. Thereafter the population stabilised, but plague continued to prevent a recovery: not by a steady cull, but in occasional large-scale outbreaks. A major visitation of the plague might strike once in a generation, and could kill a third of the population of a city in a summer. Nor were rural communities immune. Most Europeans who reached adulthood would live through, or die in, an outbreak of plague.

This extraordinary catastrophe and its long aftermath hangs over the sixteenth century. The collapse in population had obvious economic consequences: with fewer people sharing the same amount of land, landlords found themselves relatively impoverished, whereas peasants suddenly had something of a scarcity value. The aftermath of plague in Britain saw the final disappearance of serfdom and a boom in the peasantry's living standards. This is sometimes known as the peasants' golden age, but we should not get carried away. Peasant poverty had been absolute and was now merely grinding. Moreover, the price of the golden age was the ever-present threat of sudden, indiscriminating, and exceptionally painful death.

The population finally began to rise again in the 1470s or 1480s, as plague slowly retreated and the birth rate rose. By 1500 the recovery was in full spate. The sixteenth century was almost a mirror of the post-plague period. The population rose rapidly: England's population roughly doubled during the century, to over four million, more than the pre-Black Death peak. The economy grew, too, but not quite so quickly, as more marginal land came back under cultivation. Land became scarcer, labour cheaper. Generalised inflation pushed up all prices across the century – thanks to debasement of the coinage and a flood of Spanish gold – but food prices outstripped others, and the prices of necessities rose faster than those of luxuries. Whatever else this century was, it was not a peasants' golden age. The well-established inequality of wealth yawned ever wider. Landowners prospered: that included the wealthiest peasants, the yeomen, who owned enough land to feed themselves and to produce some surplus. The landless were forced into ever-deeper penury. Increasing numbers fell out of the economy altogether, to become paupers and vagrants, a source of regular moral panics throughout the century.

It was a toxic mix of factors: inflation, continued large-scale plague, rising population and growing impoverishment. Of its many consequences, two are particularly worth noticing. The first is enclosure, a long-standing phenomenon which now accelerated dramatically. It is a polite term for an ugly process: landlords' denying their tenants the use of lands which had previously been available for all ('common land') so that they could be farmed intensively for the landlords' benefit. The most notorious form of enclosure was the conversion of low-quality arable land to sheep farming. In 1516 Thomas More claimed that sheep were devouring whole villages.

In the long term, enclosure was the foundation of Britain's later prosperity, since it made much more efficient farming possible. In the short term, however, it seemed to be a means of kicking the peasantry when they were down. The violation of long-standing precedent made its injustice obvious, especially when the wider economic and demographic changes were so imperceptible. Rural anger over enclosure regularly boiled over during the sixteenth century, with important consequences for both politics and religion, but it was not enough to stop the economic logic behind the process.

The second consequence of economic change was felt in the towns, for it was there that a disproportionate amount of the population growth took place. Britain and Ireland had only one city to match the major European metropolises: London, which then as now was of a different order of magnitude from any other settlement in the islands. In 1500 London was a city of some 50,000 people, at least five times the size of its nearest rivals, Bristol and Norwich. The largest towns outside England, Edinburgh and Dublin, were smaller still. By 1600, however, London had swollen to some 200,000 souls, spilling well beyond the old City to begin the process of swallowing the surrounding counties. Other towns were growing too, but none could touch the capital. Such breakneck growth might look like prosperity, but often urban growth was a sign of despair. In the seething, unsanitary conditions of early modern towns, death rates were usually significantly higher than birth rates. Towns only grew through migration from the countryside. The rising rural population left increasing numbers landless and (therefore) destitute: the towns were their only possible destination. Towns were where the rural poor came to die. As a result, the towns became cauldrons of ambition and desperation, churning the supposedly tidy social hierarchies of early modern Britain. They increasingly frightened the respectable elites who nominally ruled them, and who struggled with limited success to impose moral and economic order. All this made the towns – and above all London – potential engines of social, political and religious instability.

Our long-sleeping peasant, therefore, was probably wise in choosing to snooze through the sixteenth century. In so doing, he avoided likely impoverishment, hunger, and early death from any number of causes. Even if he lived into old age, he would likely have done so while suffering from chronic pain or illness of some kind. In an age when alcohol was the only known painkiller, this was an unpleasant prospect. He would, at least, be poor enough to escape the attentions of the medical profession, an elite who jealously guarded their monopoly, and whose prescriptions were usually unpleasant, frequently useless and occasionally fatal.

His sister would face a slightly different mix of dangers. Women were less likely to be murdered or to engage in certain exceptionally dangerous occupations (soldiering, seafaring, construction). In exchange, they faced the sex-specific danger of maternity, along with more exotic threats such as (later in the century) the faint possibility of being hanged for witchcraft. Yet for all that, women's life expectancy at all ages was (as usual) slightly better than men's. This carried its own problems, because in an economy centred on male activity, widows were frequently left destitute. Indeed, women of all ages were more at risk of extreme poverty and malnutrition than men. These calamities drove women as well as men down the desperate path to the cities, which offered one route by which some women could survive: the thriving business of prostitution.

Diversions and hopes

We can only guess at what it was like to live in such a harsh world, although it does seem that the ubiquity of childhood deaths did not dull the pain which bereaved parents felt. Yet sixteenth-century life was not unremittingly grim, nor did peasants pass their lives in earnest discussions of enclosure, inflation and mortality rates. The towns bubbled with diversions as well as with discontent. There were improving civic entertainments, such as mystery and morality plays. There were occasional events of real grandeur, especially in London or Edinburgh, which enjoyed periodic royal entries, coronations, weddings or funerals. There were street traders and entertainers: jugglers, bear-baiters, barbers, minstrels, conjurers, salesmen, con-men. There was a booming book trade, of which we shall hear much more. And mixed with all the rest, shouting for attention, was the Church. The Franciscan friars, an urban order, had been described by their founder as God's minstrels, and their renown as preachers made them rivals for the best secular that entertainment had to offer.

If the Church was one provider of entertainment in the towns, in the villages it had a near-monopoly. The odd quack or ballad-seller might pass through, but the Church, with its highly visible stone buildings, was ubiquitous. Most people measured time not by days of the month, but by proximity to the major Christian festivals: not just Christmas and Easter, but dozens of holy days scattered through the year. The midsummer feast of St John the Baptist on 24 June was a particular highlight, marked by the lighting of bonfires. Such festivals could be raucous. The 'church ale' was one widespread custom: a kind of rowdy, alcohol-fuelled church fete, where the centrepiece was the sale of ale brewed by the churchwardens.

Festivals were moments when the normal rules of society were suspended. They were a chance for the hungry to gorge and (a pastime which united all the British nations) to drink themselves into a violent stupor. But they also meant more active reversals of the social order. In a series of events which the social scientists call 'festivals of inversion', often at Christmastime, society's strict hierarchy was deliberately mocked and reversed. As a 1541 royal proclamation disapprovingly described these events:

Children be strangely decked and apparelled to counterfeit priests, bishops, and women, and so be led with songs and dances from house to house, blessing the people and gathering of money, and boys do sing mass and preach in the pulpit.[1]

Some feared that the election of boy-bishops on St Nicholas' Day, or May Queens on May Day, mocked the social hierarchy. In truth it probably reinforced it.

For while the material conditions of our peasant's life were growing steadily worse, he was not an oppressed proletarian yearning for revolution. Occasionally, he stopped playing at inverting the social order and set about doing it in earnest. Riots and even full-scale peasant rebellions did take place. But while early modern peasants could be sharply aware of injustice, they did not seek to remake their society. The common people's daydreams took forms like the fantasy land of Cockaigne: a place of permanent festival, where there was always food and never work. No-one could conceive of a society whose backbone was not composed of agricultural labourers. Rebellion or riot usually targeted immediate, specific and limited grievances, and wore a conservative face: an attempt to restore matters to how they had once been. The archetype of the common man fighting for justice was the immensely popular figure of Robin Hood: the outlaw who remained loyal to the king. And while the Robin Hood stories mercilessly lampooned corrupt clerics and monks, most versions of the tale also stressed Robin's true piety. For it was the Church which was both the greatest force for social stability in the early modern world, and also (potentially) the greatest threat.

The Church as an institution

The late medieval Church was, and was seen as, two things at once. It was a formidable, wealthy and bureaucratic institution; it was also the city of God and the body of Christ.

The structure

The Church's institutional face is easier to pin down. By 1500, the Church's institutions in western Europe were fully mature. The continent was geographically parcelled out into dioceses (administered by bishops), which were subdivided into parishes. There were seventeen dioceses in England, four in Wales, thirteen in Scotland and thirty-two (mostly small and impoverished) in Ireland. England and Wales comprised about 9000 parishes, Scotland a further 1000 and Ireland some 2500. In theory, the network extended to every inhabited part of the islands. Most Christians met the Church principally in their parish.

A parish was a geographical area tied to a church building (the parish church) and overseen by a parish priest with responsibility for the residents' spiritual welfare ('cure of souls'). This system was not always as neat in practice as in theory. In the more remote, upland parts of Britain and Ireland, parishes were sometimes vast and parish churches inaccessible, and subsidiary church buildings ('chapels of ease') were rare. The larger English cities had the opposite problem: tiny parishes. The square mile of the City of London contained more than 100 parish churches. This provided a temptation to cross parish boundaries for churchgoing, and made it easier to slip through the net and avoid churchgoing altogether. Yet with these provisos, the parish remained the basis both of most Christians' religion and of the Church's administration.

It was also the basis of the Church's finances. Although the late medieval church had a great many sources of income, including its vast landholdings, the bedrock of Church finance was the tithe. This was a levy which in theory required that one tenth of all produce, of any kind, was owed to the parish church. The theory was sometimes threadbare; many payments had been fixed or negotiated down, and as we might expect, the payment of tithes could become a source of disputes and tension. Yet tithes were not simply taxes. Wills from this period routinely include a bequest to the parish church in token of 'tithes forgotten': a sign of the sense of moral obligation behind tithing. The taxman rarely receives such unsolicited gifts.

Tithes were due to the rector, who in principle was a resident priest with responsibility for the cure of souls in the parish. A third was due to him personally, with the rest split between maintenance of the church building and support of the poor. Commonly, however, an institution – a monastery, a cathedral, or some other foundation such as a collegiate church – had acquired the rectory of a parish church. This process, known as impropriation, meant that the parish's tithes were siphoned off to that institution to support its work. The institution would then spend a portion of the money – often only a small fraction – to pay a priest actually to serve in the parish. This priest, running the parish vicariously on behalf of an institutional rector, was called a vicar. Impropriation was widespread in England (where some 40% of parishes were impropriate), more so in Ireland (60%) and the norm in Scotland (over 85%). Impropriation has not had a good press from historians, and it certainly had some malign consequences. But in principle it could be an excellent way of taking parishes' resources and using them to support other ecclesiastical institutions devoted to education, to the care of the poor or to prayer.

Impropriation was also only one of the ways in which money could be siphoned away from a parish. Simple absenteeism was another: a rector or vicar might use a parish simply as a source of income while appointing a more lowly priest actually to serve there as curate (or, indeed, neglect it altogether). Wealthy or remote parishes were particularly vulnerable to this. Pluralism – the practice of holding several posts ('benefices') in the Church simultaneously – was one obvious cause of absenteeism, but absentees might also be students, or administrators, or in service to the king or a noble family. Such practices were technically banned, but bishops freely granted exemptions and offenders could often evade prosecution. Again, absenteeism was often a good use of resources, since it meant that deserving clerics could be found incomes, but there were obvious grounds for resentment and corruption.

The clergy

Who were these priests? In theory, men of good character and sound learning, over the age of twenty-five, who had been ordained by a bishop. Ordination was one of the seven sacraments of the Church (the rites which, it was believed, could reliably apply God's grace to a particular human situation). It set the ordained minority (the clergy, or clerics) apart from the rest (lay people, or the laity), marking them for God's service. There were over 30,000 clergy in England in 1500. Yet only around a third of clergy ever became parish priests. Every benefice in the Church had a patron – a person or institution who had the right to nominate priests to fill that benefice. The patron might be a monastery, a cathedral chapter, or a bishop; or it might be the king, or one of the nobility or gentry. Often, but not always, patrons were the heirs of former benefactors or founders. Patrons' rights to nominate were almost absolute. In principle, the local bishop could veto a patron's nominee, but this virtually never happened. Patrons, therefore, had considerable power, and here too was an opening for corruption. It was a serious offence for priests to bribe their way into benefices (the crime known as 'simony'), but it was also fairly widespread; and mere favouritism was perfectly legal. Moreover, the right of patronage to a benefice (the 'advowson') was, in law, itself a piece of property, which could be leased or sold. This structure, in England and Wales at least, was to be entirely unaffected by the Reformation – much to the dismay of the more idealistic reformers.

For the majority of priests, who did not attain parish (parochial) benefices, there were less prestigious ways to make a living. Top of the list were posts in chantries or collegiate churches. Chantries were foundations endowed by private individuals to pray for their souls. Typically, a chantry would be attached to a parish church, and it would employ a priest on a modest stipend to say Mass for the founders' souls and for all Christian souls daily, in perpetuity (or until the money ran out). Like parochial benefices, appointment to chantry posts was usually for life. There were almost as many chantry posts as parochial ones. There were also other, less lucrative and less secure posts. Priests might serve as tutors or chaplains in private households; or as curates, standing in for absentee clergy. There were guild or fraternity chaplaincies – employment by an organisation of laymen to provide them with religious services, employment which lasted as long as the employers' goodwill. And at the bottom of the ladder, there was the large clerical proletariat, those clergy who eked out a living saying occasional Masses and other services for anyone who would pay them to do so. The stereotype would have us believe that such men lurked around churches waiting to pounce on the visibly unwell, distressed or pregnant, pressing their services on them like snake-oil salesmen. This stereotype probably existed more in satirists' minds than in reality, but there is no doubt that large numbers of priests lived from hand to mouth. They might supplement their income by working as teachers, scribes, smiths, or even construction workers. Here, the sacramental barrier between clergy and laity blurred.

Few of these men were highly trained. A university education was exceptional: perhaps 10% of English clergy were graduates. 'Sound learning' meant simply being able to read the Latin service, which did not necessarily entail understanding it. A much-repeated sixteenth-century joke told of a priest who had long misread the word *sumpsimus* in the Latin service, saying *mumpsimus* instead; when his mistake was pointed out to him, he reacted indignantly, denouncing this strange new *sumpsimus* as a heretical innovation.[2] This sort of thing was good clean fun, but to focus on the educational shortcomings of the clergy is to miss the point. These men were not ordained chiefly to teach their flock, but to pray for them and to celebrate the sacraments on their behalf. It was not their learning that gave them their status, but their ordination. That status, that separation from normal human society, was marked in numerous ways. The clergy were not usually subject to the criminal law, falling instead under the Church courts' own jurisdiction. Priests were usually given the courtesy title of 'Sir', the same as a knight in the secular world. (An unlettered priest was sometimes mockingly called 'Sir John Lack-Latin'.) When performing their sacral functions, they wore holy garments, or 'vestments', derived from ancient Roman patterns. The colours of these vestments changed in harmony with those of altar-cloths and other church furnishings, with the seasons of the Church's year; it was a visible sign that the priest was not one of the people, but part of the Church itself. Priesthood was not a job from which one might retire, but a status which lasted for life. Being degraded from holy orders was an exceptional event, usually reserved for clergy who committed capital crimes. It was a medieval truism that one Paternoster (the 'Lord's Prayer') said at a priest's behest had the same weight as 100,000 said by a lay person's own initiative – just one sign of the authority which attached to priesthood.

Above all, priests were required to remain celibate for life. Clerical celibacy was not technically a doctrinal requirement of the Church, but it had long been an aspiration and from the eleventh century on it had hardened into an absolute rule. There were practical reasons for this, to do with the danger of clerical dynasties, but at heart it was a matter of holiness. Priests were set apart for God's work, and needed to be pure; whereas most medieval Christians saw sexual activity of any kind as impure. Even for lay people, marriage was second best, recommended only for those too consumed by lust to remain celibate. Priests should be uncontaminated. Of course, not all priests agreed, and the rules were not always enforced. In Scotland and Wales, it was routine for clergy to live openly with concubines, and in parts of Ireland *de facto* clerical marriage was common. In England, where the Church's discipline was rather tighter, breaches of chastity tended to be occasional and surreptitious. The lust-filled priest, who seduces virtuous wives in confession and who prefers not to marry because he would rather have the run of all the beds in the parish, was an enjoyable literary stereotype: but again, it seems, something of a rarity in real life.

Beyond the parish

The Church beyond the parish did not have much impact on the day-to-day lives of most lay people. The pope was a distant name, prayed for in the Mass. The bishop was a great lord who often was only an occasional visitor to his diocese (some bishops, especially in Scotland, literally never set foot there). His officials were seen a little more regularly. They were supposed to conduct visitations in his name periodically, ensuring that good discipline was being maintained. It did not always happen: visitations depended on energetic and conscientious bishops, capable officials, and – vitally – sound diocesan finances. In poorer dioceses such as those in Wales and much of Scotland and Ireland, visitations were simply unaffordable. The Church courts were a more regular presence. Moral offenders of all kinds might find themselves there: heretics, witches, bigamists, those accused of defamation or embroiled in disputes over wills and bequests. Sometimes clergy denounced their dissolute parishioners to the church courts, but more often it was a matter of lay people suing one another, or even of lay people suing clergy. Plaintiffs and defendants represented themselves, and the courts were accessible to the most ordinary of people. They were not criminal courts, and could not impose the death penalty. (The partial exception to that was heresy cases, in which, squeamishly, the Church required the secular government actually to conduct the execution.) They could, however, exact fines and penances or, in the last resort, excommunicate. That is, they could exclude obstinate offenders from the Church and from Christian society until they repented. Excommunicates were, in theory, ostracised during life and damned to Hell after death. In practice, the penalty was rarely taken quite so seriously – especially in Scotland, where its fearsomeness was devalued by overuse.

The other churchmen whom lay people routinely met were the 'religious', or the 'regulars': monks, nuns, friars, canons and others who followed a religious rule of life. Perhaps a fifth of all clergy were 'religious' in this sense. (Those clergy who did not belong to religious orders were known as 'secular' priests.) There was no formal requirement that members of religious orders should be ordained, and female religious such as nuns could not be (women's ordination was not dreamt of). Yet by this period virtually all male religious were also priests. This was a hugely varied group. Alongside the traditional Benedictine and Cistercian orders of monks were the urban, preaching orders of friars, the Franciscans and Dominicans; newer, more scholarly orders such as the Augustinian canons;

and many other, smaller orders, of whom the most renowned were the austere Carthusian monks.

Different religious orders interacted with the laity in different ways. The friars were actively engaged with urban life, and they included some of the Church's most gifted preachers. In particular, one subgroup of the Franciscans – the rigorous Observants – was widely revered. Monks and nuns were more withdrawn, but this did not necessarily lessen their impact. The strict discipline of enclosure was often flouted. Even if the rules were observed, the houses of the Benedictine monks (the oldest order) were usually located in towns: a visible witness of a holier pattern of life, as well as an important source of poor relief. Other orders, notably the Cistercians, had fled the corrupting influences of the urban life; but like most religious, they were landowners on an impressive scale. (Monks vowed poverty as individuals, but monasteries, as collective entities, were often exceedingly rich.) A great many people were tenants or neighbours of religious houses; these were of course business relationships which could (in the way of things) go sour. However, the regulars' place in society was ultimately defined not by their property portfolios but by their spiritual power. Their mere existence mattered even to those lay people who never laid eyes on them. It is here that we need to stop considering the Church as an institution, and see it instead as the body of Christ on earth.

Parish Christianity

Inside the parish church

We have already imagined a sixteenth-century peasant finding himself in the twenty-first century. Now picture his partner in this time-travelling exchange scheme, a modern Briton who stumbles into an English parish church in the year 1500. What would greet her eyes and ears?

We may think we know what medieval churches were like: cool, silent buildings of bare stone, dominated by organ, pulpit and altar, with perhaps a tang of incense. Yet those medieval churches which survive to our own day have undergone dramatic changes in the meantime. Late medieval churches were certainly cool – indeed, bitterly cold, with no heating and in an era which climate historians call the 'Little Ice Age'. But plain grey stone, or whitewashed walls, are a post-Reformation novelty. Most medieval churches were a pageant of colour and decoration. Normally, the most splendid example of this painting was to be found above the chancel arch, which divided the nave (the laity's church, the main body of the building where the congregation gathered) from the chancel (the holiest, easternmost part of the building). This wall typically bore a 'doom' painting: a vivid image of the Last Judgement, depicting Christ in glory, the resurrection of the dead, and the saved being received into Heaven while demons dragged the damned down to Hell. Artistically they were uneven, but the point these paintings made was unmistakable. This moment of judgement was one at which all humanity would arrive. When it came, status or wealth would count for nothing: doom paintings commonly showed kings and lords lining up to be judged with the rest, and often facing damnation. It was a visible challenge: remember, in the midst of the hurly-burly of life, that this is where we are going.

Yet the 'doom' was only a frame for the most startling image in the whole building, beneath the chancel arch: the rood loft. This object was in two parts. The base was a carved wooden screen, reaching from the floor to above head height and blocking off the chancel from the nave. The screen would include a door; it would also not be entirely solid, rather including gaps for the people to glimpse into the chancel, seeing as if through a glass darkly. It was the clearest visual symbol of the gulf between the clergy and the laity. But the screen was simply a display platform for the rood itself ('rood' being an old English word for a cross). Atop the rood screen, in every medieval church, was exactly the same tableau: a life-size wooden crucifix, flanked by life-size carvings of the Virgin Mary and of the apostle John, lamenting at Christ's sufferings as he committed them to one another's care. This direct, sometimes brutally vivid image of the dying Lord was the heart of the church building. All lines of sight led to it, for this was why Christians came to church: to see the Son of God himself.

Beyond the screen, at the east end of the chancel, was the sanctuary, enclosing the high altar. This is perhaps what would surprise our modern visitor the most, for the priest who entered the sanctuary to perform divine service was almost entirely cut off from his congregation. The words of the service (the liturgy) were in Latin, which few of the people understood. Later Protestants found this perverse, and many modern people do like-wise. It is important, however, to understand that the liturgy was not only incomprehensible: it was also inaudible, for the priest, standing or kneeling with his back to the people, behind a rood screen, would typically whisper or mutter the service – especially the most sacred parts of it. Why, after all, did the congregation need to hear and to understand him? He was not talk-ing to them: he was talking to God on their behalf. It was enough for them to know that he was doing so.

Indeed, even during Sunday high Mass, congregational participation was piecemeal and occasional. Our modern visitor might be familiar with churches where the people sit in neat rows of pews and follow the order of service, joining in 'Amens', singing, and sitting to hear sermons or readings. The late medieval service, by contrast, was an opportunity for the laity to say their own private devotions. Those who were passably literate, and passably wealthy, might use the popular prayer books known as Books of Hours. These did not contain the same service as the priest was using in the sanctuary, but instead a version of the daily liturgy said by monks, adapted for lay use. Those with less literacy or less piety would spend their time in saying their own prayers; in meditating on the numerous improving sights of the church (the 'doom', the rood and other paintings and statues); in praying at the lesser altars devoted to particular saints, which were dotted around many churches; or in gossiping and conducting business *sotto voce*. They would move about the building as they did so, for very few medieval churches had pews or other fixed furniture. The floors were open, paved with the gravestones of those who were wealthy enough to be buried within the church building itself. Those who padded from altar to altar did so over the *memento mori* of the pious dead. The sound of the Mass was therefore not silence, nor the loud voice of the priest ringing out, but a constant low hubbub of prayers, conversation, and the noise of babies and children. Churchwardens would try to keep proceedings under control: as would dogwardens, the unsung heroes of the premodern church, whose job was to expel those stray dogs who caused a nuisance.

High Mass began with a bidding prayer (in the people's native language), and ended with a blessing, but for most of the rest of the service, the priest and congregation left one another alone. The liturgy might call for responses, or singing, but participation was limited to the choir or the acolytes who joined the priest in the chancel. The low rumble of a massed congregational 'Amen' was never heard until the Reformation. Where there was music, it was performed, not participated in: plainchant or polyphony by choirs with a degree of expertise, some of whom might be priests themselves.

Our modern visitor might also be perplexed by the sermon, nowadays an invariable fixture of almost any church service. Sermons at Mass were unusual. Some clergy would deliver what they called a homily, meaning a short address of perhaps ten minutes during the Mass. But full-scale preaching was a specialist skill to which most clergy did not aspire; indeed, it required a special licence from the bishop. Medieval sermons were on a scale to daunt even the hardiest modern hearer. They were typically set-piece, standalone events, and not part of a wider service; addresses topped and tailed with prayers, which normally lasted more than an hour and commonly more than two. This called for real skill from the preacher, and real stamina from both preacher and audience: especially when the only amplification was a sounding-board and when artificial hearing aids did not exist at all. In theory, every parish in western Christendom was supposed to hear a full-scale sermon at least four times per year. In practice this varied. Urban ones were commonplace. In London, the Sunday sermon at the great open-air pulpit of St Paul's Cross was timed so that the devout of the city could attend Mass in their parishes and then come to the sermon afterwards. We rarely have evidence of the practice in more rural areas. In 1540–41, the bishop of Lincoln, John Longland, launched a systematic investigation of preaching in his huge diocese. The results show that, of 113 parishes for which figures survive, 109 heard four or more sermons during the twelve months surveyed. Of the four which fell short, only one had no preaching at all, and that village had been hit by plague that year. Yet these figures are probably not quite so glowing as they look. Of those 109 parishes, eighty-one had only the bare minimum of four sermons. Even when the parish priests themselves were the preachers, they usually stopped at four. And this was in a relatively wealthy part of England which was enjoying the focused attention of an activist bishop. It would be fair to conclude that most parishes – except perhaps in remote or upland areas – did hear sermons every so often; but that in most parishes – except in towns – they were occasional treats.[3]

The Mass and its meaning

The heart of the parish church was not the pulpit (if there was a pulpit), but the high altar. The word *altar* was used precisely: this was a conse-crated stone used for sacrifice. That sacrifice was known as the Mass, or, sometimes, simply 'the sacrament of the altar'. It is the Catholic form of the Christian sacrament variously known as the Eucharist, Holy Communion or the Lord's Supper. The Mass was absolutely central to Catholic life and devotion. It is impossible to understand late medieval religion, or the events of the sixteenth century, without some understanding of the Mass.

The Eucharist derives from one of the most mysterious events in the life of Christ. The Gospels describe how, at the Last Supper, hours before his death, Christ gave bread and wine to his disciples; told them to eat and drink; and stated that the bread and wine were his body and his blood. Finally, he told his disciples to repeat this action in memory of him. Such repetitions have been central to Christian worship since the earliest times; but their meaning is less clear. The early Church certainly regarded the ritual as intensely holy, and believed that Christ was present at celebrations of this sacrament in some particular way. One did not participate in it without the most careful preparation, for fear of eating and drinking damnation on oneself. However, there was a range of understandings of precisely what was going on, and this range remained remarkably broad for over 1000 years. Only in the thirteenth century did the western Church declare a formal orthodoxy on the subject, and even that left more leeway than is sometimes recognised. This orthodoxy, driven by reverence for the sacrament, took almost as high a view of it as possible. It was this view which was taught and – largely – believed across western Christendom by 1500.

The Catholic Mass was defined by two key, linked beliefs, both of which would become intensely controversial during the sixteenth century. First is the famous doctrine of transubstantiation. This holds that whenever a duly ordained priest correctly celebrates Mass, God performs a miracle. The bread and wine offered on the altar are physically transformed into the risen, glorified but fully human body of Christ. To be precise, their substance – their essence – is transformed (in Aristotelian philosophy, *substance* is an exact term); only their 'accidents' remained, that is, the outward appearance of bread and wine. To claim that a dramatic but undetectable miracle takes place so routinely can obviously stretch credulity, and an undercurrent of scepticism about it surfaces intermittently in the late medieval period. But there were powerful reasons for believing it. In Aristotelian terms, it made philosophical sense: nowadays, too, we believe counter-intuitive doctrines (such as the existence of atoms and molecules) because learned authority assures us they are true. Transubstantiation was a simple, literal interpretation of Christ's numinous words: 'This is my body'. And it was also an immensely attractive idea. It meant that when the sacrament was celebrated, Christ was physically, literally present in the most direct way possible; and moreover, that when believers ate the transubstantiated bread, the substance of Christ actually became part of them.

The second key part of the doctrine of the Mass is the belief that it is a sacrifice. All Christians believe that Christ's death was in some sense a sacrifice, atoning for the sins of humanity; and that that sacrifice was unique and unrepeatable. However, in Catholic eyes, when Mass is said, that unrepeatable sacrifice is made immediately present. (Hence the description of the consecrated bread as the 'Host', from the Latin *hostia*, or sacrificial victim.) Moreover, the Mass applies the merits of that sacrifice directly to the people – not just those who receive communion (that is, who actually eat the Host themselves) but also those who witness the event and those who, though physically absent, are prayed for during the service.

Congregations did not, therefore, come to Mass to hear the priest say the liturgy, or to be edified by a sermon. It was not an educational event. The Mass was about laying hold of God's power. In the jargon, it was a means of grace: a channel through which forgiveness, salvation, healing (both spiritual and, sometimes, bodily) and perhaps more worldly benefits could be obtained. It was also the closest that Catholics came in this life to the glory of God, for the Mass is the point at which Heaven touches earth and at which God incarnate, once for all, lays down his life for humanity. It is the power and the glory, and the beating heart of Catholic devotion.

To eat the body of Christ was a fearsome thing, not to be undertaken lightly. Careful preparation was needed. This meant a full, formal confession of sins to a priest, who would then impose appropriate penances and pronounce absolution. Only then, with one's soul wiped clean, could one receive Christ's body without condemning oneself. Moreover, one was supposed to fast before receiving, to ensure that the sacrament did not mingle with corruption in the gut. Then, after passing through the rood screen into the chancel, one received kneeling. The priest placed the Host directly into one's mouth, for profane hands could not touch it. As for the wine, Christ's blood: the laity never came near it. It had become an invariable practice across Catholic Europe that only the priest who was actually presiding at Mass received both the bread and the wine. This looked to later generations like clericalist exclusivity, but its origins (which are mysterious) probably lie in lay humility. Those who were taking the appalling risk of exposing themselves to Christ's piercing holiness would hardly want to do so a second time unnecessarily: and since the theologians assured them that the spiritual benefits were the same even if one received only 'in one kind', it could seem like damnable presumption to demand 'both kinds'. Or perhaps it is simply because the risk of spilling wine, and so defiling Christ's blood, was too great. Whatever the origin of the custom, by 1500 the laity had been receiving in only one kind since time out of mind.

All this meant that receiving communion was a rarity. The obligation on all good Christians was to do so once a year, at Easter: more frequent communion was a rarefied practice for the unusually pious. So when the laity attended Mass week by week – and most of them did – it was as spectators. The sacrifice which the priest re-presented on the altar availed for them whether or not they received. The climax of the service was the elevation, when the priest lifted the Host above his head in a gesture of adoration. Often he stood before a dark backdrop, so that the holy white circle could be clearly seen by the people. They glimpsed the body of Christ through the rood screen, framed by the image of the crucified Christ above it, and the image of Christ in glory above that. There was a widespread belief – tolerated if not encouraged by the Church – that to set one's eyes on the Host protected one from the danger of sudden death for the rest of that day. It testifies to the power of that moment, almost the only moment when the whole churchful of people were united in a single action: gazing, quite literally, on the body of their Saviour.

The living and the dead

It was not only those present in church who were thus united. The Mass is a sacrament of unity, drawing together all believers, including the dead. And in late medieval Christianity, the dead were a vividly important part of that community, at the forefront of believers' minds. In a time of plague and unpredictable dangers, this was perhaps unsurprising. Medieval tombs often sport grimly morbid decoration, grinning skulls reminding the viewer that death is our universal fate. But the late medieval obsession with death was not nihilistic wallowing; it was a focused and practical concern. For death was the gateway to the Last Judgement, that dreadful division of humanity which was depicted so starkly above the chancel arch: Heaven, for the saints who were purified from their sins; Hell, for the impenitent and the unbelievers. In either case, Christ's judgement would be eternal and irrevocable.

Yet most Christians did not feel themselves to fall into either of these two extremes, and this seems to have been behind the rise (during the medieval period) of a subtle complication to this fearsome simplicity. This is the doctrine of Purgatory. Based on some powerful theological reasoning and a rather more slender Biblical foundation, this doctrine offered hope to Christians who were neither incorrigible sinners nor especially heroic in their virtues. Those who died with sins unconfessed or with penances unperformed might hope for admission to Purgatory rather than condemnation to Hell – if the sins were not too grave, and the sinner was repentant. Purgatory was, literally, a place of purgation, where the sin-stained soul could gradually be cleansed until it was able to stand before God. It was therefore a place of tribulation – the purging process was assumed to be a painful one, and the torments of Purgatory were comparable to those of Hell. The vital difference was that Purgatory was temporary, and once the process of purging was complete – however many aeons it might take – the purged soul was guaranteed the eternal bliss of Heaven.

Naturally enough, most Christians – who hoped they did not deserve Hell and who did not aspire directly to Heaven – expected, on their deaths, to find themselves in Purgatory, having the accumulated muck of their earthly sins slowly scraped away by suffering. As a result, Christian practice increasingly concentrated on the practical question of how to reduce the time spent suffering in Purgatory – not only one's own expected future sufferings, but the sufferings which those Christians who were already dead were assumed to be enduring even now. Of course, to minimise one's own time in Purgatory, the most effective strategy was to avoid sin and to be scrupulous in confession and penance. But this was only the beginning. One could also do penances on behalf of the dead, to speed them through Purgatory. To go on pilgrimage in memory of one's parents, for example, was a means not simply of honouring them but of doing them a real and practical service. One travelled to the shrine of a particular saint in order to ask that saint to intercede with God on behalf of a soul suffering in Purgatory.

And here the Mass became indispensable. If the Mass was the premier channel for applying God's saving power to human need, there was no greater help to souls in Purgatory than to say Mass on their behalf. Every Mass included general prayers for the faithful departed, but it was possible to be much more specific. Those whose souls were tainted by the possession of money might make good that predicament by making provision for Masses to be said for them after their deaths: paying a priest to say one, a dozen, thirty Masses; leaving an endowment which paid for Mass to be said monthly, or annually; or, for the seriously wealthy, endowing a perpetual chantry which would employ a priest to say Mass for the souls of the founders every day. The numbers could be dizzying. King Henry VII's will required 10,000 Masses to be said for his own and for other souls. (The poor might have envied such a formidable effort, but could take comfort from the assumption that they were already closer to Christ, and that their prayers had particular power.)

Even the greatest private foundations, however, were dwarfed by those enormous engines of prayer, the monasteries. Originally, monasteries had been seen as existing principally for the benefit of the monks themselves, as they wrestled with sin and strove for holiness. They were withdrawing from the world, not taking up a role within it. Yet the world would not let them go, and the more austere their holiness, the more the laity wanted a piece of it. Bluntly, holy men (and women, to a lesser extent) attracted financial support from more worldly believers. This had, over the centuries, made the monastic houses of Britain and Ireland immensely wealthy landowners. And it also ensured that prayer for the souls of their benefactors, and for all Christian souls, had insensibly become their primary purpose. At least, the laity valued the monasteries above all as powerhouses of prayer, a ministry which the monks carried out on behalf of the whole Church.

In practice, by 1500, prayer for the dead dominated Catholic devotion in much of northern Europe. This was driven by the laity more than by the clergy. Although the Church gave lay people no formal voice in its government, lay people could still shape its priorities, not least because they provided its funding. The Church was turning into a vast network of prayer for the dead because this is what its people wanted from it.

Here, indeed, is one of the most important characteristics of late medieval Christianity: the depth of genuine popular engagement with it. It is true that this was a highly clericalised religion, with its sacred texts confined to Latin and with little formal preaching. Yet this did not mean that the laity were excluded from or ignorant of their religion. The use of a sacred and inaccessible language in worship is a feature of religious traditions the world over (Protestantism's aversion to this is very unusual). The laity may not have been able to translate the liturgy verbatim, but they knew what it signified. When (as almost everyone did) they learned to recite their Latin prayers – the Paternoster, the Ave Maria, the Credo – they could not have provided literal translations but they understood the gist and the power of the words they were using. The visual images that surrounded them in church expounded the core doctrines of creation, incarnation, atonement, penance, purgatory and judgement. An old cliché held that such images were 'books for laymen'. Those whose grasp of the faith was uncertain were subject to an annual corrective in the form of confession. Sacramental confession (which was conducted face-to-face: confessional boxes did not yet exist) was an occasion for teaching and admonition as well as for rehearsing lists of sins.

The religion of the laity was not always what respectable theologians would have wished. Important subtleties might be missed. Some lay people had a tendency to see the Church's sacraments and ceremonies as near-magical. The sign of the cross could protect against evil; a funeral Mass said on behalf of a living person could curse them. Yet we should not imagine a gulf between a superstitious lay religion and a rational clerical one. Belief in miracles, and in the power of sacraments and ceremonies to aid good Christians in this life, was perfectly orthodox. While the Church frowned on, and periodically disciplined, those who bent its rituals to blatantly magical purposes, it also robustly asserted that those rituals could bring worldly as well as spiritual benefits.

Measuring the depth and breadth of lay commitment to parish religion is not easy. Compliance with legal obligations, or lip-service paid in wills, in itself tells us very little. A more significant index, perhaps, is money. The willingness of individuals and communities to bestow serious amounts of cash on the Church is impressive.[4] Beyond their (already extensive) obligations to pay tithes and other dues, lay people dug deep into their threadbare pockets to pay for the edification and beautification of their parish churches, and for sumptuous vestments and expensive service-books for their clergy. They spent their time caring for church property (it was common for rural churches to own livestock, cared for by parishioners and providing an income for the church). They served as church-wardens – an unpaid and arduous office. These measures, of necessity, tell us nothing about those who were too poor to contribute anything. Yet at the least, they tell us that many – most? – people felt some ownership of their parish church, and indeed of their Church as a whole. This implicit covenant would be broken during the sixteenth century, but not by the people.

Satisfaction and dissent

Heresy

In 1500, Catholic Christianity was the universal religion of Britain and Ireland. Every child who survived the first few minutes of life was baptised. There was no genuine paganism left, even if some pagan festivals and sites had been Christianised. In theory, there were also no Jews, the Jews having been expelled from England in 1291. In fact, tiny underground Jewish communities do seem to have had a foothold in sixteenth-century London, but the numbers were minuscule and they remain as invisible to historians as they did to contemporaries.[5]

What England and (to a lesser extent) Scotland did have was heretics: men and women who consciously and deliberately defied the Church's teachings. Heresy greatly alarmed contemporaries and has greatly interested historians, but it is not clear that either reaction is justified. It is true that heresy could balloon into mass disobedience, schism and armed revolt. This is what happened in Germany in the 1520s, following Martin Luther's condemnation for heresy. Something similar had happened a century earlier in Bohemia, where a Czech national movement led by the dissident cleric Jan Hus had exploded into revolution after Hus was executed for heresy. In the late twelfth and early thirteenth centuries, the heresy known as Catharism or Albigensianism had taken deep root in southern France and northern Italy, and had been suppressed only after a brutal and prolonged military effort.

But not all heresy was like this. There were two distinct but overlapping kinds of heresy in Britain and Ireland in the fifteenth century, neither of which posed an existential threat to the Catholic Church. The less dangerous, older and more universal problem was of simple rationalist scoffing, curiosity and incredulity. Periodically lay people were hauled before the Church courts for claiming that there is no God; that everyone without exception goes to Heaven; that Christ was a deceiver and a whore's son; or that priests are thieves and tricksters. Shocked judges sometimes labelled these people as 'atheists', but they were not secular humanists, rationalists or materialists in the modern sense. Such 'atheism' had no philosophical or intellectual underpinning beyond a blunt scepticism, was often the product of alehouse profanity or anticlerical fury, and frequently smacks more of bravado than truth-seeking. Or, indeed, of madness: there is little to distinguish these cases from others in which suspects claimed to be Christ, or the Devil. None of this posed any danger to the Church.

More serious was the second variety of heresy, the movement known as Lollardy. The Oxford theologian John Wyclif, who died in 1384, had been bitingly critical of Catholic orthodoxy and had proposed some sweeping reforms. He condemned the wealth and institutional authority of the Church as unChristian; he disputed the doctrine of transubstantiation; and he argued that the Bible, whose importance he stressed, should be available in vernacular translations rather than kept exclusively in Latin. Wyclif was driven out of the university, but it was only after his death that a movement based on a simplified and radicalised version of his ideas began to spread across England. These dissidents – known to their enemies as *Lollards*, or 'mumblers' – proceeded to act on Wyclif's ideas, not least by producing an English translation of the Bible. They won some support amongst the social elites and the clergy. In the late 1390s and early 1400s, Lollardy briefly looked like a real danger. In 1401 a sweeping set of anti-heresy laws were introduced, which for the first time in England permitted unrepentant or relapsed heretics to be executed by burning.

Yet the Lollards' threat fizzled almost into nothing. A farcical attempted rebellion in 1414 robbed them of any remaining respectability. They were driven out of the universities. A handful were executed, but most Lollards renounced their heresies when arrested, often abjectly. It turned out that this was a movement without much fire in its belly. Improbably, however, it survived to become an established irritant on the British religious scene. From a set of idiosyncratic academic disputes, it turned into a heresy of peasants and artisans, losing Wyclif's theological sophistication even as it honoured his name and read books which were ascribed to him (often falsely). Underground, Lollardy survived in pockets across England for more than a century, and was eventually absorbed by Protestantism. There was even a Lollard presence in Ayrshire, in southwest Scotland. In England, Lollardy hung on in cities such as London, Bristol and Coventry; in rural Essex, Kent, Gloucestershire and Oxfordshire; and above all in the Chiltern hills of Buckinghamshire, the only area where Lollards seem to have formed a significant proportion of the population. Beyond the Chilterns, Lollardy was a numerically tiny phenomenon. We can name only a few hundred real Lollards, and they do not seem to have been the tip of a very large iceberg. Nevertheless, they had a stubborn durability. Official efforts against heresy lost much of their drive during the mid-fifteenth century, but when they revived under the Tudors they found a persistent, low-level Lollard presence.

What was a Lollard? Lollardy had no creed, no structures and no clergy. It was not a parallel church: Lollards had their children baptised by the parish priest like anyone else, and there is no evidence of Lollards attempting to celebrate sacraments for themselves. They typically did not absent themselves from their parish churches, even as they despised what happened there. What they did do was to gather in each other's houses, or in other safe places, to read to one another and to discuss doctrine. Reading was probably the closest thing Lollardy had to a sacred act; one result is that Lollardy has left us an amazingly rich set of textual remains. None of their books was printed until the 1520s, but the handwritten volumes were treasured, copied and recopied. They included a complete cycle of sermons which could be read in such illicit gatherings. Above all, Lollards read the English Bible which had been translated in the 1390s. This survives in enormous numbers: some 200 complete copies, and many more excerpts and fragments. It was central to their cause, and also their movement's chief attraction. Some people who were otherwise perfectly good Catholics owned copies. King Henry VI was presented with one by London's fiercely orthodox Carthusian monks. For serious Lollards, though, advocacy of the English Bible was matched by a withering scepticism towards the Church. Lollards typically denied that any object, place or person could be holy. Priests were false. Church buildings were unnecessary except as shelter. Images, paintings, holy water, the saints and the sacraments were all tricks and nonsense. The Mass, in particular, was mocked: Lollards denied transubstantiation in the bluntest terms, in contrast to Wyclif's subtlety. Indeed, crude mockery of the Church was a Lollard habit. This kind of thing could easily shade into simple rationalist scepticism, and indeed the authorities did often conflate the two. But there were some specifically Lollard themes. Images were stocks and stones; the Virgin Mary was a whore; holy water was piss; confessing to a priest was as useless as confessing to a post. One Kentish Lollard was arrested for claiming that the Host was mere bread, and that 'the knave priests did receive it before noon, and did piss and shit it at whores' arses in the afternoon'.[6]

This kind of talk was not dangerous as such. But it was, and was meant to be, grossly offensive. It provoked a reaction. That is why Lollardy, despite its isolation, theological weakness and moral cowardice, remains important. In both England and Scotland, by 1500 the Church saw the suppression of heresy as one of its key missions. Heretics were an enemy within, against whom the Church and respectable society defined themselves. 'Heretic' was a routine term of abuse, even in matters that had nothing to do with religion. In Scotland, where the real problem of heresy was somewhere between marginal and illusory, the Church had developed a hair-trigger readiness to deploy the accusation of heresy against any perceived slights or opposition. The English Church was slower to resort to this charge (with notorious exceptions). However, the pursuit of heresy had become one of the ways in which the Church asserted and maintained its power. When a new archbishop of Canterbury, William Warham, took up office in 1511, his first substantial act was a drive against heretics. At least thirty suspects were tried in the diocese of Canterbury that year, and five executed. The purpose of this purge, however, was not to exterminate heresy (much as Warham disliked heretics); rather, it was to stamp the new archbishop's authority onto his diocese. Other bishops did the same. Heretics were useful whipping-boys.

By the early sixteenth century, the Church had assumed a heresy-hunting stance. There was never a formal Inquisition established in Britain or Ireland, as there was in Spain or Italy; pursuing heretics was down to individual bishops. Yet the English and Scottish Churches were jumpier about criticism and more suspicious of novelty than would have been the case if Lollardy had never taken root. Like a minor infection, Lollardy's main impact was indirect. It did not do much damage to its host Church, but it did produce a much more aggressive immune system. The English Bible makes this plain. Vernacular translations of the Bible had slowly become available across much of Europe in the fifteenth century: German, French, Italian and other versions were printed with the acquiescence of the Church. But in England and Scotland, the Lollard heritage meant that Biblical translations were synonymous with heresy. (Simple possession of the Lollard Bible was presumptive evidence of heresy.) The Protestant Reformation broke on much of Europe unexpectedly, from a clear sky. It found England already engaged in a long and largely successful battle against its own, premature Reformation.

'Anticlericalism'

'Hard' religious dissidence in pre-Reformation Britain was marginal: anti-Lollardy was more important than Lollardy. 'Soft' dissidence is another matter. If virtually everyone was an outwardly conforming Catholic, how deep did that conformity go? Historians sceptical about the health of the late medieval church have questioned the Catholic laity's religion in two ways: first, their attitude towards the Church, and second, their knowledge of and engagement with Christian doctrine.

How did the common people view their clergy, and through them, the Church as a whole? For many years it was accepted that 'anticlericalism', or hatred of the clergy, pervaded late medieval society. This view no longer seems tenable. Colourful literary depictions of corrupt or licentious priests, by Geoffrey Chaucer and others, are much cited, but their significance is another matter. If these depictions were shocking enough to be entertaining, perhaps they are evidence that this kind of priest was rare. In any case, jokey stereotypes can take on a life of their own largely detached from reality, as lawyers and mothers-in-law know. There were, of course, real and sometimes bitter disputes between clergy and lay people, especially over tithes and other fees. Given the range of ways in which parish churches touched people's lives, this is surely unsurprising. But is this anticlericalism?

The term is an unhelpful one, belonging not to the sixteenth century but the nineteenth, when liberal and nationalist movements in France and elsewhere saw the clergy as oppressors and barriers to change. Anticlericalism in that organised, conscious sense did not exist in the sixteenth century. What certainly existed was antagonism towards some individual priests. In some cases, this translated into a generalised contempt for the clerical estate as a whole: this is particularly the case in Scotland, where widespread corruption and indiscipline did mean that many lay people despised the clergy. But this did not mean that Scotland, still less England, was simmering with revolutionary resentment. There was no obvious path leading from contempt for the clergy's abuses to a rejection of the Church – any more than modern contempt for lawyers leads to a rejection of the rule of law. Some of the most vivid anticlerical rhetoric came from other clergy, or from earnestly pious laymen. These were people who valued the Church highly, and therefore demanded the highest standards from its ministers. Up to a point, 'anticlericalism' is not even a sign of a weak Church, but of a Church which is successfully and actively policing itself. Even beyond that point, it is a normal by-product of Christian life, not a sign of a Church facing a crisis.

Clerical corruption, and disputes between the clergy and the laity, were commonplace in Scotland; they were much less so in England, although there are still a great many examples. (By contrast, much of the Irish Church was so thoroughly subordinated to lay interests that conflict scarcely arose.) In Scotland, matters may even have been deteriorating, as the Church came more nakedly under royal control. In England, they were probably improving. These problems were endemic and universal in Christendom and did not mean that the medieval Church was on the point of collapse. Of course, we know that the medieval Church *did* collapse in the sixteenth century – or at least, that it was demolished. But we are not justified in working backwards from that fact and concluding that routine friction between clergy and laity in the fifteenth century somehow exploded into open war in the sixteenth.

Is this subject therefore unimportant? Not entirely. If anticlericalism did not presage disaster, it did reveal some of the Church's fault lines and points of weakness. The willingness of some clergy harshly to criticise their own church was important. John Colet, the dean of St Paul's Cathedral, gave a notoriously forthright address to the Convocation of Canterbury in 1510, starting what his allies (including the soon-to-be archbishop, William Warham) hoped would be a major campaign against clerical irregularity and indiscipline. In the event, the results of Colet and Warham's moral crusade were predictably mixed: some abuses were dealt with and some incremental change achieved, but the transformation implied by their rhetoric was never going to be possible. However, that rhetoric of transformation, coming from such leading figures, helped to legitimise criticism and dissatisfaction from the clergy, and a generation later this would become important. 'Reform' – itself a thoroughly, admirably orthodox aim – could also become a cloak for all manner of other ambitions. Anyone with a grudge against the Church could use this kind of language to launch an attack which might win a hearing from otherwise good Catholics. And the Church's rigorous self-criticism – while laudable – meant that it was hard for such attacks to be met with an equally robust defence.

Meanwhile, the Church's actual failures (limited as they were) weakened its defence mechanisms. The shortage of preaching made perfect sense in terms of Catholic doctrine, with its emphasis on the sacraments, but this was an arrangement much better suited to situations of religious tranquillity than of controversy. The fact that most clergy were neither prepared nor permitted to preach created a gap in the religious market which could plausibly be filled by dissent. Lightly educated clergy could still be excellent pastors and ministers of the sacraments, but were ill-equipped to defend the orthodox faith in their parishes. The Church's resources were spread too thin for it easily to repel a broad-based assault.

In the face of the Lollard threat, these weaknesses had not proved too dangerous (although without them, Lollardy might well have been exterminated entirely). Yet the Lollard threat had been dealt with largely by anathematising and excluding it. Those clerics who had tried actually to debate with Lollards risked being accused of heresy themselves. This was the fate of Reginald Pecock, bishop of Chichester in the 1450s, who had written books in English against the Lollards. The very act of trying to engage with heretics was suspect, as it was seen to legitimise them. In the fifteenth-century context, Pecock's approach was probably mistaken. Debate carries its risks. In the sixteenth, when a much more serious heretical threat appeared, the persistent reluctance of Catholics to engage directly with it would prove a dangerous weakness.

Neither the English nor the Scottish Church was groaning under clerical oppression during the late fifteenth century. The clergy's undoubted shortcomings attracted some contempt and some hostility, but this is easy to exaggerate and was not revolutionary. These were not countries where there was a Reformation waiting to happen. But the tensions which did exist between the clergy and laity – more so, the tensions amongst the clergy themselves – did provide fault lines. It was not inevitable that the Church would subsequently break along those fault lines; in fact, it was unlikely that it would do so. But nevertheless, these were the points of weakness in the existing structure, where any crisis would be felt most acutely. The Church was not in danger in 1500. But it was not invulnerable either.

Notes

1 Paul L. Hughes and James F. Larkin (eds), *Tudor Royal Proclamations 1485–1553* (1964), p. 302.

2 Peter Marshall, *Religious Identities in Henry VIII's England* (2006), pp. 157–65.

3 Susan Wabuda, 'The provision of preaching during the early English Reformation: with special reference to itineration, c. 1530 to 1547' (Cambridge University Ph.D. thesis, 1991), pp. 160–3.

4 Beat Kümin, *The Shaping of a Community* (1996), pp. 65–147.

5 David S. Katz, *The Jews in the History of England, 1485–1850* (1994).

6 Corpus Christi College, Cambridge, MS 128, p. 62 (*Letters and Papers . . . of the Reign of Henry VIII* (1862–1932), vol. XVIII (ii), no. 546, p. 310).

CHAPTER 2

Politics and Religion in Two Kingdoms, 1485–1513

In the 1480s, the kingdoms of England and Scotland endured parallel crises. At the battle of Bosworth, in 1485, the king of England, Richard III, was killed, and the victor seized the crown to become Henry VII. At the battle of Sauchieburn, in 1488, the king of Scots, James III, was killed, and the victor became King James IV.

Medieval politics was not supposed to be like this, but such things had happened all too often in the fifteenth century. This chapter looks at what the victors of those two battles inherited, and how they made those inheritances their own.

Governing Britain

Kingship, lordship and elective monarchy

Over these two battles hung a pervasive, magnificent and unattainable political ideal: the ideal of kingship.

We are fond nowadays of the notion of human equality, but it was axiomatic in the fifteenth and sixteenth centuries that inequality and hierarchy were a part of the created order. The pattern held good at every level. All Creation was governed by hierarchy: a great Chain of Being descending from Christ, through the angels and the various levels of humanity, to animal, vegetable and mineral below. The same pattern could be seen in that God-given model for human society, the family. Fathers held natural authority over their wives, children and servants: natural, not absolute or tyrannical. Fathers ruled for the sake of their families' welfare (in theory).

Others within the family had authority of their own: wives over children and servants, older children over their younger siblings, servants over small children. The whole was ordered and harmonious, in keeping with God's will.

A king was father to the family of his subjects; he was God to the realm he ruled. That authority was of course expressed by bluntly practical means. The king had wealth, some military power, and fairly well-defined rights to compel service from, or grant rewards to, his subjects. He was in ultimate charge of the administration of justice. But all of these powers depended on something more intangible: the concept of good lordship. A good lord was anyone in any kind of position of authority who was just, impartial, generous and merciful towards those in his power. He rewarded loyalty, punished evildoers, shared burdens fairly and allowed the poor to eat the crumbs that fell from his table. Men would follow such a lord to the ends of the earth – and in an age when the ideal of crusading was still remembered, that was more than a figure of speech.

For the landed classes who dominated politics, good lordship also had a more specific meaning: patronage. Patronage is a confusing concept, since it is so similar to what the modern world calls corruption. Yet it was the staple currency of medieval and early modern politics, and in its own way, it worked. The word describes a relationship between a superior and an inferior for their mutual advantage. The patron – the superior, or lord – gives land, title, office or some other gift to a client, who is his social inferior. In return, the client gives the patron practical, political or even military support. It is not a contractual or formal relationship, but one of trust and obligation. It was universally recognised to be the glue which holds a stable kingdom together.

A good lord, therefore, is a good patron: generous to his clients, stalwart in their defence, just in the demands he makes of them. He is not over-generous, impoverishing himself and devaluing his gifts. Above all, he does not have favourites, elevating one family or group above their peers and breeding resentment. Patronage relationships existed at all levels of society, but kings were uniquely placed to benefit from them. For in both England and Scotland, kings alone could create and bestow noble titles. These were gifts of prestige which could buy considerable loyalty, quite aside from the wealth and power that went with them. A king whose patronage was seen to be fair was already most of the way to being a good lord.

And most people, most of the time, believed that the king – whoever he might be – was and would be their good lord. It was remarkably difficult to dislodge this belief. In England, during the great Peasants' Revolt of 1381, the appearance of King Richard II (a terrified teenager) before the rebels, and his verbal promise to address their grievances, was decisive in breaking the rebellion: what more could they have asked for? Kings, of course, worked hard to encourage this vision of themselves as the fathers of their country, but they succeeded because they were pushing at an open door. Most people were hungry for good lordship, and believed that the king, at the head of the God-given order, would provide it.

If the ideal of good lordship was God-given, so too was the primary means by which men became lords: inheritance. Again, to modern eyes, this seems perverse. Nowadays, we prefer to choose leaders through competitive election rather than relying on a roll of the genetic dice. Systems of this kind existed in late medieval Europe, and were called elective monarchies. But elective monarchies were not democracies in bud. Europe's supreme spiritual and political leaders, the pope and the Holy Roman Emperor, were both elected: the pope by the College of Cardinals, the Emperor by seven German princes and bishops. Neither example was very edifying. Papal elections often, and Imperial elections always, involved bullying, bribery and main force. One consequence was that sore losers often disputed the results. The papal schism of 1378–1417, when there were two (latterly three) rival popes, had its roots in such problems. When the kingdom of Poland became a full-fledged elective monarchy in the later sixteenth century, it produced a state of permanent internal dissent which could easily flare up into civil war.

For most Europeans, the ideal system was dynastic monarchy, whereby the crown passed smoothly from one generation to the next according to a clear and well-understood set of rules. This system was authorised by God, and by precedent from time out of mind. But it was also practical. The hereditary principle provided for a peaceful and predictable transition of power from one king to the next. It also helped to keep monarchs aware of the long-term welfare of their realms. Modern multiparty democracies would have seemed nightmarish to most medieval Europeans. Rival political parties would seem a recipe for constant faction and unrest, and governments which change every few years would seem to invite chaos, as each one used its short time in power to plunder the country with no interest in the long-term greater good.

The kingdom of Scotland provides a splendid example of how well this system could work. From the accession of Robert II in 1371, to the execution of Charles I in 1649, Scotland was ruled by an uninterrupted succession of Stewarts (the French spelling 'Stuart' was widely adopted in the 1560s). Each of those ten Stewarts was succeeded by their son (or, once, daughter). Many of them were controversial or downright disastrous as rulers. Seven successive Stewarts inherited the throne as minors, most of them as infants. Four successively died violent deaths of one kind or another. King James I of Scots spent the first eighteen years of his reign as a prisoner in England, while his uncle and then his cousin governed in his name. Yet even those with strong dynastic claims and excellent opportunities to press them almost never made serious attempts to usurp the throne. Whatever other catastrophes befell the Stewarts, their dynastic legitimacy sailed through unscathed. This was how dynastic monarchy was supposed to work. At the battle of Sauchieburn, James III was defeated and killed, not by a dynastic rival, but by an army whose figurehead was his own son, the teenage boy who became James IV.

In England, however, dynastic monarchy had virtually collapsed by the 1480s. In 1399, King Richard II had been deposed by a nobleman, Henry of Bolingbroke, duke of Lancaster, whose dynastic claim to the throne was tenuous. He, his son and his grandson succeeded in ruling as Henrys IV, V and VI, but when – for a variety of reasons – the English crown suffered a catastrophic collapse in authority under Henry VI, the claimants bypassed in 1399 began to reassert their rights. The result was thirty years of intermittent, small-scale but vicious and destabilising conflict between the 'Lancastrian' and 'Yorkist' claimants: the so-called Wars of the Roses. Henry VI was deposed in 1461 by the duke of York, whose legal claim was undeniably stronger and who now became King Edward IV. But Edward IV was himself dependent on the nobles who had fought for him, and when that coalition collapsed in 1470 Henry VI was briefly restored. After a few months, Edward succeeded in seizing back the kingdom, and his 'second reign' turned out to be a period of much greater stability. But at his unexpected death in 1483, he left the throne to his son, the twelve-year-old King Edward V, child of an unpopular marriage. Edward IV's brother, the duke of Gloucester, promptly ousted the new king, claiming implausibly that the boy and his younger brother were bastards. This new king, Richard III, made a better fist of establishing himself than later propaganda recognised, but in 1485 his numerous opponents coalesced around an alternative candidate. Henry Tudor, duke of Richmond, was almost the only living male descendant of Henry IV, but his claim was extremely stretched. By the strict rules of inheritance, as many as a dozen men then alive had a better claim to the English throne than he did. He invaded, confronting a much larger royal force, but on the battlefield some of Richard's forces changed sides and others simply withdrew. The invader was still outnumbered, but battle is an unpredictable business: Richard III was killed, and the duke of Richmond was crowned on the battlefield by his own soldiers as King Henry VII.

In other words, by the mid-1480s England had become, in practice, an elective monarchy, albeit one in which elections took place on the battlefield. Royal legitimacy was less a matter of who inherited the throne than of who could seize it and hold it. Richard III was accepted as king, at least initially, not because of his specious dynastic arguments, but because he was a competent adult male of royal blood with a wide political power base, whereas Edward V was a child. Likewise, Henry VII's legitimacy was based only partially on his dynastic claim. His royal blood made him a contender, but to turn that theoretical claim into reality, it mattered more that he was an adult male who appeared to be competent, and that the existing king was in political trouble. The political opinions of the 'electorate' (that is, the high nobility), not the genealogical facts, were the decisive element in determining the succession. Nobody liked this. But while everyone agreed that the monarchy really ought to be dynastic, agreeing which dynasty it should be was another matter.

The story of English politics in the sixteenth century is largely a story of the attempt to restore dynastic monarchy. And it is a story of a failure, for that restoration was (at best) incomplete. Sixteenth-century England was never a smoothly functioning dynastic monarchy, and anxiety about the succession to the crown was endemic throughout the period. We know with hindsight that the 'Wars of the Roses' were over in 1485, or perhaps 1487. We also know that (with one exception, in 1553) the English crown passed smoothly from one monarch to the next throughout our period. But no-one at the time knew these things. England's monarchy felt much less stable to contemporaries than it looks to us; it seemed far less dynastic and far more elective. How the successive Tudor monarchs and their subjects dealt with this problem is a major theme of this book.

Structures of government

To concentrate – as we must – on the two British kings is, potentially, to misunderstand the nature of politics in the British Isles in the late fifteenth century. For a start, 'Britain' was not at all an obvious unit of analysis. We now think of the peoples of Great Britain and Ireland as sharing a common history, whether for good or ill, but the word 'Britain' was not in common use in the fifteenth century. The kingdoms of England and Scotland both had closer ties to France than to one another. Nor can we even speak of two unitary monarchies. The islands were a crazy-paving of different kinds of political authority, overlapping and competing. This was chaotic, but not uncommon. Most of Christendom was a cat's-cradle of different political systems, shifting, incoherent and yet – most of the time – functioning. Indeed, this pattern of partial, limited and shared sovereignty is one of the most distinctive features of medieval society.

One of the most striking changes in the British Isles during the sixteenth century was the radical simplification of these structures, as idiosyncrasies, privileges and semi-independent jurisdictions were either extinguished or reduced to merely formal status. It was a century in which the authority of the 'core' of government expanded relentlessly, at the expense of the 'periphery'.

A visitor touring the British Isles in the 1480s would have found a bewildering variety of political structures. The island of Ireland was, in rather threadbare theory, a lordship of the English crown. However, real English dominance over Ireland was a 200-year-old memory. The only part of the island over which the English crown retained any effective control was the city of Dublin and its hinterland (the Pale). Much of the east and south of the island was under the rule of 'Old English' lords: that is, descendants of the Norman nobles who had first conquered the island for the English crown in the twelfth and thirteenth centuries. They spoke English; they (usually) acknowledged the formal authority of the English crown; and the crown's lieutenant in Ireland, the Lord Deputy, was normally drawn from their ranks. Yet their English overlords' distance and evident weakness gave them near-independence. (No English monarch actually set foot on Irish soil between 1399 and 1690.) Ireland also had its own parliament, although it was feebler than its English or Scottish counterparts. In 1494 it formally subordinated itself to the English Privy Council in the notorious Poynings' Law, the measure which – in retrospect – appears as the beginning of the English reconquest of Ireland.

The majority of the island, however, had no settled government at all, but was governed by (and fiercely contested between) various Gaelic lordships. In the thinly populated, physically impenetrable north and west of the island, the dominance of clans such as the O'Neills and O'Donnells was unchallenged. Occasionally a Gaelic lord might formally acknowledge English lordship, but such submissions were temporary and tactical. Neither London nor Dublin had the means to extend English control to the rest of the island, nor, it seems, did they have much desire to do so.

The dominance of the Gaelic lords extended across the Irish sea into the western half of Scotland. At the sea's narrowest point, only a dozen miles of water separate the two Gaelic-speaking realms, and in many ways it makes sense not to think of 'Ireland' and 'Scotland' but of a crescent of Gaelic lordship stretching from Connacht to Ross-shire. Close ties were retained between kin across the water, such as that between the Irish MacDonnells and the Scots MacDonalds. Yet in the 1480s, the MacDonalds had a degree of power which surpassed anything in Ireland. They held the title of Lord of the Isles, governing the whole of the Western Isles of Scotland and only nominally subordinate to the king of Scots. Even outside the MacDonald lordship, the writ of the Scottish crown ran very unevenly in the Gaelic-speaking parts of the realm.

The territorial boundaries of Scotland were contested elsewhere, too. The northern isles of Orkney and Shetland had been acquired from Denmark very recently, in 1469, and the Danish crown still technically had the right to redeem them, had it ever been able to raise the cash. More problematic was Scotland's southern border. Since the thirteenth century, the English crown had actively claimed sovereignty over Scotland, a claim which had been backed up by several serious attempts at conquest. Although an uneasy peace obtained for most of the fifteenth century, the English claim was merely sleeping, and sometimes it stirred. In 1482 a substantial English invasion penetrated as far as Edinburgh, and succeeded in capturing the border stronghold of Berwick-upon-Tweed. Berwick – once one of Scotland's largest towns – had been passed back and forth between the two kingdoms like a sporting trophy for almost two centuries, but now it changed hands for the last time, to remain (as it still does, to some eyes) a Scottish town under English occupation. The loss of Berwick stung, but it was a symptom of a larger problem: the militarisation and impoverishment of the whole Border region. Both kingdoms permitted Border families to carry out low-level guerrilla warfare over the line. If there was any law on the Border, it was the 'March law', a haphazard collection of treaties and customs for the region, shared by both realms and respected in neither. The Border was a running sore which both realms were forced to tolerate, all the more because along some of its length there was no agreement as to precisely where the frontier ran.

The Scottish kingdom's heartland was around the burghs of the east coast – Edinburgh, Perth, Dundee and Aberdeen, along with St Andrews (much smaller than the others, but the ecclesiastical and intellectual capital). The people of this settled, densely populated zone spoke the Scots language – similar, but not identical, to English. Edinburgh was, in a sense,

Scotland's capital, but in truth Scotland had little settled government. There was not much of a bureaucracy, a very thin central legal system, and almost no taxation. The king's title was king of Scots, not king of Scotland: a leader of men, not a sovereign of territory. As such, his power arose from his relationships with the aristocracy. He was not much richer than them, and his independent military resources were slight. It was only through mobilising his nobles that he could field a significant army. Parliaments met most years, and usually did what kings asked of them, but the Scottish parliament was an informal affair: a single chamber consisting of nobles and sometimes some burgh representatives, a few dozen men who knew one another well. The legal status of these parliaments' decisions was not entirely clear, and indeed the status of Scottish law itself was somewhat hazy. This is partly because justice (and, indeed, government) was administered locally by the nobility. The king's authority was not principally financial, legal or military, but moral: which is to say, unreliable but also formidable.

South of the Border, the kingdom of England was much more formal, bureaucratic and centralised. This made it an oddity. Very few European monarchs could match the authority which English kings wielded within their own borders. There had been a unified kingdom of England since the tenth century. The eleventh-century Norman conquerors had seized sweeping powers for themselves. And the extraordinary concentration of wealth, population and governing authority in the south-eastern corner of the country strengthened the country's unity, especially since that corner was the only part of England significantly at risk from foreign invasion. London's dominance is a very long-established pattern.

Yet England was not a unitary state in the modern sense. It is partly a matter of blurry edges. 'English' rule extended nebulously to Ireland, as we have seen. There were a scattering of other territories beyond the English mainland, such as the Isle of Man (technically a completely separate polity, whose overlord was the king of England and whose sovereigns were its earls). The most important such territories were the English portion of the kingdom of France. Since the 1330s, English kings had claimed also to be kings of France. In the 1420s, this cheeky claim had briefly looked as it if might mean something, but following the catastrophic defeats of the 1440s and 1450s, all that was left was the heavily fortified town of Calais, and the Channel Islands. These territories remained in administrative limbo, part of the kingdom of France yet acknowledging England's king. French-speaking populations mixed with a heavy English (and Welsh) military presence. Yet while English France was largely a memory, it remained a compelling and urgent memory. The shame of defeat and the memory of glory meant that the dream of a Channel-spanning empire still had power.

Wales was a different story again. It was under English rule, but had its own legal traditions – often based on bloodfeud, the law of the stateless. It was divided between the 'Principality', the royal lordship in the north-west, seized from the princes of Wales in the thirteenth century; and the 'Marches', military lordships whose hereditary rulers governed as conquerors, enjoying considerable independence from royal oversight. A nationalist revolt from 1400–10 had resulted in harsh penal laws being imposed, which remained in force in the 1480s. The Welsh, particularly the nine-tenths of them who spoke Welsh as their first or only language, remained an occupied people living under martial law.

England's other Celtic territory, Cornwall, had been more domesticated. Cornwall had been under direct English rule since the Norman Conquest, was represented (indeed, greatly over-represented) in the English Parliament, and was for most practical purposes simply an English county. Yet it retained its status as a duchy and had a small population of non-English speakers. It also had a distinctive political culture, shown in its remarkable readiness to defy London and also in its 'Stannery', the miners' assembly which technically retained a right of veto over English law in Cornwall and which did not finally disappear until the eighteenth century.

No other English counties retained that kind of status, although two of them, Cheshire and County Durham, had been granted extensive autonomy by the Norman conquerors and remained 'counties palatine', with independent legal and (in Cheshire's case) parliamentary structures. Most English counties had originally been created by princely fiat, and remained units which existed mainly for the sake of central government. The sheriffs who governed them, and the justices of the king's peace who ran the courts, were appointed by the king. But this did not mean that England was an absolute monarchy. For the crown to govern the counties effectively, it had to work through the local elites, which meant the nobility and the gentry. County identities were strong. When English people spoke of their 'country', they usually meant their county rather than England. A determined or wily king might sometimes corral, counter or in extremis replace the county elites, but it was never easy. And attempts to bypass or confront those elites usually failed. They knew the territory and they had the loyalty of the people in the parishes who actually made government work. Unlike their Scottish counterparts, the English nobility and gentry needed royal support to govern their localities; but the crown needed their cooperation, too. Much the same was true of the English towns, most of which had some degree of self-government, although no two towns' systems were precisely the same. Here it was usually mercantile interests which predominated, but again, a good working relationship between urban and royal government was in everyone's interests, and this meant a certain amount of give and take.

Towns and counties were both represented in the English Parliament. Like its equivalents in Scotland, Ireland and many other European territories, this was an assembly of the 'estates' of the realm: that is, its leading interest groups. The largest and noisiest part of Parliament was the county and urban representatives in the House of Commons. But at least as much authority was wielded by the smaller House of Lords: a few dozen nobles and senior clergy who sat in Parliament as of right. In the past Parliament had been a venue for challenges to royal authority, but in the Wars of the Roses it had been largely bypassed. It now tended to bolster rather than subvert royal authority. Its irregular meetings could not only provide taxation, but enact law. Quite how the statute law which Parliament produced related to common law, civil law and canon law was contentious, but statute certainly carried much more weight than mere royal pronouncement. Indeed, the intensely law-governed, even legalistic, nature of the English state is an important theme in the sixteenth century. Governments could (and did) change the law, but they could not ignore it or work outside it for long.

This patchwork of structures would be radically simplified during the sixteenth century. In 1541 Ireland was declared a kingdom in its own right – paradoxically, the prelude to a full-scale English conquest of the island by 1603. Scotland's territorial sovereignty was cemented during the period, the most dramatic single event being the suppression of the Lordship of the Isles in 1494. Anglo-Scottish tension was slower to abate. A peace treaty in 1502 proved a false dawn, breaking down in 1513 and again, very bloodily, in the 1540s; but a firmer peace from the 1560s onwards led, momentously, to the two crowns being united in 1603. By then the Scottish state was a far more administratively developed and law-governed entity than ever before. England was finally, forcibly, set free from its French obsession by the loss of Calais in 1558. The English state itself became more formidable still, with the supremacy of statute law asserted uncompromisingly and the independent power of the nobility almost entirely crushed, yet its political elite was forced to become much wider than before. Wales became, in effect, a part of England in the 1530s: it would not have any independent administrative existence for 400 years. By 1603 a multilayered, localised set of structures had given way to a single fact. Across two islands, three kingdoms and dozens of national and sub-national identities, London reigned supreme.

Church and state

Of all the political complexities of the British Isles in the late fifteenth century, the most ever-present was the Church. Church and state were separate, intertwined, overlapping, mutually dependent and – at times – mutually antagonistic. During the sixteenth century, the relationship would break down completely and reappear in wholly new forms.

There were three broad views in late medieval Europe as to how the Church should be governed, and how it should relate to the state. The first was the papal view. This ideal, which was first seriously asserted in the eleventh century and reached its apogee in the thirteenth, held that the pope was the Vicar of Christ, God's immediate representative on earth, and could by right exercise spiritual and temporal sovereignty over all Christians. In this spirit popes had deposed emperors and excommunicated whole kingdoms. The high days of papal imperialism were now past, but the claim to absolute spiritual authority remained. This included the rights, for example, to appoint to most senior offices in the Church, and to act as the final court of appeal both for the clergy themselves and in most matters deemed to be spiritually significant (such as matrimonial law).

A second, newer view of the Church was conciliarism. The great papal schism of 1378–1417 was eventually resolved, not by any of the warring popes, but by an Ecumenical Council, the Council of Constance. Ecumenical Councils are assemblies of all the bishops from across the Catholic world, along with certain other senior clergy. Such bodies had been meeting occasionally since the fourth century, and they were recognised as being the appropriate settings for settling grave doctrinal or other disagreements. However, the Council of Constance – which, in effect, deposed three rival popes and elected a new one in their place – looked less as if it was advising the papacy and more as if it was governing it. The Council itself passed a decree, *Frequens*, requiring that thereafter Councils should meet at least every ten years. A kind of constitutional monarchy beckoned. Yet over the fifteenth century, the papacy successfully faced conciliarism down. By 1500 the conciliarist dream lingered in only two countries: France and Scotland. Europe's last serious conciliarist theorist was a Scotsman, John Mair or Major, who died in 1550; and the ideal of a corporate, self-governing church remained powerful in Scotland throughout his lifetime and beyond.

A third view was in the ascendant by 1500: that kings and princes ought to govern the Church in their territories. This lay behind France's enthusiasm for conciliarism: French kings envisaged a semi-independent 'Gallican' church in which conciliar government was a fig-leaf for royal control. But some princes instead allied themselves to the papacy, allowing their loyalty to be bought in the currency of control over the Church. In 1478, Pope Sixtus IV gave King Ferdinand and Queen Isabella of Spain complete control over the newly created Spanish Inquisition, and Alexander VI subsequently gave them the splendid title of *los Reyes Católicos*, the Catholic Monarchs. Real papal authority was in retreat across Europe. The English king's right to nominate bishops went back to at least 1351; Scottish kings acquired the same right in 1487. Yet flash-points persisted. Monarchs did not look kindly on papal interference (as they saw it) in their lands. In England, the best-known symbol of this underlying tension was a peculiar law first passed in 1353, and subsequently revised, called the statute of *praemunire*. This law, in vague terms, made it an offence for English subjects to appeal to papal authority over the king's head. The contradictions were unresolved, and *praemunire* lay sleeping uneasily on the statute-book, a weapon ready to be taken up by anyone in England who wished to pick a quarrel with Rome.

And such quarrels were inevitable. Modern views (like some medieval ones) tend to see Church and state as occupying separate spheres, but the reality was that they were deeply implicated in one another's business. The Church could scarcely help being involved in politics. Its bishops and abbots were great lords, administering huge estates. Their bureaucracies could reach into the parishes in a way that the English state could not always match and that no other polity in late medieval Britain could dream of. The Church courts strayed deep into 'secular' territory on issues such as defamation, matrimony and probate. The clergy themselves were normally exempt from the jurisdiction of the secular courts, which could be a major headache for governments. More importantly, perhaps, the clerical monopoly on education and on legal and administrative skills was only beginning to loosen. Royal government still depended on the clergy. England's most senior legal officer, the Lord Chancellor, was invariably a clergyman. And some senior clerics actually held governing authority in their own right. The archbishops of Canterbury could mint their own coin; the bishops of Durham had extensive quasi-regal powers over their Border fiefdom.

And the state encroached on the Church's territory in return. Kingship was a sacred as well as a pragmatic concept. Inheritance was not a genetic lottery, but a means of recognising God's providential choice. Obedience to kings was a Christian duty. Kings were crowned by bishops, robed and given rings at their coronations like bishops, and even anointed like bishops – a sign of God's calling. This did not mean that kings were bishops, but they were not exactly laymen either: in one potent sign of this, some European kings at their coronation received communion in both kinds (see above, p. 18). Royalty had something sacerdotal about it. At their coronations, kings also swore to protect and uphold the liberties of the Church: an oath which implied both responsibility and power. It was natural enough, therefore, for kings to claim rights over the Church and dignity within it. It was also natural for the papacy to keep on good terms with kings by granting many of their wishes, and by lavishing them with titles, honours and other forms of flattery.

The dynamics of the relationship between Church and crown were different in the two British kingdoms. In Scotland, the Church as a whole was much wealthier than the king, and only loosely under royal control. Until the 1470s, parts of the Scottish Church had formally fallen under foreign archbishops (Galloway looked to York, the Isles to Trondheim in Norway), while the heartland had had no archbishop at all but was the pope's 'special daughter', under his direct authority. Given the difficulties of communication, that authority was exercised tenuously at best. In 1472, Pope Sixtus IV regularised this situation, making the bishop of St Andrews an archbishop with oversight over the whole of Scotland. In 1492 Glasgow – like St Andrews, the site of a university – was also made an archbish-opric. Scotland was coming into line with normal international practice.

The centrepiece of this normalisation was the *Indult* of 1487, James III's most valuable gift to his successors. This papal grant not only allowed the crown to nominate bishops and heads of monastic houses; it also allowed the crown to receive the income of vacant bishoprics and monast-eries for up to eight months while the nomination was confirmed. In other words, the *Indult* was less about the Church's spiritual welfare than about cash. And indeed, it marked the end of any restraint in the Scottish crown and nobility's looting of the Church. There had always been a tendency – as in much of Europe – for senior posts in the Church to go to men of high birth. Nor was this necessarily a bad thing: such men had the social clout necessary to wield their authority effectively, and often proved to be capable bishops. But in Scotland, from the late fifteenth century on, such appointments became ever more transparently about money. Some bish-ops, especially of the more remote dioceses, scarcely bothered to visit their territories, or even to be consecrated. The abuses were even plainer at the monasteries, where a recent innovation allowed lay 'commendators' to be appointed instead of abbots. Technically a steward, a commendator was in fact able to siphon off the monastery's income without the inconvenience of becoming a monk, or even a priest. By 1550, some two-thirds of Scotland's religious houses were headed by commendators. In the 1530s, King James V exploited his *Indult* rights to the full by appointing four of his infant, illegitimate sons as commendators of four of Scotland's richest abbeys. Their combined revenues almost doubled the king's annual income.[1]

The situation in England was different: more formalised, less rapacious, but perhaps no more secure. While the Scottish Church was being eaten alive by the king and nobles, the English Church retained real independence. Its bishops were a much more socially mixed group than in Scotland, France or most other countries: few were nobles, and some were very humbly born indeed. They were, of course, royal servants, but not craven ones. Most were well educated, some exceptionally so. England's two universities churned out able, careerist clerics.

The Church's power within the English state was felt above all in two institutions. In Parliament, the twenty-one English and Welsh bishops were joined in the House of Lords by many of the senior abbots (thirty-one of them at their peak, under Henry VIII). Together they normally outnumbered the secular nobility, although they rarely voted as a block. And alongside Parliament sat its sister assemblies, the two Convocations: one for Canterbury, one for York. These were the Church's Parliaments, defining canon law, discipline and practice for the English Church. They consisted of upper houses – the bishops and senior abbots – and lower houses, composed of representatives of the ordinary clergy. The Canterbury Convocation commonly met alongside Parliament (transacting its business on different days of the week, so that the bishops could attend both assemblies), but unlike Parliament it did not meet at royal command and its proceedings were not subject to royal control.

With hindsight, the potential fault-lines between Church and state can easily be seen. Nor is it wholly a matter of hindsight, because there had been regular tremors and some major upheavals along these fault-lines in the past. Yet most of the time, relations were cordial. It was in the interests of both Church and state to work together. Past confrontations had proved damaging to both sides (so would the confrontations to come). And there were principled as well as pragmatic considerations. Kings might grumble against particular bishops or popes, but they also tended to be good Christians. They took their own sacral role seriously enough that they respected the Church's authority, within its own sphere. And churchmen knew it was their duty as well as in their interests to serve their king. Church and state in the late fifteenth century were like an old married couple. Each side had its store of old grievances, but they were tied together by powerful bonds of habit, convenience, affection and loyalty. There was no reason to expect a violent breakup.

The usurper's tale: Henry VII and the restoration of stability

When Henry Tudor seized the English crown in 1485, he inherited a complex, multilayered collage of a state, headed by a monarchy which was in a state of near-collapse. He was to reign as King Henry VII until 1509, when he died in his bed and passed his kingdom on, uncontested, to his son. That, in a nutshell, was his political achievement, and it was an extraordinary one.

Challenge and survival: the pretenders

Throughout Henry's reign, England remained in effect an elective monarchy, and the new king could never be sure that the 'electors' (meaning, above all, the country's few dozen leading magnates) would continue to favour him and his dynasty. The fragility of his throne is demonstrated above all by the peculiar double episode of the pretenders.

Henry VII twice faced serious challenges to his rule, headed by two men with the oddest pair of names in English history: the so-called 'pretenders', Lambert Simnel and Perkin Warbeck. They were imposters claiming to be of royal blood: and the fact that Henry should be challenged by not one but two such men is significant in itself. The pretenders were a symptom of the extraordinary weakness of the English throne by the mid-1480s. Edward V had been deposed by an uncle whose claim to the throne was weaker than his own. Richard III was then deposed by an improbably distant relative whose claim was embarrassingly slender. Now it was proposed that Henry VII, in his turn, should be deposed by ghosts: by men who did not exist. The pretenders came to prominence because a vacancy existed for the post of pretender to the English throne. If none of the numerous real people eligible for that post were willing or able to take it up in practice, then a Simnel or a Warbeck would be found to take on the role.

The first crisis began when, on 24 May 1487, a boy aged about ten years was crowned King Edward VI in Dublin Cathedral. It was claimed that he was Edward, earl of Warwick, Edward IV's nephew, the best surviving Yorkist claimant and the only surviving direct male-line descendant of Edward III. This was certainly false – the real earl of Warwick was a prisoner in London – but it is unclear who he really was: the official account is riddled with contradictions. That account gave him the unlikely name of Lambert Simnel, although one early account calls him John. The boy was, of course, merely a front. Behind the charade in Dublin was Gerald Fitzgerald, the earl of Kildare and Lord Deputy of Ireland. The 'Geraldine' dynasty which he headed was much the most powerful in Ireland; their only real opponents, the Butlers, had been Lancastrian stalwarts driven from power under the Yorkists. Kildare feared their return to prominence, and this boy was a useful bargaining chip. Most of the Old English establishment in Ireland were persuaded to support him. A bandwagon was being started, onto which anyone who disliked the new regime in London might jump.

The most important new passenger was John de la Pole, earl of Lincoln, who was perhaps the most plausible genuine Yorkist claimant to the throne (unlike the earl of Warwick, he was an adult). A respectable army under Lincoln's command landed in Lancashire. The invasion was in Simnel's name, but had it succeeded, Lincoln would surely have dispensed with the boy's services and seized the throne himself, the third usurper in four years. So Henry VII's battlefield victory at Stoke on 16 June 1487 probably saved not only his own life, but that of the boy who was nominally challenging him. Simnel was spared, and used as an exemplar of the king's mercy. He was given a post in the royal kitchens (a menial job fit for a boy without a drop of royal blood in him), and he prospered there. He eventually became the king's falconer, married and had children, and lived at least to 1525.

This episode was briefly a real threat to Henry VII, and he treated it as such. We know with hindsight that the battle of Stoke was the last direct, full-frontal challenge that Henry would face, but at the time king himself could have no such assurance. Looking back on the affair, Henry is said to have commented caustically that the Irish would be crowning apes next.[2] That summed up two aspects of the problem nicely. First, the apes: the episode showed that if his opponents did not have a real dynastic claim, they could invent one. And second, the Irish. The lack of effective English control over the island began to appear dangerous. For centuries to come, English policy towards Ireland was driven by such fears.

And sure enough, a few years later, the Irish crowned another ape. Perkin Warbeck's name is as odd as Lambert Simnel's but much more easily explained: he was a Frenchman from the town of Tournai, and his real name was Pierrechon de Werbecque. In 1491, while in Ireland, this ambitious merchant's apprentice was persuaded to impersonate Richard, duke of York: the younger of the two 'princes in the Tower', who had disappeared during Richard III's reign. Although it was obvious they had been murdered, either by Richard III or possibly by Henry VII himself, there was no proof, and so Warbeck's claim was difficult to counter. And once again, his cause was taken up by the earl of Kildare and the Old English establishment in Ireland.

There was to be no repeat of Stoke, however. Warbeck spent the next four years on the move, trying to drum up support from the king of France and (with more success) the dowager duchess of Burgundy, who had her own reasons for loathing Henry VII. He finally attempted a landing in England, in July 1495, but the English regime was forewarned, the popular support for which Warbeck hoped failed to materialise, and the pretender was lucky to escape with his life. A second incursion, launched from Scotland the following year, achieved nothing aside from convincing King James IV of Scots to waste no more effort on Warbeck's schemes. A third and final landing, in Cornwall in September 1497, was initially more successful: 3000 men came to his banner, for Cornwall was still seething with discontent after a much more serious rebellion earlier in the year. However, he gathered no further recruits as he moved east and, when confronted with a much larger royal army, his nerve broke and he abandoned his Cornish supporters. He was captured and brought before the king, throwing himself on the royal mercy. But there was to be no pardon for this pretender. Warbeck was imprisoned, and was hanged two years later.

With hindsight, Warbeck's long and inglorious career does not suggest that he ever posed a real threat to Henry VII. Yet he was a continual headache for the regime – as was a genuine Yorkist claimant, Edmund de la Pole, who spent the period from 1501 to 1506 claiming the English throne at various European courts. Such claimants were difficult to ignore, as Sir William Stanley, Henry VII's chamberlain, knew. The Stanleys were amongst Henry's closest allies: William's brother Thomas was married to the king's mother, and the Stanleys' decision to change sides at Bosworth in 1485 had been decisive in the outcome of that battle. In 1495, however, William was suddenly executed as a traitor, on charges of negotiation with Perkin Warbeck. Stanley does not seem actually to have been plotting the king's overthrow. Rather, he had said that if Warbeck really had been

Prince Richard – the son of Stanley's old master Edward IV – then he would have found his claim hard to resist. Such scruples made even the most implausible pretenders dangerous to Henry, and so potentially valuable to his enemies. After Warbeck's failed invasion in 1495, the Spanish monarchs Ferdinand and Isabella wrote that his claim was now little more than a joke. Yet in 1499 they refused to countenance a marriage treaty with Tudor England until the joke had been taken out of the Tower and hanged. Henry VII was too insecure to allow jokes like that to continue being told.

The great question of Henry VII's reign, then, is one of survival. Given the fundamental weakness of his position, a weakness to which the pretenders are the most eloquent testimony, how did he manage to consolidate and strengthen his position? There are, broadly, two sets of answers to this question. The first is administrative, bureaucratic, and above all financial. These were the issues which consumed most of Henry's own voracious attention as a ruler, and which (because they generated copious records) have also been where most historians' attention has been focused. The second set of answers is more nebulous, and concerns questions of legitimacy and ideology.

Money and control

Henry's own priorities as king centred around that lifeblood of government, money. There is more to political power than wealth; the kings of Scotland, for example, were far more powerful than their meagre balance-sheets might suggest. Yet in England, it was at least a prerequisite for power, and during the fifteenth century it had been draining away from the crown. Henry IV's income had been approximately £90,000 per year. By the late 1450s, Henry VI's income had collapsed to around £24,000. Edward IV recovered much of the damage: his income varied considerably, but averaged perhaps £65,000. Henry VII, by the end of his reign, was regularly receiving over £100,000 per year. He died leaving a surplus of some £300,000 to his spendthrift heir.[3]

This was partly luck: triply so. First, while Henry's political inheritance was dreadfully unstable, his financial one was abundant. The Wars of the Roses had destroyed a good many of England's independent landholding families, whose lands had reverted to the Crown; and when he seized the throne Henry positioned himself as inheritor of the great duchies of York and of Lancaster. He therefore began his reign as the greatest royal landholder since the Norman Conquest. Second, unlike most of his predecessors, Henry VII was not committed to the crippling expense of pursuing a doomed war in France, for in 1453 Henry VI had had the decency to lose the Hundred Years' War finally and decisively. Instead, Henry VII inherited the fruits of Edward IV's foreign policy: Edward had launched a major invasion of France in 1475, but allowed the French to buy him off at the last minute with a substantial annual pension. Henry VII renewed this pension after a similar expedition in 1492, and thereafter he pursued a foreign policy which was modest, defensive and cheap. Third, and most importantly, Henry VII became king at the time of a generalised economic recovery. A rising tide lifts all boats; moreover, it became easier for the crown to increase the proportion of the national wealth it was seizing through taxation without provoking excessive resentment. In particular, the recovery in trade kept customs revenues buoyant, rising from some £25,000 per year in the 1460s to over £40,000 by the turn of the century.

Yet good luck was paralleled by fair judgement. Having inherited a windfall, Henry maintained a relentless stranglehold on patronage. As we have seen (see above, p. 31), wise patronage was an essential component of good lordship, but the recent royal precedents were discouraging. Henry VI, in particular, had been both partial and spendthrift. Henry VII, by contrast, erred on the side of miserliness. This had its own problems, and stirred up considerable resentment. But it had the obvious advantage of concentrating wealth in the king's hands. If noblemen died without heirs, their titles died out and their lands reverted to the Crown. Henry was extremely slow to create new noble titles to replace them. The absolute number of noble titles in England dropped steadily during Henry's reign, from nineteen shortly after his accession to twelve by 1509. Those numbers are a good proxy for the concentration of power and wealth in the king's hands.

The other means by which, notoriously, Henry asserted his power over his nobles was through vice-like exploitations of his legal and customary rights. In keeping with the so-called 'bastard feudalism' of the fifteenth century (that is, a system whereby traditional bonds of land and service were replaced by contractual, cash relationships), Henry worked hard to parlay his traditional rights into financial obligations. The trick, as Henry refined and developed it, was this. Those whom he found to have committed some indiscretion (anything from a minor infraction of a long-forgotten law through to open treason) would not normally face the full force of the law. Henry was well aware that this could spark desperation and rebellion. Instead, their offences (real or imagined) were used to bind them into a web of financial obligations in exchange for a royal pardon.

This might mean, for example, undertaking to make an annual payment to the king, in lieu of a huge fine which was shelved but never actually cancelled; or imposing restrictions on offenders' behaviour which would hamstring their ability to oppose the king. In one of the most spectacular examples, in 1507, Lord Abergavenny was indicted for retaining a private army of 471 men, and fined the impossible sum of £70,000. The king, in a show of so-called mercy, commuted this to a fine of £5000, payable in ten annual instalments – but only on condition that Abergavenny never returned to the Home Counties, where his estates lay. And yet his offence was one which most of the nobility had committed at some time or another. The idea was that the nobility would be too tied up in a legal and financial web to be able to move independently, and at the same time their incomes could be siphoned off to the Crown.

It was clever, and perhaps too clever. As expedients of this kind became a pattern, Henry VII acquired a reputation as a grasping and miserly king. This was better than being weak and over-generous, but it could still be dangerous. In the event, the most serious domestic disturbance of the reign had less to do with Henry's dynastic weaknesses than with money. Perkin Warbeck's incursion from Scotland in 1496 did little direct damage, but it scared Henry into imposing unprecedented levels of tax to deal with the supposed threat: he raised £150,000 in taxes and forced loans during 1496–97. This provoked the rebellion which Warbeck had been trying in vain to ignite. In Cornwall, that most self-willed corner of Henry's realm, resentment boiled over into rebellion. In the spring of 1497 a Cornish army which eventually numbered some 15,000 men marched on London. They picked up little help along their way, but they were not hindered either. It was a dangerous moment. Critically, Kent and London remained loyal to the king, and a royal army was mustered in time to confront the westerners at Blackheath. A pitched battle was fought on 17 June 1497, at which the rebels were slaughtered. The king, characteristically, exacted his revenge on Cornwall as a whole in financial penalties, finally restoring the duchy's traditional rights in 1508 in exchange for eye-watering fines. It was a frightening episode, and showed Henry how fragile his hold over his realm was.

Yet what is truly remarkable about the Cornish rising is that it was a one-off. There were other grumblings of discontent, and the earl of Northumberland was murdered by disgruntled taxpayers in Yorkshire in 1489. However, Cornwall aside, this resentment never boiled over into open or generalised opposition. If this was indeed an elective monarchy, in which there were numerous alternative claimants who might be expected to be less exacting, England's readiness to knuckle under to Henry's strictures requires some explanation.

Kingship and legitimacy

At root, late medieval kingship was something numinous, even religious: it was a matter of legitimacy, a quality which could be burnished by the judicious application of cash, but which ultimately could not be bought. Henry's achievement was that he asserted his right to be king in such a way that most of his subjects were persuaded to acquiesce most of the time.[4]

This was tricky, because in traditional dynastic terms, Henry's claim was feeble. He was deliberately vague on the subject. According to one chronicler, Parliament declared that the crown was due to him 'not by one but by many titles'.[5] This was, of course, an admission of weakness (normally, in a dynastic monarchy, the heir to the throne needs only one claim). Henry was forced to assemble his claim piecemeal.

Most bluntly, his claim rested on the right of battle. Crude, perhaps, but it carried real moral authority. Henry's victory at Bosworth demonstrated not only that he was a soldier to be reckoned with but that he had God's favour. Henry exploited this carefully on the day itself: hence the battlefield coronation, in the ancient Roman fashion, and using Richard III's crown. The legend that the crown had been found hanging on a hawthorn bush after the battle became part of his propaganda, his royal regalia incorporating a symbolic hawthorn bush. A good lord was, amongst other things, a lord with the power to protect his subjects: as Henry V had discovered earlier in the century, battlefield victories provide a raw legitimacy like nothing else.

This might have been enough for the Romans, but not for a country that thought itself sophisticated, law-governed and Christian. Another claim derived from Henry's key strategic decision at the beginning of the reign: his insistence on marrying Elizabeth of York, King Edward IV's daughter. This united the Yorkist claim to the throne with Henry's own personal claim. It secured Henry's dynasty, and especially the unchallenged right of any children to succeed. And children aside, Elizabeth's position as the daughter of a previous king made her an enormously potent symbol. By marrying her, Henry VII prevented anyone else from doing so and so becoming a focus of opposition. The marriage also allowed Henry to present himself, somewhat implausibly, as heir to the 'good Yorkist', Edward IV, whose throne had been seized and whose sons had been murdered by the 'bad Yorkist', Richard III. Hence the effort which the Tudor propaganda machine put into vilifying Richard, an effort whose success (thanks to Shakespeare) persists down to the present. Henry's marriage in some sense restored the old regime.

But it was a ticklish business. Parliament celebrated Henry's choice to marry Elizabeth, 'in whose person, it seemed to all, there could be found whatever appeared to be missing in the king's title elsewhere'.[6] And this of course was uncomfortably close to the truth. Elizabeth's dynastic claim to royal status was inescapably stronger than Henry's. But he could not allow himself to be merely a king consort. That would, implicitly, give her other relatives the right to inherit, and would also suggest that if she predeceased him (as in fact happened) his right to the throne would die with her. Their son, Henry VIII, could and did openly position himself as their heir of both Lancaster and York, and celebrate his doubly royal ancestry. But Henry VII could not allow his own claim to the throne to depend on his wife's. The problem is neatly illustrated by the Tudor rose, the icon of the marriage. It showed the white rose, the ancient symbol of the house of York, united with – but enclosed by and subordinate to – the red rose which had been invented to represent the house of Lancaster. Henry VIII would use the Tudor rose with enthusiasm, but Henry VII was always more measured, regularly using the red Lancastrian rose alone in portraiture and iconography. When his eldest son Prince Arthur died in 1502, his tomb in Worcester Cathedral used both roses: the Tudor rose proclaiming his doubly royal ancestry, but also the Lancastrian one asserting the superiority of his father's claim.

Henry VII was, indeed, almost the only surviving member of the house of Lancaster. As he worked to exploit this, the sacral, religious dimension of English kingship came explicitly to the fore. For one of Henry VII's recurring preoccupations was his campaign to redeem the reputation of the last Lancastrian king, Henry VI. This was not easy, for Henry VI had been a truly awful king – capricious, irresolute and inattentive to politics. But he had at least been pious, and he already had something of a reputation as a saint. Henry VII's propaganda machine exploited this enthusiastically, campaigning to have Henry VI officially recognised as a saint by the Church. It was a realistic ambition. Most of the major royal houses of Europe boasted a saint or two (France was weighed down with them). England's last royal saint had been Edward the Confessor, in the eleventh century, so another one was perhaps overdue. The wheels of papal administration turn slowly, but the campaign would surely have eventually succeeded had Henry VIII not burned the English crown's bridges with Rome.

Henry VII did his best to portray himself as following in his sainted predecessor's footsteps. He cultivated a pious image for himself – going on pilgrimage, talking (but only talking) of crusades, promoting godly clerics to bishoprics and publicly enjoying good preaching. He was also an enthusiast for one of the most earnest and rigorous religious orders in Christendom, the Observant wing of the Franciscan friars, renowned not only for their personal holiness but for their exceptional preaching. Henry founded one Observant house personally and oversaw the creation of a formal Observant province in England. Other pious acts linked him to Henry VI more directly. He poured money into Henry VI's pet foundation of King's College, Cambridge, filling the college and its chapel with Lancastrian red roses in the process. And he constructed a splendid new chapel at Westminster Abbey, intended to house Henry VI's relics – and putting himself in the place of Edward the Confessor, the Abbey's founder. The king's allies and sycophants did what they could to help spread the message. In 1486, Henry VII made his formal entry into the city of York – inevitably, a symbolically charged event. The city fathers laid on a pageant in which the first six king Henries welcomed the seventh. A pageant prepared for his entry into the city of Worcester in the same year included a figure of Henry VI hailing the new king as his nephew and, by God's grace, his heir.

The uncomfortable truth, however, was that Henry VII was only Henry VI's nephew through non-royal lineage. For the purpose of inheritance, he was a half-second cousin once removed, through his mother, Margaret Beaufort. Lady Margaret was a formidable presence throughout Henry's reign, and indeed outlived her son by two months (she had been only thirteen when he was born). In a purist dynastic monarchy, it would have been she who inherited the throne, not her son. As it was, she became in effect the leading noble in much of eastern England. But she was also important to Henry's claim. At court, she was treated as almost an equal of the queen: this was not mere filial piety, but Henry's assertion that his Lancastrian mother was at least as royal as his Yorkist wife. The king had her styled Princess, and in 1499 he allowed her to change her signature from M Richmond to Margaret R, an implicit claim to royal status. More significantly, perhaps, Henry VII turned the Beaufort family's emblem, the portcullis, into one of the symbols of English royalty, and was so successful that the portcullis can still be found on British coins. It was there on Prince Arthur's tomb, alongside the Tudor and Lancastrian roses. And it also adorned the splendid pious projects which Lady Margaret associated herself with in the last years of her life, heartfelt projects fitting for an elderly widow, but which also bolstered Henry's claim to godly kingship. The most spectacular and enduring of these were two new colleges at Cambridge University, Christ's and St John's. Her fingerprints were all

over these new foundations: Beaufort portcullises can still be seen adorn-
ing the gatehouse of St John's and the silver plate which she donated to
Christ's. Both foundations bore the influence of her confessor, John Fisher,
one of the spiritual giants of sixteenth-century England, who would in the
end be executed by her grandson Henry VIII. Nor was Lady Margaret's
conspicuous piety simply a feature of her declining years. In 1494 the pope
had recognised her as the chief promoter in England of the cult of the
Name of Jesus, a fashionable new devotion whose distinguishing feature
was intense meditation on Christ. The obvious sincerity of Lady Margaret's
religion was a formidable boost to the Tudor regime's legitimacy.

So Henry VII built his royal claim on his wife (cautiously); on his cousin
Henry VI; and on his mother. But there was one final, more nebulous but
equally significant set of claims he made, derived through his father,
Edmund Tudor, who was not English but Welsh. When Henry launched
his invasion in 1485, he landed in Wales, hoping for (and receiving) support there. At Bosworth, Henry's banners bore not the red rose or the
Beaufort portcullis, but the red dragon of Wales and – quixotic as it may
sound – the heraldic arms of the seventh-century Welsh king Cadwaladr.
This set one of the themes of Henry VII's propaganda, namely that he
was the rightful heir not only to the kingdom of England but also to the
ancient British kingdom: the heir not only of Edward III and of William
the Conqueror, but of Cadwaladr and King Arthur. This claim did not
then seem quite so preposterous as it does now. 'Britain' was – as we shall
see – a potent idea, weighted with the authority of the ages. Edward IV had
made a similar, though less wide-ranging, attempt to trace an ancient
British lineage for himself. The supposed prophecies of Merlin, King
Arthur's wizard, were much studied in late medieval England, and had even
had to be banned by statute in 1402. Henry now turned the prophecies to
his own advantage. The semi-official chroniclers of his reign, Polydore Virgil,
Edward Hall and Bernard Andre, all related how Cadwaladr, 'the last king
of the Britons', had foretold that one of his descendants would one day
reclaim his kingdom. Cadwaladr was depicted as a pious, otherworldly,
doomed prince, much like Henry VI; and the connection was made explicit
when the same chroniclers also described how Henry VI himself had
applied Cadwaladr's prophecy directly to the young Henry Tudor. The
Lancastrian and the Welsh claims were thus neatly merged together.

This was not pure invention. The Tudor family were already the focus
of almost messianic hopes from some in Wales, and had been identified
as the heirs of Welsh royalty since the early fifteenth century – a claim
which Henry researched diligently. But he also mobilised it for propaganda

purposes. Bernard Andre argued that Henry was the first truly legitimate king since Cadwaladr's kingdom had been destroyed by 'the barbarism of the English'. Henry's heraldry regularly employed the Welsh dragon: his royal arms were borne by the dragon and the Beaufort greyhound, neatly intertwining his English and British claims. A plaque was placed on Henry's father's grave calling him 'father and brother to kings'.[7] Above all, Henry linked himself to King Arthur, the legendary British king who was famed across Europe not merely for his gallantry but for his discovery of that most venerated Christian relic, the Holy Grail. When Henry chose to call his eldest son Arthur, there could be no doubt of the point he was making. It was not a common name in England, let alone for royalty; and he arranged for the birth to take place in Winchester, widely believed to have been the site of Arthur's Camelot and home to an object then believed to have been Arthur's Round Table. Contemporaries who celebrated the birth made free with the comparison between the two King Arthurs. The chronicler Edward Hall wrote that when they heard the name of the new prince, Englishmen rejoiced and foreigners trembled. That may have been an exaggeration, but Englishmen certainly paid attention. A whole series of pageants for royal entry into English cities – York, Worcester, Coventry, Bristol – explicitly linked Henry with Cadwaladr, King Arthur or both.

How much real effect did this have? It is hard to know, but one fact is worth noticing. Until 1485 Wales had regularly been one of the most rebellious and troublesome territories of the English crown. Yet while virtually every region of England rose in rebellion against the Tudors at some point or other, and there were certainly stirrings of discontent in Wales (see below, pp. 291–3), there was no armed rising in Wales from 1485 until 1642, when the Welsh took up arms in the Civil War in support of Henry VII's great-great-grandson King Charles I.

Henry's Arthurian glamour takes us into the realm of fantasy. But these fantasies were just as important as prosaic financial and legal management, because kingship and lordship is at heart a matter of fantasy. Successful kings did not merely balance their books and run tight bureaucracies. They sprinkled themselves with stardust, transforming themselves from ambitious politicians to sons of prophecy and God's anointed servants. Like all politics, kingship in an elective monarchy was a kind of confidence trick. Henry VII declared that he was rightful king often enough and plausibly enough that the prophecy came true.

But for all this, his achievement remained terribly fragile. Even by the end of Henry's reign, England was still essentially an elective monarchy.

The best proof of this is a notorious, and slippery, report of a conversation which took place in about 1499, and which we know through a report written four years later. When the king had been ill in 1499, we read, several (unnamed) 'great personages' had discussed who would 'have the rule' should the king die. They discussed two candidates, both men with some royal blood: the exile Edmund de la Pole and the duke of Buckingham. However, our informant tells us, 'none of them spake of my lord prince', Henry's son Arthur.[8]

This document is to be treated with considerable care. It is a third-hand account, and at least one of its reporters was probably exaggerating for effect. It does not mean that Henry's court was buzzing with conspirators waiting for the old man to die. Nor is it proof of Yorkist plotting, for a pure Yorkist dynast (had such a creature existed) would have recognised Prince Arthur's claim through his mother. But nor can it be dismissed as mere planning for a regency government, for neither Buckingham nor (especially) de la Pole was at all a plausible guardian of the Tudors' claims. Instead, it is elective monarchy at work. The presumption that these men seem to have shared was that their next king would have to be a competent adult male, and they were willing to consider almost anyone with royal blood in his veins.

So perhaps the key to Henry VII's success was mere longevity. He lived for long enough to leave his throne not to a twelve-year-old boy as in 1483, but to a seventeen-year-old youth, a charismatic and athletic young man who was a good fit to his new subjects' ideal of kingship. He was not an Arthur; but he was at least another Henry, bearing a name of kings. As a result, when the English political nation considered the choice of their new king in 1509, there was not a contest, but a coronation. No other candidate needed seriously to be considered. Henry VIII's succession to the English throne was smoother than that of any of his predecessors since 1422. The Tudor dynasty seemed secure. The events of Henry VIII's reign would expose that apparent security as an illusion.

'The lord of the world': James IV's Scotland and the theatre of kingship

James IV's inheritance as king of Scots might be expected to have been just as perilous as Henry VII's. He, too, had seized his crown on the battlefield, and while his right to inherit the throne was never disputed, there were other problems. Not the least of these was the taint of parricide: he had nominally led an army which had killed his own father. Perhaps worse, his leadership was indeed only nominal: he was manifestly the tool of a coalition led by the Homes of Coldingham, the Hepburns (soon to be the earls of Bothwell) and the earl of Angus, a coalition unlikely now to bow before his authority. It was certainly an explosive set of circumstances, but in the event the new king emerged from it in a remarkably strong position, not least because his youth gave him the chance to make a fresh start.

For all that James III had been an unpopular king, few Scots approved of killing him, especially not after the fact. Before the battle of Sauchieburn, his opponents had sworn an oath not to harm him, and the exact circumstances of his death remain mysterious. A parliament later that year, dominated by the victors of Sauchieburn, produced an official account of the battle, which stated that James III had 'happened' to be killed by 'vile and obscure persons'.[9] This whitewash could not prevent a national revulsion against the regicides. 1489 was a year of full-scale rebellion, in which the rallying cry for the rebels was justice for the dead king. Lord Forbes even raised James III's bloodstained shirt as his standard. The regicides also fell to quarrelling. Eventually, in February 1490, a new parliament reached a compromise, with all factions sharing power. Meanwhile, the young king fell into the background for a few years: he was twenty-one by the time he fully asserted his power in 1493–94, an unusually extended childhood for an early modern ruler. Why he withdrew in this way is not entirely clear, but he at least professed to be bitterly sorry for his role in his father's death. This penitence was most likely genuine, but it also did him no political harm, and it was the beginning of an astonishingly successful career as a theatrical politician.

James IV was a lucky king who used his luck well. His greatest windfall concerned a part of his kingdom which had been a thorn in his predecessors' side: the Western Isles and Highlands. In the early 1490s the lordship of the Isles was in chaos. The nominal lord, John MacDonald, was widely despised as the king's stooge. For much of the 1470s and 1480s, real power over the Isles had been wielded by his bastard son, Angus Og. But in 1490 Angus Og himself was assassinated. His cousin Alexander MacDonald tried to step in; so too did clan Campbell, whose power extended from their base in the southwest Highlands into the Isles, into the Lowlands, and across the straits to Ulster. The king spotted an opening and, with the support of those who were frightened by Campbell ambitions, took it. In 1493 he persuaded a parliament to revoke the lordship of the Isles to the crown, and in 1493 and 1494 led expeditions to the west in person. Alexander MacDonald was killed in 1494 – by his own kinsmen, not by royal forces. Angus Og's young son, Donald Dubh, was taken captive and would remain a prisoner for almost fifty years, until he escaped and made a last, doomed and romantic attempt to restore the lordship of the Isles in the 1540s. And the king stamped his authority on the Campbells, too, presiding in person over a trial in which some of their kin were accused of heresy. After 1494, the Highlands were neither pacified nor fully under royal control, but there was no organised centre of resistance remaining.

This marked the beginning of almost twenty years of internal and external peace, which Scotland would not see again until the union of the Crowns in 1603. Parliaments, which had been meeting almost annually, were allowed to lapse: there was no parliament at all in Scotland between 1496 and 1504, and then only three during the remaining nine years of the reign. This was not because James was a tyrant riding roughshod over his people, but because full parliaments simply did not appear necessary to a king who was master of his house. Instead, he entrenched his own political pre-eminence, and made royalty magnificent. He surrounded himself with prestigious scholars and made sure that the new art of printing gained a foothold in his kingdom (see below, p. 79). His father's splendid building programme had served something of the same purpose, but its extravagance had provoked resentment. James IV, too, recognised the political value of conspicuous consumption, but spent his money on something altogether more patriotic: a navy. This was more about prestige than sea power. A navy was modestly useful for a country with a long coastline and longer trading routes. Scotland did not, however, need a ship like the *Great Michael*, which, when it was launched in 1511, was the largest ship in Europe. (Nor could Scotland afford it: it was sold to France in 1514, once its royal patron was dead.) But it certainly put the kingdom on the map.

In 1496 the Spanish ambassador in England, Pedro de Ayala, made the bold decision to make a fact-finding visit to Scotland. He concluded that the country was poor, violent and full of fish. However, he was impressed by its king. James IV was, he wrote, 'of noble stature . . . and as handsome in complexion and shape as a man can be.' He spoke Latin ('very well'), French, German, Flemish, Italian and Spanish, as well as Scots and Gaelic. Ayala was impressed by the king's scholarship, piety, honesty and courage. His readiness to lead men into battle without thought of danger was almost foolhardy, Ayala thought, but it made him much loved. He added: 'I can say with truth that he esteems himself as much as though he were lord of the world.'[10] He was bringing civilisation to his barbarous people.

The piety which Ayala noticed was an important part of the package, for James IV knew that being a loyal son of the Church could bolster both his moral authority and his practical power. The first of those is more intangible but probably the more important. James IV, like Henry VII, was a committed patron of the Franciscan Observants (see above, p. 52). Under James, the number of Observant friaries in Scotland rose from four to nine: some of those new foundations were the king's own, including the one at Stirling to which he regularly went for Easter week and which became, in effect, his spiritual home. His personal confessor was an Observant. Like his repentance for his father's death, James's admiration for the friars seems to have been entirely genuine. That was what gave it its political power. More obviously theatrical was his habit of going on pilgrimage. Some pilgrimages became regular events for him, built into his itinerary, pretexts both for political display and for recreational travel. Yet this too was a serious business. Following the birth of a son in 1507, when he feared that neither the infant prince nor the queen would survive, James made an eight-day, 120-mile pilgrimage on foot to the shrine of St Ninian at Whithorn to pray for them. Four months later, the whole family returned there to give thanks together – prematurely, as it turned out, as the young prince would die a few days after his first birthday.

If God could not always be prevailed upon to reward James's piety, the pope proved more malleable. Successive popes bestowed a series of honours on him, culminating in the prestigious gift, in 1506, of the Blessed Sword and Hat. Soon after, in 1507–08, James made ostentatious plans to embark on a new and more spectacular pilgrimage, to Jerusalem. He went so far as to send the troublesome archbishop of Glasgow, Robert Blacader, to investigate the route. As luck would have it, Blacader died on the journey, and the king's scheme metamorphosed into something more grandiose and even less realistic: an international crusade against the Turks. As James well knew, those days were over, and in any case the king of Scots was hardly the obvious leader of a crusade. But the idea still stirred Christian hearts, and several theatrically pious monarchs had at various times found it worth their while to paint themselves in crusaders' colours. There was no risk that James would have to act on his ambitions, but crusading talk had its uses. In 1510–11, when James feared, correctly, that his two key European allies – France and the papacy – were about to come to blows with one another, his scheme for a crusade became part of his efforts to mediate between Paris and Rome, by providing a goal behind which all good Christians might unite.

James's militant piety also carried more mundane advantages. Crusading was an expensive prospect, and the king used it to extract large sums of money from the Scottish church: nearly £9000 over the last four years of the reign. How, after all, could the clergy stint in funding such an admirable project, proposed by a king who had won such honour from Rome? This was all the more so because, by that stage, the Scottish church was thick with the king's men. Archbishop Blacader, one of the leaders of the rebellion of 1488, had been the last of the old guard: by the time of his fatal pilgrimage of 1508, he had been frozen out of government. When the archbishopric of St Andrews first fell vacant in 1497, the king appointed his own brother, James, the duke of Ross. After Ross's unexpected death in 1504, the king's illegitimate son, Alexander Stewart, aged 11, became primate of Scotland in his place. The same pattern followed in many of Scotland's leading monasteries. James's veneration for the Observant Franciscans' piety distracts from his seizure of the incomes of less pure houses. This policy was not quite as rapacious as it looks. St Andrews was administered effectively enough in the young archbishop's name. Rather, it was a means of ensuring control, so that the church and its unique authority would be instruments of royal power rather than potential centres for opposition.

This period of glamorous, heavily armed peace produced real dividends for Scotland. James IV found himself able to assert his power against Henry VII's England, playing host opportunistically to Perkin Warbeck in 1496–97. Five years later he had changed tack. In 1502, he secured something which had eluded Scotland since 1328: a full-scale peace treaty with England, a treaty indeed of 'perpetual peace'. The treaty was cemented by a marriage: King James himself married Henry VII's eldest daughter, Margaret, in 1503. 'The marriage of the thistle and the rose', the poets called it: and since Henry VII now had only one surviving son, politicians in both countries were well aware that it made an eventual union of the two kingdoms a possibility.

That marriage's consequences were, indeed, to rumble on through the sixteenth century, but the peace of 1502 turned out to be less 'perpetual' than hoped. The combination of James IV's swashbuckling bravado and Henry VII's calculating caution had made for a fairly stable peace, but from 1509 there was a new king in England with a taste for some swashbuckling of his own. Henry VIII was a blustering innocent amidst Christendom's wily princes, and in 1513 he plunged into a full-scale Continental war of the kind which his father had avoided. The king of Scots was forced to choose between his new English alliance and the old French one. Inevitably, he chose glory over prudence. As Henry VIII crossed the Channel to invade France in person, the king of Scots led an army across the Tweed to ravage northern England. The Scottish host totalled some 30,000 men, outnumbering the English army which marched north to meet it under the command of the earl of Surrey. This numerical superiority, as much as James's gallantry, probably accounts for their decision to challenge the English to a set-piece battle. But battles are not mathematical calculations, and the battle of Flodden on 9 September 1513 was a catastrophe for the Scots. Cut to pieces by English billhooks, above a third of the Scots army were killed. The dead included the king himself; his son the archbishop of St Andrews; two other bishops, eleven earls, fifteen lords and a fair cross-section of Scotland's ruling class.

The disaster of Flodden overshadows James IV's reign. Was it the inevitable reward for his hubris; a sign of a new, technologically driven 'military revolution' which had left the Scots behind; or sheer bad luck? But whatever else it was, it was an aberration: a blip in a long Anglo-Scottish truce which otherwise lasted from 1483 to 1542. The peace of 1502 was a product not only of the immediate political circumstances, but of a general easing of tension between the two neighbours. England and Scotland still violently mistrusted one another. Each had its ambitions and grudges, and cross-border raiding continued. For the time being, however, neither was willing to raise the stakes much higher than that. Despite a brief clamour for revenge after Flodden, Scotland never again showed much appetite for invading England.

More remarkably, Henry VIII did almost nothing to exploit his victory, other than promoting the earl of Surrey to the dukedom of Norfolk. In Scotland (as in Ireland), English ambitions rarely extended beyond damage limitation. Usually, what the English wanted from their northern and western neighbours was an assurance that they would not be attacked – although they were willing to inflict savage pre-emptive strikes on those neighbours in the search of such assurances. The circle of mutual fear that this policy created remained a driving force in relationships between the British realms for most of the century, although from the 1540s onwards, other, nobler and bloodier ambitions would join it too.

Notes

1 Alec Ryrie, *The Origins of the Scottish Reformation* (2006), pp. 14–15, 37.

2 Michael Bennett, *Lambert Simnel and the Battle of Stoke* (1987), p. 105.

3 Alexander Grant, *Henry VII* (Routledge, 1985), pp. 43–5.

4 For much of what follows I am indebted to the work of my student Sarah Spencer.

5 Nicholas Pronay and John Cox (eds), *The Crowland Chronicle Continuations* (1986), p. 195.

6 *Ibid.*

7 J. Nichols (ed.), *A Collection of All the Wills . . . of the Kings and Queens of England* (1780), p. 389.

8 James Gairdner (ed.), *Letters and Papers Illustrative of the Reigns of Richard III and Henry VII* (1861), vol. I, p. 239.

9 Norman MacDougall, *James IV* (1997), p. 59.

10 P. Hume Brown (ed.), *Early Travellers in Scotland* (1891), pp. 39–48.

CHAPTER 3

The Renaissance

Out of Italy

The weight of history in the Middle Ages

By the late fifteenth century, Catholic Christianity had been the religion of western Europe since time out of mind; and it was time, tradition and continuity which gave late medieval Christianity much of its power. The Church was the preserver and the interpreter of the past, and the past weighed heavily on the medieval mind.

Of all the differences between modern mindsets and those of the late medieval period, this attitude towards *time* is one of the most pervasive. The medieval view of time had three facets which seem profoundly alien to us. First was changelessness. Medieval people were of course aware that the world around them changed, and that each year brought new events, but they did not share the modern assumption that change is directional or progressive. Fundamentally, the world would remain as it had always been. If it did change, it would eventually revert to its earlier state. The rhythm of the seasons mattered more than any change from year to year.

Paradoxically, this sat alongside a second assumption, about the brevity of time. We are nowadays blithely accustomed to measuring the past and the future in giddy quantities, millions or billions of years. Although some medieval and early modern philosophers did argue that the universe was eternal, until the nineteenth century most Christians held that Creation was only a few thousand years old, and that it was nearing its end. Whether that end was imminent or still centuries away, these were Heaven and earth's dying days.

This conviction led naturally to the third assumption: that the past was greater than the present. The world was not only nearing its end, it was visibly decaying into ever greater corruption, a process which could only end with a final plunge into depravity and Christ's return in glory. Anyone who doubted this accelerating collapse had only to measure the present against the past. Medieval people lived in the physical and intellectual ruins of the great classical civilisations, Greece and Rome, and they felt their inferiority keenly. It was a twelfth-century Englishman, John of Salisbury, who first quipped that scholars are like dwarves standing on the shoulders of giants: a saying which reflects the humility of the medieval mind. It was a truism throughout the Middle Ages that the ancients knew more about almost everything than the present did. The task of scholarship was principally to preserve, transmit, analyse and interpret ancient wisdom. Perhaps the worst insult which could be thrown at a medieval scholar was to call him an *innovator*. A new idea was, by definition, a wrong idea. Anything worth thinking of had already been thought of by the ancients.

This was true of secular learning, but even more so in religion. The Bible was of course the ultimate ancient text, whose authority was of a different order from anything else: this was Scripture, the directly inspired Word of God. Yet in the medieval mind, other ancient Christian authorities did not rank far below it. The ancient Councils of the Church which had formulated the Christian creeds, and the writings of the 'Fathers' (the early Christian theologians, especially those of the first six centuries), were seen as having unimpeachable authority. The Italian poet Dante, in his fourteenth-century vision of Heaven, described Christ's apostles as more like mountains than men.

Hence the power of the Church, the living representative of those mountains. The pope himself claimed to be (amongst other things) the direct successor of the prince of the apostles, St Peter. The Church's Ecumenical Councils (see above, p. 40) positioned themselves as the successors to the great Councils of the fourth and fifth centuries, bearing the same absolute authority. And the Church as a whole treasured the unbroken continuity of its ministry and its traditions from the first century onwards. Hence the value given to the word *catholic*, meaning universal: the Catholic faith was that which (in a famous fifth-century definition) was believed in all times, in all places and by all people. This was why heresy could be condemned in good conscience, for a heretic was someone who chose his own corrupt, fallible and modern judgement over the settled wisdom of the ages. Often, heretics were believed simply to be reviving heresies which had been condemned in the early Church, and on which no further debate was needed. If not, they were something worse: innovators.

The Italian Renaissance and what came of it

This historical humility was overturned by the intellectual and cultural revolution which we call the Renaissance. The idea that a 'rebirth' of sorts was taking place was current in the sixteenth century, but 'the Renaissance' is a nineteenth-century label and should be treated with appropriate care. (So too should another term coined at the same time: the 'Middle Ages', dismissing a thousand years of European history as a barren interval.) Even if we are happy with the word, almost everything about it is unclear: what it was, where and when it happened, and how many of it there were. This confusion is itself characteristic of the Renaissance. This was a slippery, restless, rhetorical and questioning movement, bubbling with contradiction.

The idea of renaissance was itself a splendidly medieval one: that learning, especially classical learning, should be reborn. By definition, a renaissance looks to the past. Historians have peppered the medieval period with renaissances, notably in the ninth and twelfth centuries: episodes in which scholarship revived and lost texts were rediscovered. The revival of learning in northern Italy in the fourteenth century was in some ways merely another such episode. The great Italian cities were wealthy enough to afford the luxury of scholarship, and their location – with access to the great monastic centres of western Europe, to the bleeding remnants of the Byzantine empire in the east, and to the hugely sophisticated scholarship of the Islamic world – gave their scholars rich pickings.

The new ingredient in the mix was politics. Northern Italy was the no-man's-land in the drawn-out struggle between the papacy and the Holy Roman Empire (an essentially German entity, despite its name). In this turbulent environment, a new kind of political structure emerged: the city-state, choosing to govern itself rather than trust in the flimsy protection of princes or bishops. Wealthy, unstable, aggressive and ferociously proud little republics sprang up: Siena, Pisa, Florence, Venice. City-states and republics were an innovation (that dangerous thing) in a continent wedded to the ideal of monarchy. But this innovation could draw on older models: the city-states of the ancient world, such as Athens and, above all, republican Rome. The Italians' most important discovery, or rediscovery, was of the importance of rhetoric and persuasion in republican politics. The high Latin style and sublime oratory of Cicero became the summit of Italian republican virtue. If Italians were to defend their new and embattled liberties as Cicero had defended ancient Rome's, they would need his skills. So would those who wished to dominate the maelstrom of Italian politics.

This was, of course, a wholly secular process. The city-states of the ancient world were pagan, and their rhetoric was a matter of persuasion and active politicking. Medieval theology, by contrast, stressed the importance of rationality, detachment and self-abasement. The principles of the Italian Renaissance – liberty, honour, the possibility of civic virtue, and the individual's assertion of his (always his) own place and reputation – owed little to Christianity. The Italians were well aware of this turn away from theology, and described their scholarship as the *studia humanitas* – the study of human authority. This is the origin of the modern term 'the humanities', then opposed not to science but to divinity. Hence the common description of the Renaissance scholars as *humanists*. This does not mean that they were atheists, like modern 'humanists' – indeed, many Renaissance scholars were intensely serious about their Christianity. But their scholarship was centred not on the dizzy heights of theology but on the attempt to revive good classical Latin.

This might seem a harmless enough project. But underlying it was a principle which was both thoroughly medieval and thoroughly corrosive to the medieval view of the world. The Renaissance humanists were not viewing the ancient past through the prism of the intervening ages. Instead, they were going directly to it. The recent past was being dismissed, and potentially challenged, on the basis of more ancient history. By attempting to recreate the ancient world, the humanists were challenging the claim of other medieval thinkers to be the faithful inheritors of that world. Their slogan – perhaps first coined in Spain, but a good description of the whole Renaissance enterprise – was *Ad fontes*: 'to the sources'. Scholarship became a race back to the beginning.

As this idea gathered force and spread beyond Italy, almost every sphere of learning was affected by it, for it provided a vaccine against the horror of novelty. Apparent novelty could now be presented as the revival of an older, forgotten truth. Here, by sometimes tenuous lines of descent, we can trace the origins of the so-called scientific revolution of the sixteenth and seventeenth centuries. Scholars such as Copernicus (who demonstrated that the Earth revolves around the Sun) and Vesalius (the father of modern anatomical studies) explicitly justified their radical assertions with reference to ancient authorities. Here, too, we can lay some of the blame for the so-called military revolution of the sixteenth century, as established patterns of warfare were torn up in the attempt to recreate Roman legions.

And while the Renaissance idea may have begun as a secular one, its implications for Christianity are obvious. To measure the present critically against the ancient past was obviously unsettling to the Church, since it inescapably questioned the Church's own interpretation of that past. This potential danger was aggravated by the humanists' methods: not theology, but philology. By immersing themselves in classical Latin (and then Greek, and eventually Hebrew), the humanists were able to read Christianity's ancient texts afresh. The best-known early achievement of this scholarship was Lorenzo Valla's debunking of the Donation of Constantine. The Donation of Constantine was a document which claimed that early in the fourth century, Constantine I, the first Christian Roman Emperor, had granted sovereignty over the Roman Empire to the then pope, Sylvester I, and to all subsequent popes in perpetuity. The Donation was not the principal foundation of the papacy's claims to authority, but it was one of the more eye-catching props to those claims. Lorenzo Valla was a philologist from Piacenza who wrote, amongst other things, a book with the marvellously Renaissance title *Of the Elegance of the Latin Language*. In an essay written in 1439–40, Valla proved that the Donation was a forgery. The Latin in which it was written was simply anachronistic. Valla concluded, as have more recent scholars, that it was concocted in the eighth or ninth centuries. Valla's work was not widely publicised until some time later, and in any case his revelation was embarrassing rather than earth-shaking. Nevertheless, it was a sign of what Renaissance scholarship might do.

By the early sixteenth century, this second Renaissance – 'Christian humanism' – was in full spate. From being a local, Italian phenomenon it had spread across Latin Christendom's network of universities, putting down deep roots in Germany and the Netherlands. And if its early phase has an icon in Lorenzo Valla, its high noon was dominated and defined by Desiderius Erasmus. Erasmus was a brilliant, sharp-tongued, penny-pinching Dutch monk who blended deeply felt piety and scholarly cattiness with an excellent feel for when to pick a fight. During the first two decades of the sixteenth century he deliberately turned himself into an international scholarly celebrity. He was no theologian – indeed, he was suspicious of theology, fearing that its abstract and divisive debates were a distraction from the Christian life. In works such as his immensely popular *Handbook of a Christian Soldier* (1504), he wrote movingly of a simple, ethical, inner Christianity, stripped of ceremonial flummery and fruitless metaphysical speculation. And his satires of that flummery and speculation could be biting. In *Praise of Folly* (1509), he compared Christ's apostles to the university theologians of his own day, observing ironically that the apostles merely detested sin, whereas it took a theologian to define it scientifically.

Erasmus' greatest *coup* was his publication, in 1516, of a Greek text of the New Testament. The original, Hebrew and Greek texts of the Bible had been incomprehensible to most medieval scholars. Since the fifth century, the standard version of the Bible in the western Church had been the Vulgate, a Latin translation ascribed to St Jerome. The vernacular translations prepared by the Lollards or by good continental Catholics in the fourteenth and fifteenth centuries were all based on the Vulgate. A return to the original texts was an obvious project for the Renaissance linguists. Erasmus' version was not the first: it pre-empted a much grander and more scholarly version of the entire Bible already being printed in Spain. (Erasmus ensured the Spanish version was banned from sale until 1520, guaranteeing his own text a clear run.) His book was an immediate success. In a famous introduction, Erasmus urged that all Christians should be Bible-readers – 'even the lowliest women'. 'Only a very few can be learned,' he admitted, 'but if they read their Bibles, 'all can be devout, and – I shall boldly add – all can be theologians.' The Bible, indeed, made scholarly theology obsolete. It taught the 'pure and genuine philosophy of Christ', stripped of all unnecessary accretions. These were eminently Renaissance sentiments; but it was also potentially revolutionary stuff.[1]

Characteristically, Erasmus did not press this too far. His inflammatory call for mass translation was made in the safe, scholarly obscurity of Latin. Yet what made Erasmus' book truly dangerous was that his Greek text was accompanied by a new translation into Latin. In this, he pointed out (with the full weight of humanist philology behind him) that the Vulgate contained a number of errors of translation, minor but not insignificant. Erasmus' translation suggested a more interior, less ritualised religion – as he himself preferred, of course. Most famously, he argued that the Greek word *metanoia* should not be translated as *poenitentia* ('do penance'), as in the Vulgate. It should be understood to mean an inner turning away from sin, rather than an outward, sacramental act of penance. Such details were not, in themselves, going to bring the edifice of medieval theology down, nor was Erasmus aiming to do such a thing. But they did eat away at that edifice's foundations. Rather than attacking established theology directly, the Christian humanists were threatening to render it irrelevant by questioning its premises. What if the whole structure of medieval theology had been built on simple misunderstandings?

The Renaissance in Britain

As with most of the great intellectual movements of the late medieval and early modern period, the British Isles were followers rather than leaders in the Renaissance. There were five universities in Britain in 1500: three small fifteenth-century establishments in Scotland, at St Andrews, Glasgow and Aberdeen (the latter two were as yet little more than diocesan colleges), and two older and more substantial English academies, Oxford and Cambridge. In the thirteenth century Oxford had rivalled Paris as the most respected academy in Europe. However, Oxford had then produced the heretic Wyclif, and its reputation had never quite recovered. Respectable patrons – in particular, King Henry VI – had built up its younger, smaller rival at Cambridge instead, and by 1500 there was little to choose between the two in terms of size, wealth or prestige. Cambridge was the more bullish of the two: it did not (yet) have a heretic to live down, and it was about to acquire a remarkable guest.

Scotland

The Scottish Renaissance was a modest affair by international standards. Yet while those small universities were not great European centres of learning, they speak of the ambitions of the Scottish elite. The university of Aberdeen was founded in 1495 by William Elphinstone, that city's bishop. Elphinstone is a textbook example of how Renaissance learning could spread through the international, Latin-speaking world of Christendom's universities. He had spent much of his youth studying in France, and had been rector of Glasgow University before becoming a bishop. His new university was consciously modelled on Paris and on other leading Continental institutions such as Bologna. He introduced a curriculum with a humanist twist (although the Greek language was not taught at any Scottish university until the 1550s). This was a novelty, for until then Scottish universities had followed the classic medieval pattern, existing principally to train the clergy in theology and canon law. Humanists, by contrast, aspired to educate the laity. In 1496, a year after the new foundation at Aberdeen, a Scottish parliament passed the so-called 'Education Act', requiring all barons and substantial lairds (a *laird* was a substantial landholder without a noble title) to send their eldest sons to grammar school until they had mastered Latin, and then to give them three further years of legal education. Like much Scottish legislation, this was never much more than an aspiration (legal training on that scale simply did not exist), but it was a very Renaissance aspiration. And lairds' education did, indeed, slowly improve. In properly Renaissance style, this education was practical and political, rather than abstract. The 1496 act aimed to give lairds legal expertise and draw them into the administration of government.

These newly educated lairds were not Renaissance humanists as such. Few of them had much Latin, let alone the ornate sophistication to which the Italians aspired. They can, however, be seen as what one scholar has called 'vernacular humanists':[2] that is, they had absorbed some of the political and cultural values of the Renaissance without actually studying the languages. This vernacular humanism had a pervasive effect on Scottish culture. It further marginalised the old, bardic traditions of Gaelic-speaking Scotland: a formidably sophisticated culture, but one whose long retreat was accelerating. By contrast, it provoked some Scots to look optimistically to the south, a thoroughly novel stance. The court poets of King James IV, who actively tried to fill his court with Renaissance scholarship, reflected the mood of good relations with England in the early sixteenth century. The finest Scots poet of this generation, William Dunbar, was kept by James on a generous stipend and fulsomely celebrated the 1503 English marriage in *The Thrissill and the Rois*. Gavin Douglas, the bishop of Dunkeld, was another of this charmed circle of court poets (usually known, in Dunbar's term, as the 'makaris' or word-builders). Douglas was strikingly pro-English in his politics; artistically, he saw himself as the heir of the great medieval English poets, Chaucer, Gower and Lydgate.

One of Douglas' habits, which was to become a Renaissance common-place both north and south of the Border, was to talk of 'Britain' or 'Great Britain'. The term was of Roman origin, and so fitted the humanists' classical pretensions better than the medieval tawdriness of 'England' and 'Scotland'. When the word 'Britain' was used in the medieval period – which was not often – it was used to mean either the historical Roman province, or one or both of Wales and Brittany. The description of the whole island as Great Britain was rare before the fifteenth century (even then, the English, as ever, tended to use 'England' and 'Britain' interchangeably). But given the Renaissance reverence for the ancient past, the revival of this ancient word could never be merely semantic. If the island of Britain had once been united (and most people believed it had been, in pre-Roman days), surely its two long-sundered kingdoms should recognise their kinship and be rejoined? The finest scholar of the Scottish Renaissance, the conciliarist John Mair, took this view. Mair's *History of Greater Britain* (the title, a typically Renaissance Latin pun, could also mean *History of Mair's Britain*), published in 1521 when he was principal of Glasgow University, emphasised that the inhabitants of Britain were Britons first, and Scots or English second. Throughout he emphasised the deep connections between the two countries and held out the possibility of a reunion.

This pro-British view is worth noting because it was almost unprecedented in Scotland. It was not, however, the common voice of the Scottish Renaissance. More typical is the view of Mair's contemporary Hector Boyis (who, in humanist style, is better known by the Latinised version of his surname, Boece). Boece was the first principal of Aberdeen University, and in 1527 replied to Mair's *History* with a *History of Scotland* of his own. While full of humanist sparkle, Boece's *History* had a pungent anti-English nationalism. It was also much more successful than Mair's version. Three different Scots translations from the Latin original were prepared in the 1530s, one of them made for King James V himself. This kind of assertive nationalism was at least as typical of the Renaissance as Mair's idealistic internationalism. This partly reflected, again, the political tang that flavoured a good deal of humanist scholarship. But it also reflected the particular priorities of the Elphinstone circle at Aberdeen. Aside from his new university, one of Elphinstone's great projects was the creation of a new liturgy for the Scottish church, the Aberdeen Breviary published in 1509–10. Like all western Christian liturgies, the Aberdeen rite was in Latin, and its essentials would have been recognisable in Poland, Spain or Cyprus; but it was also distinctively Scottish, not least in the roster of new Scottish saints whom it celebrated. It displaced the Sarum (Salisbury) missal, the English rite which had been used across most of Scotland up to that point. It was an assertion of intellectual and religious independence.

Renaissance humanism did not, of course, invent patriotism. But it did provide a veneer of sophistication for it, and a new arena in which national competition could take place. It was an arena in which the Scots, painfully conscious of their reputation as uncultured northern barbarians, strove to be taken seriously. When an Italian papal emissary named Marco Grimani visited Scotland in 1543, the earl of Moray laid on an elaborate charade to impress him. Moray proudly produced a dinner service made from the finest imported crystal for his guest. Then, at a pre-arranged moment, the servant carrying the tray stumbled, and hundreds of pounds' worth of crystal was smashed. The stereotypical Scottish lord would have killed the servant on the spot, but Moray, in a splendid show of nonchalance, simply shrugged and asked the servant to bring out some more crystal – whereupon another, identical dinner service was produced.[3] The tale may be apocryphal, but it suggests the effort and expense to which Renaissance Scots would go to confound foreigners' views of them. It is certainly true that when they encountered real Continental humanists, Scots were starstruck. One such, a perfectly competent but not especially distinguished Italian scholar named Giovanni Ferrerio, came to Scotland in 1528, where he discovered the delights of being a big fish in a small pond. He was fêted at James V's court, remained there for three years as a tame scholar, and then spent a further ten years (in two separate stints) as a tutor at Kinloss Abbey, near Inverness.

A final, important ingredient of Renaissance court culture was satire: a humanist speciality, from the Italian city-states to Erasmus. To emphasise rhetoric and persuasion, rather than mere logic, legitimised ridicule and vitriol. In Scotland, this face of the Renaissance first appeared in 'flytings', verbal tournaments of taunts and insults between two quick-witted poets, staged for the entertainment of the court like gladiatorial combat. William Dunbar's flytings were famous, and the makaris' role at court was partly to provide this sort of fun. The finest satirist of the Scottish Renaissance, however, was a court poet of the next generation: Sir David Lindsay of the Mount, whose public career stretched from around 1510 to his death in 1555. Lindsay produced formal public poetry of the kind which a Renaissance court demanded – marking, for example, the passing of the short-lived Queen Madeleine in 1537. He was made Scotland's chief herald, and was used as a diplomat (presenting a sophisticated face to the world). But he was best known, at the time and since, for his biting satires. The pitfalls and treachery of the courtier's life were an abiding humanist theme, born of humanism's fascination with the possibilities of political power and its horror of the compromises which such power necessarily meant in practice. Lindsay explored these themes in, for example, his 1530s poem *The complaint of the king's old hound*, using James V's alternate affection for and anger with his favourite hunting dogs as a metaphor for the fate of his courtiers.[4]

However, as befitted a man half a generation younger than Erasmus, the real focus of Lindsay's satires was the Church and its abuses. Beginning with scathing but orthodox denunciations of clerical immorality, indiscipline and ignorance, by mid-century Lindsay was making more searching criticisms of the Church's doctrines, practices and structures. And even merely anticlerical satire helped to create an atmosphere in which public disrespect for the clergy was licensed, at least at court. George Buchanan, a younger court humanist who would later become notorious for his near-revolutionary political theories, first made his name in the late 1530s when he composed a series of savage satires on the Franciscan friars. It was James V himself who had commissioned these, and the king then rejected Buchanan's first draft as too innocuous, demanding 'a keen satire that would sting to the quick'.[5] This was because of the king's enjoyment of verbal games, not any animus against the Franciscans – he revered the order almost as much as his father had (see p. 58). Yet games like these have consequences.

England

The English Renaissance outshone its Scottish counterpart, but it remained peripheral in European terms. The phrase 'Renaissance England' is in fact usually taken to mean the England of Shakespeare, Spenser and Jonson rather than of the early Tudors. Like the Scots, the English picked up on the new scholarly fashions. The early Renaissance was marked by an accelerating boom in education, on the back of the general economic recovery. Where the pious rich might once have founded or endowed a monastery, they now tended to endow colleges and schools, or chantries whose priests were expected to teach the living as well as pray for the dead. The days when the nobility saw reading as beneath their dignity were gone. Their children were educated by private tutors, but talented boys of all social backgrounds were increasingly able to indulge in a grammar-school education, which, for the minority who completed it, would give them a good working command of Latin. And while formal schooling of this kind was indeed only for boys, amongst the wealthy the novelty of girls' education was beginning to make itself felt too.

The royal court led the humanist charge. The university establishments, especially at Oxford, were initially resistant; but change was forced on them, partly through a series of new foundations such as Corpus Christi College, Oxford or Margaret Beaufort's new colleges at Cambridge (see above, pp. 52–3). Greek scholarship had its foot firmly in the door of both universities by 1520. As in Scotland, the new fashion in scholarship fostered an idealistic internationalism, a newly robust nationalism and a wave of satire. England, too, showed some signs of 'cultural cringe' in the face of Continental learning. In 1502 a young papal envoy named Polydore Vergil came to England, and – like Giovanni Ferrerio in Scotland a generation later – discovered that being a scholar and an Italian made him into a celebrity. He stayed for fifty years, received generous royal patronage, and produced (amongst other things) a Latin history of England which showcased England's ancient dignities for European contemporaries.

Polydore Vergil was a scholar of some note: it is even possible that Erasmus may have plagiarised some of his work. But three years before his arrival, England had been graced with its first visit from Erasmus himself. The Dutchman spent much of his life on the move, a sign of his intellectual restlessness but also of his endless search for patronage. Henry VII's court, striving to establish a reputation for scholarship, had an obvious attraction. Erasmus first visited in 1499, then again briefly in 1505, and – remarkably – spent the years 1509–14 in England. For most of this time he taught at Cambridge University, complaining bitterly about the climate; in the process he helped to put English scholarship in general, and Cambridge in particular, firmly on the international map. Early in this visit, he wrote one of his most famous books, *Moriae encomium*. The title was (as so often) a pun. It meant *The Praise of Folly*, but could also be taken to praise the London lawyer to whom the book was dedicated, and in whose house it was written: Thomas More.

More was one of a tiny handful of sixteenth-century English writers who won genuine international fame. Only his friend John Fisher and (from the other end of the century) the Puritan theologian William Perkins really bear comparison. More is the giant of the English Renaissance, and a man filled with paradoxes. His most enduring book, and the one which explained to Europe what Erasmus saw in this Englishman, is *Utopia* (1516) – a teasing hall of mirrors, at once a satire, a withering analysis of England's social ills, a work of political philosophy, and a complex joke played on the reader. In the first portion of *Utopia*, More laid out a Christian humanist critique of contemporary politics. He lambasted the callous greed and self-righteousness of the ruling classes, who would hang the starving for trying to feed themselves. He excoriated kings who cared more for war and self-aggrandisement than for the welfare of their countries. He feared that if a wise man were to become involved in politics he would find himself ignored, deceived or (most likely) corrupted. Yet like most Renaissance scholars, he could not find it in himself simply to walk away from the political world, either in the book or in his life.

The second, more famous part of the book describes a fictional island, Utopia ('nowhere') which reflects, but certainly does not constitute, More's vision of an ideal society. It runs from the idealistic (the Utopians have no private property, are peaceful and do not put criminals to death) to the satirical (prisoners in Utopia are kept in gold chains and manacles, the better to emphasise that gold has no intrinsic value and should be despised); and from the surprising (Utopia is a pagan society with broad religious toleration) to the downright weird (in Utopia, prospective brides and grooms formally view one another naked before finalising the decision to marry). The reader is never sure quite what, and how much, More really means: and this playfulness is an important part of the Renaissance style. But the basic congruence with Erasmian Christian humanism is never in doubt. While deprecating the corruption of his own kingdom, More imagines a republic of virtuous pagans, an idealised version of ancient Rome and a standing reproach to those who ought (thanks to the light of the Christian Gospel) to surpass its virtues. This republic of honest labour, good order and learning, in which all property is held in common, expands on an ancient Christian ideal: the monastery. But in keeping with the Renaissance spirit, More – who had nearly joined a monastery himself as a young man, but had married instead – does not imagine a small, exclusive, celibate community. Rather, Utopia is a universal monastery, which embraces and hallows secular work and married life. In the same year, Erasmus hoped in his New Testament that all Christians would be theologians; More hoped that they would all be monks. It was the same wish.

By the 1520s, this mischievous, restless movement was becoming a new establishment in England. Nowhere was this plainer than amongst the senior clergy. John Fisher, formerly confessor to Lady Margaret Beaufort, was the first humanist to win a bishopric (England's smallest, Rochester, in 1504). More substantial appointments followed. Archbishop Warham of Canterbury was no humanist himself, but was a generous patron to Erasmus as well as to English scholars like John Colet and Cuthbert Tunstall. Colet, the dean of St Paul's Cathedral, was a plain-speaking advocate of humanist values: he had the temerity to preach before Henry VIII that war was incompatible with Christianity, which the king, then on the point of invading France, took badly. Tunstall had been a lawyer in Warham's service, attracted Erasmus' praise, and was regularly sent abroad as a diplomat before becoming bishop of London in 1522. John Longland, a friend of More's, Tunstall's and Fisher's whom Erasmus also liked, became bishop of Lincoln (England's most populous diocese) in 1521. Edward Lee – a conservative humanist who had once worked with Erasmus, before quarrelling viciously with him – gave extensive service as a diplomat before being made archbishop of York in 1531. Tunstall, Longland and Lee all proved to be diocesan bishops in the Erasmian mould, energetically promoting clerical discipline and education while remaining actively involved in national politics.

Lee's predecessor at York was quite a different animal: the political colossus Thomas Wolsey, who was a cardinal and a papal legate, and had twice achieved the feat of holding two English bishoprics simultaneously. Those bishoprics were principally sources of dignity, power and income, and he scarcely visited his dioceses. Wolsey was more a politician than a scholar; but he, too, recognised the political power of Renaissance culture and shared some humanist values. His sophisticated and expensive tastes in music, tapestry and that pastime of princes, architecture, were well remarked at the time. He was a patron of learning, establishing a generously endowed school in his home town of Ipswich (for which he himself wrote a Latin grammar) and an enormous college at Oxford. But he also provided a larger-than-life target for the practitioners of the Renaissance art of satire. England's answer to Sir David Lindsay was the scurrilous court poet John Skelton, who in the 1510s wrote formal celebratory verse as well as vicious flytings (in both of which he showed a xenophobic patriotism). In the 1520s, he turned these considerable talents to denouncing Wolsey's power and perceived corruption, in a series of venomous satires which claimed that the Cardinal was treacherous, syphilitic and a great deal else.

Renaissance and Reformation

The relationship between this new set of intellectual preoccupations and fashions, and the religious revolution which erupted shortly afterwards, is a famously vexed question. 'I laid the egg; Luther hatched it' – so Erasmus admitted, ascribing the saying to spiteful German friars.[6] Much as he disliked the fact, it was obvious then, as it has been ever since, that there was some kind of connection. Many of the first generation of Protestant leaders were serious humanists (Luther himself was an exception, in this as in many other things). There were obvious points of contact between the Christian humanists' priorities and the Protestant reformers' programme. The overriding emphasis on the Bible, in particular the promise of making it available in vernacular languages; the contempt for so-called superstition and for clerical wealth and corruption; the emphasis on education, and on inward piety rather than external formalities – all of this was common ground. So much so that Protestants long laid claim to the Christian humanists as their spiritual ancestors.

Yet as Erasmus' disowning of Luther's hatchling shows, the connection is not at all straightforward. After several years of increasing unease, Erasmus finally and decisively broke off with Luther in 1524–25, and died a Catholic ten years later. Others who had joined him in criticisms – sometimes bitter criticisms – of the ecclesiastical establishment also refused ever formally to break faith with the old Church. Sir David Lindsay of the Mount, who sometimes went so far as to call the pope a manifestation of Antichrist, also lived and died a Catholic. Few of Erasmus' English friends ever even flirted with the new heresies. More and John Fisher were executed for their loyalty to the papacy. Lee, Longland and Tunstall all conformed, reluctantly, to Henry VIII's Reformation, but all of them worked hard to prevent any semblance of Protestantism creeping into it, both in their own dioceses and in national politics. A weak generational link can be discerned – younger humanists were somewhat more likely to become Protestants than their older brethren. Likewise, humanist Cambridge gave a warmer reception to Protestant ideas than did old-fashioned Oxford, although this may simply reflect Oxford's determination not to repeat its painful history of heresy. But there was every reason for humanists to distrust the new theologies. Far from the simple, ethical Christianity for which Erasmus had hoped, the Protestants were formulating complex and counter-intuitive theologies. In particular, their core idea of justification by faith (see below, pp. 91–2) seemed to undermine the very idea of morality. And while attacks on abuses and excessive ceremonial might be acceptable, undermining the sacraments – the very glue of Christian society – was another matter.

If humanism were simply the larval stage of Protestantism, then the course of the European Reformation would have been very different. By the early sixteenth century humanism was ascendant across western Christendom. It was not only the English and Scottish courts which had been swept by the new fashions. Europe's self-consciously Renaissance monarchs included its two most powerful sovereigns, the French king Francis I and the Holy Roman Emperor, Charles V. Yet unlike humanism, Protestantism did not sweep all before it. The Reformation was not a battle between Renaissance enlightenment and medieval obscurantism; it was a civil war within humanism. That is one reason why it was so bitterly fought.

Rather than humanism naturally developing into Protestantism, we would do better to think of Protestantism hijacking humanism and taking it in a new direction. The continuities between the two *are* real: certainly, without humanism there would have been no Protestant Reformation. Yet if Protestantism hatched from Erasmus' egg, it quickly turned out to be a cuckoo in the nest. It advocated reforms which had an Erasmian flavour and mocked the old Church in an Erasmian vein. But those reforms and that mockery were justified by a radical theological programme which did not merely go further than the Christian humanists, but actively opposed some of their ideas and added some entirely new ones.

Moreover, as the sixteenth century progressed and the battle-lines between Protestant and Catholic were drawn, both sides withdrew to some extent from the Christian humanist agenda. The playful, erudite questioning of the Renaissance had made sense when it was a matter of a few daring scholars writing clever Latin treatises for one another in a united, stable Christendom. With the continent torn by schism, it seemed both irresponsible and irrelevant. In 1559 all of Erasmus' works were placed on the Index of Prohibited Books by the grimly combative Pope Paul IV. Long before that, the Protestant danger had so alarmed Thomas More that he both wrote a series of bitter polemics and personally pursued several Protestant converts to their executions.

The contrast between the two Mores – the tolerant humanist of *Utopia* and the persecuting zealot – is unnerving to modern eyes, but there is no real contradiction. It was one thing for Latin games to be played carefully by consenting scholars with no ulterior motives; quite another for those games to be aped in public by dangerous extremists using them to destroy Christian society and damn Christian souls. More famously claimed that although superstition was bad, it was preferable to impiety. He believed, following Erasmus, that the Bible ought in principle to be made available in English; but he violently opposed doing so while the heretical disease was raging, for such strong medicine might prove fatal to patients whose orthodoxy was not robust. Ten years after More's own execution, when Europe's Catholic theologians finally gathered to give their formal response to Protestantism at the Council of Trent, it was medieval theology's sharp definitions which governed their responses, not the humanists' airy rhetoric. And this was mirrored by developments within Protestantism. Some followed the lead of the most brilliant of the Protestant humanists, Luther's friend Philip Melanchthon, who hoped for an inclusive Protestantism cautious of doctrinal over-definition. But by the end of the century, Protestants of all stripes, including (perhaps especially) those in England and Scotland, were laying out schematic, systematic theologies constructed with a hard-edged logic which echoed the precision of the medievals. The Renaissance moment had passed.

Books and printing

If the Renaissance was a movement of scholars and intellectuals, its impact was made possible by a much more mundane development: the invention of printing. Here it is traditional to notice Johannes Gutenberg, the German who first developed the technique of printing with movable type in 1454. But while Gutenberg was certainly gifted, he was less the inventor of printing than the winner of a race: his rivals were only months behind him. Printing as such – using a stamp to mark a surface repeatedly – is such a simple concept that it scarcely needs invention. Stamped metal artefacts survive from the second millennium BC. The use of inked stamps on paper was invented in early medieval China, and slowly spread westwards across the Eurasian landmass. Printed pictures – made from a single, large wood-cut stamp – were being manufactured in Europe in the first half of the fifteenth century. Gutenberg's achievement was a metallurgical one: making large numbers of cast metal stamps of individual letters, sufficiently alike that they could be set into a frame to form a page of text.

What is remarkable about printing is not its invention but its adoption. It was an idea whose time had come. Until the 1450s, books were produced by hand-copying, a process which had served scholarship well for millennia and which could quickly produce accurate copies. But it was unavoidably labour-intensive. So too was setting up a book for the printing press, but once set up, a press operated by skilled printers could produce well over 1000 copies of a printed folio page in a single day. The economics were stark. Setting a book up to print took about three times as long as hand-copying it, but once that had been done, copies could be produced at a prodigious rate for little more than the cost of the ink and paper. (Indeed, the cost of paper was the single biggest expense in book production throughout this period.) The prices of books therefore fell precipitously, and the supply increased exponentially. The result was an extraordinary, technology-fuelled boom, as Gutenberg's technical achievement was copied and improved on across the Continent. From its German heartland, printing became firmly established in Italy and France within a few years. It was a risky business. While hand-copying of books could be done on a tiny scale, printing required expensive equipment and a highly skilled workforce. All the outlay – on presses, trained printers, type, ink, paper, and binding and transporting the finished product – had to be made before a single book had actually been sold, and with no guarantee that a single book *would* be sold. The result – perhaps inevitably – was that the book boom was followed by a book bust, with large numbers of printers succumbing to bankruptcy in the 1490s and 1500s, and the industry consolidating into a few, larger centres. For those who succeeded, however, there were fortunes to be made.

Once again, Britain was peripheral to this process. It is a mark of how quickly printing had swept across the Continent that it took only twenty years after Gutenberg for a printing press first to be established in England, by William Caxton in 1475. For two or three generations, however, the English printing industry was to be dominated by foreign (principally Netherlandish) expertise. Technically, English printing remained crude compared to the more sophisticated work coming out of Paris or Venice, and indeed, when English patrons needed something large or complex printed, they usually sent the job abroad. Until 1523, the printing trade was exempt from the normal regulations against foreign merchants living and operating in England: a recognition of the English industry's dependence on foreign expertise.

This was not merely private enterprise. Governments across Europe were keen to regulate and profit from this new industry, and the printers were equally enthusiastic for official favour. Large or prestigious printing projects could be tackled much more easily if royal or noble patrons provided some of the funding up front. Indeed, publishing something really substantial – such as a full-sized Bible – was often best attempted by several different printshops working together. Governments were also alive to the potential official and propaganda uses of the new technology. Royal proclamations, for example, could now be printed and pasted up in marketplaces across the country as well as being read out by heralds, and legal texts could be circulated much more easily to local magistrates. The dangers of printing were also plain enough, but until the 1520s they did not appear pressing. Illicit books such as Lollard texts continued to circulate in manuscript (handwritten) form. It would have been hard to make money printing books of this kind, and in any case, printing (unlike hand-copying) was an industrial process which could not easily be carried on in secret.

Print prospered, therefore, with official help and under official oversight. Governments regularly backed uneconomic printing projects for political reasons. Scotland acquired its first printers in 1507, when James IV licensed Andrew Myllar and Walter Chepman to set up a press in Edinburgh. Myllar had trained in Rouen, and all their equipment – paper included – was imported. They dabbled in printing poetry in 1508: we do not know whether any of this actually reached the point of being sold. In 1510, however, they earned their keep by producing Bishop Elphinstone's Aberdeen Breviary: a prestige, nationalist project given an extra fillip by being printed in Scotland. The reality, however, was that Scotland could not yet support a genuine domestic printing industry, and printing in Scotland remained fitful and occasional until the 1560s. In Ireland, printing did not even begin until 1549 – and that too was a government-sponsored project (see below, p. 298). Likewise, there were various politically led attempts in England to establish regional presses during the later fifteenth and early sixteenth centuries, in Canterbury, Cambridge, St Albans and – a little later – Ipswich and Worcester. None survived for more than a few years.

The result was that British printing was almost completely concentrated in one place, London (indeed largely in one part of London, the immediate vicinity of St Paul's Cathedral). By 1600 regular printing was beginning in Oxford, Cambridge, Dublin and elsewhere, but London's dominance remained utterly overwhelming. This had lasting consequences. It made the book trade much easier for England's government to monitor and control. Throughout the sixteenth century, close state control of the industry was a key fact of politics, and the brief periods when that control lapsed or was evaded caused political turmoil. The contrast with France or with the Holy Roman Empire, whose decentralised and dispersed printing industries meant that dissident voices could usually find an outlet in print, is striking. Those who wished to print controversial or illegal texts were forced to do so abroad. This meant delay, expense and the practical difficulties of smuggling illegal books into the country. Later in the century, dissidents of various stripes set up mobile, clandestine presses in England, a cumbersome and difficult process which alarmed the Elizabethan regime a great deal but did not succeed in producing very many books.

London's near-monopoly of print reinforced its political and economic dominance of the islands with cultural dominance. The modern English language is based on London English: it was that which London's printers used and which therefore became the standard for written English across the islands. Other regional varieties were reduced to spoken dialects. This applied even in Scotland, where the distinctive features of the Scots language were slowly eroded by the flood of books in what they called 'Southron'. London was increasingly able to set the islands' intellectual agenda and to define their public culture. The small clique of foreigners and craftsmen who controlled London's printshops – men and women (for there were some women) whose views were by no means typical – would prove to have a great deal of power.

For print changed the world, and did so in many ways, some obvious, some not. To take the obvious first: it created a mass market for books. Books were now available in much greater numbers than ever before, and at much lower cost. Over 30,000 editions of printed books appeared across Europe before 1500 (that is, many millions of individual copies); perhaps ten times that number during the sixteenth century. This expansion fuelled, and was fuelled by, the already rising tide of literacy: once a specialist skill which had been assumed to be exclusive to the clergy, lay literacy was now very widespread, and even female literacy was rising fast (from a very low base). The explosion in books now made the effort of learning to read worthwhile. And printers, who had a business to run, always had their eye on the market. Cheap, disposable, mass-market items underpinned the entire industry, from pocket-sized books of prayers through to poster-sized single sheets containing edifying or scurrilous ballads. Cheap print of this kind gives us a rare glimpse into the lives of those outside the social elites – or at least, it tells us what the printers believed such people would buy and what they could get away with selling to them. It may also suggest something more profound: that the grip of those small elites on society and politics was weakening. It is thanks to the book trade that, in the sixteenth century, we can first meaningfully talk about 'public opinion' in England and (to a lesser extent) Scotland, although the 'public' remained a very small one.

Renaissance humanists, who so exalted education, of course approved of this spread of literacy, even if the common sort rarely read what their betters wanted them to. But the impact of printing on the scholars and humanists themselves was, if anything, more profound. We have seen how both medieval and Renaissance thought was underpinned by a profound humility towards the past, and an emphasis on preserving and transmitting the wisdom of the ancients. There was an excellent practical reason for this, namely that in the age of handwriting, preserving and transmitting that wisdom was a colossal task. It was also a battle which the medieval world had been losing. Expensive, rare, often miscopied or misleadingly edited, handwritten books were a slender thread by which to hang Christendom's scholarly tradition. Fire, flood, theft and war had steadily eroded the stock of ancient texts which were preserved. Only fragments of the vast literature of the ancient world survive to us, and most of the medieval period's own literature is lost too. The age of handwriting was an age of inexorable forgetting. The appearance of print dramatically reversed this. We know of hundreds or thousands of lost great books from before the age of print, but of none from after it. This was when European civilisation stopped forgetting and began to remember.

The Renaissance scholars could therefore set their sights higher than mere preservation. Print made books available to scholars who might previously have had to cross Europe for sight of a copy. It made standardised copies available, reducing (although not eliminating) the danger of texts being corrupted by copyists' errors. It meant that books could be illustrated with detailed and precise images, a boon to geography, medicine, mathematics and many other fields of learning.

The ancient texts which the humanists so revered were now much more widely available, and this had a real impact on their authority. Nowhere was this clearer than with the Bible, a book whose meaning subtly changed in the era of print. Christians had, of course, seen the Scriptures as having a unique, inspired authority since the earliest times. During the medieval period, however, the Scriptures were largely inaccessible, their texts in Latin and access to them restricted to theologians. And it was as plural Scriptures rather than a single Bible that the texts were seen. Manuscripts of the whole Bible were a rarity (they were physically huge); individual books of the Bible, or sets of books, were far more common. This was as true of the Lollards' illegal English Bible as of the Latin Vulgate. Print changed this in two ways. First – as Erasmus had hoped – it made the Scriptures much more widely accessible, releasing this enormous and complex set of texts from its scholarly seclusion and loosing it on a much wider public. And second, it redefined that set of texts as a single book: the Bible, or at least the New Testament, bound neatly between one set of covers. It was an immensely exciting prospect. All truth was neatly encapsulated in what (to those unfamiliar with books) looked like a small box, a box of treasures and secrets which anyone might open. To early sixteenth century people it was becoming obvious, as it had not been before, that 'the Bible' was a single entity, an accessible and unified whole. Its status as both ancient text and printed artefact gave it an authority quite distinct from that of the Church which had transmitted and preserved it. Instead, it was a standard against which that Church might be measured.

Notes

1 John C. Olin, *Christian Humanism and the Reformation* (1965), pp. 97, 100, 102.

2 Priscilla Bawcut, *Gavin Douglas: a critical study* (1976), p. 36.

3 John Leslie, *The Historie of Scotland*, ed. E. G. Cody and William Murison, vol. 2 (1895), p. 276.

4 Sarah Carpenter, 'David Lindsay and James V: court literature as current event' in Jennifer Britnell and Richard Britnell (eds), *Vernacular Literature and Current Affairs in the Early Sixteenth Century* (2000).

5 James M. Aitken, *The Trial of George Buchanan before the Lisbon Inquisition* (1939), p. xix.

6 P. S. Allen (ed.), *Opus Epistolarum des Erasmi Roterodami*, vol. V (1924), p. 609.

CHAPTER 4

Renaissance to Reformation

Henry VIII and the glamour of kingship, 1509–27

The performer king

Henry VIII is the most celebrated and most notorious of English monarchs. This is mostly because of the misadventures of his later life, when he led England into one of Europe's oddest Reformations and, in the process, went through six wives in just over a decade. However, before he became an icon of lust and religious egomania, Henry had already carefully cultivated an image as the ideal Renaissance king. He is remembered today not only for his wives but also for his portraits: Hans Holbein's images of Henry's potato-face remain instantly recognisable. This was not an accident. Attracting people like Holbein – a German portraitist who had first made his name painting Erasmus – was what Henry's court was designed to do. And his portraits defined what Henry's kingship aspired to be. Henry VIII was the first English king to have a full-length portrait painted: never before had the royal legs been depicted. This was Henry Tudor, athlete, musician, poet, lover, hunter and scholar: the whole of his being was a part of his kingship.

Henry VII could not have afforded such showmanship, but he provided the legacy which made it possible. Young Prince Henry became king in 1509, at the age of seventeen, in far easier circumstances than any of the other Tudors. His succession was undisputed. England was at peace at home and abroad. The royal finances were on an exceptionally sound footing. The new king had the leisure and the means to embark on a life of spectacle and extravagance.

He quickly moved to consolidate this position by making two moves which would become his trademarks (and which often went together): he forced through a ruthless judicial murder, and he got married. Sir Richard Empson and Edmund Dudley, two of the most graspingly efficient members of Henry VII's money-raising machine, were arrested three days after their old master's death. The charges of extortion and treason against them were not imaginary, but they were plainly scapegoats for Henry VII's increasingly miserly policies. The young king was using others' blood to signal that his would be a more forgiving and generous regime. Time would sour that message, but this much was true: Henry VIII was to prove as adept at spending money as his father had at saving it.

The marriage was to Catalina, or Katherine, of Aragon, the youngest daughter of Ferdinand and Isabella, the king and queen of Spain. In 1501 Henry VII had secured her as a bride for his eldest son Arthur – a splendid diplomatic *coup*. However, Arthur had died less than five months into the marriage, leaving the young princess in English limbo. A papal dispensation was secured permitting her to marry her husband's younger brother, Prince Henry, but Henry VII came to have second thoughts. The marriage was repeatedly postponed, and by 1509 was on the point of being abandoned. The new king, however, jettisoned his father's caution, and fifty-one days into his reign married the woman to whom he had been betrothed for six years.

The swift marriage suggests a young man suddenly released from an over-careful father's strictures. Many of his subjects felt the same. The impulse to celebrate, and to enjoy the fruits of Henry VII's thrift, was understandable. At the centre of the extended party mood of the beginning of the reign was the young king himself. He was physically huge – over six feet tall in an age when this was exceedingly rare, and with a build to match. He dressed with extravagant style, ate and drank prodigiously, gambled recklessly, and charmed or overwhelmed everyone he met. He was a recklessly powerful athlete, excelling at tennis, archery and above all at jousting, and not merely because opponents found it prudent to let him win. The court was a whirlwind of feasting, dancing, hunting, wrestling, masquing and revels of all kinds. The young king was alarmingly likely to throw himself into such festivities and to expect to triumph by his mere skill. Nor was it all animal passions. There was no royal womanising at first, and little later on. Henry was at first extravagantly devoted to his wife, and he was always sparing with his mistresses (in later life, he preferred, awkwardly, to marry his paramours). And alongside the daunting vivacity were more cultured accomplishments. Henry's learning was respectable. He had good Latin and French, smatterings of Italian and Spanish, and once even tackled Greek. He had a keen interest in the complex mathematics of astrology. He disliked writing, and his handwriting is spidery and awkward, but he could be a voracious reader (often when one of his darker moods took him). He could play the lute and the virginals (a form of harpsichord), could bash out a tune on an organ, and was a capable singer. He also wrote a fair amount of music, which is workmanlike if not always captivating; and he could manage competent poetry. If we are to believe what his contemporaries told us, he made a point of excelling in every field of endeavour which Renaissance courtliness could favour.

Perhaps we do not believe them, or not entirely; but what they said matters more than the truth. For the plain fact is that Henry VIII swiftly created a larger-than-life image of himself which contemporaries at home and abroad were enthusiastic to believe. Only occasionally do we find a chink in this armour – as, for example, when an ambassador described Henry's daughter Mary as having 'a voice more manlike, for a woman, than he has for a man'.[1] This glimpse of a contralto Bluff King Hal is appealing – and a useful reminder that the image was an image; but all monarchy is theatre, and there is no denying that Henry VIII was an exceptional performer. The illusions of splendour he wove around his court helped to place him in the first rank of European princes, a position which England's raw power would not have earned. He applied the same showman's talents to the business of diplomacy, most famously in a wildly extravagant summit of one-upmanship held in France in 1520, the so-called Field of the Cloth of Gold: a meeting which achieved very little of substance and did it with enormous panache.

Henry's royal appetite for spectacle extended above all to war, the sport of kings. Quite how seriously Henry took his military enterprises from 1512 onwards is unclear. His rhetoric was a throwback to the previous century: he was restarting the Hundred Years' War and redeeming the empty English claim to the French throne. Whether he ever earnestly believed these fantasies is another matter. In one sense, again, it is the rhetoric that mattered. Henry could and did present himself as the new Henry V. He muscled his way into the top tier of European diplomacy by sheer ambition and will-power. He was even able, in 1519, to pursue the title of Holy Roman Emperor for himself. He failed, of course, but it is remarkable that he could even make such an audacious claim without becoming the laughing-stock of Christendom.

Yet Henry's wars also show the limits of what brash theatricality can achieve. Behind the smoke and mirrors, England was a second-rate military

power, and remained one however fast Henry VIII spent his father's accumulated treasure. Moreover, Henry himself was a naive strategist, outfoxed
both by his enemies and by his supposed allies. The only really dramatic
military success of his reign was the victory over the Scots at Flodden in
1513 (see above, p. 60). It was an unexpected victory, won when Henry
himself was on campaign in France, and he entirely failed to exploit it. On
the Continent, he regularly found himself outmanoeuvred, not least by his
father-in-law and supposed ally, King Ferdinand of Aragon, as subtle and
sinuous a politician as Henry was naive and direct. A huge effort in France
in 1513, led by the king in person, resulted in the capture of the town of
Tournai: a respectable achievement, not least because it was England's first
victory in France in living memory, but neither commensurate with the
cost nor a victory worthy of a new Henry V.

In any case, Henry's new Hundred Years' War was to unravel in 1514.
As his allies deserted him, he was forced to make peace with France. The
accession in 1515 of a new French king – Francis I, whose flamboyance
and ambition matched Henry's own – raised tensions again, but Henry's
own ardour for battle was now blunted. War had proved harder, more
frustrating and much more expensive than he had hoped. The cruel truth
was that England was no match for either of the two great European war
machines – that of France, and that of the Spanish–Burgundian alliance
which was soon to be united under the Habsburg Holy Roman Emperor,
Charles V. If England was to fight France and win, it could only do so on
the Habsburgs' coat-tails. Seven years of peace, or of phoney war, ensued.
Even Henry's prize of Tournai was sold back to France in 1518.

When the renewed war finally came, in minor campaigning in 1522 and
then in earnest in 1523, it proved as empty as that of 1512–14. A planned
attack on Paris in 1523 collapsed when, again, Henry's allies followed
agendas of their own. English hopes were raised again in 1525, when
Charles V inflicted a crushing defeat on the French at the battle of Pavia,
and took King Francis prisoner. Henry hoped, naively, that his Imperial
ally would partition France with him, and let him be king of a rump French
realm. He hastily planned a huge military expedition to France to secure
his inheritance there.

This Plantagenet fantasy swiftly evaporated, and not merely because
Charles V had no interest in it. More humiliating still was the hornet's nest
of domestic trouble which Henry stirred up. The proposed expedition was
to have been funded through a 'benevolence', or forced loan, demanded
from his subjects without Parliamentary consent. The 1525 benevolence
was titled the 'Amicable Grant', an Orwellian term for bare-faced extor-

tion (such 'loans' were scarcely repaid). It was levied at an eye-watering rate: in theory, all lay people were to give one-sixth of the value of all their movable goods to the king, and all clergy twice that. The Grant was probably illegal and, in a country already smarting from war taxation, certainly unpayable. It produced that rare and dangerous political phenomenon, a taxpayer's strike. The City of London refused to pay. There were riots in Kent and East Anglia. It was said that Henry wished only to waste English money in France. The king was furious, but he had no choice but to back down. The opposition to the Amicable Grant was perhaps the only successful episode of mass political resistance throughout the century. It left Henry humiliated, forced into a peace with France, and itching for revenge against his former ally the Emperor.

The cardinal's king

Henry VIII's wars also introduce us again to Thomas Wolsey (see above, pp. 74–5). Wolsey was an English phenomenon: a man of no birth (notoriously, an Ipswich butcher's son) whose precocious brilliance had won him a place at Oxford and seen him rise in noble, ecclesiastical and then royal service, to become the new king's almoner in 1509. What makes this everyday story of clerical careerism unusual is the remarkable working relationship Wolsey and his king developed over the next few years. A court such as Henry's needed more than good cheer to function, and it was already plain that Henry did not share his father's taste for hard administrative graft. Wolsey did, and – not for the last time – Henry recognised in another the managerial talents he himself lacked. And Wolsey took pains to make himself trustworthy to his king. He never judged his master's high living (indeed, he shared many of the same tastes himself); rather, he made it his business to be a scrupulously obedient advisor. Having no independent power base, he was, and was seen to be, wholly dependent on the king's favour, with no competing loyalties. Henry was lucky to find such an extraordinary talent, and he knew it.

It was with the war of 1512–14 that Wolsey came into his own. If war is the sport of kings, it is usually chivalry and strategy which appeal to them; yet the sinews of early modern warfare were finance and logistics, and its blood was diplomacy. Wolsey took on these tedious tasks for his master, positively encouraging the king to hunt, dance and gamble while he looked after the paperwork. He was ever-present and (apparently) omnicompetent; and he received a torrent of promotions from his grateful king. In February 1514 he was appointed bishop of Lincoln; six months later, archbishop of York. In 1515 he was made a cardinal, sealing the international reputation he was earning. By then he was effectively governing England on Henry VIII's behalf. All this was possible because he was, as his modern biographer calls him, the king's cardinal: a royal servant first and last.

That said, Wolsey knew that his master was impetuous and impressionable, with a butterfly mind, and it was his duty to guide him. While no paragon of the Renaissance virtues, Wolsey did have a higher concept of statesmanship than the search for military glory. When Henry wished Wolsey to make war, Wolsey obeyed with verve and ruthlessness (the Amicable Grant was Wolsey's scheme), but his own preference was for peace. The diplomatic cat's-cradle in which England was entangled after 1514 was frustrating for Henry, but meat and drink for Wolsey, who could scheme with Italian subtlety. His greatest diplomatic triumph was the treaty of London in 1518. What might have been a simple truce with France turned into a Treaty of Universal Peace. France, England and a dozen lesser states joined in swearing perpetual amity, and – to give teeth to such idealism – they also swore to unite against any one of their number who broke the treaty. It was an internationalist vision of collective security that would not have been out of place in the 1920s. It also had Wolsey's fingerprints all over it, and gave lustre to him and his master. It was the springboard for Wolsey's (failed) attempt to become pope himself.

It was an alluring vision: universal peace, arranged by an English king (or his agent), presided over by an English pope. This offered more honour and glory to England, to Henry and to Wolsey than did a bit part in a Franco-Imperial war and the seizure of a few grubby towns. It was also cheaper, for Wolsey was painfully aware – like every attentive English administrator of the century – that England simply could not afford warfare on the Continental scale. And, of course, it failed. For all Henry's splendour and Wolsey's cunning, England simply did not have the leverage to make the treaty work. Moreover, Henry himself was only intermittently committed. He could and did talk the talk which Wolsey suggested to him, but when he scented real military opportunities, his love of peace evaporated. And while Wolsey advised and cajoled his king, he also – when pressed to it – energetically implemented policies which he himself disliked. He was a royal servant.

In the state records of the 1510s and 1520s, therefore, the king is an oddly absent figure. The ease with which Wolsey wielded royal authority can make Henry seem like the cardinal's king: at least, it was Wolsey who made it possible for Henry to be the king he was. Henry's attention to politics was, and would remain, intense but intermittent. Given the storm which he was later to bring onto the English Church and state – a storm in which Wolsey, amongst others, would be swept away – it is natural to look to this earlier phase of his life for glimpses of what was to come. There is not much to be found. His hostility to the new Lutheran heresy was unambiguous (see below, p. 95). It is only with hindsight that we may detect omens. That said, there were a few whispers of breeze which anticipate the later storm, and which help to show which parts of Henry's realm would be most exposed.

One such episode is Henry's first real domestic political crisis: the destruction of the duke of Buckingham in 1521. Buckingham was certainly a dangerous man. His lands in the Welsh Marches gave him a power base beyond direct royal control (see below, pp. 291–2); and his haughty independence ill became any subject, especially one with royal blood in his veins. An informer testified that Buckingham had listened to prophecies of the king's death, had contemplated assassinating the king himself, and had declared that Henry VIII would die without an heir. All this was undoubtedly treason; so perhaps his execution is unremarkable. Yet few contemporaries were satisfied by this explanation. There were plenty of alternatives to a beheading. Henry VII would have lamed such a man with financial penalties. Rumour had it that the root cause was a quarrel between Buckingham and Wolsey. Regardless, this is the first occasion on which we see Henry VIII's tendency to treat all opposition with high and vengeful indignation, rather than with politic pragmatism. It also exemplifies his tendency to use the axe as an instrument of policy.

Another incident touches Henry more personally. On 1 January 1511, the young king and his not-quite-so-young bride had their first child: a boy, named Henry and instantly created prince of Wales. As the court celebrated, Henry did what his father would have done: he went on pilgrimage to give thanks. He chose the shrine of the Virgin Mary at Walsingham, in Norfolk, to which Henry VII had been so devoted that he had given it a statue of himself. In February, however, the seven-week-old prince died. And Henry VIII never went on pilgrimage again. Since this was a routine (and splendidly theatrical) royal activity, it is a striking omission. It would be crass to argue that Henry's later ransacking of England's shrines (Walsingham included) was revenge on a religious system which had failed to save his son's life. Nor should it be overplayed: he had an exuberant, extravagant and lifelong enthusiasm for other traditional pieties. Yet at least, this makes clear that Henry's own religion was not entirely conventional, and that some traditions had little purchase on his conscience.

One final dimension deserves to be noticed. The young Henry VIII displayed a notable (although not exceptional) touchiness if he felt that the pope was treading on his toes. In 1516, for example, he felt this had happened over the appointment of a bishop for English-occupied Tournai, leading Henry to assert his 'supreme power . . . without recognition of any superior', and to lambast 'semblable bulls against the sovereignty of princes'.[2] This was, of course, a routine frontier skirmish with papal authority, not any kind of rejection of it. Yet it was not entirely routine to ramp up anti-papal rhetoric to such self-righteous heights. Nor was it entirely routine to assume that the English clergy owed simple obedience (and large taxes) to their king, as Henry VIII tended to do. There is no sign at all of principled antipapalism in the young Henry VIII; but there are signs of a king willing to take his own dignity and authority very seriously indeed.

The Lutheran heresy

A problem of theology

Amidst the complexity of Henry VIII's policy and diplomacy, little attention was paid to the eruption, in 1517–18, of a fierce theological spat in Germany. Martin Luther, an obscure theology professor from Saxony, denounced the legitimacy of selling papal pardons. Such pardons, by which the pope used the accumulated merits of the saints to ease the burden of penance on a sinner, had a long pedigree, as did controversy about them. The inflammatory terms of Luther's denunciation – and the amounts of money at stake – meant that his outburst provoked a counter-attack from the German theological establishment. The pope famously dismissed this as 'a quarrel between friars'. Yet a series of coincidences ensured that, instead of simmering down or being snuffed out, the quarrel blew up into a national, then an international scandal. Luther turned out to be extraordinarily stubborn, and to have been slowly developing a set of theological ideas with implications far beyond the narrow issue of papal pardons. Moreover, he turned out to be an exceptionally able publicist, using the new medium of print to mobilise wider public support for his cause. For a theologian thus to appeal, in print, to a mass audience in order to outflank the ecclesiastical establishment was quite unprecedented. The Renaissance context made that mass audience receptive, for many Germans assumed (wrongly) that the Luther affair was a battle between an honest, scholarly German humanist and corrupt, scheming, obscurantist Italians. In fact, it gradually became clear that Luther's views went well beyond established

Catholic orthodoxy, and in 1519 he was driven openly to reject the authority of the Church. He was excommunicated as a heretic, which should have been the end of him. But his local prince, the elector of Saxony, rather liked the man and was pleased that his new university had been put so decisively on the map. Luther was protected; inflammatory books and pamphlets continued to pour from his and his allies' pens, and from Germany's printing presses.

It would be some years before anything coherent enough to be called Protestantism emerged from this turmoil, but already, by 1520, Luther had formulated and expounded what would become Protestantism's central, compelling idea. This idea, simple and almost innocuous in appearance, would seep into the structures of traditional religion like water into cracks, ready to split and undermine it until it crumbled. Its dreadfully inexorable logic splintered Catholic Christianity, in the British Isles as elsewhere. We cannot understand the history of this period without understanding the idea which Luther called justification by faith alone.

Christianity addresses a practical problem: how can human beings be saved? That is, how can we ensure that, when we die, we are admitted to the perfect bliss of God's eternal presence (Heaven) and not condemned to the everlasting torment of his absence (Hell)? The common layman's view is that good people go to Heaven and bad people go to Hell, but this is only part of the answer. Mainstream Christianity (Catholic as well as Protestant) replies that we are all bad people, since we are all corrupted by sin. We can, therefore, only be saved by being forgiven. Christianity is essentially a system for providing that forgiveness, through the atoning death and resurrection of Jesus Christ, the man who is also God incarnate. This much is common ground. The question then is, how can we lay hold of the saving power of Christ's death?

The Catholic answer had, and has, several strands. True faith in Christ is fundamental. However, one must also confess and do penance for one's sins (either in this life or in Purgatory), and strive to live virtuously, a moral effort which is described as doing 'good works'. In this struggle, Catholics are sustained by the ministry of the Church, and in particular by the sacraments, those channels of grace which can bring the redemptive power of Christ's death to bear on believers. Through all this, Christians may hope at last to be 'justified'. This is a technical term meaning, literally, to be made just: to be made into a holy person free from sin. In Catholic Christianity, justification is almost synonymous with 'sanctification', the process of moral purification in this life and in Purgatory which prepares the believer for Heaven.

Luther's view was drastically different. He used the same theological sources as the traditional Catholic view – notably the great fifth-century African theologian Augustine, and the New Testament letters of Paul – but, in Renaissance style, refused to read them through the prism of the intervening ages. His reading of Augustine and Paul took one strand of their thought to its logical extreme. He began with a doctrine of 'total depravity': that human beings are not merely sinful, but are utterly corrupted, with no part of us untouched by sin's taint. In particular, our 'good works' are always contaminated by pride and ulterior motives. Therefore, Luther argued, good works can hardly contribute to justification: they merely dig us deeper into the pit of our own sinfulness. 'It must surely be something quite different which brings religion and freedom to the soul.'[3] That something is mere faith. For Luther, salvation comes only when we admit that we can do nothing to save ourselves and instead throw ourselves abjectly on Christ's mercy. It is then that Christ declares us justified, by an act of sheer grace. Justification is therefore not a process, but an event, a moment of liberation from the burden of sin. It is also a kind of legal fiction: for we are declared to be just, to be righteous, when we are obviously nothing of the kind. It is only after that decree of justification that the long, slow process of sanctification can begin.

This doctrine of justification by faith alone may seem abstract, but its practical consequences were dramatic. Once grasped, it is dizzyingly simple. Nothing at all can affect salvation other than mere faith in Christ. Our own actions, and the ministrations of the Church, can contribute nothing. And to continue to hope for salvation, or even for a helping hand, from anything other than mere faith is to dishonour Christ. If you believed that anything or anyone other than mere faith in Christ could have any role in your salvation, then Luther insisted that you were not showing the total, childlike and utterly dependent faith which alone could save. Luther's doctrine, in other words, was a call for the radical simplification of the Christian life: faith alone mattered.

So most of the structures of western Christian piety were declared either redundant or blasphemous. Luther was instinctively socially conservative, and only slowly embraced some of the implications of his doctrine, but those implications were inescapable. Works of penance were futile in this system. That threw out most of the old Church's ritual piety: fasting, pilgrimage, the veneration of relics, the recitation of set prayers. It also greatly undermined the sacraments. In particular, to Luther, the sacrifice of the Mass (see above, pp. 17–18) looked like mere idolatry. (He did not, however, reject the belief that Christ was physically present in the Mass.)

As the power of the sacraments was jettisoned, so was the distinct status of the clergy. All Christians were priests, Luther argued, with immediate access to Christ through faith. Some Christians should indeed be chosen to preach and celebrate the sacraments, but they were simply functionaries doing a job. They should be allowed to marry, for celibacy was another futile 'good work'. Monasteries, whose very purpose was moral effort, were pointless. (Luther, himself a monk, left his order and married.) And the entire doctrine of Purgatory was redundant too.

Very little of the piety of medieval Catholicism was left. Luther's doctrine appealed simultaneously to high theological principle and to low anticlericalism, and did so in a brilliant, forceful propaganda campaign with a misleadingly Renaissance flavour. By the mid-1520s the movement which had started, but which he no longer controlled, had swept large parts of central Europe.

What we call this movement is a problem. 'Protestantism' is an anachronism: the term 'Protestant' was first coined to describe those German states and cities which, in 1529, issued a *protestatio* (a legal plea) for religious toleration. Initially, 'the Protestants' meant the Lutheran princes of Germany who had formed an alliance for mutual self-defence: only gradually, from the mid-sixteenth century onwards, was the word applied by analogy to others who had dissented from Rome. Until around 1550, we are best off referring to these dissidents generically as 'evangelicals': preachers of the gospel. This was how they tended to describe themselves, and if it is an unsatisfactorily fuzzy term, it is a reminder that during the first generation or two of the Reformation, most religious identities were blurry.

Even so, with hindsight, by the mid-1520s we can discern the outlines of what would become the three major Protestant 'confessions' (in modern parlance, denominations). The first of these looked directly (although not exclusively) to Luther himself, and can sensibly be called 'Lutherans'. A second group, in northern Switzerland and southern Germany, was not dominated by any one leader, although the reformer of Zürich, Huldrych Zwingli, was its most prominent figurehead. This movement was in debt to Luther but had its own distinct flavour: more communitarian in outlook, more humanist in its methods, and with fewer scruples about systematically rewriting Christian doctrine and practice. This movement is perhaps best described as Reformed Protestantism but is commonly called Calvinism, after one of its second-generation leaders. It was to become enormously important for the British story. A third, less coherent reformist grouping had also appeared: the scattered groups whose opponents dubbed them 'Anabaptists', or rebaptisers. These radicals wanted to remake

Christian society much more profoundly than Luther or Zwingli, and their rejection of infant baptism was simply one symptom of that. Most respectable opinion was horrified by them, and they were persecuted wherever they went.

These alarming radicals are one reason why Luther's movement did not (as had briefly seemed possible) set the whole of western Christendom alight. Especially after a huge peasant rebellion in Germany in 1525, which was widely blamed on the reformers' preaching, those who wished for good order had every reason to stick to the old Church. Moreover, there were real problems with Luther's argument. His doctrine of justification may have been appealing, but it also looked very much like an innovation – and thus, by definition, an error (see above, p. 63). Moreover, the doctrine had some alarming implications. His insistence that good works and morality were irrelevant to salvation sounded awfully like 'antinomianism': the belief that good works did not matter, and that Christians should feel free to sin with impunity. Luther in fact did not mean this at all, and said so at great length, but there is no doubt that it was the message that some people heard. Some were simply horrified by this immorality; others worried that without the fear of Hell to ensure good behaviour, Christian society would dissolve into anarchy. Second, Luther's doctrine of total depravity led him inexorably to teach predestination. If we are saved by faith, he argued, then that faith must itself be a gift from God: for otherwise, it would simply be a human action, and therefore corrupted by sin. Thus it is God who gives us the faith by which we can be saved: we are passive recipients, unable even to accept God's gift without grace. Thus, the decision as to who is saved and who is damned is entirely in God's hands. We can do nothing to change our fate one way or the other. The logic here is equally formidable, but much less attractive. It was over this issue that Erasmus finally broke decisively with Luther in 1524. Later Lutherans themselves withdrew from it, although for the 'Reformed', Calvinist tradition it would eventually become central. Antinomianism and predestination were problems which continued to dog the reformers for the rest of the century.

For a variety of reasons, then, the Lutheran tide was contained. It swamped large parts of German-speaking Europe, where the nationalist appeal was strongest and where Luther's rhetoric was not muffled by translation. But to begin with, at least, it only seeped into the rest of western Christendom. Outside Germany, it was a matter of small groups of scholars, merchants and clerics who had access to Lutheran books and ideas. And almost before such groups could find their feet, the authorities of Church and state were onto them.

The arrival of heresy in England

As soon as the Luther affair came to international notice, England loudly declared its orthodoxy. In 1521 Pope Leo X formally condemned Luther's books; on 12 May of that year a public bonfire of them was duly held in London, and Bishop Fisher preached a stout sermon against heresy. This was for show. The foreign ambassadors resident in London were present. Cardinal Wolsey was trying to have his status as a papal legate extended, and a demonstration of England's orthodoxy was helpful. There were as yet no English Lutherans, and the books that were burned had probably been imported specially. Although some of Luther's Latin works had been offered for sale in Oxford the previous year, there is no other hint of incipient heresy. Later in 1521, England made an even more public statement against Luther: Henry VIII published a book against the heretic. Apparently this pamphlet – *Assertio Septem Sacramentorum adversus Martinum Lutherum* – really was the king's own project, although he was heavily coached by Fisher and others. It was no great piece of theology (one reason for suspecting that the king was its ultimate author), but it made a considerable splash, as books by celebrity authors do. It went through five editions in 1522 and 1523, in both Latin and German. It may not have stemmed the tide of heresy, but it certainly burnished Henry VIII's credentials as a good son of the Church. It earned a reply from Luther, who called Henry a pig and a drunkard: for the rest of their lives the two men nursed a mutual loathing. More to the point, the book finally clinched Henry's long campaign to be awarded a title by the pope, to match the splendid titles already bestowed on the kings of Spain and France. With an irony that would soon become apparent, Pope Leo conceded that Henry VIII was *Fidei defensor*, 'Defender of the Faith'.

In 1521, however, the threat to the true faith seemed comfortably far off. A few years later, it was lapping at England's shores for real. Early in 1526, a raid on the Steelyard, the official trading base for northern German merchants in London, uncovered a number of Lutheran books. Trade routes with Germany were an obvious entry point for the heretical infection. By then, we also find signs that Lutheranism was picking up English disciples. An Oxfordshire man named Roger Hachman was accused of heresy in 1525, having stated that 'I will never look to be saved for no good deed that ever I did' but only by merely asking God's mercy.[4] If the charge was true, it is unclear how such Lutheran-sounding ideas might have reached him. A much more ominous scandal blew up on Christmas Eve 1525, when an Augustinian friar named Robert Barnes preached in St Edward's church in Cambridge. The sermon was a sweeping denunciation of the English clergy, and in particular of Cardinal Wolsey. While not explicitly heretical, this was certainly provocative, especially because parts of the sermon closely followed some of Luther's own writings. Barnes was arrested, taken to London, and interrogated by Wolsey himself. He backed down under pressure but remained under house arrest for more than two years. In 1528 he managed to escape, having dramatically faked his own suicide. He fled to Germany, where he was to become the only Englishman to be a close friend of Martin Luther's.

Cambridge was left in turmoil. Nearly forty years later, an account of these events described how Barnes's sermon and arrest had stirred up debate about Luther's ideas across the university, and claimed that an inn named the White Horse had become so frequented by Barnes's sympathisers that it was nicknamed 'Germany'.[5] Whether or not this often-told tale is true, it is clear that over the next few years, both Cambridge and (to a lesser extent) Oxford were infected with heresy. In Cambridge, the public spectacle of Barnes's sermon was complemented by the quieter persuasions of Thomas Bilney, a diminutive, ascetic canon lawyer who later attributed his own profound conversion to Erasmus' New Testament. It has never been clear how Lutheran Bilney really was, but he stands at the head of a chain of reformist converts who had unmistakably swallowed the new German theologies. His most famous convert was Hugh Latimer, one of the century's most rousing preachers. And religious unrest in the universities was more than a few famous names. By 1530 Richard Nix, the redoubtably orthodox bishop of Norwich, reckoned that almost every priest who graduated from one particular Cambridge college 'savoureth of the frying pan, though he speak never so holily'.[6] That ugly allusion to the usual fate of heretics was more than rhetorical. England's first burning for Lutheranism had taken place in Maidstone a few weeks earlier: a priest named Thomas Hytten who had spent some years in Germany. In 1531 Bilney, too, went to the fire. But here, at least, Oxford was not to be out-done. In 1528, the staff of Wolsey's new college there, Cardinal College, turned out to include a coterie of Lutheran sympathisers. The university authorities were taken by surprise; the dean of the college had nowhere to imprison the suspects but in his salt fish cellar. Three of them died in those grim conditions, the first blood of the English Reformation.

While the trouble at Cambridge was eye-catching, the most truly dangerous event of the mid-1520s took place below the radar. William Tyndale was a priest from Gloucestershire who, during his studies at Oxford, had been attracted to Erasmus' piety; he had translated the *Handbook of the Christian Soldier* into English. Possibly he was influenced by the Lollardy which persisted in his native county, but it seems more likely that Erasmus' vision of popular Scripture simply entranced him. A gifted linguist, by 1523 he had resolved to prepare and publish an English translation of the New Testament. This was of course illegal, but Tyndale hoped that, in these enlightened times, an exception might be made, and he asked the bishop of London, Cuthbert Tunstall, for his backing. That he should have approached Tunstall – friend of Erasmus and scourge of Lollardy – is a good indication that Tyndale was then no heretic, merely a little naive. The bishop, of course, turned down such an incendiary proposal, although he too saw Tyndale as merely naive, and let him remain, untroubled, in London for the best part of a year. It was a misjudgement. In 1524, Tyndale left England, and by the time of our next sighting of him, in Cologne in 1525, he had finished his English New Testament and was seeing it through the press. Early in the process, he was denounced to the city authorities, and fled; but he simply relocated to the safely Lutheran city of Worms, where the first ever New Testament printed in English was completed in 1526.

The British Reformations did not produce any Protestant theologians of truly international stature. But Tyndale was, at least, a translator of exceptional gifts. His English New Testament – unlike the hoary Wycliffite version – was translated directly from the Greek, following Erasmus' model. Soon he would also achieve a subtle mastery of Hebrew, although he did not live to complete his translation of the Old Testament. Tyndale's Biblical translations had a vivid punchiness to them which has shaped the English language. Tyndale's Bible is more direct, and less archaic and grandiose, than the 1611 Authorised Version which drew on his work so heavily. The Worms edition of 1526 was followed by half a dozen more editions, produced in Antwerp in the late 1520s and early 1530s. These were small books, smaller than a modern paperback, and while smuggling them across the Channel was not a straightforward business it was very difficult to stop. Bishop Tunstall was at the forefront of efforts to stem the supply of New Testaments, and certainly a good many copies were seized and burned, but many more slipped through. A merry tale was later told of how Tyndale had deliberately sold a consignment of New Testaments to the English bishops, in order to finance the next print run. The reality was probably not so neat, but it is true that the bishops were trying to buy up as many copies of the New Testament as they could find, a policy which was likely to be self-defeating. Despite their best efforts, Tyndale's New Testament was finding readers.

Tyndale may not have been a heretic when Tunstall knew him, but he was now. The New Testament was not precisely Lutheran – Tyndale's theology was less forbiddingly paradoxical and more Erasmian than Luther's – but it had drunk deeply from Lutheran sources. The abortive Cologne edition of the New Testament had contained an openly evangelical prologue and marginal notes. While the later editions were plainer, Tyndale accompanied them with a series of polemical treatises in English. *The Parable of the Wicked Mammon* expounded the doctrine of justification by faith; *The Practice of Prelates* viciously attacked the English clergy; *The Obedience of a Christian Man* laid out an evangelical political theory. Nor was Tyndale alone. A small, quarrelsome and dazzlingly talented clique of English evangelicals formed around him in exile. Three men in particular stand out. Robert Barnes, after his escape, joined this group, although he was more definitively Lutheran than any of them. Miles Coverdale was the great survivor amongst them, the translator who completed the work which Tyndale left unfinished, but who was also a considerable writer and preacher in his own right. In the 1560s, Coverdale was the English Reformation's ancient conscience. John Frith, by contrast, was its lost hope: a brilliant young theologian who wrote a polemic against Purgatory and (from his final prison) a treatise on the Eucharist which went beyond Luther in questioning whether Christ was physically present at all: this was the Reformed Protestant view. Frith also, most unusually, argued for a degree of religious toleration in principle. Had he not been arrested and burned for heresy in 1533, a mere thirty years old, he might have become a theologian of the first rank.

Grassroots heretics, university reformers, and evangelical exiles: each of these posed particular problems for the establishment, but they also combined in dangerous ways. Imported books and university-educated preachers threatened to revive the torpid world of Lollardy. All too often in the late 1520s, official heresy-hunters unearthed Lollards who were reading Tyndale's New Testament or other books by the exiles. In 1526, two Lollards from rural Essex visited Robert Barnes in London, hoping to buy a New Testament from him. But, proud of their long history of dissidence, they took their old Wycliffite Scriptures to show Barnes. Barnes, they later remembered, was not impressed: he 'made a twit of it, and said, "A point for them, for they be not to be regarded toward the new printed

Testament in English. For it is of more cleaner English."'[7] Having thus insulted their heritage, he charged them the handsome sum of three shillings for a New Testament, and they happily paid up. This unsentimental attitude seems to have been widespread among Lollards, who had never tried to exploit the printing press themselves but were now happy to take advantage of it. Lollardy's theological influence on English evangelicalism was marginal at best, but socially it may have been more important. It provided early evangelicals with a ready network of hearers and protectors. More tantalisingly, many of those parts of England which were Lollard strongholds in the fifteenth century subsequently became Puritan and Nonconformist strongholds in the seventeenth century. This pattern is not easy to explain, but nor is it easy to ignore.

More alarming than a few Lollards reading imported books was the exploitation of such books by university reformers. Robert Forman was a former master of Queens' College, Cambridge, and a friend of Thomas Bilney's. By the 1520s he was rector of the wealthy London parish of All Hallows, Honey Lane. His curate there was Thomas Garrett, an Oxford man. Both were serious evangelicals, and they used their contacts in both universities to run a network for distributing heretical books. Garrett's stock, which he lent and sold to scholars in Oxford, included Tyndale, Luther and most of the leading Continental reformers. One of their associates was a porter at Thomas More's old school in London, who distributed books there and elsewhere in the City. Their customers included the prior of Reading Abbey, later a friend of John Frith's. When this network was cracked in 1528, Garrett led his pursuers on a dramatic chase across England, being finally run to ground on the outskirts of Bristol – a Lollard centre of old. He and Forman were forced to recant, but the book distribution business was hydra-headed. One over-excited informant claimed in the late 1520s that there was a secret society in London, the 'Christian Brethren', which financed the production of heretical books and circulated them amongst its members. This smacks of paranoia, but the truth was if anything worse: books were being passed from hand to hand among friends, and the distribution networks were informal, anonymous, shifting and impossible to police.

How dangerous were such movements? To ask this is implicitly to ask a 'what-if' question. If the English Church and state had never been derailed from Catholic orthodoxy, how would the evangelical movement have fared?

England's experience of the 1520s – an orthodox establishment confronting nascent evangelical heresy – was shared by (amongst others) Scotland, the Netherlands, France and Italy. German heresies won a hearing in all these regions, not least by stealing Christian humanism's clothes. In Scotland (on which see below, pp. 104–5), evangelical converts began to appear in the towns and amongst the landed elite. In France, there was a courtly and clerical pre-Reformation in the 1520s, tolerated by King Francis I. In the intensely urbanised Netherlands, radical ideas spread quickly and there was a significant dissident movement by the 1530s, including a noticeable presence of Anabaptists. In Italy, a largely clerical movement of so-called *spirituali* explored Erasmian ideas with an evangelical edge. But despite these parallels, the eventual outcomes diverged widely. Scotland eventually experienced a full-scale Protestant Reformation, propelled by English influence, dynastic accident and war. In both France and the Netherlands, heresy was fiercely repressed from the 1530s onwards, only to erupt into religious civil war in the 1560s. In all three cases, the power of the nobility to defy their sovereigns was critical. In Italy, by contrast, the evangelical movement's reluctance to engage in populist campaigning, combined with the eventual determination of the papacy to stamp it out, led to its early extinction.

England's case does not exactly parallel any of these. By the late 1520s, England's tiny, vigorous evangelical movement was trying hard to reach out beyond its intellectual ghetto, and (in part thanks to Lollard networks) having some success. To this extent England is similar to the Netherlands. But unlike in the Netherlands, the English state was centralised and had well-defined, widely accepted powers to prosecute heresy. And unlike France, England was sensitised (even over-sensitised) to the problem of heresy by the long battle against Lollardy. Italy is a closer parallel, for there, as in England, Erasmian ideas had taken deep root. Yet as we have seen, Erasmianism was not necessarily a springboard to evangelical heresy. It could also be a kind of vaccination against it, since it addressed many evangelical concerns while remaining basically orthodox. And in Italy, as in England, the authorities provided very little space for the new movement to flourish.

English evangelicalism had not yet been defeated by 1530, but it seemed well on the way. Official policy towards heresy in the 1520s fell into three distinct phases. First came the internationalist period from 1521 to 1525, when Lutheranism was merely a theoretical threat. From about 1525–29, when the threat was becoming a reality, there was a Renaissance phase, pioneered by Bishop Tunstall of London, with the backing of Cardinal Wolsey and Archbishop Warham. Tunstall, now as throughout his long career, was a firm Catholic but a reluctant persecutor. He saw evangelicals as a breed apart from old-fashioned Lollards. These heretics were in a sense Tunstall's peers: scholars, humanists, earnest for the reform of the Church. He regarded them as misled rather than as malevolent. He would certainly arrest them, but then cajole, persuade and even negotiate with them in order to restore them to orthodoxy. Tunstall invested an enormous amount of personal effort in these conversations. In one of the most high-profile early heresy cases – the first trial of Thomas Bilney, in 1527 – Tunstall repeatedly bent the rules of legal procedure, suspended the proceedings in order to give Bilney more time, and finally allowed him to make an admission of guilt which was riddled with ambiguity. Behind this policy seems to have been a hope that evangelicals could be contained in the universities and talked back into conformity.

The discovery of Forman and Garrett's book network in 1528, the alarming results of a major purge against Lollards in Essex the same year, and the continued flow of books from the exiles made it clear that this hope was false. Thereafter English anti-heresy policy entered a third, inquisitorial phase. This had the full approval of Warham, Wolsey and the king, but was led by two men in particular. Thomas More was made Lord Chancellor in 1529 and threw much of his enormous energy into heresy-hunting. In 1530, he was joined by a new bishop of London, John Stokesley, a considerable scholar but above all the king's man, and a steely enemy of dissent. (Tunstall was translated to the bishopric of Durham, an honourable posting to a diocese as yet untroubled by heresy.) More and Stokesley pursued a ruthless campaign against heretics. When Tunstall had let Bilney escape in 1527, More had commented disgustedly that the law was 'so far stretched forth that the leather could scant hold'.[8] Now he could do it his way. At least thirteen people were burned for evangelical heresy between 1530 and 1533. Hundreds more were arrested, some of them held for long periods and on occasion tortured (as the law permitted). Lists of prohibited books were published and public book-burnings held. Recantations and executions – many of them at Smithfield Market, just outside the City of London – were public, theatrical events, designed to humiliate heretics and to awe the populace with the majesty of orthodoxy and with the terrible fate which awaited impenitent heretics in Hell. As well as pursuing heresy with the law, More also tackled it in print. Between 1529 and 1533 he wrote six separate books attacking the works of evangelicals including Frith, Barnes and (at great and vitriolic length) Tyndale. Tyndale was the great enemy, whom he and the whole regime were desperate to silence. With a price on his head, Tyndale's luck eventually ran out. He was betrayed to the Inquisition in the Netherlands by an English acquaintance, and burned in Antwerp in 1536.

While it lasted, More and Stokesley's campaign was the most intense anti-heresy drive in Christendom. Evangelical heresy had a genuine foothold in England, but it was now being driven to the margins, its leaders silenced, its networks disrupted and its adherents either daunted or (in numbers large enough to set an example) killed. Its books were being countered by one of the century's most punchily eloquent prose writers in English. Frith's execution cut off its great hope. Tyndale's execution, before his Bible was even complete, should have been the beginning of the end. If events had run their course, it is reasonable to expect that by the mid-1540s evangelicalism would have become an embattled, marginal phenomenon in England, and that Lollardy would have sunk back into its rural half-life, its new books slowly becoming dog-eared. But events did not run their course. Even as this inquisitorial phase was beginning, there were signs that England might be moving in another direction. In the event, More himself was executed fifteen months before Tyndale.

Scotland: religion and politics under James V, 1513–42

While England enjoyed the dubious glories of Henry VIII's Renaissance monarchy, Scotland's political trajectory was very different. Scotland's most truly Renaissance king was killed at Flodden in 1513, leaving a seventeen-month-old son as King James V. The result was yet another long royal minority, whose effects rumbled on well after the new king began his personal rule in 1528.

The high politics of James V's minority are tangled but the outline is swiftly enough understood. There were four main players: the establishment man, the opportunist, the troublemaker and the wild card. The establishment man was the duke of Albany, the new king's cousin and also his heir presumptive. As such, he was swiftly appointed governor of the realm. However, Albany had been born and raised in France and was, for most purposes, a Frenchman. His administration was competent, and he was a conciliatory politician, but in the end he would always be France's mouthpiece. Indeed, he was detained in France until 1515 and again between 1517 and 1521: the English disliked his presence in Scotland, and at times it suited France to humour Henry VIII. Worse, when Anglo-French peace broke down, Albany found himself having to lead Scotland into another pre-emptive strike against England, in what seemed an ill-omened reprise of the Flodden campaign. So at least it seemed to his magnates, who made it clear that they were unwilling to cross the Border in 1522. In 1523 they did so only with the greatest reluctance, in small numbers and in support of a vanguard of French troops. Albany left for France in 1524 never to return, allowing his governorship to lapse by default.

His immediate heir was the opportunist: the earl of Arran, next in line to the throne after Albany himself. Arran had been Albany's ally until the abortive war with England in 1522–23 had alienated him. Shortly after Albany's departure, Arran took the twelve-year-old king into his custody, declared that his minority was at an end, and briefly pursued a pro-English policy. However, Arran quickly found himself caught between a pro-French political establishment and the most powerful noble family in Scotland, the Douglases. Archibald Douglas, the earl of Angus and head of the family, was the troublemaker of the period. Having been exiled to England by Albany, he now returned as a trusted English agent, making Arran's position untenable. Arran returned to the pro-French fold, and after a tense stand-off a power-sharing arrangement of sorts was devised in mid-1525.

It was broken by Angus a year later, when the young king was temporarily in his custody. He used this as a pretext to seize control of the government. It was transparent that the king was the Douglases' prisoner, rather than their guest, but there was little the rest of the country could do about it. Until, that is, the wild card intervened. This was Queen Margaret – Henry VII's daughter, James V's mother. She had been in a powerful position after Flodden, for James IV's will named her as regent, and she was mother to the new king and pregnant with a second royal child (who, as it turned out, died in infancy). She had forfeited this position by her swift remarriage, in 1514, to the earl of Angus. Many Scots saw her as an English stooge, and indeed she spent several long stints in England, but her path was never so straightforward. The marriage to Angus collapsed in 1517, over his adultery and misappropriation of her funds. From then on, loathing for him was her guiding principle. It was she who, in 1528, successfully plotted her son's escape from Angus' captivity, and who rallied the nobility for him. Angus was, again, driven into exile, and James V, now aged seventeen, began to rule in fact as well as in name.

Royal authority had taken a battering during the minority, and the fourteen years of James V's personal rule consisted largely of his struggle to reassert it. He succeeded, but not by subtle means. His two guiding principles were the need to rebuild the royal revenues (which had fallen by more than half during his minority) and a bitterly personal vendetta against his former captors, the Douglases. Angus and his immediate family were in exile, so James pursued their allies and clients. Communicating with the exiled earl became a capital crime. The most prominent victim was Angus' sister, burned alive in 1537 for a supposed attempt to poison the king. This was of a piece with James's generally stern enforcement of the law, a policy which was not unpopular. However, like his English grandfather Henry VII, he allowed the prosecution of crime to blur into the raising of money. As Henry VII had discovered, this worked, but also made enemies. James died suddenly in 1542, at the age of thirty. If he had lived for much longer, he might well have found that his political luck was changing.

Yet, like Henry VII, James V was more than a fiscal machine. He lacked the Renaissance flair of his father James IV and his uncle Henry VIII, but he did have a taste for fashionable scholarship. He was a patron to foreign and native scholars such as Giovanni Ferrerio, David Lindsay and George Buchanan (see above, pp. 70–2). In 1533, the elderly Erasmus wrote to James V, in search of patronage for a friend. He received it, together with an enthusiastically warm letter from the king. And like his ally Francis I of France, James V allowed some at his court to move beyond Erasmian orthodoxies. He gave licence to some fairly bitter anticlerical rhetoric. Some around the king scarcely concealed their evangelical views – including, for a while, his own personal confessor, Alexander Seton.

For evangelical ideas had begun to take root in Scotland much as they had in England. A French member of Albany's retinue was executed in Paris in 1525 for disseminating Lutheran heresies in Scotland. In 1525 a Scots parliament legislated against Lutheranism. Later that year came word of evangelical books being distributed in Aberdeen, and by 1527 English evangelical books were regularly being smuggled to Edinburgh and St Andrews. The fact that Scots readers could (usually) decipher southern English yoked the two Reformations together. Tyndale, for one, was explicitly aware that he was also writing for a Scots readership. In the early 1530s, there were even a handful of evangelical books printed abroad which had been written by Scots, for the Scottish market. At the same time, Scots clergy who had spent time on the Continent were beginning to return home filled with dangerous ideas. Because Scotland's universities offered only a basic education, study abroad was commonplace, leaving Scotland peculiarly exposed to wider intellectual currents. Yet the Scottish Church was stern in its assertion of orthodoxy. First blood was in 1528, when a young nobleman named Patrick Hamilton was burned for heresy in St Andrews. Hamilton had probably first met heresy in book form when a student at St Andrews University. He had then spent some time in the Lutheran city of Marburg, before returning to testify to his faith in his home country. His chance came quickly: he was arrested, condemned and burned after a hurried trial.

Hamilton's defiance perhaps left James Beaton, the archbishop of St Andrews, with little choice but to execute him. But there was a price to be paid. It was said that 'the reek of Master Patrick Hamilton['s burning] . . . infected as many as it blew upon' with his heresies.[9] The burning brought evangelical heresy to Scotland's attention, but it did not prevent a steady trickle of other lairds and nobles embracing evangelical ideas during the late 1520s and the 1530s. As in England, many of them were attracted less by the reformers' doctrines than by their promise to make Scripture available in the vernacular. Unlike in England, these concerns mixed with virulent conventions of anticlerical rhetoric, conventions which now (probably for the first time) became dangerous for the Church.

The pattern of defiance set by Hamilton's burning persisted. Despite the decentralised nature of the Scottish state, and the persistence of other pressing problems, James V's regime eventually managed to mount an impressively broad attack on heresy. There were a total of fourteen executions during his reign, nine of which fell in just two years, 1538 and 1539: this was an organised purge at least as fierce as that pursued in England by More and Stokesley. Books were banned and burned; more than thirty evangelicals were driven into exile; more than fifty recanted (usually forfeiting their goods to the crown in the process). Anti-heresy legislation was renewed in 1535 and again, in much more detailed form, in 1541. The king made his personal distaste for out-and-out heresy unmistakable, and presided at the first major trial of his personal rule, in 1534. If this was all there was to the story, then Scotland's evangelical movement would probably eventually have been contained.

Yet James V's policy was contradictory. This was in part because of his own ambiguities. As we have seen, he let some at his court flirt with evangelicalism, at the same time as he persecuted those who expressed such views less guardedly. More importantly, however, heresy was not a predominant or defining issue for James V. It was an occasional concern, to be tackled for reasons of conscience, prestige or diplomacy, and only when it was convenient to do so. James's overriding political concerns were to crush his domestic enemies (above all, the Douglases) and to increase his income by any means necessary. These priorities had knock-on consequences on his religious policy, which pushed him some way from simple orthodoxy.

The Lutheran Reformation was – amongst many other things – a tremendous political opportunity for almost every prince in Christendom. We have already seen how Henry VIII used it to make a theatrical display of orthodoxy and to win a papal title; a few years later he was to use it in a very different way. The opportunities offered to James V were different. His regents ensured that Scotland, too, won credit for its orthodoxy: a copy of the anti-heresy Act of 1525 was sent to Rome, prompting Pope Clement VII to praise Scotland's unswerving faithfulness. When James began to rule in person, however, the tone of Scottish correspondence with Rome changed. When asking the papacy for favours – as he did increasingly often – James invariably emphasised his determination 'to banish the foul Lutheran sect' and reminded the pope 'how sincerely and consistently' James favoured the true faith.[10] In effect, the king of Scots was turning his faithful stewardship of the Church into a protection racket. He wanted his continued loyalty to be bought, and his price was high. A series of grants and privileges were issued by Rome, the most dramatic of which came in 1531, when Clement VII granted James a tax on the Scottish church worth £10,000 Scots per year. This was nominally in order to endow James's new Court of Session, the first permanent, central law court in Scotland; but the court's real costs were a tiny fraction of the amount awarded. It was a taste of how profitable the threat of heresy could be.

In 1533 and 1534, events took a new turn which made James's policy both more lucrative and more dangerous. Henry VIII's schism (see below, Chapter 5) meant that the papacy was now keener than ever to preserve Scotland's orthodoxy. So too was the Holy Roman Emperor, Charles V, whose aunt had been snubbed by England and who now noticed Scotland's existence for the first time. Henry VIII himself tried hard to lure his Scottish nephew into following his example. James's traditional ally, Francis I of France, was therefore also forced to bid for Scotland's loyalty. Initially at least, all this attention was extremely agreeable. James cleaved to the papacy and to France but all the while was dropping hints that his continued loyalty could not be taken for granted by anyone.

Gifts and honours duly came rolling in. Charles V gave him the Order of the Golden Fleece and suggested that he marry Henry VIII's daughter Mary. Henry VIII gave him the Order of the Garter and (in 1534) a peace treaty. Pope Paul III gave him the Blessed Sword and Hat and considered stripping the ill-fated title 'Defender of the Faith' from Henry VIII and awarding it to James. And France provided profit as well as honour: in 1537 James married Francis I's daughter Madeleine. Francis had been unhappy about the marriage, fearing that travelling to and living in Scotland might be dangerous for the sickly princess; but his ally insisted on no-one less than a king's daughter, and Francis gave in. His fears were justified, for Madeleine died less than two months after she arrived in Scotland. Yet James came straight back for another French bride, and France hurried to find one. There were no more royal daughters to be had, but Mary of Guise-Lorraine was a princess of the blood who (gratifyingly) had recently turned down a proposal of marriage from Henry VIII. James married her in 1538. Both Madeleine and Mary came with very substantial dowries. When Henry VIII made another attempt to lure James into schism in 1540, with promises of looted riches, James could justifiably reply, 'There is a good old man in France, my good-father [father-in-law] the king of France . . . that will not see me want any thing.'[11]

James V's religious policy of playing hard-to-get also had advantages at home. His distrust of his nobles carried with it the danger of becoming dependent on the clergy instead, especially men such as David Beaton, who was made a cardinal in 1538 and archbishop of St Andrews in 1539. Beaton was a staunch ally of the king, but also a big political beast in his own right. It was politically useful for James to be able to threaten his clergy by periodically reminding them what Henry VIII had done. In 1540 he commissioned a bluntly anticlerical play from Lindsay, made a number of bishops sit through it, and at the end turned to them and warned them that unless they mended their ways, he would 'send six of the proudest of them unto his uncle of England'. In the same year, when Beaton presented him with a list of lords and lairds who were alleged to be favourers of heresy, the king lashed back at the archbishop for his impertinence. He cited the example of the kings of Denmark and of England, who had 'reformed' their recalcitrant bishops by imprisonment and beheading respectively; brandishing a dagger, he told the assembled bishops that he would reform them with that.[12] Nobody perhaps took this kind of thing entirely seriously, but it was a way of reminding everyone who was king, and it worked. As James pointed out to Henry VIII, he did not need to break with Rome. If he wanted the Church's wealth, he merely had to ask for it.

James V did very well out of this policy, although he was still not actually able to balance his books. Yet it was a dangerous game to play. It relied on his conjuring up the possibility that Scotland might embrace heresy, and such possibilities are not always easy to control. More immediately, the attempt to string along all of the most powerful princes in western Europe was perhaps always likely to end badly. The party ended in 1541–42, when James's relationship with Henry VIII finally broke down decisively. Henry was moving towards invading France again, his last great military fiasco; and he needed to secure his northern border. Ideally he wanted a settlement, not least to resolve an issue which had been infuriating him for nearly a decade: the Scots' willingness to harbour English refugees who were loyal to the papacy. In 1541, Henry visited the north of England in a substantial royal progress, whose purpose was both to settle a restless region of the country and to prepare for a possible Scottish war. He also, however, invited James to come to York for a summit conference (the two kings, uncle and nephew, had never met). James initially agreed to the meeting, but quickly changed his mind. His council was divided over the question, with some even worrying that he might be kidnapped. More importantly, James had promised Francis I that he would not meet Henry; and he had nothing he was willing to give Henry on the issue of the refugees. By refusing to negotiate in 1541, he gave Henry a pretext for war. The failed summit only embittered matters further, since Henry spent weeks waiting in Yorkshire for a royal visitor who never came. It was petty, but Henry was a petty man, and he did not take snubs well.

And so in August 1542 a small English force crossed into Scotland. This incursion was checked, but it was only the beginning. Scots and English forces feinted across the Border at one another through the autumn. The English revived the old claim of suzerainty over Scotland (see above, p. 36); mixed with this old nationalism was a virulent new strain of anticlerical propaganda, whose particular target was Beaton. The Scots' experience of the war was more uneasy. James, having spent more than a decade cutting his nobility down to size, now found he needed them, and they were not entirely cooperative. As in 1522–23, they were reluctant to carry the war to England; and it may be that James's elevation of low-born favourites to positions of command also fuelled resentment. This, at least, is the explanation which most contemporaries gave for the bizarre fiasco which brought a temporary halt to the war. On 24 November 1542, a substantial Scottish army which had crossed into England was unexpectedly penned into a saltmarsh by a smaller English force, against a rising tide. The so-called 'battle' of Solway Moss does not really deserve the name: the fighting was limited to skirmishes as the Scots struggled to find an escape route. In the end, the demoralised and trapped Scots force disintegrated into a rout, and dozens of the most distinguished lords and lairds amongst them surrendered to the English.

Solway Moss has too often been read as the inevitable failure of James V's regime. Certainly, James's stern policy towards his nobility, combined with a decade of public equivocation towards England, limited his ability to rally his people for war, but Solway Moss was neither inevitable nor a calamity. The real disaster happened three weeks later: James V suddenly died. Romantically inclined commentators at the time and since have assumed that he died of a broken heart, at the news of the defeat, but James's heart was made of sterner stuff. Fury would have been more in character than turning his face to the wall. A more mundane medical explanation is probable, and the grim descriptions of his deathbed agonies do not make his swift final illness sound like a disease of the imagination. Whatever the cause, the effect was catastrophic. His heir was his only surviving child, a baby girl born only six days before his death. She would inherit a kingdom in which the religious games which her father had played so successfully became dangerously real.

Notes

1 *Letters and Papers . . . of Henry VIII*, vol. XVI, no. 1253.

2 George Bernard, 'The piety of Henry VIII' in N. Scott Amos *et al.* (eds), *The Education of a Christian Society* (1999), p. 63.

3 Bertram Lee Woolf (ed.), *Reformation Writings of Martin Luther*, vol. I (1952), p. 358.

4 John Foxe, *Actes and monuments of matters most speciall in the church* (1583), p. 984.

5 John Foxe, *Actes and monuments of these latter and perillous dayes* (1563), p. 601.

6 British Library, Cotton MS Cleopatra E.v fo. 389v.

7 John Strype, *Ecclesiastical Memorials, relating chiefly to Religion and the Reformation of it* (1822), vol. I, part ii, p. 55.

8 Greg Walker, 'Saint or schemer? The 1527 heresy trial of Thomas Bilney reconsidered', *Journal of Ecclesiastical History* vol. 40 (1989), p. 223.

9 David Laing (ed.), *The Works of John Knox* (1846–64), vol. I, p. 42.

10 Robert Kerr Hannay and Denys Hay (eds), *The Letters of James V* (1954), pp. 161, 167.

11 Arthur Clifford (ed.), *The State Papers and Letters of Sir Ralph Sadler* (1809), vol. I, p. 30.

12 Alec Ryrie, *The Origins of the Scottish Reformation* (2006), pp. 44–5.

CHAPTER 5

Supreme Head: Henry VIII's Reformation, 1527–47

The break with Rome

Between 1527 and 1534, by an act of sheer political will, King Henry VIII compelled a proudly, loyally Catholic country to renounce the papacy, accept him as the Supreme Head of the Church, and join him in defying the man who was now only to be described as the 'bishop of Rome'. This event permanently changed the religious, political and social history of all the British nations, and it remains mysterious.

The story is probably the best known of the century. It begins with, and is dominated by, a question which on the face of it had nothing to do with the European Reformation: Henry VIII's determination to have his marriage to Katherine of Aragon annulled, so that he might remarry. Matrimonial law fell under the Church courts (see above, pp. 40–1), and so – ultimately – under the pope's own jurisdiction. Henry's legal case for an annulment was weak, but not entirely risible. His political case was much stronger: the Church courts, up to and including the pope, tended to give crowned heads what they wanted. A king who was determined to make trouble – and Henry VIII was as determined as any Christian prince had ever been – could bring a good deal of pressure to bear on the Church, and a sensible settlement could usually be found. In this case, however, that proved impossible. If Henry's wife had been an Englishwoman, that would have been a different matter, but she was a Spanish princess, the aunt of Charles V, Europe's most powerful prince; and she herself was implacably opposed to the planned annulment (which was inaccurately but universally known, at the time and since, as the 'Divorce').

Between 1527 and 1529 the increasingly frustrated king found that this problem, which he had expected to be resolved quickly, instead became ever more intractable. As he began to run out of space for legal manoeuvre, from 1529 on, he began to apply pressure to the English Church more generally: in effect, he was blackmailing the pope. This was not at all a stupid or a rash policy. As we have seen, James V of Scotland was to use a very similar policy to extract substantial favours from Rome right through the 1530s (see above, p. 106). By 1530 the king's 'Great Matter' was the all-consuming centre of his government, yet a resolution was as far away as ever. Cardinal Wolsey fell from grace over the king's perception that he was not pursuing the Divorce aggressively enough. Thomas More resigned as Lord Chancellor in 1532 over the question. Their place was taken by a new generation of advisers, the most politically brilliant of whom was Wolsey's former secretary, Thomas Cromwell. It was Cromwell who implemented the final, almost insanely disproportionate solution: Parliament would simply declare it illegal for *any* English subjects to appeal to ecclesiastical courts outside England.

This modestly titled Act in Restraint of Appeals (1533) was revolutionary. It effectively eliminated the pope's authority over most aspects of Christian life in England. It finally broke the king's marital logjam, allowing him to renounce one wife, marry another and have a child with indecent haste. But it was not a stable solution. The pope's response to the 1533 Act and to Henry's remarriage was to excommunicate the English king. Henry and Cromwell replied with the 1534 Act of Supremacy, which declared that he, Henry VIII, was the Supreme Head immediately under God of the Church of England.

In retrospect, the Royal Supremacy can seem the logical solution to the Divorce crisis. Yet it was hardly ideal. By taking his entire country into schism, Henry made himself a bogeyman for every orthodox Catholic in Europe. He ensured that his new marriage would always be (at best) questionable, and that, therefore, any children born from it would be of dubious legitimacy. For a monarch struggling to turn an elective monarchy back into a dynastic one, this was a suicidally dangerous thing to do, and it created problems which would swirl around his successors for the rest of the century. The costs of schism were high, and the benefits dubious. Which leaves us with two, linked questions. Why did Henry eventually settle on such a desperately risky path? And how did he get away with it?

Conscience and dispensation: two trials, 1527–29

The origins of the Divorce controversy are mysterious. We know neither who first had the idea, nor why Henry latched onto it with such sudden and unshakable determination. Possibly it was triggered by negotiations with France in April 1527 about a possible marriage between the two royal families, when questions were asked about Princess Mary's legitimacy, but it seems likely the king already had his doubts. What we know is that on 17 May 1527, Cardinal Wolsey's legatine court heard a case that the king's marriage was a sham and should be annulled. From then on, Henry's commitment to the Divorce was implacable. Why?

There were perfectly sensible political reasons for Henry to want to end his marriage. After several pregnancies, the last in 1518, Katherine of Aragon had borne the king only one surviving child: Princess Mary, born in 1516. This was uncomfortable from a dynastic point of view: uncomfortable, not fatal. There was no doubt that the English crown (unlike the French) could descend through a female line, and if there were no good English precedents of female rule, there were plenty of contemporary European examples. But female rule did have its problems – in particular, how a ruling queen might marry without attracting grave political dangers. Moreover, a single child was a slender thread by which to hang Henry's dynastic hopes. His desire for a son is well attested. He gave serious consideration to legitimising his one acknowledged bastard son, Henry Fitzroy, the duke of Richmond – even by the bizarre and incestuous expedient of marrying him to his half-sister Mary.

Yet this will not do as an explanation for the Divorce campaign, for it is a rational, politically calculated reason, and the campaign was driven by a ferocious passion that was very far from being rational. If stabilising the crown and the realm had been Henry's purpose, he would never have pursued that purpose by so extreme a means as national schism. Legitimising Henry Fitzroy or allowing the crown to pass to Mary were both risky options, but neither was as risky as declaring war on the Church.

Throughout, of course, Henry knew precisely into whose bed he would be leaping the moment Katherine of Aragon was finally driven from his own. Anne Boleyn, probably pronounced 'Bullen', was the sister of Mary Boleyn, formerly one of Henry's mistresses. In 1527 Anne, too, caught the king's eye, but – for reasons that we are forced to guess – she refused to become merely his mistress. It is likely that their relationship remained sexually unconsummated for more than five years. Perhaps for that reason, it had a dazzling intensity. These were two forceful, manipulative and exceptionally arrogant people who had met their match in each other. It was their love affair which gave the Divorce crisis its urgency. Cooler expedients such as legitimising Henry Fitzroy would not, as a papal envoy recognised, 'suffice to satisfy the king's desires'.[1] We cannot imagine Henry's 'Great Matter' without Anne Boleyn.

Yet not even Henry VIII would have taken himself and his entire country into full-scale schism merely to satisfy the royal lust. Or if he would, he was at least far too sophisticated an animal to admit it to himself. All his life, Henry had an enviable power to convince himself that what he wanted to do was in fact the right thing to do. This rendered him almost entirely free of self-doubt, and meant that persuading him to change his mind was formidably difficult. It also made him ready to assume that his opponents were also God's enemies. So rather than pursuing mere self-interest, he would deduce general principles from his own interests and apply them more widely, allowing them to take on a life of their own. As the twentieth-century playwright Robert Bolt put it, Henry had a ravenous conscience. His sense of his own rightness left destruction in its wake.

Henry's public justification for pursuing the Divorce was that he was stricken in conscience, and utterly convinced that his marriage was an unlawful pretence. This was all too convenient, and clearly not the whole truth (it does not account for his bitter vindictiveness to Katherine of Aragon). Yet it is hard to make any sense of the crisis unless we assume that Henry had convinced himself that his marriage really was unlawful.

Legally, his case rested on one verse from the Old Testament. Leviticus 20: 21 states that for a man to take his brother's wife is a violation of his brother, and that such couples will be childless. This decree originally applied to circumstances where the brother was still alive – a separate, better-attested Jewish tradition held that if one's brother died childless, there was a positive obligation to marry his widow.[2] That tradition was hard to reconcile with monogamy and was usually seen as part of the ceremonial law which had been abrogated by Christ. Yet it did make plain that marriage to a brother's widow could not be an absolute evil. The medieval canon lawyers' solution to this problem was that marriage to a brother's widow was normally banned, but not actually prohibited by God's law. The ban could therefore be relaxed in specific cases, by due authority, as it was in Henry's case. In 1503, a dispensation was secured from Pope Julius II allowing him to marry Katherine, his brother Arthur's widow.

Henry's argument, therefore, was necessarily that Julius II's dispensation was invalid. And here, immediately, two different courses were open to him, a high or a low road. Henry himself, it seems clear, always favoured the former; initially, his advisers – and especially Cardinal Wolsey – favoured the latter. Wolsey's hope was to find a technical, legal means of invalidating the dispensation. There was not much to go on, but Wolsey was a formidable operator. As he observed, the original papal dispensation had dealt with the Levitical prohibition, but had omitted the lesser problem of so-called 'public honesty' (the impropriety of marrying someone previously betrothed to a relative, whether or not the earlier marriage had been celebrated and consummated). In law this was inconsequential, for another papal dispensation could have resolved it retrospectively, and since Henry and Katherine had lived as man and wife for eighteen years, that would be the natural course. Yet it provided a possible fig-leaf for an annulment. If the pope had wanted or been free to help Henry, this could have given him some legal cover.

Henry, however, favoured another argument. He insisted that Julius II's dispensation was invalid simply because no pope had power to grant such a dispensation. In Henry's view, his marriage violated God's law, and there was an end to it. As proof, he cited the warning in Leviticus that such illicit marriages would be childless – or without sons, as cooperative Biblical scholars convinced him the passage actually meant. This approach had some moral clarity compared to Wolsey's manoeuvres. Yet it also carried serious risks. For one thing, it involved a direct challenge to papal authority, which no pope could be expected to concede easily (especially in the wake of Luther's revolt). For another, Henry's entire case depended on a point of evidence. If the marriage between Arthur and Katherine had never been consummated, then the Levitical ban did not apply. This mattered because Katherine maintained that her first marriage had in fact never been consummated. The matter was (and is) unprovable one way or the other, despite the circumstantial evidence cited by both sides. But Katherine's unbudgeable insistence certainly created a doubt.

The first trial, in May 1527, was adjourned after two weeks (and never resumed); this was probably always expected, since it was inevitable that any settlement would need papal sanction. But soon thereafter, Henry rashly tried to short-cut the proceedings. He sent a messenger to Rome without Wolsey's knowledge, asking for a dispensation to remarry pending the final settlement of his case. Of course, this failed; more seriously, in the process he admitted a serious weakness in his case. He was attempting to divorce Katherine because she was his brother's wife, but also attempting to marry Anne Boleyn despite her being his mistress' sister. Henry's own reading of Leviticus permitted this, but the canon lawyers did not agree. It also gravely weakened the moral force of his case, both abroad and in England. Anne Boleyn came to have a poisonous reputation in England, as a seducer, gold-digger, home-wrecker and heretic. There were rumours that the king had slept not only with her sister but also with her mother (rumours which, in their later and wilder forms, even alleged that Anne herself was Henry's daughter). Scurrilous nonsense, perhaps; but such rumours testify to the Divorce's unpopularity.

By early 1528 it was clear there was going to be no quick solution. Pope Clement VII's position was painfully circumscribed by the Holy Roman Emperor, Charles V, Katherine's aunt. Charles's steadfast opposition to the Divorce was grounded on family pride, on respect for the Church and for the sacrament of marriage, and also on hard politics: Anne Boleyn had been raised in France, and the Divorce smacked of Anglo-French rapprochement. Blocking it – and increasingly, frustrating Henry VIII in any way he could – came to be in Charles's interests. And block it he could, for he was now unchallenged master of Italy, and Clement would not defy him.

A brief window of opportunity opened in 1528, when Wolsey persuaded Clement to allow a legatine court to decide the Divorce in England. The king's hopes, raised by this triumph, slowly drained away. Wolsey's colleague on the legatine court, Lorenzo Campeggio, wanted to find a negotiated solution. Ideally, Katherine would have taken religious vows and become a nun, giving her an honourable exit while freeing her husband to remarry. Yet Katherine absolutely refused to do this, insisting – as she would throughout – that she was the lawful wife of the man who now reviled her. Instead, she set out to torpedo the legal process. By producing a carefully concealed alternative copy of Julius II's dispensation at the right moment, she invalidated the legatine commission, delaying the trial for months. When at last it got underway at Blackfriars in London, on 31 May 1529, Katherine denied the court's impartiality and appealed formally to Rome. She gave a bravura performance before the court. She insisted that her first marriage had not been consummated, that she had come to Henry as a virgin, and that he knew it. According to one witness, she challenged him in open court to swear an oath that this was not true, which the king (that conscience again) would not do. When news of Katherine's appeal reached Rome, Pope Clement, now reconciled with the Emperor, revoked the legatine commission. Before news of this reached England, Wolsey had already suspended the proceedings. More than two years on, Henry had achieved precisely nothing.

A new approach: 1529–32

For almost four more years the case remained in legal limbo. Clement VII was clearly inclined to rule against Henry, but he was also reluctant actually to make the decision. Better to keep the Divorce as a card that he could threaten to play either way, and to avoid provoking the fury of the English king while he could still play for time. Delay also gave Henry time to marshal his forces, to pursue other lines of attack, and to nurse his burgeoning anger.

The first casualty was Thomas Wolsey. The king's rumbling impatience with the cardinal had been growing since early 1529, fed, perhaps, by Anne Boleyn's own dislike of her rival for the king's ear. Quite why and how Wolsey fell from favour remains unclear. The king acted with precipitate speed, with disproportionate vengefulness and apparently without any immediate provocation. This was how Henry's favourites tended to fall. The fatal sign was exclusion from the king's presence. Henry apparently did not trust his own ability to resist a face-to-face appeal, and often showed real fury with his enemies by refusing to see them. After the Blackfriars trial, Wolsey was barred from access to Henry for two months. They did meet once more, on 20 September 1529, and spent an evening deep in conversation; it seemed that their tiff was over. But it was their last meeting. Henry had not merely decided that he no longer trusted Wolsey; he intended now to use the cardinal to demonstrate his new, confrontational strategy.

On 9 October charges were brought against Wolsey under the statute of *praemunire* (see above, p. 41). The claim was that by acting as a papal legate, and presiding over legatine courts (such as that at Blackfriars), he had violated royal authority. The charge was farcical – Henry himself had campaigned hard for Wolsey to become a legate – but Wolsey knew his master and knew that there was only one sensible response. He promptly admitted his guilt and threw himself on the king's mercy, formally surrendering all his offices and goods. At first it seemed that a treason charge and death would quickly follow, but in the event he was released and preserved in one – but only one – of his dignities: the archbishopric of York. In 1530 he at last visited his northern diocese, apparently intending to rebuild his power. Why he fell finally and decisively at the end of that year remains unclear. The official story was that he had been conspiring with foreign powers to block the Divorce. Henry may have believed this (and it may even have been true). It is also clear that Wolsey was not short of enemies eager to poison the king's mind against him. But Wolsey's final arrest also served to intimidate the English clergy and the pope. He was arrested in

Yorkshire on 4 November 1530, fell ill during his journey south, and died at Leicester on 29 November. He was well aware that his death pre-empted the headsman's axe, and whatever physical illness troubled him (diabetes has been suggested), his will to live had clearly gone. He died in good medieval fashion, with a show of contrition. Yet his deathbed *bon mots* also included a penetrating verdict on Henry VIII's dangerous combination of malleability and stubbornness. He advised the officer escorting him to 'be well advised and assured what matter ye put into his head, for ye shall never pull it out again'.[3]

Henry's attack on Wolsey was bitterly personal, but it was also part of a wider assault on the status of the clergy. A new parliament was summoned in November 1529, largely for this purpose. The gentry, merchants and common lawyers of the House of Commons were perhaps more easily whipped up into anticlerical resentment than any other body of men in England. That winter, the Commons passed a series of bills aimed at reforming clerical misbehaviour and restricting clergy's legal privileges: this should have been Convocation's territory, but with royal backing most of these measures were passed. In July 1530 charges of *praemunire* were brought against a further fifteen clerics, including eight bishops. In 1531 the English clergy as a body were charged with *praemunire*, for presuming to operate Church courts which did not answer to the king. This time, Henry had overreached himself and was forced to compromise. The two Convocations, of Canterbury and York, sued for pardon and accepted swingeing fines as a result (£100,000 and £17,000 respectively). Yet the price was legislation confirming the Church courts' status; and the money was not much more than they might have been asked for in taxes. More importantly, perhaps, Henry required the Convocations to accept that he was the 'Supreme Head' of the English Church, but this plain repudiation of papal authority stuck in too many consciences. A face-saving compromise was found, proclaiming Henry to be supreme head 'so far as the law of Christ allows'. That clause defused the immediate crisis. No-one pretended it solved the problem.

What, now, was that problem? On one level, these manoeuvres were simply attempts to put pressure on the pope over the Divorce. Yes, they were laden with a new rhetoric, emphasising that Henry took a dim view of clerical independence and of papal jurisdiction; but this was part of the pressure. Yet this is not quite enough. It is not merely that those who engage in such brinkmanship have to recognise that their bluffs may be called. Rather, from about 1530 onwards, Henry seems to have become genuinely attached to the idea that he was Supreme Head of the English

Church – or, at least, of the English clergy. In particular, the power of the Church courts and of Convocation (whose business was outside royal control) rankled. Perhaps the threats began as bluffs, but Henry was always a man ready to believe his own propaganda. And the focus of that propaganda began to shift. An effort in 1529–30 to secure favourable rulings on the Divorce from Christendom's great universities (a project conceived by an ambitious Cambridge theologian named Thomas Cranmer) gave way to a more explicit assault on papal authority. Officially sponsored books such as *A Glass of Truth* (1532) laid out the case for the English Church's independence from foreign interference. The Divorce was ballooning into larger issues.

The crux came in 1532. In February a parliamentary Act was passed – against stiff opposition – threatening to withhold the fees known as annates from Rome, and implicitly denying the pope's right to appoint bishops. In March, with a spontaneity which fooled no-one, the House of Commons produced a *Supplication against the Ordinaries*: a long list of complaints against supposed clerical abuses. Henry promptly sent it to the southern Convocation. When their response was less abject than he wished, he explicitly demanded that Convocation subject itself and the Church's laws to royal and parliamentary authority. The bishops refused. Henry accused them of being 'but half our subjects, yea, and scarce our subjects', and wondered if the oath which bishops swore to the pope was itself treason.[4] Most of the senior clergy – who had loyally backed the Divorce campaign – were appalled. After excruciating pressure, Convocation made its 'Submission' on 15 May 1532, with more than half of the bishops absent.

This did not give Henry his Divorce, but it did break the power of the English clergy. Thomas More promptly resigned as Lord Chancellor – one sign of how dramatic a change this was. Henry's purpose was an immediate political one, yet the Submission fundamentally changed the nature of English law. The modern constitutional doctrines of parliamentary sovereignty, and of the supremacy of statute law, can be traced back to it. Parliament's authority over religious matters was a novelty, and one which would be decisive for the rest of the century and beyond.

At this point – with English diplomacy bent quite out of its usual shape, with all other English interests long subordinated to the endless campaign for a Divorce, with England's constitution fundamentally recast and with the threat of total schism in the air – it is worth asking how Henry VIII got himself into this mess, and whether there would have been any other way out of it.

The annulment he had wanted was probably always politically impossible, at least as long as Katherine opposed it. Her obstinacy was met with increased royal fury. Henry and Katherine met for the last time on 11 July 1531, and thereafter the woman who still wore the name of queen was kept under house arrest in Hertfordshire, cut off from her husband and her daughter. Her household was progressively reduced in size and dignity. The Emperor's ambassador believed that there were conspiracies to poison her. When she did eventually die, in January 1536, it seems to have been of natural causes, but it was widely believed – including by her own physician – that she had in fact been murdered. Henry VIII publicly celebrated her death. All of which raises the question: why had he not actually had her murdered five years before, when her death would have resolved the whole issue at a stroke?

No-one was foolish enough to discuss the possibility on the record, but speculation suggests two reasons why she was allowed to live. One is political: the reaction to Katherine's murder would have been extremely dangerous. Henry might have been excommunicated as a murderer, and his subjects absolved of their oaths of obedience to him. England was still enough of an elective monarchy that it would be very hazardous for a king to be seen as a wife-killer, even without Katherine's real popularity and Charles V waiting in the wings. When Henry's great-niece Mary, Queen of Scots was widely suspected of involvement in her husband's murder in 1567, she was driven from her throne largely as a consequence.

And yet, the path of schism, which Henry eventually chose, was not obviously less risky than murder. He was excommunicated anyway, and the resulting executions of prominent papal loyalists – above all of More and of John Fisher – gave him a reputation as a bloodthirsty tyrant. But a murder would have had one great advantage over schism: the possibility of repentance. If Mary, Queen of Scots provides an alarming parallel, a subtler one is suggested by King Henry II, who was blamed for the murder of Archbishop Thomas Becket in 1170. Henry II had to do humiliating penance for his part in Becket's death, but he lost neither his throne nor his control over the Church, and Becket stayed dead. If Katherine had been murdered, Henry VIII would likewise have had to endure the discomfort and humiliation of extended (but nuanced) public repentance. Yet he was skilled at political theatre. Some luckless alleged murderers would doubtless have met grisly ends. The pope would have been immensely relieved that the whole affair was over. Once a decent pause had elapsed, Henry would have been a widower who was free to remarry, and to have children whose legitimacy no-one could doubt.

But Henry VIII was a man of conscience. He would happily murder his political enemies, but preferred to do it judicially, according to the laws he had created for the purpose. One reason for his famous enthusiasm for marriage was that, latterly, he lost his taste for taking mistresses: when a new lady caught his eye, as in 1536 and again in 1540, he insisted on marrying her and so on finding a legal means of jettisoning his existing wife. His quest for a Divorce in 1527–33 was not about securing himself an heir by any means necessary, nor about finally persuading Anne Boleyn to give in to his advances. He wanted to do these things, but to do them righteously, in good conscience. He truly believed that God was on his side. That is why this crisis was, eventually, about much more than a Divorce.

From Divorce to Reformation

One possible solution to the Divorce crisis had been threatened explicitly almost from the beginning: to refuse to recognise the pope's authority over the English Church, including his authority to settle matrimonial cases. It had remained no more than a distant threat because it was not at all clear how it could be implemented. Papal authority could be neither cherry-picked nor simply shrugged off. This 'solution' meant full-scale, open-ended national schism.

So far, the story of the royal Divorce has been entirely separate from the story of the European Reformation. Henry's Divorce crisis was a political one, of the kind which might have happened to any medieval king. This once led some historians to describe Henry VIII's schism as a political event almost entirely unconnected to the turmoil in contemporary Germany, as if it were merely a coincidence that the two sets of events happened at roughly the same time. Yet the final solution of the Divorce problem was only made possible by the German Reformation, for three reasons. The Reformation provided a diplomatic climate in which schism was possible. It provided the king with domestic allies who were critical in formulating and in forcing through his policies, in the face of considerable opposition. And it provided an ideology which allowed Henry VIII himself to secure his Divorce with a clear conscience, and to do a great deal else besides.

The diplomatic question is perhaps the most important. National schism was immensely risky. A schismatic king could find himself targeted by an alliance of Catholic powers, using a crusade against their ungodly neighbour to divide his kingdom amongst themselves with papal blessing.

Nor, in the face of such an invasion, could such a king count on his own subjects' loyalty. In 1532 MPs were warning Henry to his face that, if he persisted, 'such feuds and intestine divisions would result therefrom as to completely destroy and subvert the whole kingdom.'[5] Schism was also a near-irrevocable step. Any reconciliation with the pope would have involved renouncing any new marriage as bigamous, renouncing any children of that marriage as bastards, and reconciling with Katherine (if she was still alive). In other words, Henry was risking permanent political isolation. For the rest of his life, Henry's great nightmare was an anti-English alliance between the two great Continental rivals, France and the Habsburg Empire. When this threat looked real – as it did on occasion in the 1530s – Henry was thrown into a desperate flurry of diplomatic activity and of fortification.

What made these risks tolerable was that England was not the first schismatic territory in Europe. In 1531 a group of Lutheran states and cities in Germany allied together in the so-called Schmalkaldic League, in order to defend their religious independence against Charles V. The Scandinavian kingdoms of Denmark and Sweden were also moving in that direction: some Danish territories had rejected papal authority in the 1520s, and the kingdom as a whole finally did so in 1536. Sweden had gone into schism in 1527. Individually, none of these territories was quite so prominent or powerful as England, but collectively they counted for much more, and made an English schism possible. Their precedent was important. From at least 1528, the English were warning Rome that they might emulate the German schism. An empty threat at first, no doubt, this slowly began to seem more plausible. When it became real, the Lutherans provided obvious allies. Henry was particularly optimistic about an alliance with the Schmalkaldic League, for he and they shared a likely enemy in Charles V. Indeed, in 1541, when it briefly seemed possible that the Germans might be reconciled with Rome, Henry was ready to submit to papal authority rather than be left out in the cold. However fond he was of his schism, he would not take the risk of maintaining it unilaterally.

A second factor linking the European Reformation to Henry's crisis was domestic. Henry VIII had an exceptionally high opinion of his office, but he never committed that fatal error of monarchs, fully to believe in the powers he claimed for himself. The fiasco of the Amicable Grant (see above, pp. 86–7) was a reminder that the English crown's powers were limited. England could not be governed without at least the grudging consent of the political classes: the nobility and senior clergy, the gentry, the merchants, the scholars and the lawyers, who together made Tudor government function. And underpinning them, the wider mass of English society – especially urban society, and above all London – could not be entirely ignored. These people could make their voices heard through such crude techniques as demagoguery, vandalism, riot and full-scale rebellion.

There is no doubt that most English people, including those of the political classes, found the Divorce distasteful. It was an ugly spectacle: a king throwing over a pious, faithful but ageing wife in favour of a scheming younger model, and declaring his daughter a bastard in the process. In some cases, distaste threatened to harden into real opposition. Katherine's most outspoken defender was Bishop Fisher, but there was also a loose parliamentary grouping. In 1532 one of these MPs, the Warwickshire gentleman Sir George Throckmorton, accused Henry to his face of having 'meddled' with both Anne Boleyn's sister and her mother. That he was willing to do this – and more, able to get away with it – shows how tenuous Henry's control of the whole situation was becoming. Behind such bold figures lurked the powerful influence of the Holy Roman Emperor. His ambassador in England, Eustace Chapuys, made it his business to discover, organise and encourage as much opposition to the Divorce as possible.

Discontent at court was matched in the country. Here the focus of opposition became the tragic figure of Elizabeth Barton. Barton was a servant girl from Kent who, after an illness in 1525, began to experience trances and visions. She became a nun and swiftly acquired a considerable reputation for holiness. Both of Kent's bishops, Fisher and Archbishop Warham of Canterbury, encouraged her; the king himself met her. Such spiritual celebrities were a regular enough feature of the medieval world, but from the late 1520s on Barton began to use her fame to denounce the Divorce. She prophesied that if Henry were to remarry he would cease to be king in God's eyes, and would be deposed within a month. She had a wide following, both lay and clerical. Some of her supporters tried to have books bearing her name printed.

We can imagine scenarios in which these rumbles of dissatisfaction erupted into civil war, with a legitimist party backing the claims of Princess Mary against her apostate and excommunicated father. (Chapuys and others did imagine these scenarios, in some detail.) They did not materialise, both because the regime managed to outmanoeuvre and intimidate an opposition which was already divided, and also because the king did manage to conjure up a body of real supporters.

The defeat of the opposition to the Divorce is a masterclass in both subtle and brutal politics. The fundamental achievement was in preventing a serious opposition from coalescing in the first place. The terrible irony was that opposition was principally a matter of conscience, not of political interest. But conscience also forbade conspiracy or rebellion. As such, the king's most dedicated opponents were perhaps the men and women least well placed to organise opposition. None of them had both the skills and the stomach to organise and lead a political party against the king. The real battle was lost in Henry's subjects' hearts, subjects whose belief in the ideal of kingship was so strong that they did not wish to believe that their duties to God and to their king might diverge. Henry VIII's twenty years of magnificent political theatre proved their worth. He had made his people believe in him.

If the 'soft', ideological power of Tudor monarchy was decisive, hard power was ever present too. During the critical parliamentary vote on the Act of Conditional Restraint of Annates in 1532, Henry came into the Commons chamber and ordered the House to vote by physically dividing in his plain sight, with his supporters and opponents gathering in separate areas of the building. This procedure (then apparently a novelty, now a routine part of parliamentary practice) was an obvious means of intimidating opponents, some of whom changed their votes. There were no mass arrests – yet – but opponents were frozen out of royal favour and cut off from patronage. Against figures such as Elizabeth Barton, more brutal tactics could be employed. Investigations against her and her circle began in August 1533. In November she was arrested, and was quickly induced to confess that her prophecies had been deliberately faked. Some of her supporters were rounded up; others threw themselves on the royal mercy. Barton was made publicly to renounce her errors in London and in Canterbury, before she and five of her most prominent adherents were hanged and beheaded. Their heads were impaled on London Bridge and the city's gates. Denunciations of her as a traitor rang from every pulpit.

Yet all of this depended on there being a substantial party who were willing to fight the king's battles. Mere loyalism provided some supporters. So did political prudence: it was not only Henry who was worried by the absence of a male heir. More significantly, the king's desperation meant there were fortunes to be made by furthering his case. A generation of lawyers, administrators and theologians cut their teeth on the Divorce, and rose in royal service as a consequence of it. These were men like Stephen Gardiner, a humanist and lawyer in Wolsey's service who helped to negotiate the creation of the legatine court in 1528. This marked Gardiner out for future promotion, and in June 1529 he became the king's principal secretary. In 1531, he was appointed bishop of Winchester, the wealthiest bishopric in England, while in his mid-thirties. These were the rewards of good service.

However, Gardiner's case also shows the limits of patronage, for by 1531 he was becoming alarmed by the direction of royal policy. In 1532, he was responsible for preparing Convocation's first, defiant reply to the *Supplication against the Ordinaries*. After this, the king still respected Gardiner's usefulness, but no longer entirely trusted him. His evident unhappiness with the king's seizure of the Church led to his being replaced as royal secretary and frozen out of favour. He was the king's man, and always conformed outwardly, but reluctant support of this kind was not what Henry needed.

This was how the European Reformation suddenly became useful to Henry VIII, in the shape of England's tiny evangelical movement (see above, pp. 95–102). It was not an obvious alliance, for most evangelicals – notably Tyndale, and Luther himself – were strongly opposed to the Divorce on moral grounds. Yet when the Divorce campaign turned towards a wider attack on the Church, using Erasmian rhetoric, it began to resonate with the evangelicals' views. And so, at the same time as English evangelicals were being persecuted with some ferocity (see above, pp. 101–2), some of them also began to rise in royal favour. Hugh Latimer, who had been converted by Thomas Bilney, preached a series of sermons at Cambridge in 1529, which echoed Erasmus both in their stern moralising and in their call for the Bible to be translated. This attracted not a heresy charge but royal patronage. Eloquent attacks on the clergy's corruption, venality and obscurantism were becoming useful to Henry. Latimer preached at court in 1530, and in 1531 was given a lucrative vicarage by the king. Six months later his mentor Bilney was burned; it was a sign that Latimer was walking a dangerous line, and indeed he was himself hauled before Bishop Stokesley of London in 1532. But he continued to enjoy royal favour for his provocative preaching against 'abuses', and for his increasingly open strictures on the pope. Latimer stands out because he was the most gifted preacher of his generation, a man able to start a religious riot merely by opening his mouth. But a series of other young clerics followed the same path. Among them were Latimer's friend Edward Crome; when he was charged with heresy in 1531, he appealed directly to the king, on the grounds that he was Supreme Head of the Church. It was a sign of how useful evangelicals and the king could be to one another. Henry was flattered; Crome was allowed to make an ambiguous recantation and to prosper.

If the preachers provided propaganda cover for the regime, other evangelicals gave more strategic assistance. Three in particular were of decisive importance. Thomas Cranmer was a Cambridge theologian recruited in 1529 to give scholarly weight to the case for the Divorce, and then to the case for royal supremacy. During 1531–32, travels in Europe and conversations with evangelical reformers converted him to a decisively evangelical stance. He sealed this conversion by an illegal marriage, to the niece of a German Lutheran pastor in 1532. His scholarship, his honest conviction that the king truly was Supreme Head of the Church, and the close, trusting relationship he had forged with Henry bore unexpected fruit that same year. The aged Archbishop Warham died in August 1532. Warham had not openly opposed the Divorce, but he had become increasingly uneasy about the direction of royal policy, and was showing alarming signs of listening to his conscience. Henry now wanted an archbishop who was genuinely convinced of the case for the Divorce and against the Church. A year earlier, Stephen Gardiner might have been the man, but it was now too plain that he shared some of Warham's scruples. So Cranmer was plucked from relative obscurity and made archbishop – to everyone's surprise, especially his own. It was a turning-point. The king's union with Anne Boleyn was now, finally, consummated, either after or before a secret marriage ceremony: she was soon pregnant, providing a firm time limit to the interminable crisis. Cranmer swiftly convened a third and final trial of the king's first marriage and, on 23 May 1533, declared it annulled, refusing to allow any appeal to Rome. The three-month-old Act in Restraint of Appeals gave that refusal statutory force. The king had his way, and his longed-for child was born on 7 September – a girl, Princess Elizabeth. One of the many prices Henry paid for this victory was the installation of a patient, determined evangelical reformer as the primate of all England.

Thomas Cromwell is a more complex figure: a Putney merchant's son, himself by turns a merchant, a soldier and a self-trained lawyer. He was a sharp, cynical administrator, a man who made it his business to know everything and everyone. He caught Cardinal Wolsey's eye; in the mid-1520s he managed the foundation of Wolsey's new colleges at Oxford and Ipswich, a process dominated by the dissolution of almost thirty monastic houses to provide the funds. After Wolsey's fall, Cromwell – like Gardiner and many others – managed the transition to royal service. Like Wolsey before him, he displayed an administrative omnicompetence which quickly made him indispensable, and he joined the royal council. It was Cromwell who negotiated a ceasefire with Convocation in 1531, and the ambiguous statement that Henry was Supreme Head of the Church 'as far as the law of God allows' may have been his idea. The *Supplication against the Ordinaries*, the neutering of Convocation, the decision to assert and use the supremacy of statute law, and the legislation of 1533 and 1534 that turned the Royal Supremacy into a fact: all this was Cromwell's work. In 1534 he replaced Gardiner as the king's principal secretary, and for the next six years he enjoyed a level of power and influence comparable only to that which had been exercised by Wolsey.

It also seems clear that Cromwell was a convinced evangelical. This has often been doubted, not least by his great twentieth-century admirer Geoffrey Elton, who saw Cromwell as the founder of the modern English state, an administrative genius who rose above mere religious strife. Protestants with tender consciences have often also been unhappy about laying claim to a man whose political style was so ruthless. But Cromwell's association with evangelical religion was more than a matter of convenience. While scything his way through monasteries in Wolsey's name in the 1520s – a task he completed with verve and brutality – he also went to some trouble to protect suspected Lollards who asked for his help, an action which could have brought him no personal benefit at all. He was a friend and patron of the Biblical translator Miles Coverdale by 1527, and during the early 1530s he carefully kept open a line of communication with William Tyndale. Cranmer saw Cromwell as his most important political ally. Friends and enemies alike believed Cromwell was committed to the evangelical project, and when trouble started to swirl around him in 1539 and 1540, it was his reputation for religious radicalism which his enemies used to try to bring him down. The question is of more than biographical interest. Cromwell was the chief architect of the Royal Supremacy, and, like any architect, he expressed his client's wishes in his own distinctive way. The high road to the Divorce which was eventually chosen, and the evangelical marching music that cheered the regime on its way, both owed a good deal to Cromwell's own preferences and prejudices.

More important still was Anne Boleyn herself. Between Wolsey's fall and Cromwell's ascendancy, Boleyn was probably the closest thing Henry VIII had to a chief counsellor. Although her role is, by its nature, difficult to document, she certainly spurred the king on and helped him to think the unthinkable. And her own thinking was steadily evangelical, albeit in a courtly French rather than a tub-thumping German way. She consistently steered the king's patronage towards evangelical preachers and advisers. Latimer, Crome, Cranmer, Cromwell and many others acknowledged their debt to her. Once she was queen, her patronage of evangelicals helped to place half a dozen of them – including Latimer – on the bishops' bench.

The importance of Boleyn's support for a nest of evangelicals at court is demonstrated by one notorious incident. The two versions of this story we have (both long after the fact) are not wholly consistent, but the events probably took place in 1529. Boleyn apparently gave one of her maids an extremely dangerous book: William Tyndale's *The Obedience of a Christian Man*. The maid then gave the book to a gentleman who was wooing her. This glimpse of how heresy slipped surreptitiously from hand to hand like scandalous gossip is intriguing enough, but in this case it went wrong, and the book fell into Wolsey's hands. Characteristically, Boleyn raised the stakes: she appealed to the king. The book was returned to her, and she proceeded to lead Henry through selected passages of it. We are told that 'the king read and delighted in the book, "for (saith he) this book is for me and all kings to read."'[6]

And this is the third key point of contact between Henry VIII's schism and Martin Luther's Reformation. As well as providing diplomatic cover and domestic allies for England's king, the Protestant Reformation also gave him an ideology. If the alliance between Henry and England's nascent evangelical movement was an unlikely one, Tyndale's book contained the intellectual glue that held it together, not least in Henry's own mind. *The Obedience of a Christian Man* was a book about (amongst other things) royal authority. Against the accusation that evangelicalism was politically subversive, Tyndale (adapting Luther) argued that the pope and the clergy were the true subversives. He spiced this claim with a very high doctrine of royal authority. 'The king is in the room [i.e. the place] of God, and his law is God's law.' Whoever defies a king defies God – 'yea, though he be pope, bishop, monk or friar'. The rightful, God-given authority of the crown had been usurped by scheming clerics. As a result, Tyndale lamented, kings are 'captives ere ever they be kings, yea almost ere they be born', and are reduced to being mere 'hangmen unto the pope'.[7]

Henry disagreed with Tyndale about his marriage, but this was another matter. Henry already had a very elevated view of his own kingship and of the spiritual responsibilities that went with it (see above, p. 90). To read this when he had already convinced himself that his whole predicament was caused by papal pretensions and intransigence, and when he was beginning to suspect that his own clergy and his cardinal were thwarting God's will by opposing him – it was heady stuff. Tyndale's argument implied that the king should not only reject the pope's authority over his marriage, but over everything; and that Henry should shoulder the burden of authority over the entire English Church which God had so plainly intended for him.

The real impact on Henry of Tyndale's book is unknowable. But this is the most plausible intellectual underpinning for Henry's growing conviction, from about 1530 onwards, that the root of the whole problem was false papal claims to authority and the clergy's persistent disobedience to their sovereign. For this reason, quite suddenly, in late 1533, Henry himself and his entire regime stopped using the word 'pope' altogether, referring to Clement VII only as the 'bishop of Rome'. Clement was now merely a foreign bishop, with no jurisdiction over England. The preamble to the decisive 1533 Act in Restraint of Appeals put it in more positively patriotic terms, asserting that England was an *empire* – that is, a wholly sovereign state, acknowledging no outside overlord.

By the time it was achieved, the Royal Supremacy over the Church was more than simply a means to the Divorce. Rather, the long struggle with Rome over the Divorce had convinced Henry that Rome's authority was false. We do not know exactly when, how or through whom Henry VIII arrived at his developed doctrine of the Royal Supremacy. But whether or not it was he who had the idea, by the early 1530s it is clear that the idea had him. It became one of his core convictions that God had appointed him as the Supreme Head of the English Church.

This headship meant more than ceremonial presiding, more even than controlling appointments and administration. Henry believed he had the right and duty to determine (and to reform) the English Church's doctrine, liturgy and ceremonial practices. Martin Luther commented that Henry wished to be God, so he could do whatever he pleased. And indeed, he used his self-awarded powers with a recklessness that no pope has ever reached, attempting (for example) to rewrite one of the Ten Commandments so as to justify his own behaviour.[8]

Henry's commitment to the Royal Supremacy became inescapable in 1536, when both Katherine of Aragon and Anne Boleyn were dead, and their two surviving daughters were both declared bastards. Henry could easily have been reconciled to Rome at this point, trading a little personal humiliation for much increased international and internal security. Princess Mary's legitimacy would have had to be accepted, but there would have been no obstacle to papal recognition of his third marriage, to Jane Seymour. Yet the king does not seem even to have considered the prospect. He now truly believed that he was Supreme Head of the Church, and he would defend that status against all comers.

So does all this amount to an English Reformation? Perhaps it was the beginnings of one. The grubby tale of marital breakdown and self-righteousness is an eternal one; but only in the early sixteenth century could it have blown up into a jurisdictional dispute and into national schism. The European Reformation did not cause the English political crisis of 1527–34, but it made the eventual solution to that crisis possible. Christian humanism had given Henry VIII a taste for Biblical arguments, which made him less likely to seek a modest, legalistic solution to the crisis. Lutheran arguments about the spiritual authority of kings, filtered through Tyndale and through Anne Boleyn, gave Henry the moral confidence he needed first to bully the Church, then to threaten schism, and finally to make good on that threat. The spread of evangelical doctrines in the universities, at court and in a few other small but influential circles gave Henry much-needed allies, as the squabble over his marriage turned into a broader battle with the papacy. And the successful schisms of the German and Scandinavian princes proved that it could be done without courting annihilation either from the emperor or from God. Henry's schism was not, yet, a Protestant Reformation. But it was a Reformation made possible by Protestantism.

The Henrician Reformation

For the last thirteen years of his life, Henry VIII ruled as Supreme Head of the Church of England, and extended those claimed powers to Wales and Ireland as well (see below, Chapter 11). But what he did with that authority remains frustratingly difficult to pin down. Henry's religious policy baffled his contemporaries and has proved equally puzzling to historians. On one traditional reading, his 'Reformation' consisted of Catholicism without the pope – but this suggests that the old Church could have been beheaded and still have carried on regardless. Or alternatively, this was a sham Reformation driven by the king's lust and greed, in which religion was a mere smokescreen. Another view still would see it as a moderate Reformation, a virtuous middle way between the extremes of Catholicism and Protestantism (much of Henry's own rhetoric can be quoted in support of that view). Perhaps it had no religious coherence to it at all – one recent historian has called it 'a ragbag of emotional preferences'.[9] Or perhaps those preferences were diplomatic: one view emphasises how Henry's religious policy shifted and weaved according to England's international situation. A final approach would question whether this Reformation was Henry's at all, arguing instead that it was carried out in his name by his ministers and bishops. On this view, until 1539–40, religious policy was not made by the king so much as by Thomas Cromwell; and from then until Henry's death in 1547, the king was caught in a bloody political tug-of-war between various opposed religious factions.

The reason why all of these views persist is, of course, that all of them have some truth in them. In other words, this is a complicated subject. To find a path through it, we will look first at what Henry VIII's regime said about religion, and then at what it did.

Books and articles: the doctrinal Reformation

Henry VIII's Reformation produced four formal declarations of official doctrine, all of them problematic. First, in 1536, came the so-called Ten Articles, a summary statement of the newly independent Church's doctrine and practice which flirted with evangelical ideas, but did little more than flirt. In 1537 came a much more substantial document, *The Institution of a Christian Man*, universally known then and since as the *Bishops' Book*. This was a book-length statement of the English Church's doctrines, intended to be definitive, and assembled (as its nickname suggests) by a committee of bishops and other theologians. In some areas it pulled back from the apparent evangelicalism of the Ten Articles; in others it seemed to go further. But as a definitive guide to doctrine, it failed. The authors had disagreed vehemently with one another, and had not resolved or papered over all of these disputes. Worse, the king refused fully to endorse it, instead setting about the work of revising it almost immediately. The third statement of doctrine came in 1539, in an Act of Parliament universally known as the Act of Six Articles. This appears much more straightforward, for it reasserted six points of Catholic doctrine (chiefly relating to the Mass) and stated firmly that anyone who denied them would be counted a heretic. Yet this too is ambiguous, for the list was a partial and peculiar one which owed much to diplomatic considerations, and its enforcement was sporadic.

The last and most straightforward of these four documents was published in 1543. This was the revised version of the *Bishops' Book*, called *A Necessary Doctrine and Erudition for any Christian Man* and known, inevitably, as the *King's Book*. Unlike its predecessor, this was fully authorised by Henry and by an Act of Parliament (the Act for the Advancement of True Religion). Also unlike the *Bishops' Book*, the *King's Book* was reasonably consistent. In most (not all) ways, it was closer to traditional Catholic Christianity than the Ten Articles or the *Bishops' Book* had been. Yet the *King's Book* cannot be treated as a simple statement of Henry's doctrines either – it, too, was the product of a distinctive political moment, when the king was trying to put on a show of Catholic orthodoxy for the Emperor Charles V, and when some of his leading courtiers were engaged in a murderous plot against prominent evangelicals.

Together, these texts and other, more minor documents suggest four key marker-posts of Henry VIII's religion. First comes his sharpest difference from traditional Catholicism: the Royal Supremacy. To have the monarch as head of the Church now seems merely conventional in England, and given how much influence medieval kings had over their Churches, it is tempting to see continuity here. But Henry VIII's headship was another matter. It was a high calling bestowed on him directly by God (Parliament did not make him Supreme Head, merely recognised him as such). He was not a figurehead. His officials (who were laymen) conducted visitations and issued detailed injunctions to parishes to mend their ways, usurping the bishops' role. They ensured, amongst other things, that all references to the pope were scratched out of service books – an early act of desecration. Henry also took a leading part in theological discussions, arguing the toss with his bishops. His careful handwritten revisions to the *Bishops' Book* show him as a keen (and pedantic) amateur theologian. He even toyed with the idea that, by virtue of his kingship, he had priestly powers to ordain. The Royal Supremacy became central to Henry's own sense of honour. Anyone who dared question it risked a traitor's death. It was the hub around which the rest of the Henrician Reformation turned.

Alongside this extraordinary claim, Henry remained consistently committed to Catholic doctrine in two key areas: justification (see above, pp. 91–2) and the Mass (see above, pp. 16–19). The Ten Articles and the *Bishops' Book* were faintly ambiguous on the subject of justification, but in the *King's Book* Henry returned unequivocally to the position which he had often stated elsewhere: faith and works together were indispensable for salvation. Henry plainly loathed the Lutheran doctrine of justification, believing that it amounted to a licence to sin without fear of the consequences. As befits a king with stern views on law and order, Henry was adamant that sin should always have consequences, and that his subjects should be exhorted to lives of relentless moral effort. Archbishop Cranmer spent fifteen years trying to persuade the king to accept an evangelical view of justification, but to no avail – unless we believe the report that Cranmer finally won the argument when the king was on his deathbed, when illness had robbed him of the power of speech and when imminent death and judgement made free forgiveness seem more appealing.[10]

Likewise, Henry never wavered in his traditional view of the sacraments. His personal devotion to the Mass, in all its traditional glory, was unmistakable. He quibbled about the sacrament of ordination, which (by reserving powers to the clergy) seemed to circumscribe his own authority; and he once tried to raise matrimony, of which he was so fond, to the status of a major sacrament (until Cranmer pointed out this would mean that marriage was necessary for salvation). But overall he was as stoutly loyal to the sacraments in the 1530s and 1540s as when he defended them against Luther in 1521. His enmity towards those who denied the Royal Supremacy was almost matched by his hatred for those who questioned the sacraments. His especial venom was reserved for Anabaptists, who rejected infant baptism (an almost non-existent threat in England), and for 'sacramentaries', those who denied that Christ was physically present in the Mass.

These, then, were three of the marker-posts of Henry's religion: Royal Supremacy, justification by works as well as faith, and a traditional view of the sacraments. Hence the claim that this was Catholicism without the pope. Likewise, Henry still insisted that his clergy remained celibate (compelling Archbishop Cranmer to keep his marriage secret), and maintained the traditional hierarchy and structure of the English church, altered only at the top. Yet beneath these commanding heights of orthodoxy, the sands were shifting. The Ten Articles raised doubts about the legitimacy of the use of images and shrines, about the validity of pilgrimage, and about the practice of prayer for the dead. These doubts only deepened over the following decade. The *King's Book*, despite its general conservatism, had a sting in its tail: the final section, on prayer for the dead, admitted that such prayer was legitimate, but denied that Christians could know anything about the state of the dead or about how prayer helped them. It explicitly rejected the word 'purgatory' as a papal invention. Only the most vague and generalised prayer for the dead was now to be permitted.

This radical break with the past was justified with reference to the fourth point of Henry's religious compass: the Bible. From his first 'discovery' that the book of Leviticus condemned his marriage, to his later conviction that the Bible plainly and unambiguously taught the doctrine of the Royal Supremacy, Henry was convinced of the overriding importance of the Bible for Christian life. Even when his religion was firmly traditional, he wanted, in Erasmian style, to justify those traditions by reference to Scripture rather than to the authority of the Church. Henry's reading of the Bible directly influenced his religious policy. And now we are moving from what Henry VIII said about religion to what he did.

King Hezekiah: the Henrician Reformation in practice

If Henry VIII's doctrinal pronouncements were predominantly conservative, his actions – or his government's actions – tell a different story.

One action above all daunted his traditionalist subjects and left many evangelicals utterly convinced that he was ultimately on their side. This Biblicist king legalised the English Bible. The first full English Bible was printed in 1536. Possibly that same year, or in any case by 1538, every parish in England was ordered to buy a copy to be kept in the church for public use. By 1541 most had complied. Henry had an endearingly naive belief that anyone who read the Bible would discover the doctrine of the Royal Supremacy in its pages. When some of his subjects found other messages in the sacred text, and (worse) began to argue about them, Henry repeatedly threatened to withdraw the privilege of using the Bible, and eventually did so. The 1543 Act for the Advancement of True Religion banned Bible-reading for the lower social orders (its first draft, it seems, had excluded the laity altogether). The Act was scarcely enforced, but evangelicals' faith in their king was badly dented. Perhaps he was not quite one of them after all.

For while Henry was enamoured of the Bible, he did not learn evangelical doctrines from it. The aspect of the Bible which seems to have come alive for Henry was its model of kingship. The Old Testament books of Samuel, Kings and Chronicles described the kings of ancient Israel and Judah, kings who bore religious as well as secular authority. Henry saw himself in this mirror. He was King David, the great royal musician and poet; Solomon, the epitome of wisdom; and Hezekiah, the reformer, who had led his corrupted kingdom back to the true faith.

Henry's revival of Old Testament kingship produced one very specific preoccupation. The Old Testament writers used one yardstick almost exclusively to measure the worth of individual kings: had they suppressed idolatry? Idolatry was an ancient Christian (and Jewish) scruple, but one which had lain dormant in western Europe for a millennium. Erasmus regarded the more exuberant pieties around shrines, relics and statues as tasteless; Luther saw them as potentially dangerous distractions. But Henry arrived at a view closer to the emerging Reformed Protestant ('Calvinist') doctrine (see above, p. 93), which held that any reverence shown towards physical objects was blasphemous. Henry never went quite that far. In particular, he passionately defended worshipping the Host during the Mass, for he still believed that it was Christ's body. Yet he damned pilgrimage, and the veneration of saints' images, as 'superstition'. Twice, in 1538 and in 1541, he ordered major purges of statues and shrines which had been 'abused' in this way. Some of medieval England's most treasured relics fell to this assault. The Blood of Hailes, a phial kept at Hailes Abbey in Gloucestershire which was said to contain Christ's blood, was denounced, mocked and destroyed. The great shrine of Walsingham, which had so disappointed Henry in 1511 (see above, p. 89), was suppressed. The setting of votive candles before images of the saints was banned in 1538. The ranks of the saints themselves were thinned: a series of traditional holy days were abolished by royal proclamation, with only those saints who appeared in the Bible itself remaining. Henry preferred his subjects to be engaged in honest and productive labour than to be dissipating themselves in the worship of idols.

In one particular case, Henry's campaign against idolatry was more personal. Thomas Becket, murdered on Henry II's behalf in 1170, was England's finest home-grown saint: a martyr for the Church's independence and a symbol of resistance to royal tyranny. His shrine at Canterbury was one of the most splendid pilgrimage sites in Europe. Henry VIII pulverised it. The precious metals were melted down; the saint's relics were burned and the ashes scattered. Not a trace of the shrine remained. In Henry's view, Becket was a usurper, defying God-given royal authority in defence of the Church's own greed and corruption. To venerate him was almost to deny the Royal Supremacy. He was blotted out of Henry's Church.

The looting of Becket's shrine introduces us to the last and – perhaps – the decisive ingredient of Henry's Reformation: greed. His regime criticised the supposedly onerous papal taxation of the English Church, and with great fanfare abolished so-called 'Peter's Pence' (a duty which amounted to merely £200 per year for all England). However, as Supreme Head, Henry could not resist raiding the Church's coffers for himself. One disenchanted evangelical grumbled that the king had merely become a new pope, 'and dispensations be sold now dearer by the half than they were in the popish time'.[11] The 1534 Act of First Fruits and Tenths required all beneficed clergy to pay a tax of 10% of their annual income to the Crown, plus a fee equivalent to one year's income whenever they took up a new post. Freedom from Rome came at a price.

Above all, Henry VIII dissolved the monasteries. No previous English government had ever imposed such an extraordinary change on the country. Between 1536 and 1540, every single abbey, convent, priory and friary in England and Wales was suppressed. The religious who had served in them were turned out, sometimes with pensions to provide for their living. Their lands and incomes, which at nearly £200,000 annually were worth rather more than the king's own, were seized by Henry, in his capacity as Supreme Head.

The consequences of this slow-motion revolution were dramatic. The monasteries had been the medieval Church's powerhouses of prayer: now they were closed down. When the *King's Book* formally distanced itself from prayer for the dead in 1543, the actual practice of prayer for the dead in England had already taken a body blow. The monasteries had also been some of the Church's most prestigious and independent institutions. The great abbots had sat in the House of Lords, outnumbering the bishops; now they were gone. As for the money, no English government has ever received such an enormous financial windfall, nor spent one so recklessly. The regime made vague promises that it would use the proceeds of the dissolution for charitable purposes, but only a small fraction was ever so used. Most of it was sold at knock-down prices, or given to royal administrators and favourites. Small numbers of people made very large fortunes. The crown spent its receipts almost entirely on war – in particular, on a ruinously expensive campaign in France in 1544–46. By the end of that campaign Henry VIII's government was almost bankrupt again, and confiscated monastic lands had been parlayed into the hands of England's gentry. Where monastic houses had owned the rectories of parish churches (see above, pp. 8–10), those too now passed to the new lay owners. As a result, the crown and the gentry acquired the right to appoint huge numbers of parish clergy.

The dissolution does not seem to have been wholly premeditated. Instead, Henry appears more like someone who, having intended only to sample a box of chocolates, could not stop himself from gorging the lot. The dissolution came in waves. In 1535–36, royal visitors toured England's monasteries, looking for evidence of immorality and corruption. Their reports were used to justify a 1536 law seizing all religious houses whose annual revenue was less than £200 – supposedly in the name of reform, although poorer houses were not necessarily ill-disciplined ones. Only hindsight suggests that at this stage the regime deliberately intended a wholesale dissolution. Monks from suppressed houses were allowed to move to larger houses of their orders. Over the next twelve months, the king even endowed two new foundations. But a huge northern rebellion in late 1536, triggered chiefly by the dissolutions (see below, p. 140), changed the picture. It warned the regime to be careful, but also opened up some new possibilities. The abbot of Furness in Lancashire was charged with supporting the rebels and, to save his neck, handed the abbey over to the king. This was dubious – it was hardly his personal property – but it set an invaluable precedent. In 1538, the larger houses began to fall one by one into royal hands, most of them surrendering voluntarily. The king appointed abbots who would do this, bribed or bullied existing abbots into cooperating, and dislodged those who refused. The pliant were pensioned off generously; the obstinate were left penniless. The defiant abbots of three of England's greatest abbeys – Reading, Colchester and Glastonbury – were convicted as traitors, and (dubiously) their abbeys declared forfeit to the king. By the time Parliament retrospectively legitimised these dissolutions in 1539, they were almost over. By April 1540 not one religious house remained.

Greed is not *quite* enough to explain this. It might have led the king to devastate the monasteries, but not to exterminate them. The political costs of destroying some of the houses outweighed the financial gain they offered. For example, the duke of Norfolk was patron of Thetford Priory, in whose vault various of his family were buried. Norfolk was desperate to save Thetford, and proposed various schemes to do so. To no avail: Henry wanted every last monastery gone. Or again, there was little financial point in dissolving the nine monastic cathedrals in England, since they were promptly refounded as secular cathedrals. Indeed, if Henry's purpose had merely been plunder, he would surely have seized the cathedrals too (as plenty of evangelicals and opportunists around him urged). Likewise, chantries, collegiate churches and even England's two universities seemed like tempting fruit for a rapacious government. Yet while Henry continued to bleed taxes from the Church, there was no systematic looting beyond the monasteries. Instead, he founded six new dioceses with new cathedrals in 1540–42, dividing some of England's largest and most unmanageable dioceses. And in 1546, he founded wealthy colleges at both Oxford and Cambridge – and that in a year of desperate financial pressure.

Why did Henry VIII devour every single monastery while resisting the temptation to seize other foundations? There were particular reasons for the king to dislike monasticism. Religious orders were organisations which spanned western Christendom. English monasteries, nunneries and friaries ultimately looked to superiors on the Continent, and they were hotbeds of opposition to the Royal Supremacy – especially the best-disciplined orders such as the Carthusians and the Observant Franciscans. Between 1534 and 1540 eighteen Carthusians and as many as thirty-one Observants died in prison or on the gallows for refusing to accept the Supremacy. More than fifty other religious fled abroad rather than renounce Roman obedience. The suspicion of crypto-papistry hung around the entire monastic estate.

For evangelicals (who were well represented amongst the officials enforcing the dissolution on the ground), the monasteries' sins went much deeper. In their eyes, monks were parasites. Monasticism lavished wealth on a few individuals' blasphemous efforts at self-sanctification, while deceiving the people into believing that they could subcontract their own spiritual responsibilities to monks. One typical but inventive evangelical called monks 'purgatory horse-leeches', draining the life-blood of the commonwealth. And naturally, their corrupt doctrine produced corrupt lives. Some monks lived in 'beastly buggery', while others – remembering those who supported Elizabeth Barton – had been 'bawds and fornicators with the holy whore of Kent'.[12] Evangelicals, notably those in Anne Boleyn's circle, hoped that the king would use the monasteries' wealth to endow preaching and education. This hope became more forlorn as the spoils of the dissolution were swallowed up by the king's wars.

Henry's own view was different. He too had drunk deeply of the Erasmian prejudice that monasticism was futile and probably corrupt. He preferred subjects who laboured and paid their taxes. However, his attack on the monasteries was not meant as an attack on the Mass or on prayer for the dead as such. While he had his doubts about the industry of prayer for the dead, he never abandoned it altogether. If nothing else, he wanted Masses said for his own and his family's souls. So he would ransack the monasteries: they were temptingly wealthy, alarmingly papist, useless to the commonwealth and (or so the king was ready to believe) laced with corruption. But he would go no further.

Were these policies the king's own, or those of his advisers and administrators? We cannot know for certain. We do know that Henry's own views were forcefully expressed and that he would brook no direct opposition. He certainly believed that his government's policies were his own. Yet his attention to detail was sporadic, and a servant he trusted – such as Thomas Cromwell – could have a great deal of freedom to formulate as well as to implement policy. Henry made Cromwell his 'vicegerent in spirituals', effectively allowing him to exercise the Royal Supremacy over the Church on the king's behalf. It was Cromwell who issued the 'royal' injunctions of 1536 and 1538. There is also plenty of evidence that Henry was open to persuasion. Politicians and clergy on all sides valued having the king's ear. He would not be opposed, but he could be steered.

This was a dangerous game, however. Twice after the break with Rome, Henry turned suddenly and viciously on those with whom he had been intimate, refusing to see them and sending them to the headsman. In 1536 Anne Boleyn was caught up by a sudden whirlwind of accusations of adultery, incest and witchcraft. The great love affair ended with her execution, a hasty declaration that the longed-for marriage had never been legitimate and the bastardising of her daughter Elizabeth. This grotesque event almost defies explanation. It is commonly seen as a murderous factional struggle – a view centred on Cromwell, who turned against her with ruthless speed when the depth of the crisis became plain. Yet the truth seems messier. Anne was less attractive as a wife than as a lover, and she had recently miscarried a son. The risqué lifestyles she permitted in her household were a source for rumours which her enemies fanned and which her now-suspicious husband was ready to believe.[13] Something similar happened four years later, in 1540, when Cromwell himself – apparently at the height of his power – was suddenly arrested, barred from talking to the king and condemned. Cromwell had plenty of enemies, although probably his real offence was to lock the king into a fourth marriage (to a German princess named Anne of Cleves), overruling Henry's revulsion for Anne with diplomatic necessity. Again, however, Cromwell's fall is mysterious, and as with Boleyn, the ultimate explanation must lie in Henry's own paranoid, capricious vindictiveness. Such stories sometimes had happy endings. In 1543 Archbishop Cranmer was the target of a complex series of plots; in 1546 the king was briefly persuaded to turn against his sixth and last wife, Katherine Parr. But both Cranmer and Parr succeeded in throwing themselves on Henry's mercy, and both outlived their homicidal patron.

Henry VIII claimed that his Reformation was moderate: a sweetly reasonable middle way between popery and heresy. Yet the truly distinctive feature of his Reformation was not its moderation, nor its theological confusion, nor even its rapacity, but its bloodthirstiness. Anne Boleyn and Cromwell were only the most prominent victims. After the break with Rome, about forty evangelical reformers were burned for heresy in England. Over the same period, fifty people were executed as traitors for refusing to renounce the papacy, usually by being hanged, drawn and quartered. On 30 July 1540, two days after Cromwell's execution, three prominent evangelicals (amongst them Robert Barnes) were burned; three papal loyalists, who had long been mouldering in prison, were brought out to be hanged, drawn and quartered alongside them. The king's point was not subtle. This was *his* Reformation; those who hoped to wrest it to their own purposes did so at their peril.

Reactions and responses

How did Henry VIII's subjects respond to this extraordinary upheaval? The reactions fall into three broad categories.

Religious conservatives: active resistance, passive resistance

Opposition to Henry VIII's Reformation from his subjects was passionate, very widespread, and almost wholly unsuccessful. This is a paradox to our modern, democratic eyes, which tend to see sheer numbers as politically decisive. In fact, the nature of political dissent almost always matters more than its scale. The power of the idea of kingship, and the subtle ruthlessness with which Henry VIII exploited that power, left his opponents scattered, isolated and disorientated.

For a very few, the situation was clear: to renounce the pope was to renounce the true Church. The regime pursued these people remorselessly. Thomas More and John Fisher were beheaded in 1535. One hundred and twenty-seven people are known to have escaped into exile, where they were harassed by English agents. The presence of exiles in Scotland helped to provoke war in 1542 (see above, p. 108). The most dangerous exile was Reginald Pole. Pole, who was studying in Italy in the early 1530s, was a subtle and brilliant Christian humanist, intrigued by evangelical ideas but utterly committed to the papacy. Worse, he was a member of the royal family, from the Yorkist stock which Henry VIII still feared. In 1536 he wrote a treatise, *De unitate ecclesia*, denouncing his cousin the king, and declaring himself to be a Christian first and an Englishman second. Pope Paul III made him a cardinal, and sent him to tour European courts in an effort to mobilise a crusade against England. He became Henry VIII's greatest hate-figure. Futile plots were hatched to assassinate him. A book was commissioned and published specifically to vilify him. Mere contact with him was presumptive evidence of treason. Most of his relatives were arrested and a good many executed. In 1541, even Pole's aged mother was beheaded, perhaps the most vicious of Henry's many judicial murders.

Eye-catching as the exiles were, the threat they posed remained more potential than real. Most English people accepted the Royal Supremacy, albeit under pressure. (The stories in Ireland and Wales were very different: see Chapter 11.) Amongst the leading bishops, Stephen Gardiner, Cuthbert Tunstall, Edward Lee and John Stokesley all had doubts, but all conformed. For most lay people, the papacy did not seem worth dying for. Yet in fact, the Royal Supremacy was decisive. Once that principle had been conceded, it was extremely difficult to oppose further changes which were made in the king's name. More's and Fisher's lonely stand looked quixotic at the time. With hindsight, it seems far-sighted.

After 1534–35, therefore, opponents of Henry's Reformation within England were gravely compromised and lacked any clear cause to which they could rally. Yet opposition continued. In the autumn of 1536 a series of mass rebellions convulsed northern England. As with all peasant rebellions, these had many causes, but religion was manifestly at their heart. The largest of these rebellions called itself the 'Pilgrimage of Grace for the Commonwealth', and the 'Pilgrims' marched under a banner of Christ's wounds. They demanded Cromwell's and Cranmer's sacking and the restoration of the suppressed monasteries. Under the leadership of an obscure Yorkshire lawyer named Robert Aske, they rapidly assembled an alarmingly well-disciplined volunteer army of some 40,000 men. The king, frightened and furious, sent the duke of Norfolk north to suppress the rising. Meeting the rebels at Doncaster, Norfolk found himself badly outnumbered.

Wisely ignoring the king's shrill demands to crush the rebels, Norfolk negotiated. He promised, on the king's behalf, a full pardon for the rebels, and a Parliament to meet in the North to discuss their grievances. And the rebels believed him. Aske disbanded his army and sent them quietly home. Mere military force could not compete with the ideal of kingship. The king had made them a promise. Of course, once the rebels' army had disappeared, the promises were swiftly broken. Minor disturbances early in 1537 were used as a pretext for bloody reprisals. At least 144 people were executed, including Aske and the other leaders, and the North was placed under what amounted to martial law for the next two or three years.[14] The rebellion was used to tar all subsequent opposition to the regime as treason.

Thereafter, real opposition was limited to two forms. First was foot-dragging and passive resistance. Royal commissioners were met with sullen stonewalling. Monasteries' goods or illegal relics were hidden before they could be seized. Priests muttered against the king in confession, although they risked being denounced for this. Parish clergy deleted the pope's name from their service books as the law required, but sometimes only with a single thin line of ink. Widespread as this kind of behaviour was, it was scarcely going to stop the regime in its tracks.

More constructively, those clergy and nobles who had accepted the Royal Supremacy could help to shape what the newly independent English Church would be. Cuthbert Tunstall and Stephen Gardiner not only reconciled themselves to the Royal Supremacy, but preached and wrote earnestly in its defence. They and their allies hoped that strong royal leadership was England's best defence against heresy. They struggled to discredit evangelical leaders, and by the 1540s street-fighting between these two nascent religious parties had become a constant backdrop to politics. Conservative success in these running battles is harder to assess. Gardiner and his allies chalked up some significant victories – the *King's Book* owed much of its traditional shape to such men – but such victories were almost impossible to convert into long-term guarantees that orthodoxy would be preserved.

Evangelicals: from loyalty to frustration

For much of the 1530s, everything seemed to be going the evangelicals' way. The pope was denounced; Cromwell, Cranmer and a great many more were in power; the monasteries were falling; and – above all – the English Bible was freely set forth. Almost all evangelicals could assent joyfully to the Royal Supremacy. And they were pressing at the edges, always trying to ratchet the new orthodoxies onwards: doubting the sacraments and traditional ceremonies, undermining the clergy's authority, declaring that purgatory was false and insisting on justification by faith alone. Some reformist clergy were also beginning to marry, hoping the practice would soon be legalised.

Yet they did not run on too far. As yet, few English evangelicals embraced the 'sacramentarian' doctrines which so appalled their king. They disliked the concept that the Mass was a sacrifice (it was incompatible with their theology of justification), but they had little to say on the question of whether Christ's body and blood were physically present in the bread and wine of the Eucharist. Henry VIII devoutly believed that Christ was not only present, but present by means of transubstantiation. Some evangelicals agreed. Thomas Cranmer seems to have had a view more like Martin Luther's: that is, that Christ is physically present, but that the bread and wine are not utterly transformed. But very few explicitly embraced the more radical view of the Reformed theologians, that any presence is merely spiritual or even symbolic. When sacramentarian views were denounced in the Act of Six Articles in 1539, few evangelicals disagreed.

Nevertheless, the Six Articles exposed the fragility of the evangelicals' alliance with Henry VIII. That Act did not repeal any existing reforms, but it did warn that little more was going to happen. In its wake, a few evangelicals began to slip into exile again. At the same time, the king's failure to use the wealth of the monasteries for charitable purposes was souring his achievement in some reformers' eyes. And in 1540, with Cromwell's fall, the reformers lost their most powerful friend. Their freedoms were squeezed much harder from 1543 onwards, when the old-fashioned ortho-doxies of the *King's Book* were reinforced by a severe crackdown on evangelical printing and preaching. Worst of all, that year's partial ban on Bible-reading (see above, p. 133) felt like a betrayal.

Meanwhile, evangelical radicals and exiles, a minority within a minor-ity, felt vindicated. The evangelical exile community of the 1540s was tiny – we can name fewer than forty people[15] – but they had a powerful theo-logical and political analysis. Most of them were loyal to Reformed rather than Lutheran theologies, and were far more willing openly to confront the king. With their more moderate brethren silenced, they began to win a hearing. In the summer of 1546, with Henry VIII sickening and his minis-ters jockeying for position, there was a sudden, brutal purge against evan-gelicals. While establishment evangelicals tried to compromise their way out of trouble, as usual, the hero of that summer was Anne Askew, a young Lincolnshire gentlewoman of outspoken views. Religious conservatives at court hoped that she could be made to give evidence against her friends in high places; but she refused to break, despite cruel torture, and went to the stake noisily denouncing her persecutors. Accounts of her arrest and interrogation were swiftly published. Political moderation and doctrinal compromise were looking discredited. That same year, Archbishop Cranmer himself abandoned his quasi-Lutheran doctrine of the Eucharist and moved towards the Reformed, 'sacramentarian' views that his king so hated.

English evangelicalism was still a tiny phenomenon, but with an influ-ence out of all proportion to its numbers. It was concentrated in influential places: the royal court, the senior clergy, cities (particularly London), merchants and artisans (particularly the printing industry) and above all the universities. Few of England's centres of power were untouched by it. The reformers were passionate in their commitment and confident that God would give them the victory. They greeted one another as brethren and commemorated their dead leaders as martyrs. By 1547, they were a formidable movement.

The wider population: confusion and conformity

It is evangelical agitation and the conservative drag-anchor which attract our attention, but most people belonged to neither camp. The relentless royal propaganda asserting the Royal Supremacy, building on a long-established tradition of loyalty to the crown, made its mark. Most of

Henry VIII's subjects did not rejoice at what had been done to their Church, but found ways of squaring their consciences or their interests with it.

Confusion and bewilderment was perhaps the dominant response. If historians, with all the archives at our disposal, still cannot agree what Henry VIII's religious policies were, it is no wonder that his subjects were confused. This confusion manifested itself in two main ways, both of them helpful to the regime. First was wishful thinking. Loyalty to the crown, and the realities of power, made it natural for most people to read what they wanted to read into the regime's ambiguous religious signals. Latent good-will towards the king was probably Henry VIII's single most important political asset, and he drew on it heavily. It had some unexpected results. For example, the 1539 Act of Six Articles was a by-product of a particular diplomatic moment, and addressed only a handful of subjects. Yet for much of the population, it rapidly became a touchstone of orthodoxy. In the bewildering religious politics of the 1530s and 1540s, most of Henry's subjects seem to have been grateful for whatever reassuring certainties they could find.

Secondly, confusion precipitated withdrawal. As old dogmas were undermined, many English people retreated to religious territory which seemed certain. One clue to this comes from wills. Quite large numbers of sixteenth-century English people left wills, and wills from this period usually included a religious statement of sorts. Under Henry, a very few wills began to include explicit professions of Protestant faith. But many more abandoned traditionally fulsome Catholic language, no longer in-voking the Virgin Mary and the saints. Likewise, bequests for chantries or for other means of speeding the soul through Purgatory were eroded during Henry's reign, being partly replaced by more worldly charitable bequests. By the 1540s a large minority of wills restricted themselves to a bare assertion of faith in God. We can hardly assume that these wills were made by budding evangelicals, but it does seem that the traditional pieties no longer seemed quite so certain. The retreat from funding intercessory foundations was purely rational, since it was now likely than any such bequests would be seized by the king. Yet if the king was driving people away from traditional pieties, that had its consequences.

Indeed, under the cover of this confusion, Henry VIII's Reformation succeeded in making significant changes to his subjects' religious behavi-our. It is not merely that traditional pieties like pilgrimage were outlawed. The laity were also given newly tempting choices. From 1538, Henry's subjects were allowed to break parts of the traditional six-week Lenten fast. The opportunity was attractive to evangelicals who disdained super-stition, but also to anyone who found the traditional regulations irksome. Or again, the regime's attack on prayer for the dead – combined with shrill evangelical claims that the whole business was a confidence-trick designed to line the clergy's pockets – made it very tempting for Christians with tight budgets to spend their money on something else. Each such tempta-tion was a step away from the old Church.

Nothing accelerated this process more than the dissolution of the monasteries. It is not simply that the systematic desecration of shrines proved, crudely, that God would not instantly strike down those guilty of such sacrilege – a kind of experimental demonstration of the old religion's weakness. Equally importantly, the looting turned large numbers of English people into beneficiaries of Henry's Reformation. If these holy places were going to be looted anyway, it made sense for local people to grab what they could before the royal commissioners took everything. In some places, the formal dissolution was pre-empted by locals who stripped monastery buildings of their valuables, down to the lead on the roof and the stones from the walls. The king was of course furious, but those who had taken part in such looting were implicating themselves in his actions. More durable was the problem of the lands which were seized from the monasteries and then sold to the gentry. England quickly acquired a new class of immensely wealthy landowners who were the direct beneficiaries of the dissolution of the monasteries, and who would certainly oppose any attempt to reclaim the stolen goods they had received. Henry VIII had (unwittingly?) turned his subjects into his collaborators.[16]

Even without such worldly motives, Henry would have had his sup-porters. His theologically incoherent cocktail of policy had genuine appeal. Nationalist anti-papalism; Erasmian Biblicism; loyalty to the Mass and to other traditional pieties; a loathing of heresy; contempt for clerical wealth and corruption; and the mendacious claim to be moderate – all of these appealed to a good many of Henry's subjects. Blend them with loyalty to a forceful and charismatic king, and we can see why so many English people would still raise at least half-hearted cheers.

And some cheers were full-throated. After Henry's death, both he and his policies were genuinely mourned. In 1549, a conservative Kentish scholar named John Proctor wrote a treatise opposing what he saw as Protestant excesses, and praising how 'that noble Henry, King of Kings' had 'not without great travail and study, not without tyrannical hatred of foreign powers . . . brought home that comfortable light' of the true faith. In 1551, John Redman – a distinguished conservative theologian of long standing – wrote a similar lament for a Reformation gone astray. He described Rome as a 'filthy stinking hole' but evangelicals as 'worse than pagans and infidels'. Instead of the stubborn immobility of the 'old sort', or the reckless dashing ahead of 'the new sort', he urged England 'to amble a good gentle pace in the commandments of God'.[17]

Henry VIII, however, was no gentle ambler. He was a monster of egotism and self-righteous paranoia, perhaps the grossest tyrant ever to rule over England. Yet he was a dreadfully charismatic tyrant, whose tyranny chimed with enough of his subjects' hopes and fears to be accepted and even cherished. This was what made his Reformation possible. And this, too, gave his Reformation its afterlife, for a king's authority ultimately exists in the minds of his subjects. In Henry's case, this authority persisted long after he had departed to meet the God in whose name he had so freely ruled.

Notes

1 *Letters and Papers . . . of Henry VIII*, vol. IV, part ii, no. 4881.

2 Principally Deuteronomy 25: 5–10; *cf.* Genesis 38: 8–10; Matthew 22: 23–28.

3 Peter Gwyn, *The King's Cardinal* (1990), p. 638.

4 J. J. Scarisbrick, *Henry VIII* (1968), p. 299.

5 Pascual de Gayangos (ed.), *Calendar of Letters, Despatches and State Papers relating to . . . Spain*, vol. IV, part ii (1882), no. 948.

6 John G. Nichols (ed.), *Narratives of the Days of the Reformation* (Camden Society old series 77, 1859), pp. 52–6.

7 William Tyndale, *The Obedience of a Christen Man* (1528), ff. 33r, 78r, 79r, 80v.

8 He added a clause to the final Commandment, which forbids coveting another's property, so as merely to forbid coveting another's property 'wrongfully or unjustly'. Cranmer rebuked him for this. Bodleian Library, 4o Rawlinson 245, ff. 54v, 77r; Cranmer, *Letters*, 100, 106.

9 Diarmaid MacCulloch, *The Reign of Henry VIII* (1995), p. 178.

10 John Foxe, *Actes and monuments of matters most speciall in the church* (1583), p. 1290.

11 'A memorial from George Constantine to Thomas Lord Cromwell', *Archaeologia*, xxiii (1831), p. 63.

12 Henry Brinklow (?), *A supplication of the poor commons* (1546), sigs A3v, B3v.

13 Greg Walker, 'Rethinking the fall of Anne Boleyn', *The Historical Journal*, vol. 45 (2002), pp. 1–29.

14 Anthony Fletcher and Diarmaid MacCulloch, *Tudor Rebellions* (2004), p. 48.

15 Alec Ryrie, *The Gospel and Henry VIII* (2003), pp. 266–70.

16 Ethan Shagan, *Popular Politics and the English Reformation* (2002), pp. 162–96.

17 John Proctor, *The fal of the late Arrian* (1549), sig. B3r; John Redman, *The complaint of grace* (1609), pp. 59, 61, 68–9; *cf.* Ashley Null, 'John Redman, the Gentle Ambler' in C. S. Knighton and Richard Mortimer (eds), *Westminster Abbey Reformed* (2003).

CHAPTER 6

The English Revolution: Edward VI, 1547–53

The short reign of King Edward VI (1547–53) has long been neglected. It has been treated either as a disreputably un-English interlude, or as a period of chaotic near-collapse, best hurried through en route to the sunlit uplands of Elizabeth I's reign. Yet recent research makes the reign appear one of the most dramatic episodes in English history, when a series of profound changes were thrust on an unsuspecting country. It is the hinge on which the sixteenth century turned – for the whole of the British Isles, not merely for England. It was at least as startlingly novel and as momentous as the better-known 'English Revolution' of the mid-seventeenth century, and probably more enduring in its consequences. Like all revolutions, this one failed. Like all revolutions, it changed everything that happened afterwards.

Carnival: Protector Somerset's Reformation

From Henry VIII to Protector Somerset

The succession crisis that had dominated the middle of Henry VIII's reign finally abated in 1537, when his third wife Jane Seymour at last bore him a son (at the cost of her own life). Young Prince Edward was born not a moment too soon, for his father's health was already deteriorating. Henry suffered a bad fall from his horse in 1536, and thereafter, with his ability to exercise curtailed, his weight ballooned. Contrary to popular belief, he probably did not have syphilis, but he was troubled by a recurring ulcer on his leg and also by impotence (apparently none of his last three marriages was consummated). By the mid-1540s, although only in his fifties, he was decaying into a raddled, bloated parody of his former self. As his health failed, a new succession crisis emerged: the prospect of a child king.

Was England still an elective monarchy (see above, p. 34)? If so, would it choose a child? The last boy king, Edward V, had lasted less than a month. It was easy to imagine another usurpation. A claim could have come from England's most powerful nobleman, the duke of Norfolk; or, more likely, from his eloquent, headstrong son, the earl of Surrey. In 1543 a servant of one of Surrey's friends declared that 'if aught other than good should become of the king, he [Surrey] is like to be king'. Such talk was explosive. One of Surrey's friends fell out with him in 1546, declaring that he would rather murder Surrey himself than see a boy king in his or his father's custody. Soon thereafter, Surrey had a new coat of arms made for himself, which emphasised his own royal blood. In the febrile atmosphere of late 1546, this was folly. In December, Surrey and his father were suddenly thrown in prison and declared guilty of treason. The young earl was beheaded; his elderly father was due to follow him soon after. It was Henry VIII's last judicial murder.[1]

Even if Prince Edward secured his throne, he was a minor, and someone would have to govern in his name. During 1546 rivals were jostling for position. And when the decisions were finally made, in December 1546 and January 1547, almost all the most prominent religious conservatives were excluded from power. This was partly mere bad luck. The leading conservative nobleman was the duke of Norfolk, brought down by his son's fatal rashness. The leading conservative churchman was Stephen Gardiner, the bishop of Winchester, who had a tiff with the king over some lands at the wrong moment that winter. But able politicians make their own luck, and it may well be that the victors of this particular contest had done just that. One legacy of Thomas Cromwell's administration had been the placing of a good many evangelicals amongst the king's household servants. As Henry grew sicker, those servants became increasingly powerful. In 1545, Henry – who had always found writing tedious – finally abandoned the irksome task of signing official documents. Instead, a stamp of his signature was made, and entrusted to the chief gentleman of his privy chamber, an evangelical named Anthony Denny. The evangelical clique around the king may have steered his final decisions – or worse. The king's will, which named the regency council for his son, was signed not with his own hand, but with the stamp. There remains an outside possibility that the will was tampered with after the old man's death.

Yet conspiracy theories are unnecessary. It was always likely that – if forced to a decision – Henry VIII would place his son in evangelical rather than in conservative hands. Gardiner, the champion of the conservative cause, was widely rumoured to be a crypto-papist, and had been suspected of contact with Reginald Pole in 1541. It seemed (and still seems) likely that a government dominated by Gardiner and his allies would have led England back towards Roman obedience. And Henry's priority for his son was to safeguard his own most precious achievement, the Royal Supremacy.

The surest sign of this bias is in the provisions that Henry made for young Prince Edward's education. The prince's chief tutors in the mid-1540s included some of the finest scholars in the land (not to mention his godfather, Archbishop Cranmer). These men were not doctrinaire Protestants, but they were evangelically inclined and made no great efforts to conceal the fact. All of them were drawn from reformist Cambridge rather than conservative Oxford. Henry was willing to take the risk of exposing his son to evangelicals because, in the end, they were better than papists.

Even so, events clearly did not follow the course which Henry expected. He seems to have believed his settlement could and would outlive him. He appointed a regency council which included evangelicals, but also solid conservatives such as the Lord Chancellor, Thomas Wriothesley (pronounced 'Rithsly'), who in the summer of 1546 had tortured the evangelical Anne Askew with his own hands. With the duke of Norfolk out of the picture, the natural leaders of this council would be a group of soldiers and technocrats with no very obvious religious bias. For example, there was John Dudley, Viscount Lisle (soon to be earl of Warwick), the son of Henry VII's hated enforcer Edmund Dudley. Aside from his well-known animosity towards Gardiner, there was little to link Dudley to evangelicalism. Or there was William Paget, the secretary to the Privy Council, whom Bishop Ponet later called the 'master of practices'.[2] He could play both sides: both Cranmer and Gardiner regarded him as an ally. First among equals in this company was Edward Seymour, the earl of Hertford, one of Henry VIII's most capable and trusted generals. He was also Jane Seymour's brother and so the new king's uncle. He had nourished friendships with leading evangelicals, but as long as Henry VIII lived, he gave little sign that he was willing to support them.

By the time the old king finally died, in the early hours of 28 January 1547, these arrangements were already unravelling. His death was kept a secret for some forty-eight hours while the new realities of power were frantically mapped out. Henry's will had envisaged a regency council of equals, but Seymour and Paget swiftly secured an alternative arrangement: the council would elect Seymour as Lord Protector. He was endowed with near-kingly powers, but accountable to the council. Seymour's ascent was sealed by his elevation to be duke of Somerset on 17 February, which propelled him to the front rank of the nobility.

Seymour came to his position as Lord Protector with a reputation as a soldier, and little more. The Imperial ambassador thought him 'a dry, sour, opinionated man . . . looked down upon by everybody', with little political talent.[3] The conventional wisdom was that Paget would rule through him. The conventional wisdom turned out to be spectacularly wrong. Seymour's brief ascendancy was an exceptional period in English politics, a chaotic political carnival interrupting the long Lent of Tudor rule. He governed with a swashbuckling style which alienated most of the traditional political classes, while making a dangerous and unprecedented appeal to the wider population. His foreign policy was audacious, or foolhardy; his religious policy, revolutionary. In less than three years, all of this would come crashing about him, as his policies provoked the most widespread mass rebellions of the century. But when he was driven from office, he left an enduring memory that he had been the 'good duke' – a striking enough achievement, whether or not he deserved it.

The gospellers unleashed, 1547–49

Henry VIII's England had been governed with intense, and sometimes murderous, attention. The old king had insisted on a startling degree of uniformity in his subjects' opinions and lives. Royal visitors had inspected every church. Royal commissioners had administered oaths – in theory – to every adult male. Pulpits and printing presses were tightly controlled, and a flood of new criminal offences poured out of Parliament.

With Henry dead, the changed political mood was palpable. For some, it was as if heavy but long-familiar shackles had been suddenly removed: the sense of liberation was bewildering. For others, it was as if the medicines that had long controlled a grave disease were suddenly withdrawn: only now did it become clear how dangerous the infection was. The first parliament of the new reign, in late 1547, passed a general Act of Repeal which abolished almost all of Henry VIII's new criminal offences. The Act of Six Articles, which had become a totem of religious conservatism, was also abolished: although in fact, since the beginning of the new reign, that Act and all the legislation against evangelical preaching or printing had been effectively suspended. The regime continued to treat Catholicism with suspicion, but on the evangelical side, preachers and authors had unprecedented freedom to say and do as they wished.

The new freedoms were seized quickly. The evangelical exiles quickly returned to England. Evangelical clergy began to marry again; clerical marriage was not formally legalised until 1549, but it was clear which way the wind was blowing. Evangelical preaching was more widespread and more daring than it had ever been, even in the high days of the 1530s. Hugh Latimer – who had been bishop of Worcester in the 1530s, but had been forced to resign in 1539 – now came out of retirement. He refused to return to the bishops' bench, concentrating instead on preaching, and spent much of the reign touring the country stirring up his particular brand of evangelical trouble. But there was trouble even without his help. In Portsmouth, Catholic images were smashed in April 1547 (much to the alarm of the local bishop, Stephen Gardiner). A trickle of such iconoclastic incidents in London during the first part of the year turned into a wider wave of destruction in the autumn, culminating in the midnight vandalism of the great rood at St Paul's Cathedral on 17 November. The regime stood aside and let it happen.

The new mood was most visible in the printing industry. With official censorship almost abandoned, 1547 and 1548 saw a phenomenal leap in the output of England's printing presses. During the early 1540s, the total number of books printed in England was running at around 100 editions per year. In 1547, this shot up to 192; in 1548, to 268, a level it was not to attain again for decades.[4] The increase was driven by a dramatic boom in the publication of controversial religious material of all kinds. This was lively stuff. In 1548 an Essex pamphleteer called Luke Shepherd published a series of blistering versified satires such as *An inward passion of the Pope for the loss of his daughter the Mass*. Shepherd lampooned one Catholic priest as 'Doctor Double-Ale', a lecherous drunkard who urged Catholics to 'wash thy hands in the blood / of them that hate the Mass'.[5] One Peter Moone published a short poem mocking Catholic worship:

> In the stead of God's word we had holy bread and water,
> Holy palms, holy ashes, holy candles, holy fire
> Holy bones, holy stones, holy cruets at the alter
> Holy censers, holy banners, holy crosses, holy attire
> Holy wax, holy pax, holy smoke, holy smit[6]
> Holy oil, holy cream, holy wine for veneration
> Holy cope, holy canopy, holy relics in the quiet,
> Thus God's word could not flourish, the light of our salvation.[7]

This rumbustious material was underpinned by some more serious stuff. While satirists mocked the Mass, polemicists such as Richard Tracy and Thomas Broke wrote reasoned attacks on it, arguing that in the Eucharist Christ's body was 'eaten with the mind',[8] not with the teeth. And there was a flood of translations of works by European Protestant theologians such as Luther and Calvin: thirty-seven published in 1548, almost a seventh of the total output of England's presses that year. About a tenth of all sixteenth-century English editions of works by the leaders of Continental Protestantism were published in 1548.

The regime did not order, police or coordinate this explosion in evangelical activity (hence its creativity), but it did encourage it. Latimer and others preached at court. Almost every prominent figure in the regime acted as a patron for evangelical authors or publishers. The leading evangelical publisher Richard Grafton was given the lucrative post of king's printer. If preachers, authors or even some private citizens ran on ahead of the regime's own religious policies, it was hardly a problem. Whether by accident or by design, such radicals ended up acting as outriders for the regime, testing the ground ahead and providing political cover.

For it is clear that, from the very beginning of Edward's reign, the new regime was dominated by a clique whose faces were set firmly towards evangelical reform. Their purpose was to complete Henry VIII's unfinished Reformation, using the tools which the old king had left them – the Royal Supremacy over the Church, and the sovereignty of statute law. This new Reformation was driven by a strange but enduring coalition. On one side were the evangelical clergy, led by Archbishop Thomas Cranmer, who had been biding his time for most of his fourteen years as primate of all England. Now he was able to drive forward a programme of reform with firmness, shrewdness and – at times – a ruthlessness which belies his reputation as ineffectual and otherworldly. On the other side was the lay elite, led – initially – by the Lord Protector, Edward Seymour. When Seymour converted to the cause of radical evangelical reform is impossible to pin down, so much so that some historians have suggested that his allegiance to the evangelical cause was merely a political or a financial manoeuvre. Yet the risks of this policy were so great, and the rewards so uncertain, that it makes no sense unless Seymour's calculations were underpinned by some real belief.

The glue that held this unlikely coalition together was even more unlikely: the young King Edward VI himself. Aged only nine at his accession, it may seem bizarre to attribute any political agency to the boy. Yet we are compelled to do so, and to do so increasingly through the reign. His surviving schoolwork and correspondence gives us a compelling, and rather unattractive, picture of him. His gold-plated education brought out real academic abilities, and also a priggish haughtiness – natural enough in a precocious student, perhaps, but a fault which a king would hardly have the opportunity to outgrow. Edward VI was shaping up to be a proper Tudor tyrant. He had a boyish (and kingly) enthusiasm for chivalry and warfare, and a geekish liking for complex, rational and impractical systems. He was also, on all the evidence, sincere and committed in his evangelical faith. His quietly reformist tutors; his last stepmother, the subtly evangelical Katherine Parr; his godfather the archbishop; and the parade of preachers who were brought before him almost from the moment of his father's death, all combined to drive the reformers' gospel into Edward's bones.

The new regime's commitment to evangelical reform was tested almost at once. As much as Henry VIII had valued his hard-won Royal Supremacy, he was a political realist. He knew that the English schism was sustainable only as long as the German Protestant states maintained their own stance, and when it briefly looked as if that dispute might be reconciled in 1541, England, too, prepared to negotiate with the papacy. Within three months of Henry VIII's death, the long-feared disaster struck. The Holy Roman Emperor, Charles V, at last confronted the Protestants, and on 24 April 1547 won a crushing victory at the battle of Mühlberg. For a short while it appeared that the Protestant Reformation might be smothered altogether. The turmoil was theological as well as political, for Luther himself had died in 1546, and Charles now adroitly exploited his victory to split the enemy. He imposed a religious settlement known as the Augsburg Interim, which accepted some variation from normal Catholic practices but gave no quarter to Protestant theology. Pragmatists yielded to the Interim. A form of it was accepted by Philip Melanchthon, Luther's closest ally, whose theological brilliance was matched by an almost timorous willingness to compromise. The rejectionists appeared isolated and divided amongst themselves. There was only one, unexpected, beacon of Protestant hope: England.

In other words, almost as soon as Edward VI's government had thrown in its lot with the Protestant Reformation, that movement's international situation became desperate. Henry VIII would have back-pedalled. This new regime instead gloried in its role as the last, best hope of Protestantism. Much of this was down to Cranmer, who had spent some years nurturing contacts with the leading European Protestant theologians. He now used these to offer a lifeline to beleaguered Protestants. During Edward VI's reign substantial Protestant exile communities established themselves in England. Self-governing 'stranger' churches formed, with official permission, in London, Southampton and elsewhere: Dutch, French, and even Italian and Spanish congregations. As well as foot soldiers, there were leaders. Several major Protestant theologians found a safe haven in England. The two most important were an Italian, Peter Martyr Vermigli, an ally of the Reformed church in Zürich; and a German, Martin Bucer, the reformer of Strasbourg (then a German-speaking city).

Bucer, particularly, was a marvellous catch for Cranmer. Brilliant, verbose and elusive, he had managed the unique feat of remaining on good terms with both Lutherans and Reformed Protestants. He himself belonged in the latter camp (he was a mentor of John Calvin's), but his version of Reformed Protestantism was different from that of Zwingli: more willing to accommodate an element of mystery, and less willing to accept domination by the state. When he was expelled from Strasbourg in 1549, Bucer had several options open to him, and chose England as the most attractive. He was promptly installed as Regius Professor of Divinity at Cambridge. He died less than two years later, in 1551 (the climate of the Fens, which Erasmus had so disliked, broke his health), but in that time he had a decisive influence on the English Reformation. Bucer's reputation as a great conciliator fired Cranmer's dreams of holding an international Protestant council in England, which would reunite the sundered branches of the Protestant family. Philip Melanchthon was always the missing piece of this puzzle. Cranmer had been trying to lure him to England for years, but Melanchthon was frightened both of sea travel and of the Tudors. By the end of Edward's reign the plan seemed to be making some headway. It remains a might-have-been, but an important one for understanding England's ambitions.

More importantly, Bucer, Vermigli and Cranmer's other guests brought some theological weight to the English Reformation. They quickly realised that their hosts' scholarship had been largely cut off from the mainstream European debates, and was parochial and out of date. Bucer and the others were polite about it, but succeeded in whipping a generation of young reformers into theological shape. Partly as a result, it is from Edward's reign that we can abandon the use of vague terms such as 'evangelical' and speak more precisely of Protestants. Indeed, while Cranmer hoped to heal Europe's divides, the opposite was closer to the truth. As English Protestantism rapidly became more sophisticated during the late 1540s, divisions began to appear between two broad variants of 'Reformed' Protestantism. The new English establishment, headed by Cranmer and encouraged by Bucer, favoured the subtler Reformations of Strasbourg and Geneva, which allowed that Christ was spiritually present in the Eucharist and which favoured the doctrine of predestination. A significant group of dissidents, led by the combative former exile John Hooper, favoured the more austere model of Zwingli's Zürich, which saw the Eucharist as little more than symbolic. This potentially damaging schism was healed not in England but in Switzerland. In 1549 the churches of Zürich and Geneva produced the so-called *Consensus Tigurinus*, an agreed statement of principles which contained the dispute and restored trust between the parties. The English Reformation benefited from this act of theological statesmanship, but it did not contribute to it.

Official Reformation: the first phase

Preaching, printing, positioning England as a bastion of Protestantism, eagerly drinking in European debates and doctrines – these were the actions which led Edward VI's Reformation, but they were not how that Reformation forced itself onto the attention of the populace. Behind the religious carnival came all the authority of the law.

The landmarks of the Reformation under Protector Somerset are quickly told. In 1547, under the pretext that controversial preaching was stirring up civil disorder, all preaching licences were suspended. No-one who was not explicitly authorised by the new regime would be permitted to preach. (Exactly the same thing had been done in 1534, when the Royal Supremacy was first established.) In order to fill the empty pulpits, an official Book of Homilies was published on 31 July 1547: a collection of twelve sermons, edited and partly written by Cranmer himself. Royal injunctions issued on the same day required all clergy to read these Homilies aloud to their people. Amongst other things, the Homilies painstakingly spelled out the key Protestant doctrine of justification by faith alone. No more Henrician ambiguity: this was simple, mainstream Protestantism. How influential the Homilies really were is hard to judge. Priests who disliked their message cannot have enjoyed being the archbishop's mouthpieces. However, in the wake of Henry VIII's Reformation, few would have been so foolhardy as actually to disobey.

The royal injunctions covered more than the Homilies. Taking a cue from the sporadic iconoclasm which had already begun, the regime now ordered its clergy to 'take away, utterly extinct, and destroy all shrines, covering of shrines, all . . . pictures, paintings, and all other monuments of feigned miracles, pilgrimages, idolatry and superstition: so that there remain no memory of the same.'[9] This would strip almost every English and Welsh parish church of what had once made it holy. For the moment, roods and altars were exempt, but the zealous were already attacking them, and in 1549 they too came under direct assault. Eventually even gold and silver plate were melted down – a testament to the government's financial desperation as well as its religious zeal. In most places, the destruction was careful, ordered, calm and thorough. Virtually all English and Welsh medieval religious art was destroyed. (A partial exception was stained glass, for one did not smash windows lightly. Often they were simply painted over: it was better to lose light than heat.) To modern sensibilities, this is an appalling holocaust, but it was not an act of barbarism. These things were destroyed because they were seen to be blasphemies: objects falsely claiming to be holy and so dishonouring God. They had not merely to be removed, but desecrated and destroyed. This conviction did, at least, recognise the power of religious art. A Protestant iconoclast who destroyed a statue because it was an idol was closer to the spirit of those who had made it than is a modern museum-goer who admires it because it is pretty.

Alongside this, new legislation completed the process of dissolution which Henry VIII had left unfinished. During 1548, all chantries, collegiate churches and other foundations which existed principally to pray for the dead were suppressed. The doctrine of Purgatory (see above, pp. 19–21) was now theologically unacceptable, and the foundations which had supported it were temptingly rich targets. There were no exceptions: even Henry VIII's own lavish chantry was taken. Where it could be proved that foundations had had more respectable purposes – education, for example – they were sometimes partially re-established; but the informal educational and other services which most chantry priests provided simply disappeared. Like the dissolution of the monasteries, the dissolution of the chantries left a sour taste: plunder in the name of reform. At one stage, Cranmer had actually opposed the legislation in Parliament.

Actual worship changed more slowly. Cranmer had been working steadily on liturgical reform for more than a decade, but the early results were piecemeal. A new English litany had been brought in in 1544. At Easter 1548, communion was ordered to be distributed to the people in 'both kinds' (see above, p. 18). A swathe of other ceremonies, such as the use of holy water, were abolished the same year. Yet the Latin Mass was still in use. Cranmer's work finally bore more substantial fruit in 1549, in the first edition of the famous Book of Common Prayer.

The 1549 Prayer Book was a strange compromise. It was probably always intended as an interim measure: a half-way house to a properly Protestant liturgy. Its purpose was to ease the shock of the new, and also to split the opposition. It succeeded tolerably well on the first count, and spectacularly so on the second, so much so that it has continued to divide and confuse Anglicans down to the present. The book was old wine in a new skin. Its outward form was disorientatingly novel for most English people (and simply foreign for the Welsh: see below, pp. 302–3). It provided new orders for the principal public services of worship, all entirely in English. The priest was to speak these English words aloud and distinctly, and the people were to sit still and listen. In place of daily Mass, there were now to be daily services of 'morning prayer' and 'evening prayer', loosely based on the old services of Matins and Evensong. It was expected that, on the rare occasions when the Eucharist was celebrated, the people would always take communion – a dramatic break from the past. All of the new services, the book's preface boasted, were resolutely Biblical, and indeed the main purpose of the new daily services seems to have been to expose the public to as much of the English Bible as possible.

Yet beneath these obvious novelties of form persisted some important continuities of theological substance. The book accepted – grudgingly – that the new communion service could still be described as 'the Mass'. It still included various critical elements of the Mass. The sign of the cross was made over the bread and wine by the priest during the prayer of consecration. The priest was still to place the elements directly into the believer's mouth, and as he did so he was to say, 'The body of our Lord Jesus Christ which was given for thee, preserve thy body and soul unto everlasting life.' The words were, at least, compatible with the doctrine that Christ was physically, objectively present. Cranmer himself no longer believed this. Nor did most of his allies, many of whom were disappointed by the 1549 Prayer Book. Yet Cranmer knew what he was doing, and he had already waited long enough to be patient for a little longer.

1549–50: the hinge of the Edwardian regime

The end of Seymour's Protectorate

The 1549 Prayer Book was to be the last substantive achievement of the Reformation under Edward Seymour. That summer and autumn, a series of disasters overtook him, of which the most obvious was war. In the last years of Henry VIII's reign, Seymour had been prosecuting a grimly inconclusive war in Scotland on the king's behalf, in order to compel a marriage alliance between the infant Scottish queen, Mary, and the young Edward Tudor, prince of Wales. Seymour had repeatedly disagreed with Henry VIII about tactics during this war, and had been prevented from fighting it with the subtlety and single-mindedness which he thought necessary for victory. When he became Lord Protector, he was determined to have another crack at Scotland.

The resulting war was a disaster for all concerned (see below, pp. 209–12). The years 1547–49 saw the most sustained and brutal Anglo-Scottish warfare since the 1330s. The Scots suffered major battlefield defeats and terrible devastation, but, as they called on French aid, they slowly beat back the invaders. By the summer of 1549 it was clear that, despite the immense effort poured into the war, the English cause in Scotland was lost. England's possessions in France itself were also under intolerable pressure. The humiliation was bad enough: Seymour was made to look weak (for losing the war) and foolish (for voluntarily embarking on a war which he could not win). But the financial damage was worse. The war was ruinously expensive: its total costs have been estimated at over £1.3 million, of which less than a quarter was paid for by taxation.[10] Vast debts were run up, and the regime was finding it difficult to borrow any more. By July 1549 the Exchequer had entirely run out of cash. And this was after, in an attempt to eke out his finances, Seymour had presided over the serious debasement of English coinage (reducing the amount of silver in coins so as to be able to mint more). This inevitably produced that most destabilising and capricious of economic problems, galloping inflation.

This financial and economic crisis intertwined with the second problem of 1549: the matter of the 'commonwealth'. As we have seen (see above, pp. 4–5), this was a period in which the living standards of most of the population were falling; in which increasing numbers of the poor were being driven off the land by enclosure and overpopulation; and in which inflation and seizures of land were steadily redistributing wealth to the landowning classes. These changes were usually ascribed to moral rather than economic causes: it was all down to the greed of rapacious landowners. This argument, which had been made by the Christian humanists, was now picked up with verve by Protestant preachers like Hugh Latimer. Crucially, Seymour himself publicly supported this kind of rhetoric, and also made some efforts to try to turn it into a reality. Royal commissions in 1548 and 1549 made high-profile attempts to stem the process of enclosure, and stirred hopes (in the event, false hopes). Seymour was, no doubt, sincere about this. It also helped to legitimise his religious programme: his Reformation would relieve his subjects of earthly as well as spiritual oppression. And it had its political advantages too, for it allowed Seymour to court a wider sphere of political popularity than English rulers would normally contemplate. To others in the political establishment, this looked dangerously naive. Paget lambasted those whose 'spiced consciences' and 'womanly pity'[11] led them to play such games with the poor: games which could not truly better the lot of the common people, but which could whip them into disorder.

Unfortunately, Paget was at least partly right. It took more than preachers' denunciations or even enclosure commissions to change deep economic realities. The fiscal crisis caused by the Scottish war produced high taxes and debasement-fuelled inflation. The dissolution of the chantries felt like simple plunder dressed up in religious justification. There were incidents of unrest in Hertfordshire, Middlesex, Essex and Norfolk in the summer of 1548, with popular anger focused as always on enclosure. By 1549, a generalised economic crisis was looming, sharpened by the rabble-rousing preaching which Seymour had openly encouraged.

The result was the most dangerous episode of civil unrest in England in the entire sixteenth century. In the event, there was little bloodshed, but at the time it seemed as if the entire country might collapse into anarchy. All over the south of England – in Norfolk, Suffolk, Cambridgeshire, Hertfordshire, Essex, Kent, Middlesex, Surrey, Hampshire, Berkshire, Buckinghamshire, Oxfordshire, Wiltshire and Somerset (and also in the east riding of Yorkshire) – groups of peasants left the land, assembled themselves into camps, and sent demands to their local gentry and to the Lord Protector. Some also attacked local gentry, tore down fences and plundered private estates. (Another, slightly earlier rebellion, in Devon and Cornwall, was largely separate, although it shared some of the same social grievances: see below, pp. 165–6.) The campers' demands echoed those of the preachers: no enclosure, lower rents, no debasement. One Kentish rebel leader even adopted the name 'Captain Commonwealth'. Some campers also echoed the evangelicalism of the commonwealth preachers: perhaps this was simply the sort of language they thought would get them a hearing, or perhaps it testifies to those preachers' success in linking economic and religious reform.

Seymour's regime was taken entirely by surprise. Brutal repression was the normal Tudor reaction to civil unrest, but with the Scottish war unravelling, Seymour had neither the troops nor the money to do this. It would also have been a reversal of his existing policy, for the 'campers' were largely taking him at his word, and indeed were explicitly appealing to him. His response was, therefore, an inconsistent mixture of negotiation, bluster and repression which confused everyone. It was the element of negotiation which most alarmed the rest of the political elite. Letters were exchanged with the rebels in which Seymour vowed to take their grievances seriously. Evangelical preachers were sent to urge them to good obedience. It worked, or almost worked. Most of the campers were persuaded to return home more or less peacefully, and there was little bloodshed. Only in Norfolk did the 'camping time' turn bloody. The shift of economic power towards landowners had been particularly harsh there (there were even attempts to reintroduce serfdom), and the anger of the rebels was matched by the ruthlessness of John Dudley, the earl of Warwick, who was sent to suppress them and who shared none of Seymour's interest in compromise. This rising – 'Kett's Rebellion' – was smashed in a full-scale battle at Dussindale, southwest of Norwich, on 27 August. Casualties on both sides ran into the thousands.

In the short term Seymour's regime survived the 'camping time', but its political credibility was badly damaged. It was not merely that he had been almost powerless to act against the campers, and also against the separate rebellion in the south-west. The rest of the governing class feared that his populist posturing had provoked the crisis, and (after the fact) despised the way he had negotiated with the rebels rather than facing them down. Even this, however, need not have been fatal for the Protector. What made it so was that Seymour was already alienated from most of the political elite which had once supported him.

There was a litany of complaints. Seymour had spent extravagantly on vanity projects (London's Somerset House was the flagship of these) while failing to spread patronage around in the way that the ideal of good lordship demanded. More fundamentally, Seymour's autocratic political style made his fellow councillors feel that he was behaving like a king, not a Lord Protector. Perhaps the most troubling incident was his decision to have his own brother, Thomas Seymour, arrested and executed in early 1549. Thomas' ambitions had certainly ruffled feathers. In 1547, he had married Henry VIII's widow Katherine Parr with indecent haste. When she died in childbirth, Thomas turned his attentions to the fifteen-year-old Princess Elizabeth, and there were rumours of an attempted rape. But it was Thomas' arrogance rather than any real or supposed crimes which led to his death. This shocking act of fratricide was the more serious because Edward Seymour himself was so clearly manifesting the same flaws. One of the sparks to his dispute with his brother was his insistence that his wife should take formal precedence over that of Thomas, even though the one was merely the duchess of Somerset and the other the dowager queen of England. It was a symbol of what power was doing to him. In theory, he was chosen by the regency council to govern on their behalf, but he had come to act as if authority was his by right.

As a result, when the political reckoning came from the linked crises of 1549, Seymour had already acquired a substantial roster of enemies. Instead of negotiating his way out of trouble, he held his ground and raised the stakes as his remaining allies slipped away from him. Finally, in an act which he clearly believed was bold, on 6 October he absconded to Windsor with his nephew, the twelve-year-old king. In Scotland, when the earl of Angus had attempted a similar stunt with the young James V in 1526, he had been able to keep it up for some two years; Seymour's kidnap lasted for less than a week. Even Cranmer – Seymour's most loyal ally, both by instinct and by calculation – could not swallow this. Seymour surrendered on 11 October rather than making a futile attempt to fight. He was deposed as Lord Protector two days later, and never replaced. The councillors whom he had so alienated would not make the mistake of setting someone else in his place.

Seymour's own failings as a politician are clearly fundamental here, but this unhappy tale also points to a deeper problem: the sheer difficulty of regency government under the shadow of a political colossus like Henry VIII. For forty years, English politics had revolved around a larger-than-life king. His sudden absence created a painful political vacuum. All the symbolism and authority of royalty was attached to a nine-year-old boy. The regime made full use of this: the preachers who had once lauded Henry VIII as a new Hezekiah (see above, p. 133) swiftly anointed his son as a new King Josiah, the boy king of ancient Judah who had restored Jewish worship to its ancient purity. But preachers' rhetoric could not hide the fact that, for many practical purposes, there was no king. The reason why it was so easy for Edward Seymour to assert quasi-royal authority was that there was a hole at the heart of the English state. Both the administration and the wider political culture expected autocratic rule, not consensual, conciliar government. Seymour had, in effect, royal responsibilities without full royal authority. Others might have navigated these difficulties more ably or more humbly than he did, but there was truth in the Biblical proverb which was so often quoted early in Edward's reign, and which so enraged his regents: 'Woe be unto thee, O thou land whose king is but a child.'[12]

Religious opposition and its failure

That mischievous quotation was a gift to those who opposed Edward VI's Reformation. And it is here, rather than in the crises of war, rebellion and political style, that we might have expected opposition to the new regime to focus. In 1547–49, Seymour's regime had unleashed a series of dramatic religious changes on a largely conservative country, and (as the crises of 1549 made painfully clear) had done so from a political position which was much weaker than that of Henry VIII. The project seems impossible. Evangelical reformers had gained power at the old king's death in what amounted to a palace coup. It was a flimsy springboard from which to bounce a reluctant nation into a religious revolution.

In fact, religious conservatism in the reign of Edward VI is one of the most extraordinary features of this extraordinary reign: extraordinary because it remained almost wholly quiescent. Only in 1549 did it make any real appearance on the political scene, and then it failed to achieve anything of substance. This was partly down to the regime's good judgement, in splitting and isolating potential enemies of the new order; but it owed much more to good luck.

From the beginning of the reign, it was apparent that the most dangerous opponent of the new religious policy would be Stephen Gardiner, the bishop of Winchester. Gardiner had already become a hate-figure for evangelicals, who reviled him as Wily Winchester, the scheming Machiavelli of crypto-papistry. He did not quite deserve this reputation; but he could be ruthless, and as a writer and preacher, his eloquence easily matched the best of the evangelicals. Indeed, he was one of very few religious conservatives who was willing to engage directly with the evangelicals in print. Gardiner spent much of Edward's reign fighting a doomed rearguard action against Seymour's and Cranmer's reforms.

Gardiner's key argument was unnervingly powerful, at least in 1547. Henry VIII, Gardiner argued, had arrived at his religious settlement after the most careful debate and had thrown the full weight of royal authority behind it. The regents for an under-age king simply did not have the right to change that settlement. Only King Edward himself could do that, when he came of age. It was an unnerving line of attack because it amounted to a claim that Seymour and the regency council did not, in fact, rule with full royal authority. If Gardiner had won this argument, it would have hobbled the new regime's power in every sphere of government, not simply religion.

Many of the senior clergy and of the landed elite shared Gardiner's doubts, including some on the regency council. So did many of the population at large. It is not difficult to imagine situations in which these fears could have precipitated the formation of a serious opposition faction. Such a faction could have blocked the new regime's ambitions in Parliament, and forced Seymour to stand down as Lord Protector or to abandon his religious policies. It did not happen. Why?

This was Tudor England, so a part of the explanation is brute force. In September 1547 Gardiner was arrested, and aside from five months of closely watched liberty in 1548, he spent the rest of the reign in prison. This silenced him as a preacher and – importantly – as a voice in Parliament, although it did not stop him from writing and publishing. (Keeping prisoners incommunicado was almost impossible in the sixteenth century.) In 1551, after a long legal process, he was formally deprived of his bishopric. Nor was he alone. One by one, the other bishops loyal to Henrician conservatism were forced out of office: prominent amongst them Edmund Bonner, bishop of London, in 1549, and the old soldier Cuthbert Tunstall, bishop of Durham, in 1552.

This purge had begun with a softer target. Richard Smyth was the Regius Professor of Divinity at Oxford, and one of the few who had joined Gardiner by writing in defence of traditional religion. He published three polemics in 1546 and 1547, one of which ran to three editions. Smyth's books drew heavily on the writings of John Fisher, and as a result were formidable. He himself was less so. He was arrested, and on 15 May 1547 made a humiliating formal recantation at Paul's Cross in London. This was itself quickly published, in two editions. Discredited, Smyth withdrew abroad, where he soon disowned his recantation, but the damage had been done.

Meanwhile, the regime's tame polemicists and their wilder allies were developing two consistent lines of attack on their opponents. First, all religious conservatives were accused of 'popery'. This conveniently flexible term could be used to imply that almost any aspect of traditional religion was a covert attack on the Royal Supremacy, and therefore (as Henry VIII had established) treason. Secondly, the regime mounted a ferocious attack on 'Anabaptists'. This is odd, for hardly any real Anabaptists ever seem to have been found in England. The term was and is used to describe a range of different radical sectarian movements which had a following in Germany, the Netherlands, Bohemia and elsewhere. Edwardian Protestants seem to have worked themselves up into a full-dress panic about Anabaptists based on very little evidence. Almost every major Edwardian writer produced an anti-Anabaptist tract at some point. Indeed, two alleged Anabaptists were arrested and burned for heresy in 1550, although they seem to have owed more to Lollard radicalism and their own makeshift theological ingenuity than to any Continental traditions. The panic was real enough, but the danger of Anabaptism was not that it might take over England. Rather, the fear was that it might discredit 'mainstream' Protestantism by association. By vehemently denouncing (and executing)

Anabaptists, the new Edwardian establishment asserted that its Reformation was not anarchic or heretical. Good order in church and state would still be preserved. By striking at the Anabaptists on one side and the papists on the other, the regime could present its own radicalism as virtuous moderation.

The executions of those two Anabaptists have become notorious: this was the 'blooding' of English Protestantism, when it lost some of its innocence. What is much more remarkable is that there were no parallel executions of Catholics. Despite all the tirades against papistry, and despite the draconian treason laws, not a single English subject was executed for loyalty to the papacy under Edward VI. The tone was set at the very start of the reign, for the duke of Norfolk had been due to go to the block on the morning of 28 January 1547. But Henry VIII died hours before, and it seemed more prudent to spare him (he remained a prisoner for the rest of the reign). High politics in the reign of Edward VI was significantly less homicidal than under Henry VIII. Even Seymour himself survived his deposition in 1549 (for a time). But the most obvious beneficiaries of this change of mood were Gardiner, Bonner, Tunstall and other conservative leaders. Although kept prisoner, none of them was killed. In similar circumstances, Henry VIII would certainly have found a way of disposing of them. Why this more merciful policy was adopted is not clear. The absence of Henry's vindictive righteousness must be significant; and a fragile regime was unwilling to act more aggressively than was strictly necessary. But whether by accident or by design, this policy helped to box in the regime's religious opponents. A few martyrs could have boosted traditional religion. Instead, the regime's measured behaviour made it that much harder to oppose.

However, the main reason why there were no Catholic martyrs was that few Catholics had the stomach for martyrdom. By 1547, everyone remaining in England was openly committed to the Royal Supremacy over the Church. It was extremely hard to attack the regime's actions without implicitly denying the Supremacy. Gardiner, as we have seen, did find a way of doing this, but it was of limited use. His argument undermined the authority of all regency governments, which nobody liked. Moreover, as the young Edward grew up and his own Protestant views became unmistakable, it became obvious that pinning conservative hopes on the king was futile. Worse, it was counter-productive. The universal faith in good kingship made it possible to believe – as one Hampshire conservative put it, in his cups – that 'when [Edward] cometh of age, he will see another rule, and hang up a hundred of such heretic knaves'.[13] Such hopes inclined them to wait patiently while their Church was destroyed around them. Edwardian conservatives hated what was happening, but were at a loss to know how to oppose it. As a result, most of them were driven into a miserable silence, pinning their hopes on mirages, dazed by the speed at which principles they had conceded were being used to overthrow their world.

Despite the unprecedented freedom of the press in 1547–49, hardly any religious conservatives ventured into print. What could they say, beyond name-calling? The few who did – like John Proctor in 1549 (see above, p. 144) – did little more than lament the passing of a Church whose restoration seemed hopeless. Their allies in Parliament were equally daunted by the power of the Royal Supremacy: the regime never faced serious opposition there. It was the same story in the universities. After the Henrician conservative John Redman, the master of Trinity College, Cambridge, was persuaded in 1549 to accept both the new Prayer Book and the 1547 Homilies, no-one else in Cambridge was willing to stand up for the old faith. On his deathbed in 1551, Redman admitted to much more pervasive doubts: he now claimed that he did believe in justification by faith after all, and he had serious misgivings about the Mass. Traditionalist friends who were at his side found their faith gravely shaken as a result. Even Gardiner was caught in this trap. During his drawn-out negotiations with the regime, his loyalty to the Royal Supremacy forced him to concede a great deal of ground. Like Redman, he yielded to the 1549 Prayer Book: he thoroughly disliked it, but it bore the king's name and Parliament's approval, and he could not find sufficient grounds to defy it.

This was Cranmer's triumph, and the vindication of his decision to preserve a fiction of doctrinal continuity in the 1549 Prayer Book. As Henry VIII had done, Cranmer now split his potential opponents into learned theologians (worried about doctrine) and the wider population (more concerned with outward forms). This did not prevent widespread opposition to the new order, but it left that opposition leaderless. The result showed itself in 1549. At much the same time as southern and eastern England were being convulsed by the 'camping time', a much more determined and focused revolt broke out in Cornwall, that traditional site of dissent. The Cornish rising, which quickly spread to Devon, reflected a range of grievances, but its focus was the new Prayer Book. As the rebels' demands stated, the new liturgy seemed like 'a Christmas game', a nightmarish carnival made permanent. Even they did not ask for the restoration of the papacy, but for the Act of Six Articles and other laws that had been in place under 'our sovereign lord King Henry VIII' to be restored (without addressing the fact that they now had a new sovereign lord).[14] The rebellion was a serious and a frightening one for the regime, but it ended as peasant rebellions almost always do. Lord Russell led an army which confronted the rebels in early August, rescued the besieged city of Exeter, and eventually brought them to battle at Sampford Courtenay on 16 August. Some 4000 rebels were killed, plus those executed during the subsequent reprisals.

The failure of the 'Prayer Book rebellion' left the traditionalist cause in much worse disarray than before. As numerous official propagandists from Cranmer down hastened to emphasise, the rebellion proved that traditional religion was inherently seditious, and that both tradition and sedition were 'popery'. For the rest of the reign, while the regime encountered local foot-dragging, obstructionism and reluctance, there was no more open resistance.

The last chance for religious conservatives came in the autumn of 1549. The collapse of Seymour's regime had little to do with religion (although the Prayer Book rebellion helped to underline Seymour's weakness), but conservatives seemed well placed to benefit from his fall. Among Seymour's leading opponents were pragmatists such as Paget, and established conservatives such Wriothesley, who was now earl of Southampton. In the background was the powerful figure of Princess Mary: Katherine of Aragon's daughter, aged thirty-three, next in line to the throne and a Habsburg princess. She was an obvious alternative regent for her young brother. It was the most dangerous moment for the evangelical project in the whole reign.

In the event, the struggle for power following Seymour's deposition was won decisively by John Dudley, the earl of Warwick. Dudley's victory over the Norfolk rebels had enhanced his authority. He also had a power base in the young king's own household. His private religious views (if he had any) are a mystery, but political logic pushed him into a Protestant stance. He and Wriothesley had been, in effect, joint leaders of the coup against Seymour, and were now therefore rivals for power. Wriothesley apparently hoped to bring in Mary as regent, which would certainly have meant a change of religious policy. But there were by now powerful forces in the regime which favoured continued Protestantism. Several nobles, many of them of very recent vintage, were committed reformers. Amongst these, of course, was Seymour himself, who for all his offences was still the king's uncle and the duke of Somerset. Dudley's boldest stroke was his decision to spare Seymour's life, and to release him in January 1550. The reconciliation would not last – Seymour was ultimately executed in 1552, for supposedly plotting against Dudley – but for the time being it put

Dudley at the head of a broad faction, and left Wriothesley, who was dogged by illness, isolated. Dudley became Lord President of the Council. After a nasty wobble, the government of Edward VI remained as committed to the Protestant cause as before.

Neither Dudley's triumph nor his commitment to the reformist cause was pre-ordained. The eventual outcome was a throw of the political dice. Yet the dice were loaded in the reformers' favour, and not only by fifteen years' worth of purges of Catholic sympathisers from government. The decisive factors in 1549–50 were, it seems, the views of the two members of the royal family involved. Mary, as a regent, would inevitably reverse Seymour's Reformation; while the young king was sympathetic to the Protestant cause and actively hostile to his sister. Imposing her as a regent against his will would not have been impossible, but it would cut against the grain of monarchy. Dudley was thus able – indeed, compelled – to position himself as the defender both of the king and of the Gospel. As so often in Tudor politics, it was the monarch's own views which were ultimately decisive.

Lent: the Duke of Northumberland's Reformation

Consolidation and division: the official Reformation

John Dudley is traditionally cast as the bad duke to Edward Seymour's good duke – or, sometimes, vice versa – but the two men are not easily comparable. Dudley had himself created duke of Northumberland in 1551, but he never became Lord Protector, nor did he rule as absolutely as Seymour had. He was merely Lord President of the Council, and to some extent maintained conciliar government. Moreover, the king was no longer merely a name. He took an increasingly active interest in government, making a considerable nuisance of himself at times. Although Edward was still legally under his councillors' tutelage, Dudley was temperamentally inclined to yield to his royal master.

Dudley patiently extracted England from the worst of the messes he had inherited from Seymour. Peace with Scotland and France was concluded in March 1550, on abject terms. England was left with nothing in Scotland and also had to yield up Henry VIII's last French conquest of 1544, the city of Boulogne, for a modest ransom. It was a humiliating end to Henry VIII's and Seymour's adventures, but it was at least an end to them. The royal finances began to stabilise. Dudley also attempted to revalue the debased coinage in 1551: somewhat ineffectually, but there was at least no further debasement. Domestically, something like normality returned. Censorship of printing returned, albeit Protestant print was still strongly encouraged. The populist 'commonwealth' agenda faded, although Latimer and other preachers continued to worry at it.

Meanwhile, Cranmer's reforms proceeded apace. In 1550 came a new Ordinal, a form for the ordination of priests and consecration of bishops, which ran much more plainly counter to Catholic doctrine than anything in the Prayer Book. (Gardiner, who had swallowed the Prayer Book, could not accept the Ordinal.) As the conservative bishops were prised out of office, they began to be replaced with genuinely radical figures. Cranmer's young chaplain Nicholas Ridley became bishop of London. The returned exile John Hooper, a keeper of the pure flame of Zürich's Reformation, became bishop of Gloucester (not without trouble: see below, pp. 169–70).

Cranmer's sights, however, were now set towards the next great wave of reforms, which surfaced in 1552–53 in three forms. The last, but most important, was a statement of the Reformed English Church's faith, which after long delay appeared as the Forty-Two Articles in June 1553. Despite some intense infighting over the details of the Articles, it was always plain that they would be a Reformed Protestant statement; in their final form, they owed much to Martin Bucer, Peter Martyr Vermigli and the other Protestant refugees. By then, those doctrines had already been given tangible form in another great reform, the 1552 Book of Common Prayer. This completed – or at least advanced – the project which Cranmer had started in 1549. Much of the book was unchanged, and to the inattentive layperson the differences might have seemed matters of detail; but theologically the new book was in a different world. The most drastic changes were in the communion service (no longer 'Mass'). Communion was now celebrated not at an altar but at a 'holy table' in the nave of the church. Most importantly, the doctrine of Christ's real presence was now unambiguously excluded. When the bread and wine were given to the people (ordinary leavened bread, not wafers, and placed into their hands), the minister was to say, 'Take and eat this in remembrance that Christ died for thee, and feed on him in thy heart by faith, with thanksgiving.' The bread was now 'this', a mere object. Christ was to be received by faith in the heart, not by the power of the sacrament in the mouth. The transition to Reformed Protestantism was complete.

Entwined with doctrinal and liturgical reform was legal reform – in Cranmer's mind, at least. Since the neutering of Convocation in 1532 (see above, p. 118), the English Church's law had limped on piecemeal, despite several attempts at a comprehensive review. This finally happened in 1552, when Cranmer, aided by Vermigli and others, produced the so-called *Reformatio Legum Ecclesiasticarum*: a comprehensive Protestant code of Church law, drawing on the best Continental examples. Its provisions included permitting divorce in cases of adultery or cruelty, and a renewed anti-heresy law. It also provided a comprehensive system of moral discipline, based on that pioneered by Bucer in Strasbourg. This would have meant the Church actively policing the people's morals, and using private exhortation, public penitence and (ultimately) the threat of exclusion from communion in order to keep the Christian community pure. It was an immensely attractive idea to many Reformed Protestants. Yet significant numbers of people might well end up excluded from such a Church, making it less like a national Church and more like a sect. Moreover, for the Church to claim such powers of discipline for itself seemed to usurp the role of the state. This may be one of the reasons why the *Reformatio* remained simply a proposal. When it was put before Parliament in 1552, it was defeated in the House of Lords. An attempt to revive it in 1571 would also fail. The Church of England's law would remain a jury-rigged variant of medieval canon law, and (uniquely amongst Protestant states) English law would make no provision for divorce until the nineteenth century.

The failure of the *Reformatio* is one of the clearest signs that, by 1552, the Protestant coalition within Dudley's regime was under serious strain. It was Dudley himself who blocked the *Reformatio* in Parliament: this may reflect mere personal friction between him and Cranmer, as well as his fears that Cranmer wished to assert too much ecclesiastical independence from the state. A parallel dispute arose over the 1552 Prayer Book. For all its theological radicalism, the pattern of worship laid out in the book still had a traditional feel in places, and some ceremonies were retained. In an essay appended to the Prayer Book, Cranmer defended this by positioning himself between those who were 'addicted to their old customs' and those who were 'so newfangled that they would innovate all things'. Some ceremonial, he insisted, was necessary to maintain 'order and quiet discipline.'[15] Increasingly, however, other Protestants regarded this as pandering to popery. The first major dispute had arisen in 1550, when the radical John Hooper was appointed bishop of Gloucester. He refused to wear the traditional bishop's rochet and chimere for his consecration, thinking them popish. It was a minor issue, but the dispute over it became a major trial of strength, for the first but not the last time (see below, p. 268). Bizarrely enough, it led to Hooper's being imprisoned for some weeks in early 1551, until he gave in and agreed to wear the offensive items. It was a Pyrrhic victory for Cranmer's policy of trying to keep England's Reformation in step with itself.

In 1552, the matter of the dispute was more momentous. Traditionally, communion had been received kneeling, out of reverence for Christ's bodily presence. Although the 1552 Prayer Book did not teach either Christ's presence or veneration of the sacrament, it retained the use of kneeling. Some Protestants, however, preferred communion to be received standing, or even seated at a table, in a literal re-creation of Christ's Last Supper. One such was a firebrand Scot named John Knox. From 1549 to 1552, Knox had been minister to Scottish Protestant exile congregations in the north-east of England, where he had felt free to ignore the strictures of the distant and politically enfeebled bishop of Durham. Rather than following the 1549 Prayer Book, he had devised his own liturgy, which included the practice of sitting to receive communion. Dudley, rather than bringing Knox into line, encouraged him. He brought Knox to London, and even considered appointing him as bishop of Rochester to be 'a whetstone to sharpen the archbishop of Canterbury'. When the 1552 Book was close to completion, Knox ostentatiously denounced the use of kneeling, forcing Cranmer into a furious rearguard action. Cranmer won this confrontation on points; a last-minute rubric added to the book explained that the use of kneeling did not imply veneration of the sacrament. Knox, perhaps the most tactless public figure of the sixteenth century, quickly alienated Dudley, who described him as 'neither grateful nor pleasable'.[16] But the fact that Cranmer was having to fight such battles at all showed how ill-tempered the Protestant coalition was becoming.

The future of the Edwardian Reformation

Edward VI's death in the summer of 1553 brought the Protestant adventure to a sudden end, and leaves us with some unanswerable questions. Where was the process of Reformation headed? And how would the English people have responded to it?

The regime's destination was clearly a fully Reformed Protestant settlement, despite the division between those (like Hooper and Knox) who wished to strip out every remnant of traditional religion and those (like Cranmer and Bucer) who would have been willing to retain some remnants of the old ways. The 1552 documents give a much stronger appearance of finality than the 1549 Prayer Book, but they might not have been its last word. Cranmer's recent biographer Diarmaid MacCulloch speculates that, in due course, a third Prayer Book might have followed, its ceremonial content slimmed down and its Reformed doctrines more unmistakable. Some traditions which had survived into the early 1550s would no doubt have met their end. The office of bishop would probably have survived, as a means of royal control over the Church, but the bishops' estates would have been plundered still further (Dudley looted them mercilessly). They would likely also have been stripped of their remaining sacramental trappings, and perhaps (as in some Lutheran states) renamed superintendents. The cathedrals, whose survival through Edward's reign was a masterful feat of inertia, could surely not have lasted much longer. In due course, some kind of canon law reform would doubtless have been enacted, although how far it would have gone towards a comprehensive system of discipline is another matter.

Popular reaction to the Edwardian Reformation is equally opaque. It is clear enough that Catholicism had been comprehensively outmanoeuvred. Despite all the widespread affection for the old ways, there was simply no realistic way of reasserting them. By 1553 English Catholicism seems to have been firmly set on a road to oblivion. It is hard to see any alternative to its slowly draining away, over a generation or two. But how strong was Protestantism? There is good evidence that many people simply withdrew in confusion and distaste from the religious controversies of the time, trying to find ways of living Christian lives which honoured their king, quieted their consciences and avoided trouble with the law. It is also obvious that the Edwardian Reformation, like the Henrician Reformation before it, was primarily a political event: a Reformation from 'above' rather than from 'below'. The changes were not driven by any popular clamour for Protestantism.

But we cannot quite leave it there, for the regime's changes did not simply fall on deaf ears. The explosion of Protestant print during 1547–49 tells us something about demand as well as about supply. Although many of the printers had Protestant sympathies, they were also businessmen, and they printed books in order to sell them. Likewise, there is good evidence of preachers attracting substantial crowds. Of course, this evidence can be overread. The boom in evangelical print tells us more about London than England, and in any case, buying a scurrilous squib against the Mass does not make someone a doctrinaire Protestant.

What the explosion of evangelical activity under Seymour's Protectorship does prove is that there was widespread *interest* in what the Protestants had to say. There are good parallels for this from other episodes in the European Reformation: occasions when a long period of religious repression, followed by a sudden release of pressure, produced a burst of evangelical activity and of public curiosity about the new doctrines. Such waves of Protestant liberation swept (with varying levels of force) across Scotland in 1543, France in 1560–62, and the Netherlands in 1566. Just such a wave swept across England in 1547–49. Henry VIII's anti-papal propaganda, his flirting with evangelicalism, and the reformers' insistent positioning of themselves as the moderates between papist and Anabaptist extremes had their effect. They did not necessarily win converts, but they did win a hearing.

It is here that the language of the 'commonwealth' becomes genuinely important. The views of the commonwealth preachers – attacking landlords, hoarders, speculators and enclosure, while advocating charity, education and mercy to the deserving poor – were very widely shared. Evangelicals and traditionalists alike could agree on such questions. It was a key achievement of Edwardian evangelicals to make this agenda their own. It was an achievement eased by official backing, and fuelled by the evangelicals' readiness to add parasitical, corrupt clergy to their list of targets. Even religious conservatives admitted 'there was never . . . so much exhortation to charity . . . so much persuasion to aid and succour the poor', even if they grumbled that this was all verbiage and hypocrisy.[17] For the truth was that, in the bewildering religious confusion of the late 1540s, everyone could at least agree on the commonwealthmen's platitudes. The willingness of the campers of 1549 to use the regime's evangelical jargon proves not that they were Protestants but that they had accepted the new political and religious terms of trade. When Protestant preachers were sent to pacify these assemblies, they were (mostly) given a respectful hearing. By wrapping themselves in the commonwealth's colours during a period of intense economic crisis, the Protestants won themselves a crucial degree of legitimacy.

And when the outlines of the new settlement began to emerge, it was not without its attractions. Although austere, the new religion was much cheaper to maintain than the old one. In place of the sumptuous furnishings of Catholic worship, all that was now needed was a Bible and a Prayer Book. Hard-pressed parish ratepayers would have seen the advantages. For the less cynical, worship in the vernacular had a real appeal. The Prayer Book and the Homilies made attending church an occasion for learning and edification – values which Renaissance culture prized enormously, but to which the old Church's worship had paid little attention.

It is even possible that Protestant worship could be fun. In the old Church, music had been for choristers and clergy, and the people listened rather than participated. In 1549, a Protestant courtier named Thomas

Sternhold published a short selection of so-called metrical psalms: verse paraphrases of the Biblical psalms in English, to be sung to ballad tunes. Similar verses had been deployed by Continental reformers from Luther to Calvin and (importantly) Bucer. England embraced them with enthusiastically. Although Sternhold died later the same year, his collection – augmented by a friend – went through a dozen editions in 1549–53. Rival versions appeared. English congregations had never sung before: now, it seems, they did with gusto. Metrical psalms lifted the otherwise word-weighty Protestant services, and also provided a sense of unity. Their voices joined, parish communities could feel that, if they were being taken unwillingly into a new world, they were at least making the journey together.

Elective monarchy revisited: the Jane Grey debacle

In the event, that journey was rudely interrupted by high politics. On 6 July 1553, Edward VI died, aged fifteen, probably of tuberculosis. Although he was not the perennially sickly child of legend, he had been ill the previous year, and a cold in February soon developed into something worse. For the last three months of his reign, he and those around him knew that he was dying. He lasted rather longer than his doctors expected. When it came, his death provoked the worst succession crisis of the sixteenth century, a crisis which tells us a great deal about the country that he was ruling.

Until early 1553, the succession had looked straightforward. A statute of 1543 had established the matter, and Henry VIII had confirmed it in his will. Edward, his only surviving son, was to succeed him. If he should die without heirs, the crown was to pass to Henry's eldest daughter, Mary. If she too should die childless, her successor was to be her younger half-sister Elizabeth. In other words, in 1553 Mary Tudor was the heir apparent. Yet it was not so simple. Both Mary and Elizabeth were technically illegitimate, as the children of marriages which had subsequently been annulled. The 1543 statute named them regardless, but it was irregular for illegitimate children (let alone illegitimate women) to inherit. More pragmatically, Mary was the last person that either Edward himself or his government wanted to succeed, for she was known to be hostile to both Henry's and Edward's Reformations. There was, therefore, a strong temptation to change things.

And so, in the last weeks of the king's life, a scheme was drawn up by which Edward's cousin Jane Grey would be his heir. Virtually the whole political establishment consented to it. Dudley was at the head of the queue, and on 25 May 1553 he married his own son to Jane Grey. After

Edward's death, however, this arrangement unravelled with astonishing speed. Mary, then in Norfolk, refused to recognise Jane's claim and declared herself queen. She quickly mobilised an army from her local supporters, but it turned out to be unnecessary. London turned in her favour and the forces loyal to Jane drained away. Councillors, too, seeing how the wind was blowing, quickly changed sides. Dudley, Cranmer and a few others were left entirely isolated. Jane's 'reign' lasted for thirteen days. It was the only successful English rebellion of the century.

What does this episode mean? It has usually been interpreted as a sign of John Dudley's arrogance and folly. This no longer seems tenable. First of all, the scheme was not doomed to fail. It is true that it was illegal under the 1543 Act – although had Edward lived long enough for a parliament to ratify it, that problem would certainly have been solved. Yet even without that authorisation, all Edward was doing was claiming the same power as his father to nominate his successor. Excluding Mary should hardly have been controversial, since her illegitimacy was well established in law. And the scheme was very widely accepted. The fatal mistake was that Mary herself was allowed her liberty. If she had been safely tucked away in the Tower of London, her rebellion would have been impossible. It remains surprising that Dudley – soldier as he was – neither secured Mary nor prepared for a challenge from her. But then, very little in her career up to that point suggested that she would act so swiftly and decisively.

Secondly, the scheme was probably not Dudley's at all. Early in 1553 he was still assuming that Mary would succeed. Plotting coups within the royal family would have been quite out of character for such an obsessively obedient royal servant. By then, however, the first versions of the scheme had already been drafted by King Edward himself. Edward's animosity towards his eldest sister is well documented. Dudley had with difficulty prevented a major row with the Habsburgs in 1551 when Edward had insisted that Mary should be banned from hearing Mass. The first versions of Edward's 'device' for the succession excluded all women, on principle. This, plus the taint of illegitimacy, got rid of Mary (and Elizabeth). The children of Henry VIII's sister Margaret were excluded on the grounds that they were foreigners. That left the descendants of Henry VIII's younger sister Mary – all of whom, unfortunately, were women. This Mary's daughter Frances Grey, marchioness of Dorset, herself had three daughters, and it was on these girls that Edward pinned his hopes. If one of them should manage to produce a son, there would be an heir who was male, unimpeachably legitimate and (it could be assumed) Protestant.

If such a boy had been born, the mere fact of maleness might have been enough to secure him the throne. The trouble came as Edward's sickness worsened faster than the Grey girls could marry and fall pregnant. The 'device' was now hurriedly revised – probably still on Edward's own initiative – to claim that, in the absence of male heirs, Jane and her sisters could inherit. To include them, while excluding all other women (including Jane's own mother, Frances, who was still alive), deprived the 'device' not only of maleness but also of logic. Jane was being favoured, it seemed, because she was a Protestant, because she was married to Dudley's son, and because she was not Princess Mary.

The result was a contested election to the English crown. For all the Tudors' achievements, this fact alone proved that they had not yet turned England into a secure dynastic monarchy. Ironically enough, it was Henry VIII's matrimonial adventures which created the problem, adventures which had been undertaken partly in search of dynastic security. In a properly stable dynastic monarchy, the 1543 Act itself would have made no sense, for the succession would not have been needed and could not have been altered by statutory intervention. As things were, the political nation (a body which had been expanded significantly by the events of the previous two reigns) had a choice to make. On Jane's side were Protestantism, the political establishment, unquestioned legitimacy of birth and the direct support of the recently deceased king. On Mary's side stood her latent Catholicism, popular distaste for Dudley, the widespread view that her parents' marriage *had* been legitimate, the 1543 Act, and her father's will.

This mix of factors was mutually reinforcing. The rejoicing that greeted Mary's accession clearly reflected the relief of large numbers of Catholic Englishmen and women that their Protestant nightmare was over. Yet in the end this was not a Catholic *coup*, but a legitimist restoration. The niceties of law mattered less than the nation's sense of just succession. Above all, Mary's succession depended on her hated father, who still loomed so large in his former subjects' minds. The crisis of 1553 is a story of Henry VIII's will triumphing over Edward VI's from beyond the grave. The old tyrant had a long arm. He had ended his son's religious revolution, and he was not finished playing with his children's fate yet.

Notes

1 National Archives, SP 1/175 fo. 85r; Susan Brigden, 'Henry Howard, Earl of Surrey, and the "Conjured League"', *Historical Journal* vol. 37 (1994), pp. 507–37.

2 John Ponet, *A shorte treatise of politike power* (1556), sig. I3v.

3 Martin A. S. Hume and Royall Tyler (eds), *Calendar of Letters, Despatches and State Papers relating to . . . Spain . . . 1547–49* (1912), pp. 19–20.

4 Andrew Pettegree, 'Printing and the Reformation: the English exception' in Peter Marshall and Alec Ryrie (eds), *The Beginnings of English Protestantism* (2002), p. 172.

5 Luke Shepherd, *Doctour doubble ale* (1548?), sig. A6r.

6 A mark or stain, either literal or moral.

7 Peter Moone, *A short treatise of certayne thinges abused* (1548), sig. A2v.

8 Thomas Broke, *Certeyn meditations, and thinges to be had in remembraunce* (1548), sig. B3v.

9 *Iniunccions geuen by the kynges Maiestie aswell to the clergie as to the laitie of this realme* (1547), sigs C2v–3r.

10 W. K. Jordan, *Edward VI: the Young King* (1968), pp. 392–3.

11 Andy Wood, *The 1549 Rebellions and the Making of Early Modern England* (2007), pp. 23–4.

12 Ecclesiastes 10: 16 (Great Bible).

13 John Bale, *An expostulation or complaynte agaynste the blasphemyes of a franticke papyst of Hamshyre* (1552), sig. B1r.

14 *A Copye of a letter contayning . . . the articles or requestes of the Deuonshyre & Cornyshe rebelles* (1549), sigs B6r, B7r.

15 Joseph Ketley (ed.), *The Two Liturgies, AD 1549 and AD 1552* (1844), p. 155.

16 C. S. Knighton (ed.), *Calendar of State Papers of the Reign of Edward VI* (1992), nos 747, 779.

17 Thomas Paynell, *Twelue sermons of Saynt Augustine, now lately translated into English* (1553), sig. A3v.

Two Restorations: Mary and Elizabeth, 1553–60

After Edward VI's death, no English government would make such a brash attempt to impose religious novelties on its subjects until the 1630s. The religious policies of Edward's two successors, his half-sisters, were both defined by their attempts to restore previous settlements. Mary (ruled 1553–58) made an energetic and controversial attempt to restore Catholicism to England, an attempt which was cut short by her death. The policy of Elizabeth (ruled 1558–1603) was more cautious but no less relentless, and centred on a partial restoration of Edward VI's Reformation. The contrasts between these two restorations are obvious. Mary was Catholic, Elizabeth Protestant; Mary was forthright, Elizabeth subtle in her violence. Mary's Church avoided and Elizabeth's pursued theological debate; Mary's was closely tied into Continental affairs, affairs which Elizabeth strove to keep at arm's length. Above all, Mary's failed and Elizabeth's succeeded.

Yet there are parallels too. The attitude of the sovereign was always decisive. These were also England's first reigning queens since the twelfth century, and they dealt with the problems of female rule in similar ways. Both, too, were their father's daughters. While neither of them had any wish to restore his policies, they could not shake off his legacy. Nor could either act independently, for England – and England's religion – was entangled in the wider webs of European diplomacy.

Mary

Mary's reign is the most tantalising and controversial period of the sixteenth century. To her defenders down the centuries, many of them Catholic, the reign is England's great lost hope: a chance to turn aside from schism and return to the unity of Christendom, a chance cut short by her untimely and childless death. To her more numerous detractors, who have been predominantly Protestant, the reign is a brutal, backward-looking dead end, a doomed project whose most memorable feature was the execution by burning of some 300 Protestants. The argument cannot be resolved, since it is not really about what happened, but about what would have happened had Mary lived longer. The plain fact that her restoration *did* fail looms inescapably over the reign.

Religion, marriage and their consequences

The strengths and weaknesses of Mary's position were defined by the manner in which she became queen. Outwardly, her position after the Jane Grey debacle was unassailable. Her enemies had been forced into the open and defeated. Yet such a decisive victory was possible only because she found herself at the head of a broad coalition. The political nation had decided she should be queen, but this did not mean that she had unfettered political freedom. On the contrary, she had debts to those who had supported her during July 1553.

This mattered because it was not then clear precisely what her religious policy would be. Her devotion to the Mass was well known, and her loyalty to the papacy widely suspected (not least because it was Rome which had defended her parents' marriage and her own legitimacy). Yet she had – under intense pressure – eventually conformed to Henry VIII's Reformation. When she became queen, she became, in law, Supreme Head of the Church of England (the last monarch to hold that title). Many conservatives, as we have seen, wanted to do no more than to return to Henry VIII's Reformation. While it was plain that Mary would reverse the Edwardian changes, it was not immediately clear whether her intended Year Zero was 1547, 1529 or somewhere in between. This ambiguity meant that, in the euphoria following her victory, all her subjects except hardened Protestants could celebrate her accession. It also means that that euphoria should not be overread as Catholic loyalism.

In fact, Mary's own intentions were fixed from the beginning. She planned a full restoration of papal authority. In August 1553, in an echo of her father's rhetoric, she urged her subjects to live in harmony together, 'leaving those new-found devilish terms of papist or heretic'; but she also explicitly stated that such tolerance would last only 'unto such time as further order . . . may be taken'.[1] All existing preaching licences were swiftly revoked, and Catholic voices heard again in pulpits. The conservative bishops who had spent the latter part of Edward's reign in prison were immediately released and restored to their sees. Stephen Gardiner was not only reinstated as bishop of Winchester, but made Lord Chancellor. The duke of Norfolk, who had spent the whole of Edward's reign in prison, was released and restored to his lands and titles, although Mary could not give him back the health which his long imprisonment had broken. The Catholic exiles began to return. Laws could not be changed so swiftly, but officious or over-clever Protestants who attempted to enforce the Edwardian religious legislation rapidly found themselves overruled.

As for the Protestant establishment: the Jane Grey fiasco had damaged it badly. Archbishop Cranmer was deeply implicated in that plot, and Mary was able to have him condemned for treason – although she spared his life, for now. John Dudley, the duke of Northumberland, was condemned to die. In a sweet victory for the new regime, immediately before his death Dudley made an abject recantation of his heresies and a tearful profession of the true Catholic faith (enough to save his soul, in Catholic eyes, but not his life). A string of leading reformers – Hugh Latimer, John Hooper, John Bradford amongst many others – were arrested during August and September 1553. Others fled the country, the beginning of an exodus of Protestant refugees which would eventually number close to a thousand people. Those reformers who remained found themselves harassed when they preached, and unable to have their books printed. For now, it stopped at harassment and imprisonment, but English Protestants had a lugubrious persecution complex and fully expected that there would be worse to come.

Yet the country cannot be divided neatly into the queen's Catholic supporters and her Protestant opponents. The Privy Council she appointed was deliberately broad and inclusive, and even her informal kitchen cabinet of key advisers included William Paget, who had been at the heart of Edward VI's regimes. When Parliament eventually assembled, the tensions in the new regime became clearer. Mary was to face more difficulties in the House of Commons than any of the other Tudors. Her first two parliaments even refused to reinstate the old heresy laws. Where her Catholic restoration threatened to trespass onto questions of property, the gentry and burgesses of the Commons became particularly agitated. One problem above all delayed the formal reconciliation with Rome until the very end of 1554: Church property seized under Henry VIII and Edward VI, such as monastic and chantry lands. Most of the members of the Commons had benefited from this plunder, and they were unwilling to buy reconciliation by returning their ill-gotten gains. Mary, bolstered by papal envoys, was adamant that they should do just that, but it was the Commons who won this particular stand-off. The regime eventually guaranteed to respect the new owners' rights. England accepted, even welcomed, the Catholic restoration, but not at any price.

If that was a defeat for Mary, it was felt even more deeply by the man who would become her closest adviser. Reginald Pole, theologian and cardinal of English royal blood, had been Henry VIII's favourite bogeyman in the 1530s. Since then, he had risen in the world even as his native country had sunk deeper into heresy. He was a leading voice at the Council of Trent, the Catholic Church's much-delayed systematic response to Protestant critiques. In 1549 Pole had been a leading candidate for the papacy, and had been defeated by only two votes. England's return to the Catholic fold should have been his life's crowning mercy. He was sent as papal legate to negotiate the terms of the reconciliation. Naturally, in due course he replaced Cranmer as archbishop of Canterbury. His influence in Marian England is easy to underestimate, for he wrote no books during this period and very few of his sermons survive. But it is also true that during his long exile, he and England had become foreign to one another. Pole was devoted to Mary, but deeply distrusted many of her advisers. He had limited respect for those who had conformed while he himself had chosen exile. In particular, he had misgivings about Stephen Gardiner, who had not only accepted the Royal Supremacy but had written a powerful Latin treatise in defence of it. (In 1553, an enterprising Protestant dug this out and published an English translation, in a successful attempt to embarrass the new regime.) After months of negotiations, Pole finally landed in England in November 1554. When Gardiner died a year later, Pole's influence expanded in turn.

Religion was not the reign's only political fault-line. Alongside her commitment to the papacy, Mary was also determined to restore another feature of England's old order: the long-standing alliance with her mother's family, the Habsburgs, the alliance of which she herself was the living symbol. She planned to do this in the traditional way, through a royal marriage. Once she had been spoken of as a possible wife for her cousin, the Holy Roman Emperor, Charles V, but Charles was now married and was an old man. Mary was instead to marry his son Philip, the heir to his Spanish realms, eleven years younger than herself. Since the Habsburgs were (at least in their own eyes) Catholic Christendom's greatest bulwark against heresy, this was a splendidly orthodox project, but that was not the whole story. The Spanish marriage was never popular in England, at any level. When the queen's plans became known in late 1553, it marked the end of her political honeymoon.

Indeed, the marriage provoked the most alarming crisis of Mary's reign: the rising at the end of January 1554 known as Wyatt's rebellion. Its leader, the young courtier Thomas Wyatt, was a Protestant, as were many of his accomplices; but Protestantism as such had neither the support nor (yet) the will to foment a rebellion. It was the threat of a bloodless Spanish conquest which produced a movement able to stir up much of Kent, and which then, frighteningly, persuaded the City of London's own trained bands to join it. Of course, the rebellion was suppressed. Afterwards, the regime claimed that it was the work of Protestant fanatics and French agitators. Both claims were true, but they were not the whole truth. Plenty of good English Catholics also disliked the Spanish marriage.

It was here that Mary's gender weakened her. It had once been questioned whether a woman might succeed to the English throne, but this question had been settled by default. Between the death of Edward VI in 1553 and the death of Mary, queen of Scots in 1587, all of the leading candidates for the English throne were women. But, as Elizabeth and the Scottish queen would also discover, ascending the throne was the easy part. Marriage was the great conundrum for any ruling queen, since the very essence of early modern marriage was a wife's subordination to her husband. For Mary to marry the future king of Spain threatened that England would become a province of Spain, especially if they had children. In the event, Mary's government finessed the situation with some skill. The marriage treaty of 1554 was a triumph for English diplomacy, which not only secured England's jurisdictional independence, but stipulated what any children of the marriage would inherit. The plan was for Mary and Philip's heirs to become sovereigns of England and of the Netherlands (then under Spanish rule) but not of Spain itself, potentially creating a formidable cross-Channel realm whose natural heart would have been in London.

To that extent, then, the rebels' fears were misplaced. But there is no escaping that the Spanish match produced the closest international alliance of England's century, and that the consequences were mostly malign. England was, once again, sucked into the Habsburgs' decades-old war with France, which also triggered a new war with France's ally Scotland in 1557. The Habsburg alliance generally had the better of the fighting in the late 1550s, with a single exception: England's last remaining Continental stronghold, the city of Calais, succumbed to a French siege in 1558. England could not afford to pay for a counter-attack. The Habsburgs' failure to come to Calais' aid, or to secure its return as part of a peace treaty, seemed to prove that English fears about the Spanish match were well grounded. Like most 'special relationships', this one was not, when it counted, an alliance of equals.

The Spanish match had one further, unpredictable but highly damaging effect on Mary's government and religious policy. Reginald Pole's papal candidacy in 1549 had been torpedoed by the dark warnings of another cardinal, Gian Pietro Carafa. From a humanist, almost Erasmian background, Carafa had become bitterly suspicious of any apparent weakening of conservative Catholic orthodoxy. Pole, he argued in the conclave in 1549, was altogether too sympathetic to heretics, if not actually a heretic himself. Carafa was also deeply suspicious of the Habsburgs, whom he suspected of wanting to conquer Italy and make the popes little more than their personal chaplains. In 1555, Carafa himself was elected pope, taking the name Paul IV. His two feuds – with Pole and with the Habsburgs – together turned the papacy into a consistent enemy of Mary's regime in the later 1550s. Pole was stripped of his legatine powers in 1557 and accused of heresy later the same year. It latterly became almost impossible for Mary to fill vacant bishoprics (for papal approval was now needed once again). Carafa's concerns were not groundless, but his pursuit of them was disproportionate and counterproductive. While she was trying to restore papal authority, Mary's single most troublesome opponent was the pope himself: the irony was not lost on contemporaries.

One final piece of the political context needs to be borne in mind. In 1557 and 1558, as the unwelcome wars were gathering pace and as the quarrel with the papacy was becoming more serious, England was also faced with two linked internal crises: harvest failures and epidemic disease. Heavy autumnal rains in 1555 and 1556 led to two pitiful harvests, rocketing food prices, and pockets of starvation in 1556–57. Then, in 1557 and 1558, two waves of influenza swept the country. Tens of thousands died, perhaps as many as one-twentieth of England's population. Mary's government was not, of course, even remotely responsible for these disasters, but it was affected by them: through deaths, loss of tax revenue and the need to divert scarce resources to poor relief. They also undermined its moral authority, for – especially combined with a national disaster such as the loss of Calais – these disasters could look uncomfortably like divine judgement being visited on England. Anyone inclined to entertain such thoughts would find Protestants eager to argue the point.

Every government has to deal with unexpected crises, and if the disasters of 1557 and 1558 have an air of doom to them, that is because hindsight knows that they were also the last years of the reign. Mary's authority remained undoubted until the end. But her position was not unassailable; nor was she able to devote as much of her time and resources to her religious policy as she would have liked.

Rebuilding the Church

Our view of Mary's positive attempt to restore English Catholicism to its former glories has been transformed by recent scholarship. Where once her policy was dismissed as backward-looking and desultory, it now appears to have been carefully thought through and pursued across a wide front. This does not, of course, mean that it was working.

In the religious battles of the sixteenth century, Catholicism's many advantages (tradition, wealth, ritual depth) were countered by two strategic weaknesses. The first was material complexity. A pre-Reformation parish church was filled with elaborate and expensive items: screens, roods, pattens, chalices, vestments, altars, candlesticks, stoups, sepulchres, and much more. Most parishes' stock of these items had been built up over generations. On a larger scale, the same was true of the Church as a whole: the work of the religious orders depended on the wealth which they had slowly accumulated. Catholicism without any of this material support was of course possible, but it would be, literally, impoverished. Protestant worship, by contrast, needed no material props beyond a few books; and destruction and plunder were far quicker and cheaper than replacement and rebuilding. The battles played out in church buildings between Catholic and Protestant were asymmetric warfare which favoured the reformers. The physical damage done to the old Church during the reigns of Henry VIII and Edward VI was not easily reversed. And that physical damage mattered, for Catholicism was a richly textured religion of the senses, as against the austerity of Protestantism's word-based piety.

Catholicism's second strategic weakness was its claim to define theological orthodoxies authoritatively. Protestantism was a discursive tradition from the beginning, and remained so; but open-ended theological argument was not Catholicism's natural state. This is not because Catholics were unable to defend their positions – John Fisher, Thomas More or Stephen Gardiner were second to none as debaters. Rather, the very act of defending their positions undermined those positions, for any public argument naturally invites its hearers or readers to be judges. Protestants were perfectly happy with this; Catholics could not be. To engage in a public debate with their doctrinal opponents legitimised those opponents, and required the reading public to make up their own minds about doctrines which the Church had authoritatively defined. Protestants were challenging their Catholic opponents to wrestle in the mud. Even if Catholics won such a bout, they would be contaminated by it. Yet remaining silent in the face of Protestant attacks was hardly preferable.

These two strategic weaknesses broadly determined the Marian regime's effort to rebuild English Catholicism, an effort which had two central planks. First was the physical and institutional restoration of what had been destroyed. Some of this was easy. Most clergy were able to say Mass, and liturgical texts could easily be provided. A fair amount of the material losses which parishes had suffered could be quickly made good too, for some items had been hidden by conservative laypeople in local communities and could be swiftly returned to their rightful places. But rebuilding was nevertheless an arduous task, one whose financial burden fell almost entirely on parishioners. Paying for such work of restoration would have been a tall order at the best of times, and the late 1550s were not the best of times. And the politics were not straightforward either. The crown, having seized huge amounts of Church property, now wanted its subjects to pay to replace them: and this with another Protestant as heir apparent, who might be expected to seize it all again. A certain thriftiness would have been only natural.

Given these difficulties, the regime's success in rebuilding parish worship is remarkable. A comprehensive study of all the surviving parish account-books from the reign has demonstrated almost universal compliance with the minimum level of repair which the regime required. 'Most of the parishes . . . decorated their churches more than the legal minimum required', despite the very considerable costs.[2] This astonishing success in the parishes contrasts sharply with other spheres of religious life. Only a dozen monasteries were refounded under Mary, all but one (Westminster Abbey, the queen's flagship project) on shoestring budgets. Likewise, very few chantries were re-established. Mary and Pole were both personally eager to see a revival of monasticism, but the parishes were the first priority.

What does the success at parish level tell us? It is clear that significant numbers of the local elites were willing to pay for the Catholic restoration, whether out of personal conviction or out of social and political obligation. It also bodes well for the Church's ability to regenerate itself on the ground, for re-equipped churches were a pre-requisite for the rebuilding of lay Catholicism. Yet on that measure, the work left to be done far outweighs that which was managed in the five years of Mary's reign. A hasty, skeletal framework of the old religion was reinstated. In place of carved

roods, some parishes used painted canvases. Gravestones were cannib-
alised to make altars. To notice such makeshifts is not to suspect laxity –
if anything, they testify to the pious ingenuity of lay people attempting
the near-impossible. But restoring the full splendour of Catholic worship
would have been a labour of generations. Such was certainly the experience
of Catholic renewals across Europe. And some losses could never be made
good: the shrines and relics, objects whose very age marked their holiness,
were gone forever. English Catholicism was permanently the poorer.

Alongside restoring structures and institutions, the second thread of the
restoration was rebuilding the faith. In this case, the effort was not simply
to undo the Henrician and Edwardian changes, but to harness and redirect
some of them. In the front rank of this effort was Edmund Bonner, now
restored as bishop of London. Bonner was a tough-minded, energetic
administrator who in the 1530s had been a protégé of Thomas Cromwell's,
but whose increasingly plain conservatism had led to his deprivation in
1549. Bonner was an enthusiast for the new technology of printing, and
sponsored a string of key publications. The centrepiece was a book entitled
A Profitable and Necessary Doctrine, which – like Bonner himself – serves
as a hinge between Henrician and Marian England. It was a revised version
of the 1543 *King's Book* (see above, p. 130), the last and fullest statement
of Henry VIII's doctrines, now, of course, brought fully into line with
Catholic orthodoxy. *A Profitable and Necessary Doctrine* also included
fourteen homilies, which drew directly on the set which Cranmer had
published in Edward VI's reign (see above, p. 155) but, again, were revised
to provide firmly traditional views of justification, the Mass and the nature
of the Church. Marian priests were being provided with sermons which
could be read from pulpits in order to broadcast the truth to the people.
Both texts were widely circulated. In 1555, the queen's printer produced at
least five print-runs of the *Profitable and Necessary Doctrine*, in addition
to eight print-runs of the homilies alone – well over 10,000 copies in total,
enough in theory for every parish in England to own one. While Bonner
had no authority to mandate the use of such texts outside his own diocese,
he and the regime clearly intended that they should be so used.

Bonner's project provides important clues to the regime's strategy.
Printed books, it appears, were at best ancillary in that strategy. The heart,
again, was the parish church, and the priest within it. Bonner's books were
available to all who wished to buy them, but their target audience was the
clergy, whom he aimed to equip to rebuild the faith. Likewise, Cardinal
Pole saw the sermon, not the book, as the primary means by which true
doctrine was to be communicated to the English (the common assertion

that he was wary of preaching is quite mistaken).[3] It was a shrewd strategy. Books are inherently discursive and disputatious, a cacophony of voices competing for the bookbuyer's loyalty. By contrast, the sermon as a medium is inherently authoritative: a single voice speaking for the Church, six feet above contradiction. It allowed Catholic doctrine to be taught without issuing an invitation for its merits to be discussed.

The religious publications of the Marian regime, then, included sermons aplenty, liturgical works, devotional treatises, and the works of the ancient Fathers of the Church. Almost all of these works were prepared by clergy. They tended to meet heresy with blunt condemnation rather than with sustained engagement, argument or mockery. Only one author produced full-throated Catholic polemics in Mary's reign, and he is the exception that proves the rule. Miles Huggarde was a layman (in fact, a hosier) and author of seven passionately Catholic pamphlets, most famously a vicious polemic called *The Displaying of the Protestants*. He won official favour, being made hosier to the queen in 1553 and later being actively supported by Pole, but he was his own man. Much of his best work was written during Edward's reign, when he had no immediate prospect of being able to publish it. This was not the kind of work which the regime chose to commission. Indeed, when its more favoured authors did produce works with a controversial edge, the regime was slow to use them. Nicholas Harpsfield, the archdeacon of Kent who was part of Pole's inner circle, produced two key texts of religious controversy in Mary's reign: a damning and precise account of Archbishop Cranmer's vacillations while in prison, and a vivid biography of Thomas More which helped cement More's reputation for sanctity. Neither work was published in Mary's reign. In each case we can guess at the reasons – Cranmer's story was dangerously double-edged, and the More biography might have embarrassed some senior people in the regime, who had been implicated in his death. But the regime's slowness to print controversial texts, even when they were handed to it, speaks of a wider and more deliberate policy. Both of Harpsfield's books circulated in handwritten copies, widely so in the case of the More biography. This was the old Renaissance way, and it was Mary's, and above all Pole's, vision of how religious controversy should be conducted: carefully, behind closed doors, not through the megaphone of the printing press. The wider reading public were expected to learn, not to argue. One side-effect of this was a significant decline in printing. The industry shrank under Mary, and many of those who had built their business on religious controversy either left the country or withdrew from the trade altogether. The remnants were subject to new regulation.

The success of this publicity strategy is hard to assess. Historians naturally overestimate the impact of printed books (which still survive for us to read) and underestimate sermons (which are lost as soon as they are preached). Even so, however, it seems in retrospect that the decision to evade religious controversy carried a heavy cost. In France, a decade later, the old Church was to respond very differently to an alarming Protestant advance. French Catholic polemic of the 1560s and thereafter was as vitriolic, furious and unbalanced as anything Protestantism produced; but what French Catholicism may have lost in dignity it made up in success. The French religious wars were won as much by words as by muskets, and alongside its battles and riots was vicious book-to-book combat. But that kind of lowbrow street-fighting was not Cardinal Pole's style.

English Protestants, by contrast, excelled at it. From the beginning of the reign a stream of polemics poured out. There were some valiant attempts at clandestine printing in England, but most of this production took place abroad. It was not an easy business. English-speaking typesetters were rare and paper was expensive. Even when books were printed, smuggling them in was tricky, and earning any kind of money from them trickier still. Print runs were short, books small, and prices high. Even so, the books poured forth, unrelenting in their venom: *The Hunting of the Romish Wolf, A True Report that Antichrist is Come, The First Blast of the Trumpet against the Monstrous Regiment of Women*. The regime struggled heroically to intercept them, but books are easily concealed and the government's resources were limited. Books were the most visible sign that the Protestant problem was not simply going to go away. If the regime was unwilling to shout its opponents down, it would have to tackle them in other ways.

The Protestant problem

Mary's regime is notorious for its hardline policy towards Protestantism. Arrests of prominent Protestants began almost immediately. Once the medieval heresy laws were eventually restored, the burnings began. Between 1555 and 1558 some 285 men and women were burned alive for heresy, and another thirty or so died in prison. By modern standards of mass killing, the number may seem small, but while it lasted this persecution was as intense as any which sixteenth-century Europe had seen up to that point.

The burnings have long been seen both as the reign's defining feature (hence the seventeenth-century nickname 'Bloody Mary') and as its defining failure. With hindsight, it is easy to see the persecution as self-defeating, a gruesome propaganda gift to the regime's enemies. It is argued that those initially sympathetic to the Catholic restoration were alienated by the regime's cruelty. Our own revulsion at this policy – which is appalling by any modern standards, and seemed brutal even to many contemporaries – naturally leads us to believe that it was doomed. Unfortunately, history rarely has such moral clarity.

The potential propaganda value of the executions for Protestants was unmistakable. Burnings were public displays, staged for the edification of the people. Fire symbolised the Hell for which unrepentant heretics were destined; the victims' extended sufferings both dehumanised them and provided a stern deterrent. Yet Protestants proved effective at stealing the show. A willingness to die, and to die cheerfully with Christ's name on one's lips, was the most powerful possible testimony to the strength of one's faith. Eloquence at the stake, an established reputation for holiness of life, or obviously pitiable personal circumstances could all give the victims mastery of the propaganda stage. So did genuine atrocities, such as the notorious incident in Guernsey in which a pregnant Protestant woman gave birth as the flames were rising about her, only to have her newborn child flung back into the fire. Protestants were quick to claim the regime's victims as martyrs, and to interpret their sufferings as spiritual triumphs. The martyrs' letters from prison were treasured, and their example quoted. There were even signs of an effort to publicise their sufferings more systematically. During the reign, the Protestant exile John Foxe – who himself believed that religious offenders should never be executed, a most unusual position – began compiling the book that would become his life's work. First published in Latin in 1559, and then in English in 1563, Foxe's *Acts and Monuments* (universally known as the Book of Martyrs) ensured that Mary's reign was remembered chiefly for its bloodshed.

It is worth emphasising, then, that Mary's regime had little choice but to adopt a policy of persecution, and that that policy was strikingly effective. Committed Protestants were a small minority of the English Church and people, but they were energetic, vociferous and implacable in their opposition to the regime. If a stable Catholicism were to be restored, these people simply had to be silenced. This was hard. Exile did no more than muffle their voices. Placing pressure on the exiles was difficult; the regime's attempts to sequester their property in England was blocked by the House of Commons, jealous of property rights as always. Nor was imprisonment an adequate solution. Tudor prisons were notoriously porous, principally because prisoners were required to pay the costs of their own incarceration and could thus virtually become their own gaolers' employers. It only took a little bribery to ensure that prisoners could send and receive letters, receive visitors and even make short trips outside. Even the most closely guarded prisoners managed at times to obtain writing materials and to smuggle letters out. The prison writings of Marian prisoners fill several volumes in their modern editions, testimony both to their quantity and to how their words were cherished by other Protestants. If neither exile nor prison would shut these people up, what else was left?

Another line of reasoning led in the same direction. English heretics had a long tradition of breaking under pressure. Medieval Lollards had been exceptionally timorous heretics, virtually never persisting in their errors when recantation could have saved their lives. Protestants in the reign of Henry VIII had been only a little braver. A few had stood firm, but many more – including leading figures – had tried to negotiate their way out of heresy charges, with varying degrees of success and of principle. Mary's regime plainly expected the same pattern to continue. John Dudley, facing death, followed the script precisely. So did several others, including John Cheke, formerly one of Edward VI's tutors. Had large numbers of others joined them, matters would have turned out very differently. While Protestants could repackage executions as martyrdoms and make some use of them, recantations were irretrievable disasters. The appearance of humiliated men earnestly renouncing their Protestant errors reinforced every Catholic claim about heretics: that they were wilful, insincere and self-seeking. A string of high-profile recantations could have produced a terminal collapse in Protestant morale.

The regime worked hard to procure such recantations. The leading Protestant prisoners were not summarily condemned, but interrogated painstakingly over weeks or months, often by very senior clergy. The dedication with which the regime wooed such intransigent figures is testimony to recantation's political importance – and also its spiritual significance: this was a struggle to rescue souls from the jaws of Hell. And yet, unprecedentedly, many Protestants held firm, particularly the leaders. Under Henry VIII, matters had been different: the king's policy was ambiguous, and the evangelicals' beliefs often ill-defined. Now things were plainer, and the divide sharper. The exiles exhorted those in England to stand firm. Prisoners wrote to one another with the same message. Once the executions had begun, their precedent provided another motive to remain steadfast.

There was one partial, tantalising exception, an episode which marks Mary's worst single error. Archbishop Cranmer was the regime's prize prisoner. Already condemned as a traitor for supporting Jane Grey, he was kept alive to face trial for heresy too. It was a lengthy process, partly because a duly consecrated archbishop (however heretical) could only be tried by papal commission. Kept in isolation and under relentless pressure, Cranmer slowly crumbled. He had never been as combative as some of his co-religionists. Moreover, his Protestantism had been built around a very high doctrine of the Royal Supremacy, and now his queen was commanding him to return to Roman obedience. Over the winter of 1555–56, he signed a series of recantations, each more unambiguous than the one before. The regime was on the verge of a spectacular *coup*: Cranmer publicly renouncing his heresies.

The opportunity was thrown away – it seems, by the queen herself. Mary was determined that Cranmer should die, and as a heretic, not merely a traitor. Her loathing for him is understandable, for it was Cranmer who, more than twenty years earlier, had pronounced her parents' marriage void and led England into schism. Yet as a penitent heretic, his life ought to have been spared. The decision to kill him anyway looks unpleasantly like personal vengeance. Perhaps the manifest injustice of the sentence changed Cranmer's mind. Or perhaps the knowledge that his death was unavoidable removed the temptation to try to buy his life with a recantation. In any case, he returned to his Protestantism in the most decisive fashion possible. Declaring at the stake that his right hand, which had signed the recantations, would burn first, he held it steadily in the flames until the smoke overcame him. It was the single most vivid – and memorable – demonstration of Protestant sincerity at any of the burnings.

However, even without spectacular recantations, the executions had their effect. English Protestantism was decapitated. Men like Cranmer, Hugh Latimer, John Hooper, John Bradford and John Philpot were of some use to their fellow Protestants as martyrs, but this hardly compensated for the loss of a whole generation of preachers and theologians. The effectiveness of this policy is clear from the profile of those executed over the period. In 1555 and 1556, most of the victims were preachers, theologians and senior clergy. Cranmer, burned on 21 March 1556, was the last of these. Gardiner and others had wished to stop there; but Gardiner died in late 1555 and Mary, Pole and Bonner chose instead to press their advantage. The focus now shifted to lay Protestants who gathered in secret to hear and spread the word. Such conventicles were (correctly) seen by the regime as critical to the Protestant resistance. The attack on conventicles tended to produce mass executions, as whole groups were rounded up, and so the rate of executions climbed, peaking in the summer of 1557. From then on it began slowly to fall. Burnings continued until the very end of the reign, but by 1558 it was clear that the supply of Protestants to be burned was not going to rise exponentially. Brutal as it was, the policy of persecution was at least successfully keeping the Protestant minority under control.

The impossible question again: what would have happened had Mary lived longer? English Protestantism would not have been eradicated quickly or easily. Its partisans were not numerous, but they were exceptionally determined, they had some powerful friends, and the exiles' literary hyper-activity was likely to continue. Executions would have continued for the foreseeable future, monthly if not weekly events. Indeed, the regime might have had to become considerably more ruthless. There are numerous accounts from Mary's reign of Protestants saved from arrest or condemna-tion by legal niceties or by the squeamishness of individual officials. Due legal process was deeply ingrained into the English state. A more inquisit-orial approach might have proved necessary if the regime was to move beyond suppression to extermination, which would have been politically difficult. Yet this is simply to question quite how and when the inevitable defeat of Protestantism would come. In France and the Netherlands, Pro-testant minorities launched civil wars in the 1560s. It is hard to imagine the same thing happening in fiercely centralised England. Even if open rebellion or resistance of some kind had been attempted, it would certainly have met a swift and bloody end. The moment for a Protestant rebellion had been Wyatt's rebellion of 1554, and it had failed. From then on, if political stability was granted, the neutering (and, perhaps, the extinction) of English Protestantism was simply a matter of time.

One other factor was working in the regime's favour. The Protestants' energy and verbosity made them dangerous, but also made them quarrel-some. Without the firm leadership which had contained those quarrels in Edward's reign, serious splits began to appear. The most notorious of these splits took place in one of the largest exile congregations, in the German Lutheran city of Frankfurt. John Knox, the Scottish firebrand who had agitated against the 1552 Prayer Book, carried his campaign with him into exile. Much of the Frankfurt congregation shared his concerns, but a vociferous minority wished to maintain visible continuity with Edward VI's Church. The split became acrimonious, and Knox and his allies were outmanoeuvred. In 1555 his enemies persuaded the Frankfurt city authorities to expel him, and he fled to Geneva. This spat had long-lasting consequences. Knox became pastor of a new exile congregation in Geneva, which ditched the Prayer Book entirely and set about translating John Calvin's thoroughgoing Reformation into a British context. In 1558, Knox and his English friend Christopher Goodman horrified other exiles with a pair of pamphlets calling for open rebellion against Mary. The bad blood left by the Frankfurt stirs was to persist for generations.

A parallel drama was being played out in the English prisons, where a dissident Protestant faction, led by laymen, was vociferously denying the doctrine of predestination. To the remnants of the clerical leadership left over from Edward's reign, this was a grave error which undermined the whole basis of Protestantism. The dispute quickly became vicious. Prisoners awaiting death wrote furious polemics against one another. By 1558 the 'orthodox' Protestants had succeeded in discrediting the 'Freewillers', but the dispute shows how easily Protestantism could splinter. The regime deliberately tried to exacerbate this schism, repeatedly postponing the execution of 'Freewiller' leaders so that they could continue to stir up trouble. Had Mary lived, this is how English Protestants would have faded from view: with their hands at one another's throats.

The end of the regime and the transfer of power

Catholic hopes, then, were reasonable enough. But between them and their fulfilment lay an obvious problem: the continuity of the regime. Mary had become queen on the basis of her father's will. That same will provided that, should she die childless, the crown would pass to her half-sister Elizabeth, a known Protestant. It was an impending disaster for Mary, one which was in plain view throughout the reign, but nevertheless one which her regime was unable or unwilling to prevent.

Mary did of course act swiftly to secure a Catholic succession, by marrying. A child would have transformed her political prospects, and her longing for one is in any case unmistakable. Twice she believed she was pregnant; on the first occasion her pregnancy was publicly celebrated and widely believed until the very end. False pregnancies were not uncommon in the age before blood tests (possibly they were symptoms of the cancer which eventually killed her). Her conviction that God would give her a child, and give England an heir, apparently made her reluctant to consider contingency plans. But she was thirty-eight years old when she married. The odds were never in her favour.

A child was the best solution to the succession problem, but not the only one. Another was to dispose of Princess Elizabeth, and this was actively considered. After Wyatt's rebellion, there was widespread suspicion that Elizabeth had been involved. Elizabeth herself always denied it, and no firm evidence has ever surfaced, but it still seems inherently likely. She was arrested and imprisoned; Simon Renard, the Spanish ambassador, urged that she be executed as a traitor. That would have been bold, but it was perfectly possible. William Paget suggested a less bloody solution: marrying Elizabeth off to some appropriately distant foreign prince (the duke of Savoy was suggested). This would have made her a foreign subject and (arguably) ineligible to succeed – although it could not entirely guarantee her disappearance.

Neither of these things was done, and that decision not to act was the queen's own. She had no great love for her half-sister, as their personal history would suggest, but latterly they had been on passably good terms. Mary also lacked their father's taste for shedding royal blood. An execution would have been politically risky, at least without proof (real or fabricated) of Elizabeth's guilt. Mary would undoubtedly have been labelled a tyrant by many of her subjects, and perhaps also by her own conscience. Instead, she chose the next best solution: keeping Elizabeth as a closely guarded prisoner. In 1555, however, when Mary was confident that she was pregnant, she felt secure enough to release Elizabeth into a loose house arrest – a grave error, in retrospect. The young princess used her straitened position shrewdly, allowing herself to be seen but not heard by the people in the surrounding area and opening discreet channels of communication with potential political allies. A decorous silence was her best policy, for it allowed England's deep reserves of wishful thinking about good lordship to settle around her. She did nothing to give anyone reason to oppose her. And so, indeed, when Mary died in November 1558, Elizabeth succeeded virtually unopposed, and did so – once again – on the strength of Henry VIII's will.

That Mary should have allowed Henry VIII's order for the succession to remain intact is, on the face of it, bizarre. A simple Act of Parliament would have been enough to overturn Henry VIII's will, and since – in Catholic eyes and in English law – Elizabeth was undoubtedly illegitimate, there was every reason for doing this. There was also a plausible alternative candidate. Margaret Stewart, *née* Douglas, the countess of Lennox, was the only child born to Henry VII's daughter Margaret's second marriage, to the earl of Angus (see above, p. 103). She was a firm Catholic; she had been living in England since the mid-1540s; and she was a close friend of the queen. Moreover, she had that most valuable political asset, a son (Henry, Lord Darnley: at the age of twelve, his personal failings were not yet evident (see below, pp. 225–6)). Mary favoured Lennox openly, granting her ceremonial precedence over Elizabeth. Lennox herself was keen to press her candidacy. It seemed only natural.

Why did it not happen? Henry VIII, who disliked Lennox, had firmly excluded her from the succession, citing doubts about her legitimacy. More seriously, to choose Lennox and her descendants would mean excluding the sole living descendant of Margaret Tudor's first marriage: Mary Stewart, the queen of Scots. A case could be made for excluding her, as a foreigner; but a similar case could be made against Lennox (she had been born and raised in England, but was a foreigner's daughter and a foreigner's wife). And for Mary Tudor's regime, the queen of Scots was the worst possible successor. To be sure, she was soundly Catholic, but she was even more soundly French. She had been at the French court since 1548, and on 24 April 1558 she married the French dauphin, Francis. If she and her husband succeeded to the English crown too, it would create a vast Franco-British empire which would tip the European balance of power decisively away from Spain and the Habsburgs. Philip – by 1558, King Philip II of Spain in his own right, and King Philip of England through his wife – would not allow his English ally to be swallowed up by his French enemy. Yet if the regime legislated to exclude two obvious candidates (Elizabeth, Mary Stewart) in favour of a third, more politically acceptable one (Lennox), did it not run the risk of repeating the Jane Grey debacle? One did not need to be a keen observer of Tudor politics to notice that attempts to fix the succession frequently backfired.

So Elizabeth became, perversely, the least bad option: the candidate with the best chance of resisting a French claim. And if her religion was less than ideal, it was not obvious that her personal religious views would be decisive. Elizabeth would, as queen, naturally be at odds with a France that was disputing her right to the crown, and would therefore be forced to maintain the Spanish alliance. Philip II's own plan was to maintain his English alliance on almost the same terms by promptly marrying Elizabeth. As well as Philip, Elizabeth would have Cardinal Pole to reckon with: primate of all England, and a man of royal blood himself. Her room for manoeuvre would have been very limited. During 1558, as it became clearer that Mary might not live long, a rational Catholic could well have concluded that the best hope for securing Mary's restoration lay with Elizabeth.

It was not a foolish hope. The steadfastness which Mary's senior clergy showed in 1558–59 (see below, p. 200) is a testament to her achievement. Whatever else can be said of Mary, she was the saviour of English Catholicism. She rescued it from its paralysing Edwardian self-doubt, equipping it to survive as a combative minority for generations. But events conspired against her. If Mary alone had died in the autumn of 1558, some kind of continuity might have been possible. But the epidemics of that year stripped her regime bare, and her quarrels with Pope Paul IV meant that replacing deceased bishops was slow and difficult. Of the twenty-six bishoprics in England and Wales, nine were vacant at the time of Mary's death: four candidates had been nominated by the queen, but not yet approved by the pope. Above all, Pole himself died of influenza on the very same day the queen did, 17 November. Against all expectation, the new queen Elizabeth had a chance to become mistress of her own house.

Elizabeth

Elizabeth inherited a kingdom reeling from lethal epidemics, still suffering from food shortages, with (as usual) a near-bankrupt government, and locked into a damaging war with France and Scotland. Her own accession gave the war an additional twist, because as soon as Mary was dead, the French claimed the English throne for themselves, in Mary Stewart's name. It was in this perilous context that the new queen had to confront the question of religion.

The path to the 'Settlement'

Elizabeth's own religion is an enigma, as indeed are her views on most other questions. Her political style was to be indirect, to delay (always delay), to feint and cloak her real opinions, to be as inconsistent and capricious as her contemporaries expected women to be, and to allow others to speak for her so that she could distance herself from what they said. Almost nothing of what she said or did can be taken at face value, in this or any other area. Still, the outlines are tolerably clear. She was, apparently, a conviction Protestant of sorts. Like her father, she was unswerving in asserting her own authority over the English Church, although she never wielded that authority with his recklessness. She had no patience with what she saw as superstition; she welcomed the translation of the Bible and of the liturgy into English; and (we can put it no more strongly than this) she seems to have accepted most of the central doctrines of Reformed Protestantism. She also shared the family taste for moderate amounts of good preaching. And yet, her Protestantism was of a curiously dated kind. She was not the last Henrician – such doctrinal idiosyncrasy was simply no longer possible – but she was, perhaps, the last of the old-fashioned evangelicals.

Henry VIII's Reformation had maintained most of the core doctrines of Catholicism, while making dramatic changes to the practices and institutions of religion. Elizabeth's preferences were a mirror image of this. She was happy to adopt Reformed Protestant doctrines more or less wholesale, but she was much more reluctant to let go of traditional ceremonial and structures (she approved of crucifixes, for example). This seems to be a matter as much of taste as of theology. Her view of the clergy, for example, was highly traditional: she liked the old titles, some of the old vestments, and even balked at the idea that they might marry. It is a testament to Elizabeth's political skill, and to her luck, that by the time she had been queen for a year a religious settlement which bore strong resemblance to these preferences had been enacted into law.

From the first days of the reign, Elizabeth gathered a group of advisers around her who shared a distinctive religious flavour. These were cautious, patient, conviction Protestants – indeed, noticeably more forthright in their Protestantism than she was. Foremost among these was the man who would dominate the reign: William Cecil, later to become Lord Burghley, who had been a talented young administrator in Edward VI's reign and now became secretary to Elizabeth's Privy Council. Cecil and Elizabeth were a formidable political team. They frequently disagreed, but they also respected one another, and knew how to manage and use their disagreements effectively. But Cecil was only the leading figure of a close-knit group of friends and colleagues who now formed the heart of the new regime. The most notable of the others was Nicholas Bacon, who became Lord Chancellor. These men (all of them men) were Protestants, but most of them had, like Elizabeth herself, conformed outwardly to the Catholic restoration. If they had an intellectual home, it was not Geneva but Cambridge, where their friendships had been formed. They had been Edward VI's tutors and his advisers. Many of them had been close to Martin Bucer, the great conciliator of the German Reformation, who had spent the last eighteen months of his life in Cambridge; or to John Cheke, the scholar who had recanted under Mary and died soon thereafter. They were scholars and humanists – 'Athenians', they called themselves – but also nationalists. Cranmer's dream of uniting the Protestant world under an English banner appealed to them. They blended a blunt political pragmatism with some of the old Edwardian idealism about the reform of the commonwealth. Like the Marian regime, and unlike the Protestant exiles, they wished (in vain) to see politics as a matter for private and civilised discussion between learned men, not a public shouting-match conducted through the printing press. But like the Marian regime, this air of calm should not be taken to imply that their views were lukewarm or malleable.

The new regime's religious policy was dictated by this mix of daunting circumstance and subtly opinionated personnel. The burnings, of course, ceased. The queen made a few symbolic changes immediately, such as ending the use of candles in her private chapel. As was becoming habitual with new regimes, she revoked all preaching licences. She allowed a few departures from the Latin service, such as the use of the litany, the Lord's Prayer and the Creed in English. But she was much cagier about the future direction of policy than Mary had been in 1553. A series of position papers laying out possibilities were written over the winter of 1558–59 by several of the 'Athenians'. The overriding concern of these authors was how to enact a Reformation which would be tolerably Protestant but which would nevertheless maintain some kind of national unity. One of these manifestos compared filling the English with good religion to filling a bottle with water:

Glasses with small necks, if you pour into them any liquor suddenly or violently, will not be so filled, but refuse to receive that same that you would pour into them. Howbeit, if you instil water into them by a little and little, they are soon replenished.[4]

From its earliest days the regime was concerned both to enact a Protestant settlement, and to ensure that Protestant radicals did not run too far ahead. Cecil and his allies remembered how, in Edward's reign, Protestant agitators had forced the pace of change. This was not going to be allowed to happen again.

The new regime, and Elizabeth in particular, found the views and the style of some of the Protestant exiles distasteful and inexpedient. Their displeasure centred on John Knox and on Geneva. Knox and Goodman's tracts of 1558, which had urged rebellion against Mary Tudor (and especially Knox's, which had deplored all female monarchy), permanently tainted Geneva and anyone associated with it in Elizabeth's mind. In fact, virtually no-one shared Knox's views, and the other exiles hastened to distance themselves from him. One of them, John Aylmer, hurriedly wrote a rebuttal of Knox. Aylmer's book was a classic mixture of inclusive Protestantism and exaggerated nationalism, which moved on from denouncing Knox's sedition to urging the English to rally to their queen against all her foreign enemies. 'You have God, and all his army of angels on your side', he wrote to his fellow-countrymen (summarising this in a notorious marginal note – 'God is English'). But Aylmer's loyalism was tempered. He insisted that queens must be tempered by good counsel, and while he would defend Elizabeth from Knox's attacks, he would not say a word in Mary's posthumous defence.[5] It was better than Knox's ravings, but Elizabeth would still not be drawn into this kind of world-view. Aylmer's book received a cool welcome, and to begin with she kept even the more cautious exiles at arm's length.

The reason was clear enough. In the first few months of the reign, the regime's great religious project was to win as many of the existing clergy as possible over to a new settlement. This possibility was taken extremely seriously. After all, many of the Marian bishops had served under Henry VIII and had accepted his schism: Archbishop Heath of York, Bishop Tunstall of Durham, Bishop Bonner of London and others. To persuade them to follow their monarch once more should not have been too hard. This, it seems, was the main reason for Elizabeth's odd choice to be her archbishop of Canterbury. Matthew Parker was a Cambridge scholar of long standing, and a friend of the 'Athenians'. His Protestantism was both undoubted and understated. He had been a chaplain to Anne Boleyn (who, he recalled, had before her death asked him to care for the orphaned Elizabeth), and had preached at Martin Bucer's funeral. During Mary's reign, his 'exile' had been a house a few miles outside Cambridge which his friends in the university arranged for him. He was both reluctant and underqualified to be primate of all England. But in 1558–59, Elizabeth did not need a politician, an administrator, a theologian or a pastor at Canterbury as much as she needed a conciliator. Parker never concealed his distaste for Catholic doctrine, but his learned and generous career in Cambridge meant that he was probably better trusted by leading Catholics than any other prominent Protestant. If anyone could bring them round, he could.

Soon enough it became clear what the regime was trying to achieve: a package of religious legislation which would restore aspects of Edward VI's Reformation. Yet this aim was under pressure from both sides. Exiles were now returning, and speaking freely – some much too freely. And when religious legislation was first brought before Parliament in February 1559, the bishops in the House of Lords voted it down *en bloc*, preventing Elizabeth even from repealing the heresy laws. Thus bloodied, the regime adopted more patient tactics. A formal disputation was staged at Westminster at Easter between eight Catholics and eight Protestants: ostensibly this was an act of disinterested inquiry to assist Parliament in its decisions, but it was transparently rigged, with the order of proceedings favouring the Protestants, and the Catholics denied access to books or time to prepare answers. When the Catholic bishops walked out in disgust, the regime used this as an excuse to imprison them, thus keeping them out of the House of Lords.

Fresh legislation was introduced in April: a bill reinstating the royal headship of the Church, and another reinstating a variant of the 1552 Prayer Book. They contained some important novelties. The queen's title was altered from Supreme Head to Supreme Governor: a cosmetic change, but it soothed some worried consciences, Protestant as well as Catholic. More significantly, the Prayer Book had some of its spikier Edwardian edges smoothed off. The earlier, 1549 book had implied that Christ was physically present at communion, while the 1552 book had replaced the relevant phrase with an unambiguous statement of a spiritual presence. The new Elizabethan book, in a compromise which was theologically dubious and liturgically impractical, simply mashed the two statements together, requiring the priest to recite both formulae in full to every communicant. It was an unwieldy solution.

These minor changes may possibly have been intended to win over Catholic opinion, but they plainly did not do so, and it seems unlikely that the regime hoped they would. If they were aimed at a specific audience, it was more likely a foreign one: that elusive Protestant international. The Lutheran states of Germany – whose right to practise their religion had been granted by a defeated Emperor Charles V in 1555 – were watching English affairs closely. The duke of Saxony wrote to Elizabeth urging her to adopt something 'near' to a Lutheran confession of faith. She replied promising to do so, professing enthusiasm for alliance with the Lutheran princes.[6] This was disingenuous. The proposed Prayer Book, like its Edwardian predecessors, was plainly a Reformed Protestant document, and indeed Lutheranism as such now scarcely existed in England. However, these changes – moving away from Henry VIII's kind of royal supremacy, and shoving a cumbersome ambiguity into the communion service – made it possible to hint to the Lutherans that the door was still open.

Neither this nor the regime's other manoeuvres made the parliamentary battle of April 1559 a straightforward one. The most nail-biting race was the vote in the Lords on the Act of Uniformity, authorising the Prayer Book. It passed by 21 votes to 18 – much too close for comfort, and a margin achieved only by the strong-arm tactics which kept several bishops away from the chamber. A second defeat would hardly have forced Elizabeth to return meekly to Rome, but it would have emboldened her opponents and left her policy in limbo. She might, in the end, have been compelled to offer full toleration to Catholicism: an outcome which nowadays might seem desirable but which, to any sixteenth-century observer, would have meant potentially catastrophic instability.

The steadfastness of the Catholic bishops took Elizabeth's regime by surprise, very much as the Protestant leaders' stubborn refusal to recant had surprised Mary. The days of compromise were over. Yet the regime did not give up hope. With the newly minted law now on its side, Elizabeth turned to her chosen conciliator, Matthew Parker, to win the dissenters over. He spent most of the rest of the year working on them, spending long hours in private debate with at least ten individuals. He had high hopes for the now-frail Bishop Tunstall of Durham, who had stayed away from Parliament, but it came to nothing. Tunstall died a Catholic in Parker's custody later that year, aged 84 (Parker, a gentleman and a scholar, paid for his funeral himself). The other Catholic bishops vanished into prison (some of them to remain there for decades) or into exile. One prominent Catholic did break: Richard Smyth, who had retracted his Catholicism once before, in 1547. But now, as before, Smyth fled abroad and renounced his recantation as quickly as he could. Only one of Mary's bishops conformed: Anthony Kitchen, who had been bishop of Llandaff since 1545. It is an interesting exception, for Kitchen was no mere timeserver. He had voted with the other bishops in the Lords; he refused to take the oath of supremacy until a specially worded variant was prepared for him; and he even refused to take part in Parker's consecration. Although his health was failing, he continued to administer his remote diocese according to his own lights, and with almost no resources, until his death in 1563 at the age of 86. There would not be another Catholic bishop in England or Wales for 300 years.

Parker's failure was disheartening, but probably inevitable. The world had changed, and conversions were no longer so easy. In particular, English Catholics had fallen for tactics like this before. Most of them had conformed to Henry VIII's schism because it appeared to change little. They had had leisure to learn from that mistake. If they acceded to a compromise, it would twist into full-blown Protestantism under their noses. Edward's reign had seen a ratchet of progressive change, with a further development every few months. By reinstating a version of Edward's Reformation, the new regime was implicitly signalling that the ratchet would resume. Catholics had no illusions about this. The exiles and other advanced Protestants certainly expected it. Most in the regime, including Cecil himself, expected it. The English would be filled with Protestantism, slowly but relentlessly. The new laws looked like a temporary compromise, the consequence of a particular political moment. No-one believed in 1559 that they were a permanent 'settlement' of religion. No-one, that is, apart from the queen.

For the most bizarre feature of Elizabeth's reign – and perhaps of the whole English Reformation – is that against all odds, the legislation of 1559 and the detailed royal injunctions which followed later the same year did form an enduring religious settlement. An adjusted version was soon in place in Elizabeth's other realm of Ireland (see Chapter 11). Some of the gaps were filled in later. A revised version of the Edwardian articles of religion was passed, and the Edwardian Homilies were revived and supplemented with a second volume. However, during the remainder of Elizabeth's forty-four year reign, the English Church's structures and practices saw no major changes. In the twenty-first century, the Church of England's practices are still recognisably derived from that febrile moment of failed compromise in 1559. Elizabeth restored the Edwardian Reformation, but she restored a still image of a moving process. Despite being placed under extraordinary pressure at times, she absolutely refused to accept any significant changes to that snapshot. This was partly because she felt change had gone quite far enough already, but more because the process of change itself alarmed her. She did not wish to see a relentless Reformation, with policy led by wild-eyed radicals who would take a mile if given an inch. Instead she had an unfinished Reformation, frozen in time.

Implementing the Reformation

Elizabeth had apparently hoped for an inclusive religious settlement, stretching from the more pragmatic Protestant exiles to genuine tradition-alists. When this failed, the vacuum was filled by the exiles, who ended up securing some two-thirds of the newly vacant bishoprics. Those exiles who had stood up for the Prayer Book and for continuity – men like Richard Cox, now bishop of Ely – were naturally among them. So too, however, were less 'safe' figures such as John Jewel, the new bishop of Salisbury, who became one of the most eloquent defenders of the new settlement. And some bishoprics went to genuine zealots. Edmund Grindal became bishop of London, an appointment which would end in tears. Most radical of all was James Pilkington, who was sent to the remote and deeply conservative diocese of Durham to see what he could make of it. These appointments partly reflect the differences between Elizabeth and her counsellors, for Cecil and others were distinctly friendlier to the radicals; yet such appointments always had the queen's consent. They reflect the sheer talent of some of these men – the new Church needed men like Jewel, Grindal and Pilkington. However, they also reflect the limits of Elizabeth's freedom. She could make the rules of her new Church, to some extent at least. But she could not determine its spirit.

This became clear in a series of skirmishes during the first year or two of the reign, as the outlines of the new settlement were filled in. Most significant, perhaps, was a fight which was over before it had begun, over clerical marriage. Elizabeth never disguised her distaste for clergy who married, but she could not prevent the practice. The best she could do was allow bishops to veto their clergy's choice of wives, and even this regulation was often ignored. The queen's views were simply overwhelmed by events. Most of her senior clergy were already married, including Matthew Parker. It was a *fait accompli*. Much the same can be said of another early struggle, not so close to the queen's heart but far more visible in parish churches. This was over metrical psalmody (see above, pp. 172–3). Psalms sung by whole congregations to lively ballad tunes had been a novelty in Edward's reign, and the Marian exiles had worked hard to produce a complete set of such psalms. They did not sit very well with the dignity of the Prayer Book service, and the Act of Uniformity made no provision for their use. Later in 1559, however, the royal injunctions permitted the use of a metrical psalm before or after the daily service, and this grudging loophole became the basis for a huge revival in psalm-singing. In 1560, Jewel described crowds of 6000 roaring out psalms in unison before sermons at Paul's Cross in London. Once again, the queen's own preferences could not entirely control what was happening on the ground.

Clerical marriage and the psalms were practical matters, but a more momentous battle was fought over a symbol: the crucifix in the queen's private chapel. For most Reformed Protestants, any reverence for a physical object – especially a statue or painting – was idolatry, a gross offence before God. To use a crucifix in church was to dishonour Christ and worship a piece of wood. Elizabeth did not agree. Her view was more like that of her last stepmother, Katherine Parr, an old-school evangelical who had described the crucifix as a 'spiritual book' on which Christians should meditate.[7] Elizabeth's habit of placing a crucifix on the altar in her private chapel was politically explosive, and when she considered permitting her subjects to do the same in their parish churches, her bishops closed ranks. Even Parker, in his quiet way, made it clear that he could not serve in such a Church. The queen was forced to back down. She retained her own crucifix, but no-one else was allowed to do so. Even so, she only hung onto it by her fingertips. On at least four occasions, anonymous iconoclasts stole into the chapel and destroyed the offending object. The regime replaced it, but did not dare pursue the vandals. Gleeful Catholics mocked the inconsistency, while Cecil continued to receive letters from worried Protestants reminding him that idolaters were threatened with 'great peril of God's wrath and displeasure'.[8] Like much of the rest of the Elizabethan 'settlement', this was less a settlement than a ceasefire line.

However, these skirmishes can distract from the scale of Elizabeth's (and Cecil's) achievement. A Reformed church was established without the civil war which the regime evidently feared. Grudging consent was still consent. Two decisions can stand as symbols of this achievement. On the one hand, there was the decision to return to iconoclasm (her own crucifix apart). Quietly and without fuss, the Edwardian campaign of destruction was re-enacted. The parishes which had strained to restore the material apparatus of Catholic worship in Mary's reign now promptly demolished it again. The regime kept this process orderly and unobtrusive. In particular, it barred Protestant agitators from unilaterally attacking stone altars, which had forced the pace of change under Edward. Yet its commitment to iconoclasm was real, and by the mid-1560s the destruction was almost complete. There was very little resistance.

At the same time, however, the new Protestant Church accepted both the structures and the personnel of the old Church. There were obvious reasons for retaining the office of bishop: bishops were appointed by the queen, and were therefore a central instrument of state control of the Church. But while they were stripped of much of their wealth, and largely excluded from high politics, they remained *bishops*, mitred and rocheted lords of the realm, rather than Protestant superintendents. Their cathedrals, too, again escaped the cull, partly because Elizabeth liked old-fashioned church music. Canon law and the Church courts remained unchanged; an attempt to reintroduce Cranmer's failed canon-law reform in 1571 was blocked by the regime. Everyone understood that the 1559 settlement represented a sharp break with the past, but in legal and administrative terms, continuity with the past was maintained, and that continuity mattered. Parish clergy continued to be appointed by their traditional patrons, many of them now lay people, and their posts continued to be regarded as property, of which they could be deprived only by due process of law. As such, and as always, the parish clergy were the great drag-anchor on religious change in Tudor England, for as long as they were willing to conform outwardly to the religion of the moment they were allowed to remain in post. Only Mary had made any effort to break this pattern, when in 1554 she sacked clergy who had married (some 15% of the total). In Elizabethan England, clergy whose instinctive loyalties were plainly Catholic were allowed to remain in post across the country. Building a

Protestant ministry would be the work of generations, and the regime did not wish to hurry.

Francis Bacon famously and justly commented that Elizabeth did not wish to make windows into men's souls. Outward conformity in matters of order, rather than an inward unity of faith, was her goal. The Act of Uniformity required simply that clergy use the new Prayer Book service, and that the people attend it. Those who failed to turn up, and could not produce a 'lawful or reasonable excuse to be absent',[9] were to be fined a shilling for each offence. That could soon add up, but it made dissent into a misdemeanour rather than a crime. It also gave the language a new word for those Catholics who absented themselves for reasons of conscience and were consequently fined: 'recusants'.

During the first decade of the reign, however, the regime's policy towards Catholics was even softer than this suggests: less a matter of not looking into souls than of 'don't ask, don't tell'. This was prudence rather than tolerance, for the regime was genuinely afraid of the Catholic rebellion which excessive zeal might provoke. The result was an unaccustomed period of relative religious peace. Only gradually did it become clear that this Reformation, unlike the three that had preceded it, was probably here to stay. Elizabeth had cautiously but successfully led her subjects into a new world. It remained to be seen what they would make of it.

Notes

1 Paul L. Hughes and James F. Larkin (eds), *Tudor Royal Proclamations 1553–1587* (1969), p. 6.

2 Ronald Hutton, 'The local impact of the Tudor Reformations' in Christopher Haigh (ed.), *The English Reformation Revised* (1987), p. 129.

3 Eamon Duffy, 'Cardinal Pole preaching' in Eamon Duffy and David Loades (eds), *The Reign of Mary Tudor* (2006).

4 Louise Campbell, 'A diagnosis of religious moderation' in Luc Racaut and Alec Ryrie (eds), *Moderate Voices in the European Reformation* (2005), p. 40.

5 John Aylmer, *An harborowe for faithfull and trewe subiectes* (1559), sigs L4v, P2r, P4v.

6 National Archives, SP 70/4/283: I owe this reference to David Gehring.

7 Katherine Parr, *The lamentacion of a sinner* (1547), sig. D2v.

8 National Archives, SP 12/36 fo. 77r.

9 Gerald Bray (ed.), *Documents of the English Reformation* (1994), p. 332.

CHAPTER 8

Reformation on the Battlefield: Scotland, 1542–73

Like the English Reformation, the Scottish Reformation was a political event. In England, however, the fixed point of religious change was always the crown's authority. In Scotland, the Reformation happened despite of and in opposition to that authority. The result was that Church and state in Scotland were at odds with one another for a century and a half, and that Scottish Protestantism came to nourish a myth of pristine, apolitical purity. Yet the Scottish Reformation was as deeply political as its English counterpart, with which it was so closely entwined. And while it began as a movement of opposition to the state, it eventually led to the Scottish crown asserting its authority more effectively than ever before.

Regency, 1542–58

The crisis of 1543

The drama of the Scottish Reformation proper begins with the sudden death of James V in December 1542, shortly after the battle of Solway Moss (see above, pp. 108–9). James's heir was an infant, which was scarcely a problem for the Scots – long royal minorities had become unpleasantly routine. She was also a girl, which in itself was not a problem either: everyone agreed that this week-old baby was the rightful queen of Scots. What made Queen Mary's accession awkward was its timing. Scotland was at war, and the fiasco of Solway Moss had left large numbers of senior Scottish nobles in English hands. Others, notably James V's enemies the Douglases, were already in English exile.

A reigning queen – even an infant – presented a tempting opportunity to anyone with an interest in Scotland. If she lived long enough to marry, her husband would expect to become king of Scots, and to pass the kingdom on to their children. All over Europe, principalities were being swallowed up in this way. The long-independent duchy of Brittany had recently been absorbed into the French state through just such a dynastic union. The Habsburgs' expert playing of the marriage game had created a cat's-cradle of an empire comprising Spain, the Netherlands, Austria, parts of Italy and a good deal else. Scotland was now ripe for the plucking. Everyone was interested, but the English had a head start, thanks to geo-graphical proximity, a moment of military superiority, and the availability of a plausible future husband (Prince Edward, then aged five).

It briefly seemed that both countries would agree to a marriage. After two weeks of political confusion, the regency of Scotland was settled on James Hamilton, the earl of Arran: son of the earl who had briefly held power in the 1520s, and now next in line to the throne. Arran swiftly set about trying to secure a marriage treaty with England. This may seem a strange policy, given the Scots' well-established antipathy to the English, but he was not alone in favouring it. A royal marriage offered the prospect of an honourable, long-term peace between the two realms. Moreover, the accession of a reigning queen so close in age to the Prince of Wales looked to some like divine providence. A marriage might also have had advant-ages for Arran. He hoped that with an absentee queen, he and his family might become viceroys. It made more immediate political sense too. Scots captives and exiles were returning from England, all of them pledged to work for the marriage. More particularly, Cardinal Beaton, the archbishop of St Andrews, was adamantly opposed to the plan. Beaton was also Arran's main political rival.

Above all, negotiating with England was a way of playing for time, time in which to wriggle out of a very uncomfortable military position. To this extent at least, Arran's policy worked. The negotiations for the marriage took half a year, being made more difficult by Henry VIII's insistence on terms which were little short of conquest. Eventually, grudgingly, Henry withdrew some of his more outrageous demands, and the treaty of Greenwich was duly signed. However, Arran had overplayed his hand. Mounting opposition to the treaty – led by Beaton and by another possible claimant to the Scottish throne, the earl of Lennox – forced Arran into a swift and total reversal of policy at the beginning of September 1543. Henry VIII was furious, but it was now too late to return to war that year, and his planned invasion of France was pushing Scotland down his list of priorities. But Arran was humiliated, too. He survived in office, but for the time being he did so on Beaton's sufferance. Scotland was set back on its familiar, anti-English course.

Politically, 1543 was a passing moment, but it had a lasting religious impact. During the first months of the year, Arran gave active encouragement to evangelicals in Scotland. From the beginning of his regency, he let it be known that he was 'a great favourer of the Scripture' – a Protestant sympathiser.[1] He briefly imprisoned Cardinal Beaton. He sponsored two evangelical friars to preach in Edinburgh, and encouraged other burghs to do likewise. He persuaded a parliament to relax some of the anti-heresy laws and – most significantly of all – to legalise the English Bible. In the midst of his other negotiations with the English, he ensured that large quantities of English Bibles were in fact shipped north.

This policy was not driven by religious conviction. Throughout his long career, Arran showed a very politic flexibility on religious matters (and, indeed, on almost everything else). Rather, this was political theatre performed for an English audience. Henry VIII had been badgering the Scots to imitate his Reformation for nearly a decade, and for a new governor of Scotland who needed to keep the English sweet, it made sense to oblige. Arran shamelessly played up his agreement with and interest in Henry VIII's settlement, and made English ambassadors sit through stage-managed sermons. The problem was that Scottish evangelicals would not stick to the part which Arran had scripted for them. As England would discover in 1547, the death of an adult king and the sudden lifting of religious repression can produce an explosion of unauthorised religious activity. By the summer of 1543 Arran was becoming alarmed by what he had unleashed. In June a decree was issued 'for remedy of scandalous bills, writings, ballads and books that are daily made, written and printed', in particular those attacking the Mass.[2] Heretical books were suddenly everywhere. Whole towns were said to be turning to the new doctrines. There was also a spate of anticlerical violence, some of which looked like iconoclastic zeal. In early September 1543, when it became apparent that Arran was going to abandon both his pro-English and his pro-evangelical policies, east coast towns from Aberdeen to Edinburgh were swept by riots. In Dundee, which was worst hit, the burgh's two friaries were destroyed.

1543 became a lost moment of hope for Scottish evangelicals, when they came up for air and conceived ambitions which they could not then fulfil. The evangelical party which remained at the year's end had acquired some important new converts, and some bitter political experience. As the English ambassador to Scotland observed, the country was now divided between a smaller, Protestant and pro-English party, and a larger, Catholic and pro-French party. Those two parties and their backers would spend the rest of the decade at one another's throats.

The 'Rough Wooing'

Outmanoeuvred and outraged by Arran's diplomatic and religious two-step, Henry VIII resolved to renew his interrupted Scottish war. This much was inevitable (the Scots had no illusions on that score). But there were two different Scottish wars now available to Henry VIII. He could simply have resumed the war of 1542, a relatively low-key affair whose purpose was simply to bloody the Scots enough to keep the Border quiet. This would have made some sense, for England's main military ambitions now lay elsewhere. In 1544, a joint Anglo-Habsburg attack on France was envisaged, and Henry did not want the Scots to spoil his long-anticipated party.

However, an alternative, subtler, more ambitious policy was being touted by several of Henry VIII's self-proclaimed friends in Scotland: notably the Douglases, now returned from their long English exile. The idea was to stir the two factions which had emerged from 1543 into full-scale civil war, and to support the Protestant faction. This would have been a many-stranded policy: the provision of weapons and money for pro-English Scots, the garrisoning of some Border and coastal towns by English troops to provide refuges and bases of operations, bribery and coercion of uncommitted or wavering Scots, and a flood of propaganda to promote both the Protestant and the pro-English cause. In other words, a classically Tudor mix of soft and hard power. The aim: to secure a new and more lasting marriage treaty and bind the two realms into a permanent union. It was an ambitious plan, but not a foolish one. Henry's ablest general, Edward Seymour, the earl of Hertford, strongly supported it. A judicious mixture of persuasion and coercion could well have persuaded the weight of Scottish opinion to accept an honourable, godly alliance with England.

Henry VIII chose neither of these two options. Instead, he attempted a mixture. He wanted the marriage, but would not pursue it with the subtlety or patience necessary. The attack on Scotland which he ordered for the spring of 1544 was primarily a punitive raid, aimed at keeping the Scots out of the French war, and in this it succeeded. But this army was ordered to proclaim that this attack was a punishment for the Scots' faithlessness in breaking the marriage treaty. Seymour, commanding the army, planned to spare pro-English lords from attack, to accept those lords' offers of loyalty to Henry, and to leave garrisons behind him in order to protect such loyalists. Yet Henry explicitly forbade him from doing any such thing, ordering him instead to 'put all to fire and sword, burn Edinburgh . . . and as many towns and villages about Edinburgh as you may . . . putting man, woman, and child to fire and sword without exception, where any resistance shall be made.'[3] Such genocidal fantasies were, fortunately, impractical, but Seymour did his best, launching an ambitious amphibious attack on Edinburgh, burning much of the city. His forces then marched back to England overland, destroying everything they could.

This brutal raid effectively put paid to the Douglases' subtle strategy. England's long reputation for high-handed violence in Scotland was powerfully reinforced, and the pro-English party discredited. Yet although Henry VIII was not willing to pursue the marriage alliance intelligently, he still continued to demand it on the grounds that he was Scotland's natural overlord. Predictably, this failed miserably. The war began to go sour for England. A Scottish victory in a minor battle at Ancrum Moor in February 1545 rallied the Scots' morale, and another major English raid that autumn achieved nothing more than destroying crops and alienating those of the local population who survived. Worse, the French war was going sour for England too. The city of Boulogne fell to a massive English assault in September 1544, but its defences were all but destroyed in the process and the English were hard put to hold it. The French were now besieging English forces in Boulogne, and also sending some troops to aid their old Scottish allies. When – to England's relief – the treaty of Ardres was concluded with France in 1546, Henry's Scottish ambitions were quietly abandoned.

And there matters might have lain, had Edward Seymour not become Lord Protector of England on Henry VIII's death in 1547. Seymour had always been far more committed to wooing the Scots into an alliance than his old master, and he now reopened the Scottish front with vigour. For the first time, a substantial propaganda effort was attempted. Seymour himself wrote an *Epistle or Exhortation to Unity and Peace*, and tried to have it circulated in Scotland: one of a series of pamphlets (many of them by Scots) which spoke not of an English conquest of Scotland but of a free union between two equal countries to form a new entity called Great Britain. As we have seen (see above, p. 69), it was an idea which had its attraction in Scotland. The novel twist was Seymour and his allies' insistence that the glue binding this new country together would be Protestantism. The hope was that Scottish humanists and Protestants would throw in their lot with the pragmatists who argued that an honourable union was better than a devastating war.

And indeed, when Seymour led an army north in the autumn of 1547, he tried to have it conduct itself differently. When it seized provisions from the local population, he at least apologised. He tried to differentiate between friendly and hostile lords. But it was too late. The patterns of the war were already set. The English forces and their commanders were not trying to support one side in a Scottish civil war, but were engaged in their traditional activity of invading and devastating Scotland. Nor were the Scots now willing to be pushed into an English-sponsored civil war. Arran pulled together the largest army ever assembled by the independent Scottish kingdom to face the invasion. His 26,000 men faced off against Seymour's 16,000 at Pinkie, seven miles east of Edinburgh, on 10 September 1547. The Scots' numerical advantage, however, was outweighed by English artillery, particularly the heavy ship-board guns that could fire a considerable distance inland. The battle was a bloody rout: some 5000 Scots were killed, and another 1500 taken prisoner. The choicest captive was the earl of Huntly, one of Scotland's most powerful nobles. Taunted by his captors on the battlefield as to what he now thought of the marriage alliance, he is said to have replied that he would accept the marriage, 'but I like not this wooing'.[4]

After this victory, Seymour established a string of garrisons deep inside Scotland, as far north as Dundee. Large parts of southern and eastern Scotland were now effectively under English control. Yet England's high hopes quickly seeped away. Militarily, Scotland was a tough nut to crack. Its dispersed population and decentralised politics meant that converting battlefield victories into lasting conquest was tricky. It also boasted some of the most formidable fortified strongholds in Europe: even after Pinkie, Seymour knew better than to attempt a direct assault on Edinburgh Castle. Winning round large numbers of Scots proved impossible. Scottish Anglophobia ran too deep, and the brutal behaviour of the English armies belied Seymour's soft words. Instead, the Scots turned to their old allies, France. The new French king, Henry II, was willing to invest heavily in Scotland. Renewed French help arrived in June 1548. The following month, a treaty pledged the queen of Scots not to the English king but to the French dauphin. To seal this promise, the five-year-old queen was actually shipped off to France. England's main war aim now looked unattainable, and its armies were forced onto the defensive. The garrisons Seymour had erected fell one by one to the French during a bitterly fought war in 1548–49. When a peace was finally agreed in 1550, it was an unmitigated, humiliating defeat for England.

For the Scots, the reckoning was more complex. For Scottish evangelicals, the 'Rough Wooings' were a missed opportunity, as their hoped-for English allies turned out merely to be incompetent butchers. Yet the Scots reformers made the best of what opportunity they had. Some retreated to England, especially after 1547, when Seymour welcomed them (for a time). And in Scotland itself, the chaos of the wars gave them a good deal of room for manoeuvre. The evangelical George Wishart spent much of 1544 and 1545 on an extended preaching tour across a wide swathe of the country, supported by sympathetic magnates. And the evangelical cause was assisted more directly by the damage of the war itself. English forces, correctly seeing the Scottish clergy as steadfastly anti-English, deliberately targeted them, and church buildings, throughout the conflict. Seymour's regime could not pursue iconoclasm in Scotland as systematically as it did in England, but in both countries it inflicted lasting damage.

Evangelical activism and English-sponsored violence combined in the most bizarre episode of the wars. During 1544–46, although Arran nominally remained governor of Scotland, it was Cardinal Beaton who actually dominated the Scottish regime, and the English backed several attempts to assassinate him. In 1546 one such attempt succeeded – without English help, as it happened, although the assassins certainly assumed that Henry VIII would reward them. They were a gaggle of lairds – some with personal grievances against the cardinal, some of them earnest evangelicals wishing to avenge George Wishart (who had been captured and burned on Beaton's orders earlier the same year). Having murdered the cardinal, they then succeeded in barricading themselves into his castle in St Andrews. They held it against all comers for nearly a year. The earl of Arran did not grieve for Beaton; and he was restrained from assaulting the castle because his eldest son, whom Beaton had been keeping as a hostage, was now in the assassins' hands. For a while in early 1547, a weird truce held, during which time several Protestant preachers (including the young John Knox) were able to operate openly from the castle, spreading the word to the surrounding towns. But this surreal peace could not hold. The English gave the 'castilians' warm words but scant help. In July, a small French fleet arrived, and an artillery bombardment forced the 'castilians' to surrender within hours. Their lives were spared, but they were taken captive – the commoners, including Knox, being used as galley slaves.

So at St Andrews, as elsewhere, Scottish reformers' hopes were defeated by English ineptitude and French military might. But the defeat was not total. Beaton's death in itself was a serious blow to the Scottish Church, and those few months of freedom, during which Knox and others had preached openly, had left their mark. By the end of the war in 1550, Scotland had a new religious landscape which was not quite congruent with its new politics.

French Scotland, 1550–59

The price of Scottish victory in the Rough Wooings was that the 'auld alliance' with France was not only renewed but reinvented. The Scots queen was as tempting to the French as to the English. The treaty of Haddington in 1548 pledged her in marriage to the French dauphin, Francis, and placed her in French custody until she was of age (exactly the kind of arrangement England had been trying to secure). The earl of Arran, who had briefly managed to reassert his authority after Beaton's murder, now had to accept that he was a junior partner in governing what was effectively a French province. He remained as governor for the time being, and was given a splendid French title (duke of Châtelherault) and accompanying lands, but real authority was slipping out of his hands. In his place was the new French ambassador, Henri Cleutin, the seigneur d'Oisel; and, above all, the young queen's mother, James V's widow, Mary of Guise.

Guise was the linchpin of the renewed alliance. Her status as queen mother carried some weight, and she had proved herself a clear-sighted and level-headed politician during the 1540s. Above all, she was a French princess. In 1550, she travelled to France with some of Scotland's leading nobles for an extended conference to sketch out Franco-Scotland's political future. Guise herself evidently wanted to stay in France, with her daughter and in her home country. King Henry II, however, recognised that she was a unique asset. In 1551 she was sent back to be (in effect) his viceroy in Scotland. This was formalised in 1554, when the minority of the twelve-year-old Queen Mary was formally ended. Now she was not a child queen, but an absentee, and her government was conducted not by a governor but by a regent: Mary of Guise.

Guise's political aims were clear, simple and broadly shared by most Scots. She wished to see the Franco-Scottish alliance cemented into a permanent dynastic union, a union which would (in due course) see her grandchildren ruling over a united Franco-Scottish realm. Her triumph came in 1558, when (after some alarming wobbles from the French side) the long-planned marriage between Mary and dauphin Francis finally went ahead, and when a Scottish parliament granted Francis the crown matrimonial. This made him king of Scots, a title which – in principle – he would

have been able to retain even if his wife had predeceased him. The arrangement was not universally popular in Scotland. The presence of a small
French standing army in Scotland caused some friction. The disdainful or
patronising attitude of some Frenchmen towards their small but proud ally
occasionally grated. So did Guise's attempts to introduce a taste of French
governance, especially when her subjects feared she was trying to raise
taxes. An exasperated Guise commented: 'They will not endure it, and say
that these are laws of the French, and that their old laws are good.'[5] Some
of the nobility resented being edged out of power in favour of Frenchmen.
Most seriously, the Scots elite disliked being drawn into wars purely for
French advantage. In 1557, a planned invasion of England was stymied
when Châtelherault and others refused to cross the Border. Flodden had
dulled the Scots' appetite for such adventures, as the duke of Albany had
discovered in 1522–23. Guise – humiliated and frightened by this mutiny –
was furious. The road to Franco-Scottish union was not without its pitfalls. But these were all second-order gripes and disagreements. Few Scots
questioned the basic policy.

It was through this dynastic lens that Guise viewed Scotland's religious
conflicts. Her priority was to unite the Scots behind the French alliance,
regardless of their religious views. There was no resumption of the persecution of the 1530s. Only two Protestants were burned during Guise's
ascendancy, in 1550 and 1558, and she was not involved in either execution. Instead, the Protestant nobility were brought into the regime. When
she became regent in 1554, she sacked the royal treasurer – Archbishop
Hamilton of St Andrews – and replaced him with the earl of Cassilis, a
stout Protestant. She turned a blind eye to those nobles and lairds who
kept Protestant preachers in their own households. Even some of those
who had been captured at St Andrews in 1547 were politically rehabilitated. Unlike some of her French relations, Mary of Guise seems genuinely
to have had limited interest in religious differences as such. Admirably
pragmatic, perhaps, but this was also a fatal blind spot. It was religious
politics which would be her undoing.

For Guise's inclusive policy was not Scotland's only religious policy.
After Cardinal Beaton's murder, Governor Arran had nominated his own
illegitimate half-brother, John Hamilton, as the new archbishop of St
Andrews. The nomination smelt fishy, but Hamilton turned out to be a
formidable prelate (if not a model of holiness). He immediately embarked
on a programme of internal reform, quite different from Cardinal Beaton's
anti-heretical trench warfare. Two general provincial councils of the Scottish Church, in 1549 and 1552, decreed a series of disciplinary measures.

The clergy's behaviour, morals, education, dress, income and even the fact that some of them were wearing beards came under scrutiny. It was the most serious and constructive attempt for over a century to respond to anticlerical worries. Implementing such reforms was trickier than decreeing them, but some real steps were taken here too, not least in the establishment of an impressive new college at St Andrews for training clergy.

More controversially, Hamilton showed some doctrinal flexibility too. The 1552 provincial council licensed a new, vernacular catechism for use in all Scottish parishes. Like the English formularies and homilies of the 1540s and 1550s, this was an attempt to bypass clerical incompetence and transmit true religion directly to the people. The catechism is plainly Catholic, but it is Catholicism of a particular kind. The papacy is hardly mentioned. Instead, it is laden with the language of conciliarism (see above, p. 40). The discussion of issues such as the sacraments and justification remained Catholic but drew heavily on evangelical phrases and ideas, and downplayed many of the doctrines which Protestants found most offensive. The limited evidence we have of other books published and sermons preached in 1550s Scotland suggest that this conciliatory tone was widespread. Hamilton and his allies were even ready to pick public fights with more conservative churchmen in order to demonstrate their reasonableness: in 1552, he won a set-piece confrontation over the use of the Lord's Prayer, which he insisted should be addressed to God alone, not to the saints.

In other words, from 1549 the Scottish Church wore a new face: humble, self-critical, and – on both disciplinary and doctrinal matters – open to change. There were obvious reasons for this change of tone. Large numbers of Scots, especially in the landed and educated classes, had become alienated from the Church by the 1540s. A more reasonable approach might help win them back. Other territories across Europe were attempting similar experiments in religious compromise in the 1540s and 1550s, and Hamilton drew heavily on their experience – in particular, on the work of Hermann von Wied, a reforming archbishop of Cologne.

Hamilton also recognised that, if this policy were to succeed, it was vital to provide clear boundaries to the new doctrinal freedom which he was opening up. Sweet reason needed to be balanced by prosecution of those heretics who remained unpersuadable. The problem was that Guise would not permit it. Any resumption of persecution went against Guise's own, rather different policy of conciliation. Moreover, Guise was inherently suspicious of the Hamiltons as a group, for it was they who stood to inherit the crown if Queen Mary should die childless. When, in 1556, she did recommend to the pope that several senior clergy be placed in charge of reforming the Church, she pointedly omitted Archbishop Hamilton and his allies from the list.

The Scottish Church was left looking introspective, self-doubting and defenceless. That, combined with Guise's policy of tolerance, provided a crucial breathing space for Scotland's Protestants. Long-standing Protestant legend has it that a network of formal underground congregations – 'privy kirks' – were formed during the 1550s, but there is in fact almost no evidence for this. What did happen is that sympathetic noble and lairdly households became the focus for informal gatherings of evangelicals, who assembled to read the (still legal) English Bible, to pray, and to hear the Word preached. Some nobles kept evangelical household chaplains; there were also travelling preachers.

One of these was John Knox. Knox returned to Scotland in 1555 after a series of adventures. He spent two years as a French galley slave and four as a preacher in Edwardian England, before winding up on the losing end of a nasty dispute among Protestant exiles in Frankfurt (see above, pp. 170, 191–2). Now he returned reluctantly to his homeland, and spent a year criss-crossing the country, attempting (with limited success) to convert his fellow Scots to a stark, Calvinist version of Reformed Protestantism. In reality, the Scottish evangelical world was far more diverse than this. Only a few were willing radically to separate themselves from the old Church as Knox wished, and some of those embraced more egalitarian or informal structures than Knox liked. The principal significance of the visit is that it happened at all. Knox was able to spend a year travelling in Scotland reasonably openly, and he won a hearing from a wide range of lairds and nobles. In 1556, when his arrest was mooted, Guise arranged for him to be warned. He escaped abroad, and the ecclesiastical authorities were reduced to burning him in effigy. The Protestants were growing bolder. They had every reason to believe that neither the queen regent nor Hamilton's Church had the stomach to oppose them.

The Scottish Revolution, 1558–61

An unexpected war

In 1558–60 this religious–political situation suddenly blew up into a crisis which became the defining moment of modern Scottish history.

It began with Protestant boldness. In December 1557 five Protestant nobles signed a band for mutual protection, the document later known as the 'First Band of the Lords of the Congregation'. In fact, such bands were common enough in Scottish politics, although this pointedly omitted the normal clause insisting that the signatories would not act against royal authority. The signatories then sent Guise a set of ambitious but not impossible requests. They asked to be allowed to host Protestant sermons on their estates (which they and many others were already doing); and they also wanted prayers in the vernacular to be used in parish churches. That last request went beyond anything which Hamilton's reform programme had suggested, but not miles beyond it. When Guise had a group of reformers from Dundee rounded up the following summer, they presented her with a similar set of demands. She gave the petitioners what they felt was a fair hearing, and promised to lay the question before the parliament due to meet that winter. Religious compromise was in the air. Effectively, in return for minimal conformity to a stripped-down national Church, Protestant lairds would be allowed to host worship on their own lands. There was a possibility that Scotland would become a religious patchwork, with estate-by-estate Reformations. Similar piecemeal, aristocratic Reformations were soon to emerge in much of central and eastern Europe.

The compromise stayed tantalisingly out of reach. When the promised parliament duly met, it gave Dauphin Francis the crown matrimonial: this was Guise's great triumph, and gave her a freer hand to deal with domestic opponents. Moreover, the accession of Elizabeth to the English throne that November threatened to revive the Scottish Protestants' alliance with England. In April 1559, the international situation changed, with a firm peace at last concluded to the long war between France and the Habsburgs. Henry II of France had made peace in part because he was alarmed by the growth of Protestantism in his own realms, and he ordered Guise to clamp down on religious dissidence. At the same time, Protestant hardliners were determinedly trying to thwart any compromise. A small iconoclastic riot in Edinburgh in September 1558 had polarised opinion; so too had an anonymously circulated bill demanding that all Scotland's friars hand their property over to the poor. Protestant preachers like John Willock insisted that no compromise with popery was possible. The old Church seemed to agree. Another general provincial council met in March 1559, and while it reaffirmed Hamilton's existing reform programme, it rejected Guise's suggestion that it permit the vernacular in worship. She had no room left to forge a compromise, and in April 1559 she summoned Willock and four other preachers as heretics.

A settlement still seemed possible. The Protestant lairds regarded the summons as an invitation to negotiate, and planned to escort the preachers to Guise. The preachers had other ideas. They had recently been joined, again, by Knox: forbidden by Elizabeth from returning to England, he had reluctantly come back to Scotland instead. Now, on 11 May, he preached an inflammatory sermon at Perth which triggered a full-scale iconoclastic riot. Guise, inevitably, regarded this as an act of rebellion, especially since some royal tombs were damaged. The Protestant lairds, now styling themselves 'the Congregation', mobilised to defend themselves. More or less by accident, a religious rebellion had broken out.

Guise, who had handled secular Scottish politics so adroitly, was suddenly badly out of her depth. The rebellious lairds posed a limited threat. They were few in number, and while some could field creditable forces, these were feudal levies who could not be kept in the field for longer than a few weeks. Yet Guise's mishandling of the situation over the summer and autumn of 1559 eventually united most of the political nation against her. When she made a truce by which Perth would be returned to her control, and then violated its terms, she lost the support of the remaining Protestant lords. Soon the Congregation had occupied Edinburgh, a splendid but unsustainable victory. Another truce followed, and again Guise was seen to have violated it, for she began bringing in large numbers of French troops and constructing a formidable fortified base at the port of Leith, near Edinburgh. The Congregation were able to persuade large numbers of Scots that this was a prelude to French conquest and tyranny, and so to broaden their movement from a religious revolt to a war of patriotic self-defence.

Guise nevertheless seemed well placed to win such a war. When the Congregation remobilised and again occupied Edinburgh in October 1559, they were in belligerent mood. They declared Guise deposed as queen regent, and prepared to assault Leith. But their makeshift forces were quite incapable of tackling the heavily armed French. The few skirmishes were dreadfully uneven and the Congregation quickly abandoned Edinburgh again, this time in a near-rout. Viciously punitive French raids on the Protestant heartlands in Fife and Ayrshire followed through the winter of 1559–60. The rebels' cause seemed lost.

Outside events saved them. First, France was losing its ability to fight a war in Scotland. Henry II had been killed in a grisly jousting accident in July 1559. This left Francis and Mary as king and queen of France as well as of Scots, and left Mary of Guise's brothers, the duke and cardinal of Guise, effectively in power. But the sudden removal of Henry II's strong hand led – as had previously happened in Scotland in 1543, and in England in 1547 – to an explosion of religious dissidence. The dramatic growth of Protestantism in France frightened the new regime there. In March 1560, a Protestant plot to seize the young king himself at Amboise was uncovered. The Guise brothers, fighting off such threats, could not offer their sister in Scotland the reinforcements she needed. Most of the few they did send were shipwrecked en route.

Meanwhile, the new English regime was inching its way towards intervention in Scotland. The Congregation had been begging the English for assistance since the very beginning of the revolt, and Elizabeth I's chief minister William Cecil was keen to help; but the queen herself, always both cautious and parsimonious, was very reluctant. Only in January 1560 did substantial help arrive: a naval blockade of Leith, followed by an army in April. It was not a huge force, but Elizabeth avoided the mistakes which had defined her father's and brother's disastrous Scottish wars. She and her commanders on the ground went out of their way to treat their Scots allies with deference and courtesy, and made clear their wish to withdraw as quickly as possible. That, and the brutality of the French army, was enough to win over most Scots. Guise's forces were quickly bottled up in Leith, where they were besieged from April to July 1560. Although they were able to repel assaults, their hopes of resupply or reinforcement were melting away. Worse, Guise herself was gravely ill with dropsy, and died on 11 June. France sent not an army but ambassadors to negotiate a surrender.

An unexpected peace

The treaty of Edinburgh which followed was a defining event in sixteenth-century Britain. In it, Francis and Mary were made to renounce their claim to the English throne, and (in vague terms) to recognise Scotland's religious liberties. Scotland's governance was committed to a council of Scots nobles, which would plainly be dominated by the Congregation. Above all, this meant three young Protestant noblemen. Lord James Stewart was an illegitimate son of James V, and a pugnacious and effective politician who would be a pivotal figure in Scottish politics for the next ten years. Archibald Campbell, earl of Argyll, could field the largest private army in the British Isles and was passionately committed to the cause, although his raw power was not matched by his political skills. And the duke of Châtelherault's son (who bore the courtesy title of earl of Arran) was second in line to the Scots throne, after his father, and was a fervent

Protestant. All three were profoundly committed to the English alliance. England, for so long the auld enemy, was now Scotland's partner in a Protestant amity which would endure in various forms down to the present. Scots – and, to a lesser extent, the English – began once again to talk of 'Britain': a humanist and evangelical ideal, but now, as never before, grounded in political reality. It was a new world.

The defining feature of this new world was religion. Throughout the 1559–60 war, the Congregation had been fighting for religious liberty, and at the end of the war it seemed likely that that was exactly what they would get: the freedom to practise their religion alongside Catholicism. Their king and queen, after all, were still Catholics, and no one was talking about deposition. The treaty of Edinburgh insisted that Church property looted during the war be restored, and reserved the question of a religious settlement to Francis and Mary.

But this was not how it turned out. In August 1560, a parliament met to select the new governing council. But this 'Reformation parliament' was a distinctly irregular assembly. Citing a threadbare fifteenth-century precedent, it was flooded with Protestant lairds – 106 of them turned up to participate, despite their having only attended Parliament in ones and twos (if at all) since the 1480s. This was a revolutionary assembly in constitutional dress, and its actions make it the hinge on which modern Scottish history turns. In defiance of the treaty, the parliament decided to commission a Confession of Faith from the Protestant ministers. The dominant voice among those ministers was now that long-established troublemaker, John Knox.

Knox had no interest in religious coexistence. His model was the pure Reformed Church in Geneva, a Church established in law which compelled obedience from the entire population. The Confession of Faith was the first step. It was a rousing statement of Reformed theology, flung together with indecent haste. Stripped of a few of the more politically pointed comments which Knox wished to make, it was put to a vote in Parliament on 17 August 1560.

To everyone's surprise, the Confession swept through unopposed, on a wave of revivalist emotion. Lairds and nobles competed to pledge their blood in its defence and lamented their former sins. Of nearly 200 present on 17 August, only nine registered any dissent, mostly by abstaining rather than daring actually to vote against it. The bishops were paralysed. Archbishop Hamilton abstained, claiming feebly that he had not had time to read the document. The Congregation were discovering how complete their victory was, for the fight had gone out of Scottish Catholicism. A decade of public self-questioning and a year's association with French tyranny had profoundly discredited the old Church, especially compared to the fierce certainties Knox preached. After the Confession was passed, the parliament swiftly finished the job with two short Acts prohibiting Scots from recognising the pope's authority, and banning Mass from being celebrated in Scotland. This was Protestant triumphalism, not compromise.

Yet the revolution was incomplete. Proclaiming a new theology was not enough. During the spring and summer of 1560, the preachers had also drawn up a 'Book of Discipline': a structural blueprint for a new, national, Reformed Church. In place of priests and bishops, there would be readers, ministers and superintendents. The old Church's property would pass to its reformed successor. And – critically – this new Church would be responsible for policing the morals of the entire nation through 'kirk sessions', courts of moral discipline in every parish. Such kirk sessions had already been created in key towns during the 1559–60 war: most notably in St Andrews, where there was a functioning kirk session from October 1559, disciplining adulterers as well as overseeing the formal penances of Catholic clergy. Thirty-eight priests publicly proclaimed their conformity to the new religion at St Andrews in early 1560. If the Confession was the Scottish Reformation's spirit, the Book of Discipline was its backbone.

Hence the bitterness of Knox and his allies when, over the winter of 1560–61, the Book of Discipline was gutted by another, more conventional parliament. While content to allow kirk sessions to flourish (which they did – see below, pp. 256–60), the leading lairds and nobles balked at the ministers' financial ambitions. The wealth of the Scottish Church was already largely under their control, and the Book of Discipline would have had them relinquish this. They refused, insisting that the financial structures of the old Church remain in place while the new one found its own funding. The fact that some of these same nobles were themselves very generous in providing such funds hardly eased the blow.

So in 1560, Scotland, like England, had an unfinished Reformation, but unfinished along very different lines. The Reformed Church itself was as pristine in its doctrine and practices as Knox could have wished, although not yet as severe in its structures as some later precisians would require. Yet it survived on a shoestring, eking out an existence in the burghs and a few rural areas, but ill-equipped to spread across the whole country. It was desperately short of ministers, having taken the brave decision that only men of approved learning and doctrine could act in that role. In most parishes, if there was any service at all, it was led by a 'reader', licensed to do no more than read the Bible and the new, skeletal liturgy (adapted from that of the Anglo-Scottish Church in Geneva). The Book of Discipline proposed that ten superintendents be appointed, to take responsibility for planting new churches across the country; but what was expected of these men was superhuman, and only five of the posts were ever filled. Alongside this vigorous but struggling Church was the still-walking corpse of Scottish Catholicism. Its clergy were banned from celebrating Mass, and were in theory excluded from their parish churches (although such rules were easier to proclaim than to enforce). Yet they retained their titles, their vicarages and other lands, and their tithe incomes. Monastic houses were broken up as communities but continued to function as propertied corporations. The bishops remained in office, including Archbishop Hamilton himself. Indeed, three of them now came out as Protestant converts, and effectively did the job of superintendents in their dioceses.

This frustrating and confusing situation, in which two structures jostled with one another, was to persist in various forms for over a century. In the winter of 1560–61, however, Scottish Protestantism also faced a more immediate problem. On 5 December 1560, Francis – king of France and of Scots – died of an ear infection. Since he and Mary were childless, the union between Scotland and France was dissolved, to the relief of both English and Scottish Protestants. Yet Queen Mary was now a free agent again. During the spring of 1561, it became clear that she was not going to remarry quickly. The Catholic, French-raised, eighteen-year-old widow would have to return to the newly Protestant and pro-English land where she had been born and of which she was still queen.

A tragedy of errors: Mary and the Scots, 1561–73

Playing the queen, 1561–67

The situation Mary faced on her return from France in 1561 called for consummate political skill. Ruling Scotland had never been easy; the Scottish crown had moral authority but little financial or military muscle. To inherit what was (in effect) a foreign land, run by a clique who had defeated her adopted home country and her mother in war; to do so while adhering to a religion whose practice was now illegal; and all against the backdrop of worries about the rule of female monarchs – this was formidable. It is a credit both to Mary and to Scotland that it worked as well as it did.

Three factors weighed in Mary's favour. First, the profound loyalty of most Scots to the crown and to the Stewart dynasty. Neither of the Protestant noblemen who might conceivably have attempted to seize the throne (Lord James Stewart and the duke of Châtelherault) ever made any open moves to do so. Either their own loyalism or, more likely, that of their peers made any such scheme impossible. In 1561, Scotland had been without a reigning monarch for nineteen years, and was hungry for one. The deep belief in good lordship meant that, like any monarch, Mary started with a fund of political and popular goodwill. The second factor favouring her reinforced this. Although her political judgement was very uneven, she excelled in one key area: the theatre of monarchy. Like her great-uncle Henry VIII, she was physically imposing, knew it and used the fact: a six-foot redhead whom contemporaries found beautiful and who could charm crowds as well as individuals. Here, at least, the French court had given her good training. She could use set-pieces such as royal progresses and entries to good effect. It was an important skill. It is testimony to her reputation that Elizabeth I never dared meet her. The English queen supposedly feared both that the comparison would not flatter her, and that she would be unable to resist her Scottish cousin's charms.

Finally, Mary began her rule in Scotland with one excellent decision, a decision which provided the political credit which she was to live off for four years and more: to accept her half-brother, Lord James Stewart, as her principal adviser. There were siren voices in 1561 urging Mary to lead a Catholic counter-revolution, landing in conservative Aberdeenshire and mustering an army. Mary sensibly declined. Too close a dependence on Lord James might have seemed dangerous, but Mary correctly calculated (or luckily guessed) that she would be able to remain her own woman. The arrangement was that Mary would rule as queen, in name and in fact. But she would not interfere with the new religious status quo, nor with the new political rapprochement with England. She would be allowed to remain a Catholic, and – despite the parliamentary Act of the previous summer – to have Mass celebrated for her in private, the only legal Mass in the kingdom. And she and her subjects would have the chance to get to know one another.

Both Mary and Lord James were as good as their word. Mary issued a proclamation stating that, while she would not ratify the Reformation parliament's religious Acts, she would not attempt to change the new religious status quo. And she was allowed her Mass; Lord James personally barred the door of her chapel to the outraged Protestants who were determined to prevent such idolatry. The issue provoked a nasty split between purist and pragmatic Protestants. The purists' self-appointed spokesman was Knox, now minister of Edinburgh, whose natural mode was as a prophet denouncing corruption. Over the next few years Knox came to see Lord James and the other Protestant pragmatists as traitors and backsliders. The queen's Mass was at the centre of his fury. It was more dangerous, he memorably preached, than ten thousand Catholic soldiers, because it would bring down God's wrath on the whole nation. This wild-eyed stuff was positively embarrassing for the secular Protestant elite. Mary had, through her reasonableness and the moderation of her demands, succeeded in breaking apart the Protestant coalition which could have been united against her.

And so, for four years, Mary's status as Catholic queen of a Protestant nation caused her very little trouble, as if her Catholicism were simply a personal foible. Rome and France were dismayed. She tolerated Protestantism; she included numerous Protestants in her council, and counted some of them as close friends. Lord James, in particular, she showered with favours, making him first earl of Mar and then earl of Moray. In 1562, she faced the first serious domestic crisis of her reign, pitting her against the earl of Huntly. Huntly was the most stalwart Catholic amongst the senior nobility, who a year earlier had offered to support her in arms. But his family, the Gordons, regarded the north-east of Scotland as their territory, and Mary (in typical Stewart fashion) wanted to bring them to heel. When she visited the north-east in the autumn of 1562, dispensing justice as she travelled, the Gordons either miscalculated, misunderstood the situation, or panicked. Mary was barred from the royal burgh of Inverness, interpreted this as rebellion, and quickly mustered an army. Huntly failed to mobilise any supporters and found himself facing a hopeless battle at Corrichie on 28 October 1562. He was taken prisoner after the rout, and – saving Mary considerable bother – promptly died in a fit of rage.

Huntly's fall was spectacular, but less of an achievement than it seemed. Mary could boast of a more solid achievement in Church affairs. The weird half-life of the Catholic Church and the desperate straits of the new Reformed Church created an opportunity for Mary, which advisers like William Maitland of Lethington helped her to exploit. By the 'thirds of benefices' scheme, erected in 1562, the crown 'assumed' one-third of the value of every benefice in the Church. This enormous tax was justified on the grounds that the queen would use the proceeds to fund the new Reformed Church. It was politically flawless. The Protestant nobility could hardly oppose it; it made the queen the new Church's paymaster and patron; and it also gave her a substantial and regular source of cash. Best

of all, it deepened the rift in the Protestant camp. Knox predictably denounced an arrangement by which 'two parts [of the benefices are] freely
given to the Devil, and the third must be divided between God and the
Devil.'[6] And the scheme's success was an invitation to extend it. The quiet
seizure of all Church property beckoned.

However, Mary's early success was more fragile than it seems, for it
was not what she herself counted as success. She was queen of Scots, and a
dowager queen of France, but she was also the great-granddaughter of
Henry VII and she cherished a hope to become queen of England. When
Mary Tudor had died in 1558, Francis and Mary had claimed the English
crown, on the grounds that Elizabeth was illegitimate and Mary was
next in line. The treaty of Edinburgh in 1560 had renounced that claim,
but – chiefly for that reason – Mary always refused actually to ratify the
treaty. She did not (at this point) expect to remove Elizabeth, but Elizabeth was childless and a decade older than Mary. Mary made it her prime
political objective to be accepted as heir to England. By pursuing a pro-
English policy – the policy which Moray, Maitland and her other Protestant advisers wanted for ideological reasons – she hoped eventually to be
rewarded by being recognised as Elizabeth's heir. Moreover, ruling in
Scotland gave her the perfect opportunity to demonstrate that she *could* be
a good queen to a Protestant realm. If Scottish Protestants were pleasantly
surprised by her rule in 1561–65, there was a reason for it. Mary was
trying to impress the neighbours, and was on her best behaviour.

It was, therefore, Elizabeth who brought this period of stability to an
end. Her steadfast refusal to recognise an heir was reinforced when she
made the insulting suggestion that Mary marry the recently ennobled earl
of Leicester, Robert Dudley, widely believed to have been Elizabeth's own
lover. Mary did not take that bait, realising that playing nice with Elizabeth was going nowhere. But instead of putting her southern ambitions
aside, she started to pursue them more directly.

In 1565 Mary was, at twenty-two, one of the most eligible widows in
Europe, and marriage was an obvious way to bolster her claim. Given her
overriding interest in her English claim, she made what might seem like a
shrewd choice. Another plausible alternative candidate for the English
throne was her cousin Henry Stuart, Lord Darnley, the son of Margaret
Douglas (see above, pp. 193–4) and grandson of Margaret Tudor. Although
his claim was ranked behind Mary's in strict order of primogeniture, he
was a man and had been born in England. He was three years her junior,
and was (if he was anything) a Catholic who was willing to conform to

Protestantism. A marriage to Darnley, uniting their two claims, was a formidable prospect. Elizabeth's open disapproval only made it more attractive. Darnley came to Scotland in January 1565. Mary spent much time with him, and persuaded herself that she was in love with him. They married at the end of July, without even waiting for a papal dispensation.

The Darnley marriage was an unmitigated disaster for Mary, for two quite distinct reasons. First, it immediately turned Scottish politics into a hornet's nest. Darnley's father was the earl of Lennox, long in exile, and long the rival of the duke of Châtelherault and of the Hamiltons. The marriage rehabilitated him, at the same time as it ousted the Anglophile Protestant establishment of Moray, Maitland and their allies. Lennox's new assertiveness and Moray's fears accelerated to the point where civil conflict seemed possible. In the event, the Anglophiles were isolated and unwilling to confront the queen, and Moray fled to England without a fight. The brief, sham rebellion of the autumn of 1565 – the 'Chaseabout Raid' – gave Mary an illusion of victory, but Scottish politics were gravely destabilised, and her new base of support was far narrower than the old one.

This, in itself, need not have been catastrophic. The real disaster was Darnley himself, who proved to be more arrogant, inconstant, short-sighted, petulant and incompetent than any other British politician of the century, excepting only those who were actually insane. In a personal monarchy, this mattered deeply. In particular, it cruelly exposed the weakness of female monarchy in the sixteenth century. If a queen consort had had personal failings of that order, she would simply have been slapped down and, if necessary, kept in genteel confinement for breeding purposes. But Darnley was now – in his own and his father's eyes, at least – king of Scots, and regarded his wife as subject to him. As she tried to broaden her political base, Darnley instead pursued the Lennox Stuarts' interests. He reacted to opposition (not least from his wife) with fury. Within months he had acquired an impressive list of enemies.

Mary's marriage to Darnley lasted for just over eighteen months, a period of chaotic and bewildering political turbulence. An interlude of sudden public support for Catholicism in late 1565 was followed by Mary's equally sudden abandonment of the Lennox Stuarts. For a time in early 1566 it appeared that she was bypassing the nobility entirely, and trying to limit her political circle to her own household. This led to her first direct brush with political violence, for a gang of nobles organised by the Douglases and helped by Darnley barged into her private chambers and – in her presence – murdered the Italian musician who had become her French secretary, David Riccio. Riccio's supposed crimes were largely imaginary, but the incident was a warning of the explosive pressures which were building up in Scottish politics. Mary succeeded in restoring an illusory stability for much of the rest of 1566, much helped by her pregnancy, and even more by her successful delivery of a baby boy on 19 June. He was baptised with Catholic rites and named James, the name of kings.

His father did not attend the baptism, a further sign of his utter failure to understand his political role. The problem of Darnley became intense over the winter of 1566–67, and was eventually solved by the most notorious murder of the century. Towards midnight on 9 February 1567, the house outside Edinburgh where Darnley was staying was entirely destroyed by a huge explosion. His body was found in the grounds of the house, apparently suffocated. The murder remains deeply mysterious, and Mary's involvement in particular is hotly debated. The problem is not a lack of suspects or of evidence, but an excess. Almost every leading figure in Scottish politics had reason to loathe Darnley. If Mary was not directly involved, it was because those who plotted the murder chose not to involve her, not because she would have regretted the outcome. There was a desperate need to be rid of Darnley, and the marriage could not be dissolved without bastardising the infant prince. Murder seemed the only option.

And indeed, Darnley's death offered the prospect of a return to stability. If Mary's judgement and sense of political theatre had not deserted her, she could have emerged from the whole episode strengthened. She failed, however, to appreciate that a murdered king was a wholly different animal from a living Darnley. It was understandable that she should feel personal relief, even euphoria, at being rid of such a menace; but fatally, she made no attempt to conceal these feelings. The prime suspect for the murder was (and remains) the earl of Bothwell, a stoutly anti-English lord who had been almost the only nobleman loyal to Mary's mother during the war of 1559–60. Instead of using Bothwell as a scapegoat, Mary made him the favourite of the moment. He was tried for the murder – that much was unavoidable – but she ensured that the trial was a whitewash. Riding high, Bothwell decided to consolidate his position by marrying the newly widowed queen himself. Several leading magnates, Lennox and Moray among them, prudently withdrew abroad. Bothwell bullied some of those who remained into accepting his marriage to the queen in principle. Hastily discarding his own wife, he abducted the queen and married her (by the Protestant rite) on 15 May 1567, on his terms if not against her will.

Conceivably, a king could have got away with murdering his wife in order to marry a woman who had been complicit in the murder. For a queen, it was quite impossible. It was not simply that Mary's behaviour (protecting and favouring an unrepentant murderer) was the very antithesis of good lordship. The prospect of Bothwell as king of Scots was almost as unpalatable as that of Darnley. The coalition against them mobilised with impressive speed. The forces which she and Bothwell were able to scrabble together faced off against a larger rebel army at Carberry on 15 June 1567. As so often in Scottish politics, the confrontation did not actually tip over into large-scale bloodshed. Mary surrendered, and Bothwell fled abroad (he died in prison in Denmark in 1578). Mary was led back into Edinburgh, with well-drilled crowds shouting abuse at the murderess, and then imprisoned in Lochleven Castle. After bitter disagreements between her captors, she was compelled to abdicate in favour of her infant son.

How had it come to this? She had made some disastrous errors. Her folly after Darnley's murder was suicidal, and the decision even to marry him was rash, although no one foresaw quite how unmanageable he would be. Yet to focus on Mary's own actions risks missing the larger picture. She had less room for political manoeuvre than any other British monarch of the century. Her religious position was, in the end, incidental to her fall, but it did ensure a steady level of background hostility towards her from both religious extremes. More importantly, her troubles mercilessly expose the weakness of female monarchy. Any marriage she made was of necessity destabilising (although Darnley and Bothwell were bad choices by any standards). As well as her husbands, she was also gravely undermined by her son. James's birth was a dynastic triumph, but his existence meant that Mary could seem to be no more than keeping the throne warm for him. Worse, it created a reversionary interest. As James III had discovered in 1488, in a dynastic monarchy the existence of an heir can facilitate rebellion. There was now a good and legitimate alternative to Mary – an infant, yes, but Scottish politics was well accustomed to minority rule. Mary was the only female monarch in sixteenth-century Britain who produced a child, and she was deposed barely a year after his birth. Having borne a son, she had outlived her political usefulness.

King's men and queen's men, 1567–73

Mary's deposition did not resolve the political chaos in Scotland, any more than Darnley's murder had. Unlike the murder, the deposition was not irrevocable. The crisis of 1567 triggered six years of civil war between the 'king's men', who favoured the infant James VI and his regents, and the 'queen's men' who hoped to restore Mary.

The first beneficiary of Mary's deposition was her half-brother and erstwhile favourite, the earl of Moray. Returning from exile at precisely the right time, he appeared as the white knight poised to rescue Scotland from its homicidal maelstrom, and swiftly installed himself as regent. Knox, with uncharacteristic good sense, buried his differences with Moray and threw his fiery rhetoric behind him; for after six years of limbo, the Reformed Church now had unambiguous government backing. In December 1567, a parliament acting in the young king's name did what Mary had always refused to do, and ratified the Reformation parliament's Acts. The new regime also tried to justify Mary's deposition (beyond mere accusations of murder and adultery). During 1567 Moray's in-house humanist scholar, George Buchanan, drew up his tract *The True Law of Kingship*, which reduced monarchy to a kind of elective figurehead and explicitly proclaimed a right to assassinate tyrants.

Not all Scots shared Moray and Knox's triumphal mood. In May 1568, Mary dramatically escaped from captivity, and the size of the army which rallied to her made the new regime's fragility plain. The battle of Langside on 13 May 1568 was a real battle. Mary was defeated, but her forces had outnumbered those of her opponents and the defeat was not in itself disastrous. What made it so was Mary's panic. Her only previous personal experience of fighting had been the merry farce of the Chaseabout Raid; this bloody business was altogether different. She fled south-west and, in an appalling miscalculation, decided to cross into England and throw herself on Elizabeth's mercy. This decision precipitated a twenty-year crisis in English politics (see below, pp. 235–6). However, the one course of action which Elizabeth was never going to take was to restore the Scottish queen to full and independent sovereignty. For the rest of her life, Mary was a prisoner and a pawn in others' strategies.

The eventual victory of the king's men may seem inevitable from that moment, for the queen's men had no queen to restore. But this did not make Moray's regime any more popular. His close alliance with the English, especially during England's show trial of Mary for Darnley's murder, made him look like a traitor. As well as the usual Catholic suspects, his opponents included the Hamiltons, who (with some justification) regarded the regency as rightfully theirs; the earl of Argyll, a staunch Protestant but a legitimist who was personally close to the queen; and Protestant pragmatists like Maitland of Lethington who favoured a compromise. For compromises were possible. If Mary were to be returned from England trussed up in an appropriate marriage, she could be kept on a tighter leash (the young duke of Norfolk was spoken of as a possibility, an idea which unfortunately went to, and eventually cost him, his head). Moray's Anglophile policy appeared craven rather than staunch, and the suspicion that he was after the crown for himself was growing. The gathering crisis was resolved on 23 January 1570 in the traditional Scots way. Moray was shot dead by a Hamilton sniper as he rode through Linlithgow.

The king's party almost collapsed. For much of 1570 Scotland seemed to lack any effective government at all, the civil war disintegrating into a series of local feuds. It was, as in 1560, English intervention which turned the corner. The earl of Lennox returned from his English exile at the head of a small army, and was promptly made regent for James VI. He set about fighting a nasty little war, principally against his old enemies the Hamiltons, bolstered by further English military help. Archbishop Hamilton of St Andrews, the Catholic reformer of the 1550s, was now a leader of the queen's party; when Lennox captured him in 1571 he tried and hanged him. Lennox himself was killed in battle later the same year. A new regent, the earl of Mar, was promptly appointed, but the war seemed no closer to resolution. During the winter of 1571-72 Edinburgh itself was fought over, with the castle being held implacably for the queen.

Finally, England moved from advocating compromise to full support for the king. Fear of Catholic conspiracies convinced Elizabeth that it would be folly to reinstate Mary on any terms. Such fears were apparently vindicated by the St Bartholomew's Day Massacre in France in 1572, in which thousands of Protestants were murdered by Catholic mobs. Prophets of doom like Knox had been forecasting such horrors for years, and their insistence on seeing every conflict in apocalyptic terms began to seem reasonable. Mary's religiously diverse coalition began to break up. The beginning of the end was Argyll's decision to come to terms in 1572. Regent Mar died later that year, but at least did so of natural causes. His successor, the earl of Morton, imposed a decisive but not vindictive peace settlement early in 1573. Even then, he could not make it stick without English help, for the diehards in Edinburgh castle refused to surrender, and a three-month siege was necessary to complete the victory.

It was a fitting end to Scotland's thirty-year political–religious spasm. After 1573, Scottish politics was as turbulent and violent as always, but certain truths were now inescapable. Scotland was decisively a Reformed Protestant kingdom, and its diplomatic alignment was decisively with England and against France – however contentious the details might be. By contrast to England's state-led affair, Scotland's Reformation appears more 'popular' – even as a Reformation 'from below'. But while this is true, the Scottish Reformation did not come from very far 'below'. Popular

Protestantism largely followed political and military events, rather than leading them. In the towns and cities, which elsewhere in Europe (even in England) were the cradles of religious change, there was comparatively little agitation. Dundee acquired a reputation for radicalism early on, and there were Protestant cells in Perth too, but the two other large towns – Edinburgh and Aberdeen – were bastions of conservatism, before and after 1560. The queen's men still found widespread support in Edinburgh in 1571–72, despite (or because of) a decade of Knox's preaching. Change was led not by the mass of the population, but by the landed elite. The Protestant convictions of these lairds and nobles were real enough, but they were reinforced by more pragmatic considerations. They had substantial holdings of Church lands to defend, and they were very sensitive to any infringements of their traditional liberties, infringements which they feared Catholic or French tyranny might bring. All of which meant that when Protestantism came to Scotland, it came not to bring peace, but a sword.

Notes

1 National Archives, SP 1/175 fo. 17r (*Letters and Papers . . . of Henry VIII*, vol. XVIII, pt. I, no. 27).

2 National Archives of Scotland, CS7/1 fo. 368r.

3 Joseph Bain (ed.), *The Hamilton Papers*, vol. II (1892), p. 207.

4 Marcus Merriman, *The Rough Wooings* (2000), p. 8.

5 John Pollen (ed.), *Papal Negotiations with Mary, Queen of Scots* (1901), p. 430.

6 David Laing (ed.), *The Works of John Knox*, vol. II (1846), p. 310.

CHAPTER 9

Gaping Gulfs: Elizabethan England and the Politics of Fear

The politics of Elizabethan England was dominated by events which did not happen. With hindsight, the forty-four years of Elizabeth's reign appear to be a time of amazing political stability. The faces remained the same: William Cecil, later Lord Burleigh, was Elizabeth's right-hand-man until his death in 1598. Even thereafter, despite the tumultuous rise and fall of her young favourite the earl of Essex, William's younger son Robert Cecil ensured that there was more continuity than change. Religious policy scarcely changed throughout the reign. The most pressing question of high politics – the queen's marriage – was eventually resolved by inaction, when it finally became clear that she would not marry at all. Elizabeth's foreign policy was not quite so static, but its themes were consistent and can be quickly summarised: she was poor, she knew it, and she had no interest in crusades or martial glory. She spent most of her reign resisting cries for intervention to defend her fellow Protestants, beleaguered in Scotland, France and the Netherlands, and when she did succumb she did so to the most minimal extent possible. Only in the 1580s was she finally sucked in by the Continental wars of religion. It was also in the late 1580s that she was forced – again after two decades of resistance – finally to end the saga of Mary, queen of Scots, which had dominated domestic politics for nearly thirty years.

Whether we call this stability, prevarication or paralysis, it was how Elizabeth liked to govern. On those rare occasions when real action was taken, it was usually preceded by months or years of royal deliberation and obstruction. Yet the fascination of Elizabeth's reign is that this stable, placid picture is not the one which her subjects saw. They saw a world of dangers crowding in on every side, in which England's apparent security was a dangerous illusion. The political world of Elizabethan England was one of fear – and also of frustration at the queen's apparent unwillingness to act. It was a potent combination.

Marriage and the succession: the long crisis

From elective monarchy to monarchical republic

Throughout her reign, Elizabeth was plagued by the same, perennial problem that had vexed her sister, brother and father: the succession. She was unmarried and childless. In the event, she was to live until the age of 69, but no-one knew this at the time. For forty years, England was a heartbeat away from a succession crisis. In 1562, the queen contracted smallpox and was gravely ill. Had she died, there would have been a contested succession, with one of the strongest candidates being the Catholic Mary Stewart, queen of Scots. For the Elizabethan political establishment, that was a nightmarish prospect. Mary's succession hovered over English politics like an axe.

Mary was not the only claimant, and it would have been perfectly possible for Elizabeth to follow her father and brother's example by taking steps to regulate the succession. Any of her parliaments would gladly have obliged. But Elizabeth steadfastly refused to do this. To name a successor, she declared, would be to weave her own shroud – and, as her brother's experience showed, it might not work. She was equally cagey about the other obvious solution to the problem, marriage. She insisted that the decision of whom, when and whether she would marry was hers alone, and responded furiously if pressed on the matter. The question of the succession dominated the entire reign, and Elizabeth simply would not answer it.

Elizabethan England, therefore, was not merely an elective monarchy (see above, p. 34). It was an elective monarchy caught up in permanent, unofficial campaigning. Elizabeth was denying her subjects the single greatest benefit of dynastic monarchy, namely political certainty. This raised the temperature and broadened the arena of politics in a way that permanently altered the English state. Henry VIII's Reformation had widened the scope of England's political classes, and during 1547–49 Edward Seymour's populist politics had widened them further still, bringing people who had usually been politically excluded to bear on affairs of state. John Dudley's regime had backed away from that policy, and Mary's had sharply reversed it, reasserting the dominance of a small political elite

– with mixed success. Elizabeth now widened the political arena again, not by deliberate policy but through the ever-present succession crisis. Much as her subjects might have liked simply to accept her good lordship and their own place, febrile political uncertainty made it difficult to do so. Widespread public attention to high politics became a habit in Elizabeth's reign, a habit which England has never subsequently broken.

Indeed, 'elective monarchy' is no longer an adequate term to describe what the English polity was becoming during Elizabeth's reign. Patrick Collinson describes Elizabethan England as a 'monarchical republic'.[1] Elective monarchy became enmeshed with Christian commonwealth of England – and that powerful word *commonwealth* was used to translate the Latin *res publica*. Thomas More, like the Protestant idealists of Edward VI's reign, had used the word 'commonwealth' to make a moral point: the king should order society for the benefit of all. But now there was no king, only a queen, and a queen whose realm seemed so vulnerable that the good government of the commonwealth could not simply be left to her. The queen's gender, her counsellors' fears, their humanist and Protestant theories of government and – above all – her stubborn inaction gave those counsellors a leading role in the formulation and execution of policy. This was not an arrangement like Wolsey had had with Henry VIII, whereby he simply took over the running of government on the king's behalf. Elizabeth never allowed her ministers to do that. Rather, and this was the secret of her political success, she acted as the opposition to her own regime. This worked surprisingly well, for although both queen and counsellors found it intensely frustrating at times, they also ultimately trusted one another. But it also set up a wider dynamic which changed, or further changed, the nature of the English polity. Politics in a monarchical republic could not be confined to the council chamber, nor even to the Parliament house. Her counsellors – and not only her counsellors – discovered that they were 'citizens concealed within subjects'.[2] This remained, intensely, a *monarchical* republic; but the monarch's affairs were now the concern of all the commonwealth, whether she liked it or not.

The marriage problem

Elizabeth never married. At her accession, aged twenty-five, no-one would have predicted this, and it is very unlikely that she took a deliberate decision to remain unmarried until (at least) the early 1580s. However, she did treat every possibility of marriage with caution, deploying the political power of playing hard to get. And there were a great many possibilities.

There were the Habsburg marriages – Philip II of Spain or Archduke Charles of Austria – which would have renewed England's oldest alliance, but which would have made the maintenance and defence of Protestantism difficult. There were the French marriages – the first and less serious candidate from this stable being Henry, duke of Anjou, who later became King Henry III of France, a possibility which would have drawn England into the turmoil of France's religious wars. There was a Swedish marriage – Eric XIV, king of Sweden – which would have united England to another Protestant kingdom. The possibility was popular, but Sweden was somewhat beneath Elizabeth's dignity and she never took the match very seriously. The same, but more so, could be said of the earl of Arran, a Protestant who was second in line to the Scottish throne. Elizabeth was entirely uninterested in this possibility, even before he fell into madness in 1561. And there were numerous Englishmen. Most noblemen of the right age were rumoured to be candidates at some point or other. Much the most serious of these was Robert Dudley – son of John the duke of Northumberland, and grandson of Edmund, Henry VII's enforcer. Elizabeth and Dudley were close friends (she created him earl of Leicester), so close as to give rise to rumours, especially when his wife died in convenient and suspicious circumstances. She seems to have agonised over the possibility of marrying him, but to have decided, in the end, to preserve both her political independence and her future marriageability. And so, as each favoured candidate took his predecessor's place, the years ticked by.

If Leicester was the first genuinely serious candidate for Elizabeth's hand, the last was Francis of Valois, who was made duke of Anjou in 1576, after his elder brother Henry became king of France. For nearly five years, from 1578 to 1582, the Anjou match was a live political possibility. As a last chance to resolve the succession problem, it was a long shot – Elizabeth was forty-five years old when the match looked most like succeeding, in 1579. The French doctors who examined her as part of the negotiations declared that she was fertile, but the odds must have been against her bearing a child. However, the Anjou match had a genuine political appeal. An alliance between Protestant England and a Catholic France convulsed by religious civil war might have bolstered the centre ground in a rapidly polarising continent. Moreover, Anjou was a genuine crossover figure. Although a Catholic, and heir apparent to the French throne, he had previously fought alongside the French Protestants against his brother King Henry III, and was aiding the Dutch Protestants in their own war against Spain. And on a personal level, Elizabeth found the match (or at least the courtship) very appealing, responding to doubts from her ministers with sincere and well-calibrated bouts of tearful fury. Her Protestant subjects, of course, were horrified by the prospect. In 1579 a barrister named John Stubbe wrote a book condemning the planned match – *The discovery of a gaping gulf, whereinto England is like to be swallowed by another French marriage.* Men like Stubbe saw gaping gulfs all around them. With the nation's survival hanging in the balance, it was not enough to keep quiet and trust the queen. Elizabeth did not appreciate unsolicited political advice, particularly not in print, and particularly not on this subject. Stubbe had his right hand cut off for his pains (when it was done, he cried 'God save the queen!' before fainting from shock). But Stubbe was right, and ultimately Elizabeth knew it. The true gaping gulf was that which was opening up between Protestant and Catholic Europe. It would take more than a marriage to bridge it.

And if there was no marriage, and no child? On the face of things, the person with the best genealogical claim to succeed Elizabeth was Mary, queen of Scots. It was a possibility most English Protestants were desperate to avoid. The problem only sharpened after 1568, when Mary was in English custody. There was, of course, only one foolproof way to exclude her from the succession: to kill her. Elizabeth, reluctant to start a round of royal bloodletting and always wary of irrevocable actions, steadily refused. Mary's trial in 1569 for murdering her second husband ended in an inconclusive verdict, which could be used to justify her continued imprisonment but not her execution. In 1571, a plot brokered by an Italian merchant named Roberto di Ridolfi came to light, which would have seen Mary married to the duke of Norfolk and installed on the English throne. Norfolk, a fool rather than a villain, was beheaded, and Elizabeth was begged to do the same to Mary. Her bishops warned that if she showed 'unreasonable clemency' God would condemn her.[3] Parliament debated bills allowing Mary to be executed if anyone rebelled in her name, or pre-emptively pardoning anyone who might murder her. But Elizabeth would not budge.

Only in 1585, with the international situation one of hair-trigger tension and with fears that Mary would be the beneficiary of any Catholic invasion, was Elizabeth bounced into accepting a new treason law. The so-called Act of Association laid down that anyone who 'compassed or imagined'[4] a plot to assassinate the queen should be tried by a special court; and that, if an assassination succeeded, a similar special court should decide on the succession. In early 1586 Elizabeth's spies learned of just such a plot, organised by a Catholic gentleman named Anthony Babington. While intercepting his letters, they allowed Babington to proceed. In this way they secured the smoking gun: a letter from the imprisoned Mary explicitly endorsing the plan to murder Elizabeth. Babington's plot never posed a real danger. Rather, it was the means by which the subtle Protestant zealot Sir Francis Walsingham, Elizabeth's secretary of state and spymaster, fenced the queen in. She could not prevent the Scots queen from being tried and convicted under the 1585 Act. Yet Elizabeth was still deeply reluctant to sign the death warrant. She was frightened of taking responsibility for it – hence her suggestion that Mary's gaoler, Sir Amias Paulet, murder his prisoner. (Paulet, a tough-minded Protestant who was eager enough to see Mary dead, flatly refused to do such a thing.) Yet she agonised about the moral consequences too. In the end, she claimed that she was tricked into authorising the execution, and it may even be true. Mary was beheaded on 8 February 1587, at the age of forty-four, having spent nearly half her life as a prisoner. However reluctantly, Elizabeth had finally done something.

The extended Mary crisis left its mark on England. With Elizabeth manifestly unwilling to solve the problem, England's anxious Protestants were forced to take matters into their own hands. England had, as this book has argued, been an elective monarchy in practice since the fifteenth century or earlier. Only in Elizabeth's reign did it contemplate becoming one in theory, too. The merits of dynastic versus elective monarchy became a favourite set-piece of humanist disputation (even if, by convention, such discussions always concluded that the hereditary principle was best). The question was debated before Elizabeth when she visited Oxford in 1566, much to her displeasure. In 1575, the Protestant preacher at a London mayoral election provocatively asked whether monarchs should be elected too.[5] One unmentionable fact was that Elizabeth's own succession depended on statute (the 1543 Succession Act) rather than on heredity, since in law she was illegitimate.

Despite the abstract terms in which such discussions were couched, it was plain they were of immediate political relevance. Others tackled the subject more directly. In 1563 John Hales, a bureaucrat and former Protestant exile, wrote a treatise arguing that Mary, as a foreigner, could not succeed. His book sparked a furious debate, to which over a dozen surviving tracts testify – all unpublished, for such matters were too sensitive to address in print. By the 1580s, this debate had reached fever pitch. The 1585 Act of Association, startling enough in itself, arose in a wholly unprecedented fashion. The so-called Throckmorton plot of 1583 (in which Mary may have been involved), and the assassination of the Dutch Protestant leader William of Orange on 10 July 1584 (a forcible reminder of how devastating religio-political murders were), concentrated English fears as never before. In the autumn of 1584 Elizabeth's Privy Councillors drew up a Bond of Association, by which they pledged themselves 'to pursue to utter extermination' anyone plotting to assassinate the queen or hoping to benefit from her death. But this was more than a touching demonstration of councillors' loyalty. Thousands of God-fearing Protestants across England solemnly swore the Bond's oath. The subsequent Act was explicitly a legal form of the Bond, and it was swept into Parliament on the back of (in effect) a mass petitioning campaign. This was organised, popular and populist politics on a scale never seen before.

The Bond of Association was a sign of just how far the slow-burning succession crisis had pushed politics out of its normal course – if anyone could now remember what 'normality' was. Like the reaction to the proposed Anjou marriage, it showed a mass willingness to become involved in politics and, if necessary, to save the queen from herself. Neither the councillors who formulated the Bond nor the subjects who signed it were demagogues or radicals. Yet the danger was too extreme for constitutional niceties. If the queen would not do what she manifestly had to do, then the humble whisper of counsel would become more insistent until, if necessary, she was shouted down.

How far was this a matter of Elizabeth's gender? The commonplace that good monarchs should take counsel was felt to apply especially to a queen. Some at least of her counsellors clearly felt that they had a greater right to press their views on a female ruler. In some areas – especially the masculine sphere of war – Elizabeth sometimes found it genuinely difficult to maintain full control of her affairs. It is also true, of course, that if Elizabeth had been a man, the question of marriage would have been far less vexed (as she herself observed, a king of England would have been able to deal with Mary by marrying her). Yet this should not be overplayed. Mary Tudor had not been faced with political voluntarism on this scale. The most that can be said is that Elizabeth's gender made her subjects more forthright in offering her unwanted advice.

More significant, perhaps, is the new political culture of Protestantism. As Mary Tudor had discovered, underneath the high Protestant doctrine of obedience was a mulish insistence on conscience. Few embraced the radical resistance theories advocated by Christopher Goodman, John Knox and George Buchanan, but Protestants certainly believed that they must sometimes speak out in defiance of their rulers. They had also learned to use mass politics in Edward's reign, when their books and sermons had made the running for the regime. The awkward loyalism of a John Stubbe, who presumed to lecture the queen in public about God's will for her marriage; or of the Bond of Association, which was so earnest to protect the queen that it took her laws into its own hands – this has something distinctively Protestant about it. And as Mary Tudor had also discovered, these people were difficult to silence.

Elizabethan England did not have a fully fledged 'public sphere' of the seventeenth- and eighteenth-century variety. There were no newspapers; printshops were still firmly controlled; and there were no spaces for public debate equivalent to later coffee-shops. Yet there was nevertheless a steady hubbub of public interest in politics. If there were no newspapers, there was theatre. Throughout the reign, but especially from the 1580s, there was a rising fashion for historical plays. These frequently included pointed allusions to contemporary politics, whether in the eyes of the authors, the audiences or the regime. One such play – Shakespeare's *Richard II*, about a deposition – was deliberately staged by the earl of Essex's supporters immediately before his doomed rebellion in 1601 (see below, p. 311). This explosion of theatrical culture, and the wider 'English Renaissance' of which it was a part, cannot be put down simply either to the wider political crisis or to the restless, questioning, awkward political culture of Protestantism. But nor can we imagine such a Renaissance without them.

'By halves and by petty invasions': war and rumours of war

Elizabeth's accession coincided with a major reorientation of European politics. The treaty of Câteau-Cambrésis in April 1559 ended the long, bloody struggle between France and its Habsburg enemies. France's Scottish province saw a rebellion in the name of religion the following month, leading to a war of religion in which both France and England intervened (see above, pp. 217–18). In a harbinger of things to come, Spain contemplated intervening in this war, in support of its old French enemies. By then, the long-suppressed religious strains in France itself were showing. 1560–62 were years of breakneck growth for French Protestantism, growth which was checked only when France's Catholic nobles took up arms in defence of their faith in 1562. For the next thirty-five years France was convulsed by a series of religious civil wars, punctuated by unstable truces. By the 1590s, France was less a European superpower than a European battleground, in which Catholic and Protestant powers were fighting a proxy war.

At the same time, Catholicism was consolidating. At the final sessions of the Council of Trent in 1562–63, the old Church decisively rejected constructive compromise (of the kind which had failed in 1550s Scotland) in favour of a blunt rejection of Protestantism. Philip II of Spain – who had once been king of England – disliked some of the implications of Trent, but he was unflinching in his defence of Catholicism: no sixteenth-century ruler was plainer or more obviously sincere in his religious convictions. A whisper of Protestantism in Spain itself in 1558 had been stamped out ferociously. But Philip's other great territory, the Netherlands, was a different matter. This wealthy, cosmopolitan and populous collection of states had had a lively and diverse Protestant presence since the 1520s, despite bloody and sustained religious persecution. Rising opposition to the persecution amongst the Netherlandish elites culminated in the sudden collapse of the government's authority in the spring and summer of 1566. After a brief 'Wonderyear' of free preaching and a storm of iconoclasm, a Spanish army brutally reimposed control. But Protestant exiles were now resisting in arms. Five years of guerrilla war and piracy exploded into full-scale armed revolt from 1572 onwards. It was the beginning of a Dutch religious war which was to last until 1648, and which was to divide the Netherlands permanently into a Protestant north (the modern Netherlands) and Catholic south (Belgium).

The established Protestant states of Europe – in Scandinavia, Germany, the Swiss Confederation and the British Isles – were not of necessity involved in these wars. Indeed, the Lutherans stood aloof from all of them, although they followed events with close interest. Amongst Reformed Protestants (or, as they were beginning to be called, Calvinists), the mood was different. The French and Dutch wars pitted Reformed Protestants against Catholics, and the Reformed had lively international networks. They hosted one another's exiles, translated one another's books, sent missionaries and received refugees. Preachers across the Reformed world urged that their embattled brethren be supported, with prayers, with money and – if possible – in arms. This call was heard particularly keenly in the largest and most powerful Reformed Protestant territory: England.

It was not only preachers who felt that England had an obligation to fight to defend its Reformed brethren abroad. Elizabeth's own regime was filled with men who felt that the battle against the Romish Antichrist was an apocalyptic struggle. Even William Cecil, politician to his fingertips, felt the power of this argument – particularly in his younger days. The earl of Leicester, Elizabeth's favourite and nearly her husband, was outspoken on the subject. So too was his stepson Robert Devereux, the earl of Essex, the impetuous favourite of Elizabeth's last years. Beneath the cool pragmatism of Elizabeth's regime was the hot blood of Protestant zeal.

But not for Elizabeth herself. Her reluctance to see the world as divided along religious lines – much less to fight according to those lines – was almost as frustrating to her loyal and godly subjects as her refusal to define the succession. Indeed, the subject is still controversial. The queen's stubborn refusal to be dragged into what she saw as unnecessary wars, in the face of almost universal pressure to do just that, is evidence of (according to taste) her penny-pinching and indecisive myopia, or her shrewd and level-headed prudence. Inevitably, both views have a good deal to recommend them. Together, they perhaps help to account for one undoubted fact of Elizabeth's foreign policy: it succeeded. Scotland was secured as a Protestant ally. France's Protestant-friendly king, Henry IV, was eventually placed securely on his throne. The Dutch Protestant rebellion succeeded, or at least survived; and the war with Spain, when it finally came, saw one decisive English victory as well as exacting a steady toll on Spain's American empire. (In one other arena of conflict – Ireland – the military victory was even clearer, but the political damage was so severe as to upset the reckoning: see below, pp. 305–13.) And all this happened without bankrupting the regime. Some of these successes happened despite Elizabeth rather than because of her. There was also an element of what her partisans called providential deliverance, and what looks to historians like dumb luck. But neither providence nor luck is a trivial political asset.

How the Elizabethan regime manufactured its luck can be seen in the first great foreign policy crisis of the reign, the Scottish war of 1559–60 (see above, pp. 217–18). When that conflict first broke out, the peace of Câteau-Cambrésis had only just extracted England and Scotland from the larger Franco-Habsburg war into which both countries had been dragged by their allies. England was still smarting from the loss of Calais in that war. Elizabeth was insecurely on her throne and the mortar had not yet set on her religious settlement. It was not a time for foreign adventures. When the embattled Scottish Protestants called on England for aid, the queen's response was chilly – not least because John Knox, one of her least favourite people of any religion or nationality, was in the thick of their counsels. Many of Elizabeth's counsellors felt differently. Cecil, once a protégé of Edward Seymour, shared some of his old master's British Protestant idealism. Where Elizabeth saw danger, he saw opportunity: not only to defend the true faith, but a once-in-a-lifetime chance to secure England's northern border by breaking the Franco-Scottish alliance.

Yet Elizabeth had no patience with idealistic arguments for Protestant solidarity, and little enthusiasm for supporting subjects in rebellion against their lawful princes. She was also (as always) painfully aware of how little she could spare the cash for a Scottish adventure. When a small injection of money (£1000) was sent north, only to be stolen en route, Cecil took more than a week to work up the courage to tell Elizabeth of the mishap. When she did, finally, agree to intervene, it was on much more pragmatic grounds. A decent-sized French army was now in Scotland, digging itself in, and that posed an immediate threat. (Some Scots hoped to match the capture of Calais by taking back their own lost town, Berwick.) Cecil finally persuaded Elizabeth that an intervention in Scotland was simple self-defence.

Even then, it was done carefully. First a small naval force was sent, with orders to blockade the French fortifications. The ships were to defend themselves, but if possible not to fire the first shot. If they did, the admiral was ordered to pretend that this was done on his own initiative, because of his outrage that the French were claiming sovereignty over England. It was only when this force had successfully throttled France's supply lines that a land army was sent north. Thanks to a judicious application of force and diplomacy, the English won a decisive victory without fighting a full-scale battle. Cecil himself went north to negotiate the treaty – and also managed to persuade his queen to abandon her demand that the French return Calais as part of the deal.

How did the Elizabethan state win this victory, the very foundation of its subsequent security? There was luck – the unexpected weakness of France as it began to be eaten away by its own religious turmoil. Perhaps there were also missed opportunities: an earlier intervention might have hastened the victory. But Elizabeth's manifest reluctance to intervene was itself powerful. It convinced her Scottish allies, in the face of centuries of contrary experience, that she did not nourish hopes to conquer Scotland. The punctilious behaviour of her forces, and their rapid withdrawal after the victory, maintained that goodwill. Her caution also helped to ensure that the conflict did not reignite a general war; and her and Cecil's close attention to military detail ensured that the operation stayed on budget. The French felt not merely outgunned but outmanoeuvred by the novice English queen. In the spring of 1560 the long-term English ambassador in Paris believed that, in little more than a year, French views of her had been transformed: 'She is now rather envied and feared than pitied and condemned.'[6]

This set the pattern for her foreign interventions for the rest of the reign: reluctant, tardy, always more attentive to national security than to pan-Protestant idealism. Yet in the face of militant Catholicism, those two motives became hard to disentangle. If supporting the Dutch rebels, for example, was not a matter of godly solidarity, it was one of enlightened self-defence: for if the Netherlands had come fully under Spanish military control, the threat to England would have been immediate. (The purpose of the Grand Armada of 1588 was, indeed, to ferry a portion of the Spanish army in the Netherlands across the English Channel.) It was better to fight proxy wars than real ones. Hence the other feature of Elizabeth's wars: their finely calibrated level. Elizabeth favoured careful, limited, deniable and semi-detached interventions. Refugees were welcomed, and a blind eye was turned to their fundraising and military activities unless they became too provocative. When the city of Geneva was threatened in 1582–83, Elizabeth allowed (even encouraged) private fundraising to support its defences, but no more than that. Or again, between 1567 and 1572 the irregular navy of the Dutch rebels – the so-called 'Sea Beggars' – was permitted, grudgingly, to operate from English ports, which kept the rebellion alive. The provocation was enough to end Spain's alliance with England, but not enough to spark a war. Similarly, the regime often placed men of known Protestant zeal in forward positions, apparently expecting them to act independently. Francis Drake, part-time slave-trader and the queen's favourite pirate, helped to turn harassment of Spanish shipping in the Atlantic from a private enterprise into a self-funding instrument of state policy. He was also a zealous Protestant who buoyed his crews' morale with tales of Catholic atrocities. In all these cases, the regime became skilled at knowing how much provocation it could safely offer its enemies – and at rapid back-pedalling on those occasions when it went too far.

Direct intervention was rarer. Even in Ireland, supposedly her own realm, Elizabeth's wars were parsimonious (see Chapter 11). Only once before the 1590s did English forces intrude on the French civil wars, sending 3000 men to hold Le Havre and Dieppe for the Huguenots (French Protestants) in 1562. The experiment was not a success. It was the earl of Leicester's project, and he had sold it to Elizabeth as a means of recovering Calais. The episode ended with Huguenots and French Catholics joining forces to expel the English, and all sides were left feeling ill used. For nearly thirty years thereafter, English intervention in the French wars was limited to miserly loans (often laundered through third parties), private initiatives, and endless diplomacy. Cold wars and proxy battles were much more Elizabeth's style.

But cold wars have a habit of heating up, and proxies of being sucked in. Philip II's insistence that his wars were wars of religion dragged England into them whether the queen liked it or not. It turned out that men like Leicester and Walsingham, who mirrored Philip's zeal, were better able to understand the world that that zeal had made. The crisis came in the mid-1580s – at the same time, by no coincidence, as the domestic crisis over Mary, queen of Scots, reached its height. The beleaguered Dutch rebels had been begging for direct help for a decade, but all they had received was a few English volunteers, some diplomatic cover, and half-promises of money and soldiers which quickly evaporated. In the early 1580s, the Anjou marriage negotiations briefly held out the possibility of a general anti-Spanish alliance comprising France, England and the Dutch rebels, but without such comprehensive diplomatic cover Elizabeth was not prepared to act, and all the Dutch had were warm words and a little money. The assassination of William of Orange – the rebels' *de facto* leader – in 1584 seemed to presage disaster. Spanish armies were grinding northwards. Anjou's death earlier the same year was almost as damaging, for it left a Protestant (Henry of Navarre) as heir apparent to France. The French Catholic League, whose purpose was to exclude the heretic from the throne, quickly became formidable and allied with Philip II. Far from an anti-Spanish alliance, a universal Catholic crusade now threatened, with the crumbling Dutch rebellion as the first, and perhaps only, line of defence. All this happened against the backdrop of renewed plotting involving Mary, queen of Scots and of Catholic missionary activity in England (see below, pp. 248–50). Excitable Protestants had been warning of a vast Catholic conspiracy for decades, but it now seemed alarmingly plausible. Drake's privateers were already involved in something like an undeclared naval war against Spain. On 20 August 1585, in the treaty of Nonsuch, Elizabeth finally and reluctantly committed herself to military support of the Dutch rebels, and thus to open war with Spain: a war that would last for the rest of her life.

Elizabeth fought the war much as she had conducted peace: carefully, hesitantly, delaying decisions and (as a result) avoiding both catastrophes and opportunities. Military aid to the Dutch rebels was real enough, but hardly decisive. Financial aid to the French Huguenots was miserly, although it helped them to stave off disaster. Elizabeth was determinedly trying to negotiate a peace even as the Spanish were planning an invasion. Philip II's patience with England's meddling was wearing thin, and was only reinforced by his outrage at Mary, queen of Scots' execution. For Philip, his 'enterprise of England' was a religious duty upon which he felt certain Providence would smile. This attitude, as much as the 'Protestant wind' and the actions of the English navy, accounts for the failure of the Grand Armada of 1588. Although Philip's army was fearsome, and the

Armada itself a fair match for England's navy, the Spanish were operating in unfamiliar waters at the end of long supply lines, and the plan was complex. There was little room for error or for unforeseen events, those two perennial companions of war. Philip, knowing God to be on his side, had not felt the need to make contingency plans, nor would he countenance changing the strategy when things began to go wrong. In this way a series of minor mishaps – bad weather, miscommunication, and some English harassment – were able to scatter the Armada completely. Worse (from the Spanish viewpoint), the distraction of the English campaign gave the Dutch rebels a critical breathing space, in which they were finally able to halt the Spanish reconquest. England had at last provided decisive help to its allies, if not in quite the way Elizabeth had intended.

Thereafter, the war settled back into a familiar Elizabethan pattern, and was conducted – as the privateer Walter Raleigh disgustedly said – 'by halves and by petty invasions'.[7] The mediocre performance of English forces even in smaller encounters suggests that Elizabeth was wise to shun glory-seeking. Rather than being in the forefront of the Protestant war effort, England was its reserve, an unreliable supply of men, money and materiel. In the summer of 1589, Henry III of France was assassinated, making his kingdom the focus of attention once again. The French civil war was now fiercer, but also simpler, than ever before: pitting the new King Henry IV, and his Huguenot and legitimist supporters, against the Spanish-backed Catholic League. England provided real help to the embattled king, but it was not enough. In 1593, Henry IV publicly admitted that he could secure his throne only by converting to Catholicism. This allowed him (eventually) to defeat the League, reunite France and grant legal toleration to the Huguenots. It was more or less the outcome for which Elizabeth had hoped from Anjou more than a decade earlier, and it defended English interests very adequately. Yet it was hardly a decisive victory, nor one for which England could claim very much credit. The Spanish war continued: fighting in the Netherlands and northern France, and raids against Spanish shipping and ports aimed both at loot and at blocking a further naval assault from Spain. But only in Ireland did this last phase of the war have any dramatic effects (see below, pp. 309–12).

So Elizabethan England neither led a Protestant crusade nor fell into the clutches of the popish Antichrist. Rather, it managed to secure a defensible line against the Spanish threat, a line which ran through the Netherlands and France rather than through the Channel or the Irish Sea; and it managed to blunt some of Spain's ambitions. The privatised, self-funding style of warfare which Elizabeth's parsimony favoured gave England a foothold in the Atlantic and, over the next century, was to mutate into North American settlements in the name of commerce and religion.

Yet Elizabeth's wars, and her efforts to avoid them, look more old-fashioned than new-fangled. In raw military terms, England was gravely outclassed. Spain could be contained only because it was fighting at such long range and on so many fronts (not least its struggle against the Ottoman Turks in the Mediterranean). Elizabethan warfare was low-level and often privatised because it was all that the English state could manage. The Armada campaign itself painfully illustrates this. The military preparations made for a possible Spanish landing were ingenious, under the circumstances, but the regime deliberately waited until, or beyond, the last possible moment to mobilise its forces, so as to keep the bills down. It worked – in the end, the land forces were paid for the equivalent of slightly less than one day's service[8] – but this might not have seemed so wise had they been called upon to fight. Was this recklessness on Elizabeth's part, or reluctance to waste money on defences which would in any case have failed?

One final curiosity can serve as a symbol of the confusions and contradictions of Elizabethan foreign policy. Following the Scottish campaign of 1559–60, Elizabeth decided to make the border stronghold of Berwick-upon-Tweed impregnable. The Elizabethan walls of Berwick, most of which still survive, would have made the town almost invulnerable to assault by the military techniques of the time. They also took a decade to build and cost almost £130,000 – ten times as much as her regime ever spent on any other military building.[9] But at no point in Elizabeth's reign or thereafter were they remotely necessary. Is this the ultimate indictment of the Elizabethan state, which starved more urgent military projects of funds in order to fight the last war? Or does it testify to a level-headed prudence, more akin to Henry VII than to Henry VIII, which preferred averting dangers to chasing opportunities, and prioritised defence over aggression?

Catholicism, 'popery' and the enemy within

If the succession and foreign affairs both posed dreadful threats, what made them worse was their possible intersection with a third possible catastrophe. Elizabeth's English or Welsh Catholic subjects might rise against her, as her Irish Catholic subjects repeatedly did. The Catholic enemy was domestic as well as foreign. This threat never coalesced into a mortal danger, but – as the Gunpowder Plot of 1605 showed – it was not entirely imaginary either. And even if it had been, the imagination is a powerful thing. Everyone in the Elizabethan elite knew that England's religious politics had repeatedly, unexpectedly and dramatically reversed themselves during the 1530s, 1540s and 1550s. It might happen again all too easily.

In reality, English Catholics were frozen out of power throughout Elizabeth's reign and long afterwards. They appear to history as a doomed community of exiles and rural gentry, powerless and divided. But this was very much how the Protestant exiles had appeared during Mary's reign, before Providence had delivered England back into their hands. The apparent ease with which the English political establishment became a Protestant establishment under Elizabeth was deceptive, and everyone knew it. Excluding Catholics from power made them invisible, but this made them more frightening, not less. Invisible or not, it was clear that Elizabethan Catholics were far more powerful than Marian Protestants had been. There were Catholics – some unabashed, some wearing thin veils of conformity – at every level of English society and in every corner of the realm. The highest nobility included open Catholics, such as the earl of Arundel, who briefly seemed a realistic husband for the queen. A few even made their way into the House of Commons, although overall that body's religious mood loyally reflected that of the regime it served. The county elites were filled with open and closet Catholics. And among the clergy of the established Church were thousands of men who had been ordained under Mary or Henry VIII, and whose obedience to the new settlement was suspect. Catholicism was particularly strong in the 'dark places of the kingdom',[10] unlit by the radiance of the Gospel – Wales, the north of England (especially Lancashire), and other remote areas. But it was present everywhere. Cecil took a close interest in the problem, trying hard to monitor the scale and the patterns of Catholic allegiance. But while recusants – open non-conformists – could be (and were) counted, they were the tip of an iceberg. Below them were the 'church papists': those who conformed outwardly to the established Church while remaining to some degree Catholic. This phenomenon was of course unquantifiable. The regime initially felt itself to be – and, to some extent, was – a fragile Protestant crust on a Catholic nation.

Elizabethan Catholics were very different from their Henrician and Edwardian forebears, for Mary's restoration had given them back their sense of themselves. Whereas Edward VI's Catholic subjects had met the Protestant advance with bewildered and disempowered silence, the Elizabethans regrouped and fought back. Like Marian Protestants, Elizabethan Catholic exiles quickly gathered into communities which became hot-houses of theological productivity, the most important being at Louvain. When John Jewel, the newly minted bishop of Salisbury, tried to prove Catholicism false in his so-called 'challenge sermon' of 1559, it was a challenge that the Louvain exiles were ready to answer. The exchange between Jewel and his main opponent, Thomas Harding, is one of the great set-piece encounters of the English Reformation, between two first-rate theological writers, and Harding emerges from it with some honour. Another contributor to that debate, William Allen, in 1568 secured the Catholic hierarchy's backing for a college at Douai. The English College was not only an institutional home to Catholic exiles; it was a springboard for an active missionary campaign to return England to the old faith.

Jewel and Harding's literary fireworks in the 1560s were not accompanied by much actual persecution of Catholics. Even the recusancy laws were enforced very patchily – in part because the courts were often staffed by officials with divided loyalties. Only the clergy were actively pursued during the 1560s, as the newly established courts of High Commission began systematically to hunt down and destroy Mass books and banned images, and to discipline priests whose nonconformity was too blatant. Even then, relatively few were actually dismissed. The queen had no taste for purges; and depriving clergy was, legally speaking, not a simple matter. But fundamentally, this hesitant policy towards Catholics reflects the new regime's fears. They did not wish to start a fight with an enemy whose strength they could not estimate. Better to wait, and to allow time, conformity and generational change to take their toll.

This phoney war came to an end in 1569–70, and (as so often in Elizabethan England) the trigger was Mary, queen of Scots. Some in both England and Scotland saw her captivity as an opportunity to settle the English succession by binding her into a safe marriage. The duke of Norfolk was spoken of. The plan originated with solid Protestants, but some Catholics were enthusiastic for it, in part because Norfolk had a reputation (probably unjustified) for crypto-Catholicism. The queen, however, squashed the idea sharply, throwing Norfolk into prison to underline the point. Two northern noblemen – Norfolk's brother-in-law the earl of Westmorland, and Westmorland's own brother-in-law the earl of Northumberland – took this badly. Both were Catholics of one kind or another, and both had been marginalised by Elizabeth's regime. Panicked by Norfolk's arrest, they stumbled, almost by accident, into open rebellion in November 1569. Mass was celebrated in Durham Cathedral, and they raised a small force, intending it to be the nucleus around which a full-scale Catholic rebellion could form. Their plan was to liberate Mary, marry her to a Catholic, and compel Elizabeth to recognise her as heir to the throne.

It was the storm which the regime had been dreading for a decade; when it came, it did little more than rattle the windows. The earls won few recruits, the rapidly assembled royal army had no difficulty outnumbering them, and the Scottish queen was quickly whisked out of their reach. The earls ran out of money, their forces began to disintegrate even before they reached York, and they fled to Scotland, hoping to join the 'queen's men' in the ongoing civil war there. In fact they promptly fell into the hands of the regent, the earl of Moray, who was delighted to curry Elizabeth's favour by imprisoning them.

The 'Northern Rebellion' was a fiasco, but one with grave consequences: and not merely because it made English Catholicism seem a paper tiger. On 27 April 1570, Pope Pius V lent very belated support to the defeated rebels in his bull *Regnans in Excelsis*. This declared Elizabeth to be a heretic, 'the pretended queen of England and the servant of crime', and excommunicated her.[11] It was, of course, hardly news that Elizabeth was not a Catholic, and expelling her from a Church she had left a decade earlier may seem comically self-important. However, the bull went on to declare that, as a consequence, she was deposed as queen. It not only absolved her subjects of any duties towards her, it demanded that they 'do not dare obey her orders, mandates and laws', on pain of excommunication themselves.[12] Copies of the bull were smuggled into the country. One was nailed to the door of the bishop of London's palace by night. Rome had declared war on Elizabeth, and was conscripting her Catholic subjects to be its soldiers.

The battle duly hardened. The legal space permitted to English Catholics steadily shrank. From 1569, magistrates were required to swear to the Royal Supremacy and the Inns of Court were purged. In 1571 a new treason law was introduced, which, following Henry VIII's precedents, treated Catholics as traitors serving a foreign power. The 1571 parliament also took steps to seize exiles' property – a sanction at which Mary's parliaments had balked. During the crisis over the 'prophesyings' in the later 1570s (see below, p. 271), Puritans did their best to whip up a moral panic about Catholic infiltration. This resulted, in 1577, in an attempt at a full-scale census of English recusancy and, in the same year, in the execution of a Catholic for treason on purely religious grounds – the first such execution since 1544. Predictably enough, the generalised panic of the early 1580s was felt in this arena too. In 1581 the fine for recusancy was increased 400-fold, from a shilling to £20. The following year, it was made treason for a priest ordained abroad to set foot on English soil.

As significant as the legal tightening was the spread of anti-Catholic propaganda. We can doubt whether the English became genuinely Protestant during Elizabeth's reign, but its public culture certainly became bitterly anti-Catholic. Preachers inveighed not only against 'papists' – those who acknowledged Rome's authority – but against 'popery', any remnants of Catholicism that had survived the Reformation, remnants which the zealous could find almost everywhere. Helped by the Northern Rebellion and *Regnans in Excelsis*, the regime worked hard to associate Catholicism with rebellion, treason and foreign conspiracy. The centrepiece of this effort was John Foxe's *Book of Martyrs*, first published in English in 1563 and regularly expanded thereafter. Foxe's monumental volume lovingly detailed the sufferings of the true martyrs for the faith, principally but not exclusively under Mary. Its most memorable characters, however, are not the martyrs themselves (whom Foxe reduced to a tedious and saintly uniformity) but their persecutors. A riot of grotesques and villains leap off the pages: bloody Bonner, wily Gardiner of Winchester, Wolsey the vainglorious and corrupt, and many more, tracing the battle between Christ's saints and Antichrist's legions back to the dawn of Christianity. The *Book of Martyrs* was placed on open access in some churches, alongside the Bible, and seems sometimes to have been read aloud in services by Protestant clergy who grew bored with the official Homilies. Many of its tales became common currency, some of them reprinted in cheap abridgements, and they kept the memory of Catholic atrocities fresh. Foxe's book also provided a framework through which new horrors could be interpreted. The St Bartholomew's Day Massacre of 1572, the plots around the Scottish queen, the troubles in the Netherlands – all appeared as facets of a terrible conspiracy, whose head was the pope and whose target was that chosen nation, England. Foxe himself was no nationalist, but for many of his readers and interpreters it seemed natural to associate Englishness with the true faith and Catholicism with foreignness, and to defend Christ and the queen in arms against both.

These were paranoid fantasies, but the threat was real. Plots and conspiracies aside, the Catholic missionary effort stepped up dramatically in the 1570s. Books were now being supported by priests, trained at the Douai seminary (which moved to Rheims in 1578) and at a new English college in Rome itself, founded in 1576. By 1580 100 missionary priests had arrived in England; 500 more followed by the time of Elizabeth's death. In 1579 the college in Rome was taken over by the most earnest and ambitious missionaries in the Catholic world, the Jesuits. The Jesuits were relentlessly demonised by the regime, a backhanded compliment to their effectiveness. The first two English Jesuits slipped into the country in 1580. One of them, Edmund Campion, was caught and executed with the customary brutality, and became the highest-profile Catholic martyr of Elizabeth's reign; the other, Robert Persons, a wily survivor, escaped to torment the regime with his sharply judged pamphlets for the next thirty years. The missionaries suffered fearsome casualties: at least 131 were executed, mostly in the 1580s, along with at least sixty of their lay supporters. But they also achieved a measure of success. English Catholicism did not reverse the Protestant tide, but it was not swept away, nor was it broken into scattered islands. The priests sustained networks of contact and mutual support, moving surreptitiously from one gentry household to the next. The Jesuits, in particular, led an attack on 'church papistry', which they saw as an unacceptable compromise. Catholic books continued to arrive from the Continent; there was even an authorised English Catholic New Testament in 1582. Occasionally, temporary, clandestine printing presses were set up in England itself – an impressive feat for such a cumbersome business as printing, although it was an achievement which Puritan dissidents were matching (see below, pp. 274–5). None of this permitted the active proselytisation of the English population – a highly dangerous enterprise – but it kept English Catholicism alive and kicking.

Mere survival is a real enough achievement, but with hindsight English Catholicism in Elizabeth's reign still looks painfully weak. This was not merely a matter of numbers. Like the Marian Protestants before them, Elizabethan Catholics demonstrated that no religious minority is too small and embattled to quarrel. In the late 1590s English Catholics were riven by a bitter dispute over jurisdiction. William Allen, now a cardinal, was the acknowledged leader of the English Catholics, but his strategy had always hinged on spectacular political change: invasion and overthrow of Elizabeth. By the time of his death in 1594 this seemed like a mirage; it also played into the Elizabethan regime's hands, for it made Allen and his allies look like traitors to their queen. While the Jesuits continued to favour this confrontational approach, some of the missionary priests who were 'seculars' (that is, not members of a religious order) shared the view of many lay English Catholics that it was better to try to find a way of coexisting with the regime. This dispute – a matter both of high strategy and of low rivalry between secular and regular priests – might normally have been settled by a bishop banging some heads together, but the Catholic Church in England had no bishops. It was a missionary province in hostile territory. This suited the Jesuits well, giving them as it did almost a free hand. That position was confirmed in 1597 when the cardinal-protector of England appointed George Blackwell, a secular priest friendly to the Jesuits, as 'archpriest', with jurisdiction over the secular clergy. Some of his new charges, resenting what they saw as a Jesuit takeover, appealed to Pope Clement VIII to replace Blackwell with a bishop – symbolic of a more settled Church. Some of these 'appellants' also openly declared their loyalty to the queen. The dispute dragged on for five years. Clement quickly ruled in Blackwell's favour and the appellants submitted, but Blackwell was not satisfied, charging the leading appellants with schism and attempting to suspend ten or more of them. Eventually it was Clement himself who had to bang heads together, in 1602 confirming Blackwell in office but ordering him to keep the secular priests and the Jesuit mission separate. The spat died down, but it had done its damage. The row was very public, and the regime had, of course, done its best to stir up trouble, putting known antagonists in prison together and even permitting some of the appellants to travel to Rome to put their case.

Yet for all the damage it could do, the Elizabethan regime also gave English Catholics three lifelines, helping keep Catholic hopes alive and the Catholic voice heard in national politics. First and simplest, the regime took them seriously. It debated with them and persecuted them. In the 1550s, Queen Mary's regime had refused to dignify the Protestants with an answer, and so yielded the field of debate to them; now Elizabeth's regime did answer its mockers, and so elevated their importance. Neither option was a good one. Likewise, the more zealous Protestants' attacks on 'popery', real or imagined, of necessity kept the 'papists' at the forefront of religious politics.

Second, the nature of the regime's own politics provided an opportunity for Catholics. For even as persecution of Catholics gathered pace, it was clear that this was not a government of zealous Protestant ideologues, but a regime driven as much by low politics as by high principle. This attack began with a bang, with the notorious 1584 book known as *Leicester's Commonwealth*. It was and remains anonymous, although the Jesuit Robert Persons may have had a hand in the project. Whoever wrote it, it was the gutter press at its best: a vicious, muckraking broadside against the earl of Leicester. Leicester was an easy target, and his mockers struck home with precision. The charges against him, of which the high points were two supposed murders and three supposed adulteries, were well informed, well documented and either demonstrably true or strikingly plausible. The attack on this one nobleman, however, was less important than the allegation that England was, indeed, Leicester's commonwealth: his corruption was symbolic of the whole regime's depravity, in particular through his supposed affair with the queen.

The authors of *Leicester's Commonwealth* accused their target of 'atheism', claiming that he was 'never seen yet to say one private prayer within his chamber in his life'.[13] Against the most dedicated Puritan in the queen's inner circle, this was a bold charge, but it was to become central to the Catholic critique of late Elizabethan politics. In Catholic eyes, Elizabeth's counsellors' actions were so little informed by morality or faith – and so much by Machiavelli and their own lusts – that they amounted to a denial of God. This was not, therefore, a battle of Catholics against Protestants, but of principle against rapine, and faith against faithlessness. It was insidiously plausible. Not only Leicester, but the conformist establishment at the heart of the regime – men such as William and Robert Cecil, Francis Walsingham, and Archbishop Whitgift of Canterbury, men who were concerned to defend the Elizabethan settlement by any means necessary – could easily enough be depicted as cold, unprincipled, power-hungry villains of the worst kind. As elective monarchy shaded into monarchical republic, and the role of counsel was asserted ever more strongly, the 'republic' those counsellors were making could be described as a treacherous conspiracy against the commonwealth and against the queen herself. The evident brutality of the persecution of Catholics helped to support this argument, and the regime's insistence that it was done for political rather than religious motives played into Catholic hands too. The hard years of the 1590s – cruel taxation, the burdens of war, and the twin natural disasters of a grave outbreak of plague and a series of failed harvests – sweetened no-one's view of the regime. And the Catholic critique even resonated with the views of more forward Protestants. Some of the bitingly political plays which dominated the English stage in the 1590s could easily be read as implicit endorsements of these criticisms: a phenomenon all the more alarming when the plays were not written by open or covert Catholics. The Catholic critique had struck a nerve.

The third lifeline for Catholics was, of course, the succession. For almost thirty years, Catholics were in the position to which they had become accustomed ever since Henry VIII's Divorce campaign: in the arguments over succession and legitimacy, they had by far the stronger *prima facie* case. While Protestants contorted themselves to justify excluding Mary Stewart, and as the queen steadfastly ignored the issue, Catholics were able to argue simply and straightforwardly for Mary's hereditary right. There was no need to play with dangerous ideas of elective monarchy. In 1587, of course, these positions were dramatically reversed, for

Mary Stewart's execution left King James VI of Scots, a sound Protestant, as the leading candidate for the throne. Protestants promptly lurched back towards dynastic legitimism and Catholics began exploring elective alternatives. Yet Elizabeth still refused to name an heir. There was a decent legal case for arguing that James could not succeed, and the other candidates included suspected crypto-Catholics (Arabella Stewart, James's cousin) and open Catholics (Isabella, the daughter of Philip II of Spain). So Catholic commentators continued to try to stir things up. Robert Persons' spuriously even-handed *A Conference about the Next Succession* (1595) was a Catholic manifesto for elective monarchy, adopting many of the arguments so painstakingly developed by Protestant theorists and turning them against them. The fact that so many of the candidates were possible favourers of Catholicism gave some weight to Persons' and other Catholic voices, despite their exclusion from power. Even James VI felt the need to drop hints that he might tolerate or tack towards Catholicism. When someone like Persons spoke, it was as well to listen. As everyone knew, if a real succession crisis came, the sleeping Catholic giant might wake, and only then would his strength be tested.

Notes

1 Patrick Collinson, 'The monarchical republic of Queen Elizabeth I', *Bulletin of the John Rylands Library*, vol. 69 (1987), pp. 394–424.

2 Patrick Collinson, ' "The state as monarchical commonwealth": "Tudor" England', in *Journal of Historical Sociology*, vol. 15, no. 1 (2002), p. 94.

3 Patrick Collinson (ed.), *The English Captivity of Mary, Queen of Scots* (1987), p. 45.

4 G. R. Elton (ed.), *The Tudor Constitution* (1960), p. 77.

5 Robert Crowley, *A sermon made in the chappel at the Gylde Halle* (1575). I am grateful to Paulina Kewes for this reference and for discussions on the subject.

6 Joseph Stevenson (ed.), *Calendar of State Papers, Foreign Series . . . 1559–60* (1865), no. 1066.

7 Christopher Haigh, *Elizabeth I* (1988), p. 140.

8 Neil Younger, 'If the Armada had landed: a reappraisal of England's defences in 1588', *History*, vol. 93 (2008).

9 Jane Dawson, 'William Cecil and the British dimension of early Elizabethan foreign policy', *History*, vol. 74 (1989), p. 213.

10 J. E. C. Hill, 'Puritans and the "dark corners of the land" ', *Transactions of the Royal Historical Society*, 5th series, vol. 13 (1963), p. 92.

11 G. R. Elton (ed.), *The Tudor Constitution* (1960), p. 416.

12 Ibid, p. 418.

13 Anon., *The copie of a leter, vvryten by a Master of Arte of Cambrige* (1584), p. 198.

CHAPTER 10

Reforming the World of the Parish

By 1560, England's and Scotland's political establishments were committed to the Protestant Reformation. In particular, they were committed to the Reformed Protestantism of Zürich and Geneva, and to making that Reformation a reality in the lives of the people. And that was where agreement ended. The debates over exactly what kind of Reformations there would be in England and Scotland were bitterly divisive. English Protestantism contained a vocal and energetic minority, who called themselves the 'godly' or the 'elect' but whose many mockers and enemies called them 'Puritans' or 'precisians'. These 'Puritans' believed that England was divided between a truly Christian minority (that is, themselves), and a wider population still sodden with the dregs of popery. Neither the structures nor the morals of the English Church had yet attained the purity for which they hoped. But to understand their worldview, we need to begin with the country that many of them saw as the ideal to be followed: Scotland.

Protestant Scotland: from kirk session to presbytery

A disciplined Church

The Scottish Reformation's success in embedding itself in parish life is one of the most mysterious events in the sixteenth century: for that success was remarkable. Few records survive from before 1560 that allow us to peer into the daily life of Scottish parish churches, but as Reformed churches were established, they formed 'kirk sessions' (see above, p. 220). Their records give us an extraordinary picture of Reformed Protestantism in action.

The 1560 Scots Confession of Faith had declared that one of the distinguishing marks of a true Christian Church was godly discipline. On this
view, a Church was not merely a collection of individuals. It was the bride
of Christ, his chosen and covenanted people, called to holiness. It was also
a light to the world – that is, it ought to be demonstrably virtuous, to refute
the Catholic claim that Protestantism was moral anarchy. To achieve this,
they turned to Matthew's Gospel:

*If thy brother trespass against thee, go and tell him his fault between thee
and him alone: if he hear thee, thou hast won thy brother. But if he hear
thee not, take yet with thee one or two, that by the mouth of two or three
witnesses every word may be confirmed. And if he refuse to hear them,
tell it unto the Church: and if he refuse to hear the Church also, let him be
unto thee as an heathen man, and a publican.*[1]

Reformed Protestants took this as a literal pattern for their collective life.

The system of discipline which emerged in Scotland, modelled closely
on that in Calvin's Geneva, centred on the kirk session: an assembly
of ordained ministers and lay 'elders'. These elders were pillars of the
community who took responsibility for policing the people's morals –
including one another's. The people were encouraged to report grave or
public sins, but the elders were also responsible for actively seeking out
such sinners. The Reformed Scots service-book, the *Book of Common
Order*, required that kirk sessions should assemble every Thursday 'diligently [to] examine all such faults and suspicions, as may be espied'.[2]
Those suspected of moral offences would be visited privately by members
of the kirk session. If they proved obstinate, they might be summoned
before the session and formally reprimanded. If they were still unrepentant,
the procedure could be repeated publicly before the whole congregation.
The more discreet stages of the process might be bypassed for notorious or
public offenders.

Such penitence was designed to be humiliating. The penitents' stool,
where offenders sat so that the whole congregation could see them and
marvel at their folly, became a fixture in post-Reformation Scottish churches.
Penitents would be clothed in sackcloth, go barefoot, or wear signs de-
scribing their offences. Yet kirk sessions were not courts of law, and did
not punish as such. They applied moral and social pressure to secure
repentance and reconciliation. Those of us with modern concepts of liberty
and privacy tend to bristle at the thought of a kirk session: busybodies
judging others' morals. Yet in a society with no privacy and little concept
of individual liberty, this made some sense. For example, sexual miscon-

duct (inevitably, the bread and butter of kirk sessions) was not simply a private affair. Extramarital sex produced illegitimate children, the costs of whose care would usually fall on the parish. And while the kirk sessions' handling of illicit sex reflected the wider society's double standard on these issues (unchastity was widely seen as a mere foible for men and the defining, unforgivable sin for women), they did at least make attempts to identify, and discipline, the fathers of bastards as well as their mothers. Nor were the kirk sessions' attitudes to their people forbiddingly judgemental. The kirk session minutes document the care which elders frequently took in pacifying quarrels or in attempting to help those whose lives were in turmoil. Patching up family quarrels was a particular concern. The Reformed system of discipline could be paternalistic in the best sense.

Yet if the kirk session was not quasi-totalitarian, neither was it a kind of institutionalised counselling service. Its primary purpose was neither social control nor social harmony, but godly order. Alongside sexual offences and quarrels, the mainstay of its business was religious offences. Those who missed sermons, who arrived late, or who talked or fell asleep during them; those suspected of work or of inappropriate recreation on a Sunday; those who did not send their children to be catechised – all such people could expect a visit from one of the elders. Likewise those who disparaged the new faith (or its ministers), or showed any signs of sympathy or nostalgia for the old. Such offences did not need to be overt. For example, the Reformed church in Scotland (showing a zeal unmatched anywhere else in the Reformed Protestant world) suppressed all traditional feasts, fasts and festivals, making no distinction of days aside from Sundays. However, many lay people persisted in marking 25 December as if it were still the popish festival of Christmas. The elders might come knocking that morning, and woe betide you if they found a goose in your oven. Such disciplines could not, of course, make people into good Christians or save their souls. Only God's decree of predestination could do that. But it was the elders' responsibility to ensure that God was honoured by at least the outward reverence of all the parish, and that sinners did not lead the righteous astray.

This might seem a radically new experience for most lay people, but the shock of the new should not be overestimated. For one thing, kirk sessions did not spring into being fully formed; although since their records are our main source, we know frustratingly little about the processes that led up to their establishment. It was a matter of decades before a reasonably comprehensive network of kirk sessions was in place across the country – an impressive enough achievement, but not one performed with a click of John Knox's fingers. What is reasonably clear is that the creation of a functioning kirk session depended on two separate elements being present: first, a committed minister, who would provide the diet of preaching which both justified and underpinned the kirk session's discipline; and second, a lay elite who were willing either to co-opt the Reformed Church, or to be co-opted by it. This second part of the process inevitably involved some compromise, as the ministers' zeal accommodated itself to existing social realities. This was made painfully clear in Edinburgh, where, uniquely, a pre-1559 clandestine Protestant congregation had developed a kirk session of its own. This congregation, a small and socially undistinguished gathering, tried to take advantage of the victory of 1560 to assert its authority over the whole burgh; but it failed entirely. The burgh's merchant and professional oligarchy swiftly took control of the new establishment and marginalised the early converts. Before long the kirk session was staffed principally by trained lawyers. Although the kirk session was structurally separate from the secular magistracy, the overlap of personnel between them meant that the two became different faces of the same social elite.

Edinburgh was a religiously conservative town, but the same process of taming Reformed zeal can be seen in a town like Perth, where the Reformation rebellion had first broken out. Although there is no indication of lingering Catholicism in Perth, the new system bedded down there only slowly. The earliest kirk session records surviving for Perth date from 1577, and although the session had certainly been functioning for some years by then, it seems to have been doing so in an *ad hoc* fashion. Here, too, the kirk session's membership reflected the town's political structure and its political divisions. Perhaps this seemed like contamination: the Reformed Church was becoming simply another forum for local politics. Yet it was only through adapting itself to local political structures that the new Church could get under Scotland's skin. As a result, there were compromises. The first of Perth's kirk session records, from 1577, refers to a Corpus Christi play recently staged in the burgh. The session clearly disapproved of this, yet did not confront it directly. Instead, they were often inclined to use such routine breaches of discipline as a way of funding their extensive poor-relief efforts, through imposing fines on offenders.

In other words, even once it was established, the kirk sessions' discipline was never so relentless in practice as it was in theory. Perhaps it never could have been. At the edges of every community are the misfits, the awkward, the incapable and the pitiable, and kirk sessions – like any local magistrates – were forced daily to take decisions over quite what to pursue when dealing with such people, and what to overlook. Moreover, the kirk sessions did not attempt to impose a total cultural revolution. They targeted the religious practices which they found most egregious, but allowed a good deal of the ritual life of the parish to persist or to resurface in different forms. For example, baptisms, weddings and burials had been liturgically and theologically transformed; but liturgy and theology are only small parts of the communal marking of births, marriages and deaths. Other festivities and rituals around these and other events continued much as before. Some practices were tolerated even more directly. When the *Book of Common Order* was translated into Gaelic, its translator added a prayer for use in blessing a ship going to sea. As the best recent study of discipline in the Scottish Church puts it, 'when Reformed ministers and elders threw out the popish bath water, they were careful to keep not only the baby, but also some bath toys to keep it happy'.[3]

As a result, in much of Scotland the kirk sessions achieved more than compliance: they achieved respect. The Church's elders, who were also almost everyone's social betters, were seen to be working painstakingly to preserve the peace and to correct antisocial behaviour. The system's inbuilt safeguards against hypocrisy also helped. Elders were formally required to look for faults 'not only amongst others, but chiefly amongst themselves',[4] and in particular to give minute attention to any shortcomings in their minister's life or teaching. Many of them did indeed discipline their own members readily. The response to this regime went beyond grudging compliance. Even those who, for reasons of illness or distance, were excused from attendance at sermons frequently made an effort to be there, and to be seen to be there. For if the kirk session was oppressive for the minority who crossed it, it was also a source of moral reassurance and approbation for the rest of society. To be in good standing with the kirk session was valuable testimony to one's moral character. Kirk sessions became arbiters of reputation.

This was most apparent at the celebrations of the Lord's Supper, the Reformed sacrament of the Eucharist. Originally intended to be held four times a year, it was in fact usually celebrated only once or twice. These set-piece events, often spread over two or more Sundays in large parishes, were again a mix of the new and the old. The liturgy, based on that which Knox and his congregation had devised in Geneva, was stark in its opposition to the old Mass. Sacramental confession had been abolished too. Yet the minister and kirk session would now examine the people to decide who might be admitted to the sacrament, a process which must have felt somewhat like confession to those on the receiving end. The chosen ones would be given a communion token – often a simple button of leather, or the like. These tokens were bluntly functional, but they were heavy with meaning. More than a sacred meal ticket, a communion token was a marker of moral standing. A believer might even feel a twinge of pride at holding one, however much the preachers warned that such pride was the devil's snare.

And if the kirk sessions had a stick to wield, after all their exhortations, this was it: excommunication. This was a well-established punishment, known as 'cursing' in pre-Reformation Scotland, when its overuse had devalued it considerably. The Reformed Church reinforced it with the full weight of the kirk session. To be excommunicated was not simply to be excluded from communion, but to be cut off from all traffic with good Christian people. All members of the Church were expected to avoid any but essential dealings with excommunicates. Wives were to shun their husbands, and children their own parents. Business dealings with them were forbidden. Those who broke the exclusion risked censure themselves. Although the practice was, again, messier than the theory, excommunication was a genuinely fearsome threat. The pressure on an excommunicate to repent and to petition for readmission to the Christian community was strong; and such offenders would be expected to demonstrate that their repentance was heartfelt.

This system worked well, then: almost too well. Kirk sessions became formidably powerful, and the more scrupulously and responsibly they exercised that power, the more powerful they became. In Reformed societies across Europe, these powers were a focus for controversy. Even in Geneva, Calvin had secured the Church's right to excommunicate offenders only after an extended and nasty struggle with the city council. In other Reformed territories, such as the Netherlands, only a minority of the population were ever full members of the Church – making the social exclusivity of membership more appealing but the decree of excommunication less alarming. Scotland was the only territorial state which achieved a universal system of discipline where the power of excommunication was firmly in the Church's own hands. This was a source of considerable pride to some Scots Protestants. It was also one of the factors underlying the bitter ecclesiastical quarrels of the half-century after the Reformation.

Bishops and presbyteries

From 1560 to 1689, the Scottish Church was engaged in a protracted and often vicious internal battle over apparently minor issues. The problem was one of Church government, not of theology. One party – which tended to be supported by the crown – favoured the retention of bishops. The other, led by ministers claiming to be the heirs of Reformed purity, favoured more conciliar forms of Church government. From the late 1570s, these purists advocated the creation of structures they called 'presbyteries', and as such they themselves were called 'Presbyterians'.

A presbytery was an elected council (consisting of 'presbyters', from the Greek for an elder), chosen by the churches in a particular geographical area, whose responsibility was to oversee and govern those churches. Its function was, in other words, very like that of a bishop. The differences were twofold. First, bishops were seen as having an intrinsic authority over their fellow clerics, bestowed by consecration and symbolised by their status as lords of the realm who sat in Parliament. Presbyteries, by contrast, were composed of ordinary ministers, who remained formally equal to one another and to all other ministers, and who held office for a limited period. The principle that all ministers are equal became one to which Presbyterians rallied. This issue concealed a second, more practical difference. Bishops were appointed by the king, but presbyteries were elected by the churches under their care. In other words, the battle between Episcopalians (the supporters of bishops) and Presbyterians was about royal power. How much control ought the state to have over the Church?

For a Church which had first established itself by rebellion, and then maintained itself for six years under the doubtful protection of a Catholic queen, the obvious answer was: not much. John Knox insisted that monarchs owed their authority simply to divine providence, and could command obedience only insofar as they obeyed God's will. He repeatedly showed himself ready to denounce or oppose rulers he disliked to their faces (once reducing Mary, queen of Scots, to tears). The *Book of Discipline* – Knox's project – insisted that everyone should be subject to the Church's discipline, 'as well the rulers, as they that are ruled'.[5] Knox was no theorist, but after his death in 1572 a more thorough set of demands was worked out by the scholar Andrew Melville.

Melville, like Knox, had spent time in Geneva; unlike Knox, he had a head for administration. It was under his oversight that a *Second Book of Discipline* was created in 1578, clarifying several issues which the first book had left uncertain. The *Second Book* vigorously asserted the near-complete independence of the Church from state control. The symbol of this was the General Assembly, the supreme governing body of the Scottish Church, an institution which had taken shape informally during the 1560s. The Assembly had then functioned as a focus for Protestant opposition to the queen, and had of course operated independently of her. It now had no wish to lose that independence. The *Second Book* therefore asserted that General Assemblies 'ought always to be retained in their own liberty', and needed no royal permission to meet. The one role which the crown might have, the *Book* admitted, was that in emergencies a king might intervene to reform or purge the Church of error. But in more settled times, 'where the ministry of the church is once lawfully constituted, and they that are placed do their office faithfully, all godly princes and magistrates ought to hear and obey their voice, and reverence the Majesty of the Son of God, speaking by them'.[6] And this did not apply only to the General Assembly. In principle, a kirk session could call *any* sinner in Scotland before it, regardless of rank. God is no respecter of persons. As Melville reportedly said to James VI's face in 1596, it was Christ who was king of the Scottish Church, 'whose subject King James the Sixth is, and of whose kingdom not a king, nor a lord, nor a head, but a member!'[7]

Unsurprisingly, those in authority had a different view. It was easier for the Melvillians to write manifestos than to bring these structures into being. For most of the 1567–73 civil war, the Scots Church remained a strange hybrid, a half-finished Reformed Church alongside the still-functioning husk of its Catholic predecessor. The General Assembly believed that the structures and revenues of the old Church should come under its control; the various regents for the young James VI wished to continue treating ecclesiastical offices as their own property. Regent Mar's unilateral appointment of a new archbishop of St Andrews in 1571 stirred up so much resentment from the ministers that it became urgent to find a compromise. The resulting agreement – the Concordat of Leith, in 1572 – initially met with widespread approval. Even Knox, in his final illness, accepted it. The Concordat allowed for bishops, who would be nominated by the crown but examined by ministers, and who would be under the General Assembly's oversight after their appointment. This was not terribly different from the system of superintendents which had been half-erected after 1560 (see above, pp. 220–1), although some Protestant consciences recoiled from certain dregs of popery – the old diocesan boundaries, the wealth and lordliness of the bishops, and indeed the title 'bishop' itself.

The Concordat failed because the General Assembly could not hold the crown to its side of the bargain. Neither the earl of Morton, regent from 1572 to 1578, nor the bishops whom he appointed, honoured the Concordat's spirit, inflaming the suspicion of those ministers who had always disliked it. It was in this mood that the Assembly drew up the *Second Book of Discipline*. That *Book* did not propose presbyteries as such, but did urge that elders in different churches work together for mutual support and correction. In 1579, the Assembly suggested using the 'exercises' which had emerged in both Scotland and England as a forum for this (see below, p. 271). Political change made the task seem more urgent. The earl of Morton had been deposed in 1578, and the twelve-year-old king declared an adult. However, real power was slipping into the hands of his French-raised kinsman Esmé Stuart, soon to be the duke of Lennox, who was a Catholic. In 1581 the Assembly ordered the creation of thirteen 'model' presbyteries in a block of territory across the central Lowlands, prototypes for a network of some fifty which they hoped might cover the whole country. It was the 1560s all over again. Rather than overturning the authority of the bishops, the Reformed Church was simply going to bypass them.

However, while the Assembly responded to Esmé Stuart's pro-Catholic, pro-French regime by reasserting its independence, Scotland's Protestant nobility took more direct action. In 1582 the young king was kidnapped in the so-called 'Ruthven Raid', and a group of Protestant nobles and lairds seized control. Stuart was banished, and died shortly afterwards. However, the fifteen-year-old king was in no mood to be treated like this. While James's own Protestant convictions were never in doubt, the Ruthven Raid sealed his distrust of Presbyterian zealotry. He already had ample reason to be suspicious of the mulishly independent political culture which Knox, Melville and others had cultivated. These were the men who had fought a war against his grandmother and deposed his mother. A particular hate-figure for James was his former tutor, George Buchanan, who had justified Mary's deposition in almost republican terms. James had received a formidable education at Buchanan's hands (he joked that he had learned Latin before he learned Scots), but also some formidable beatings. When James escaped from the Ruthven Raiders, after less than a year, he began seriously to assert his independence. He and his new favourite – James Stewart, whom he made earl of Arran – were too shrewd to seek vengeance on the Ruthven Raiders directly, but they did act to bring the Presbyterians to heel. The result was a series of parliamentary Acts in 1584 which the ministers dubbed the 'Black Acts'. Rather than a negotiated compromise like the Leith Concordat, this was a full-scale assault. The Black Acts reaffirmed the Protestant Church's doctrines and practices, but suppressed the presbyteries, subjected the General Assembly to royal control, and placed sweeping new powers in the bishops' hands. Clergy were required to subscribe to the Acts. Some two dozen who refused chose exile in England instead.

Politically, this worked. The point had been made, and James's authority asserted – an authority which became all the more real when he cast Arran off in 1585. Ecclesiastically, however, such a hardline position was unsustainable. The presbyteries were restored in 1586, to work alongside bishops. They slowly spread, numbering over forty by the early 1590s and covering the bulk of the country. The bishops' powers were more eroded than abolished. In 1592, James recognised the presbyteries' and the General Assembly's supremacy in a parliamentary Act which the ministers dubbed the 'Golden Act' – prematurely. For the king continued to see himself as the Church's overlord and protector. He still insisted on his right to regulate when the General Assembly met, although he was careful to use that power circumspectly (requesting, for example, that it reschedule meetings from the morning to the afternoon so that he might be present). Radical Presbyterian sentiment flared up again in 1596–97, provoking a confrontation in which the king again outmanoeuvred his opponents. Yet he was not so foolish as to believe he had defeated them decisively.

James's view of his position was made clear during the other great political–religious crisis of the early 1590s: the witch scare. In 1589 James married a Danish princess. When the happy couple sailed back to Scotland, they were caught in a dangerous storm which (in accordance with warnings he had received earlier) James feared might be the work of witches. It sparked a large-scale witch-hunt which crossed much of the country and which ebbed and flowed for most of the 1590s. James himself was to write a book on the subject (one of many this most literary of kings produced), and he interrogated several suspected witches in person. According to the earliest published account of these trials, one such witch confessed to having asked the Devil why he wanted to drown the king of Scots. The Devil replied that 'the king is the greatest enemy he hath in the world'.[8]

This was the kind of testimony that James VI wanted: that he was no mere member of Christ's Church. Nor would he accept the Presbyterian insistence on the inherent equality of all Christian ministers, an equality which seemed to deny not only his own distinctive role but also the whole hierarchy of Christian society (indeed of Creation). He would tolerate the existence of presbyteries, but not the abolition of bishops. During the 1590s, as he made his succession to the English throne seem inevitable (the achievement his mother had never managed), Puritans and Presbyterians in England hoped that he might bring some of the Scots' radicalism south with him. It was wishful thinking. In 1604, as a newly minted king of England, he famously and bluntly rebuffed such hopes by asserting, 'No bishop, no king.' In James's experience, this was not a debating point. It was a statement of fact.

Puritans and conformists in England

During the reigns of Elizabeth I in England and James VI in Scotland, jealous eyes looked from each country at the other. James and his allies in Scotland envied the Elizabethan regime's control over the English Church. Likewise, a noisy minority of English clerics and lay people looked long-ingly at Scotland, where a purer and more complete Reformation had been enacted. Not all of these 'Puritans' were actual Presbyterians, wishing to abolish episcopacy. But there was much else for Puritans to admire in the Scots Church. The plain simplicity of Scottish worship contrasted starkly with the Book of Common Prayer's ceremonious complexity. The General Assembly's freedom, even though mitigated by royal oversight, was scarcely imaginable in England. Above all, perhaps, English Puritans envied the congregational discipline exercised by kirk sessions. For those who thought that such discipline was a distinguishing mark of a true Church, England's failure to embrace any such system was damning indeed.

However, Elizabethan Puritans could only envy the Scots. Their own government spent forty years repeatedly facing down their attempts at reform. Clergy were deprived; careers ended; even an archbishop of Canterbury was broken, as successive waves of Puritan agitation dashed themselves on the rock of Elizabeth's monumental stubbornness. The experience of zealous Protestants during her reign was an arc from hope, through frustration and anger, to resigned defeat. But this is not the whole story. If the pressure for further Reformation made no progress at national level, the parishes were another matter. While Puritanism did not trans-form England's public life in the way that it hoped, it had more impact on its wider culture than is often acknowledged – indeed, more than the Puritans themselves liked to admit.

The long struggle against the Settlement

As we have seen (see above, pp. 201–3), plenty of the English Church's senior clergy in the early 1560s had grave reservations about its structures and rituals. Their choice nevertheless to accept office in it can be viewed cynically: dignities and regular incomes have their appeal. But the choice also made strategic sense. Experience suggested that reformation was a process, and as long as it was moving in the right direction, most Pro-testants could accept some compromises. The new Church's core beliefs were unequivocally Reformed Protestant. The most authoritative Reformed theologians in Europe – notably Peter Martyr Vermigli, who had spent much of Edward VI's reign in England – urged their English friends to conform.

This is an important point, because during the seventeenth century the English Church would mutate into something distinct from Reformed Protestantism, and assert an 'Anglican' identity for itself. These Anglicans then rewrote the history of the sixteenth century in their own image. The peculiarities of Elizabeth's Reformation made this rewriting possible, but we should not be deceived by it. To describe the sixteenth-century English Church as 'Anglican' is anachronistic. This was a Reformed Protestant Church. It had important idiosyncrasies, but every Reformed Protestant Church in Europe had some idiosyncrasies. Reformed Protestantism was not a franchise to be imported wholesale. There was wide agreement that while some religious questions were essential, others were 'matters indifferent' – *adiaphora*, in the Greek term popularised by the Lutheran Philip Melanchthon. On such matters, Christian practice could legitimately vary. The concept of *adiaphora* permitted considerable variation in the practice of religion. It also, in principle, allowed English Protestants who disliked aspects of Elizabeth's Reformation to conform without staining their consciences. In practice, however, the concept of *adiaphora* caused as many problems as it solved – for the questions of what was truly 'indifferent', and of who might regulate it, remained open.

If there was space for consciences to be flexible about details of religious practice, there was no such space on another issue. One of Henry VIII's many legacies was that English Protestantism retained an exceptionally high doctrine of obedience. And this was before 1558–59, when Protestants were providentially liberated from Catholic tyranny by the accession of Elizabeth, a queen who was clearly God's gift to her people. It was her subjects' duty to obey her, not to second-guess her. Moreover, maintaining the unity of the Reformed Church in England was also a matter of supreme importance. Given Protestantism's well-deserved reputation for being quarrelsome, this is worth stressing. Virtually every English Protestant wished to maintain a single, national Church, into which all English people would be born: not voluntary congregations, still less a plurality of churches. Puritans were not (with very few exceptions) separatists. Their loyalty to the established Church was put under immense pressure at times, and they certainly strained at the bounds of conformity. Yet they were also convinced that schism was a grave sin, and very few were willing to abandon visible unity until the Church itself broke down in the 1640s. For the time being, the English Church was an argumentative family, headed by an obstinate matriarch. Her spiritual children might fight bitterly with one another and even grumble against her, but that did not mean they were ready to run away from home.

The first set-piece confrontation between Puritans and the regime unfolded in the reign's first meeting of the Convocation of Canterbury, in 1563 – almost the last occasion on which that ancient assembly seemed like a possible locus of power. The 1563 Convocation secured one undoubted triumph. Edward VI's Church had set out a formal definition of its doctrine in the Forty-Two Articles. Convocation now approved a lightly revised version of this text. A short group of articles denouncing Anabaptist radicals were dropped, for that threat no longer seemed pressing. Most of the other revisions were cosmetic, although the new text was slightly more flexible on the issue of predestination. The article on the Eucharist was revised much as the Prayer Book had been: a flat rejection of the Lutheran doctrine of Christ's presence was replaced by a somewhat more ambiguous text, although – at the last minute – the assembly agreed to omit that article altogether, as an unnecessary insult to potential Lutheran allies. So in the end Convocation adopted Thirty-Eight Articles. Eight years later, Parliament was to approve these, plus the omitted Eucharistic article, establishing the Thirty-Nine Articles in law.

The Articles were, and were seen to be, a statement of solid Reformed Protestantism, akin to the 'Confessions' adopted by the Reformed Churches of France, Scotland and the Netherlands in the 1560s and 1570s. Two differences between the Articles and those Confessions are worth noticing, however. First, the Articles did contain some wafer-thin cracks of theological ambiguity. This was not unusual in texts of this period. By the early 1580s, the Scots Confession, too, looked insufficiently precise, and in 1581 the so-called 'Negative Confession' was drafted – a text designed specifically to make it impossible for Catholics to affirm it. Yet Elizabeth did not permit any such clarifications and developments. The Thirty-Nine Articles' cracks remained, cracks into which later theologians could work their chisels. Second, these were Articles, not a Confession. They were imposed by authority, not a statement of a Church's or a people's faith. Paradoxically, this made them less powerful. Initially, clergy were not compelled to subscribe to them (as they had been to the Forty-Two Articles). In 1571, Parliament did require clergy ordained before 1558 to subscribe, which put Catholic bitter-enders under pressure, but this did nothing to ensure conformity among Protestants.

These were quibbles, however. The English Church's Reformed Protestant identity, already unmistakable from its liturgy and Homilies, was now formally proclaimed. Naturally enough, the 1563 Convocation also set itself to reforming the popish elements surviving in that liturgy. A slate of six proposed reforms tackled several particular Reformed bugbears, including pipe organs, holy days, traditional vestments, signing with the cross in baptism and kneeling at the Eucharist. The battle in Convocation's lower house was hard fought, with the bishops – and behind them, the queen – twisting arms mercilessly to defeat the proposals. In the end, the lower house rejected them by fifty-nine votes to fifty-eight. If there was a moment when 'Puritans' as a distinctive group appeared within the English Church, this was it. They would become familiar with the taste of defeat.

Needless to say, the wafer-thin defeat in Convocation did not end Puritan disquiet. The first conflict to boil over was that over clerical dress. It may seem a strange subject to become excited about, and even to smack of clerical narcissism. No one argued that vestments were theologically significant. All sides in this quarrel agreed that they were *adiaphora*, things indifferent on which good Christians might legitimately disagree. But the queen insisted, as a matter of obedience, that her clergy wear a stripped-down version of traditional clerical vestments when preaching or presiding at divine service. The ornate sacramental vestments of the old Church were gone, but Elizabeth wished her clergy to retain a surplice (a plain white gown worn over the outer clothing) and a black cap. The royal injunctions of 1559 had indicated this, although with some ambiguity. That ambiguity led many of the more 'advanced' clergy to take a different path. They did not wish to conduct worship in ordinary civilian clothing – that would lack order and dignity – but in academic dress, including a degree hood where appropriate. They wished to be Protestant ministers distinguished by their learning, not Catholic priests endowed with sacramental power.

Puritan clerics found the vestments issue genuinely troubling. Those who had been in exile had seen the simple purity of Reformed worship in Zürich or Geneva. Now they were being asked to dress up in a pale imitation of popish frippery. To stand before their congregations actually wearing this get-up implicated them personally and directly. It was, they feared, a visible sign of continuity between the reformed and the unreformed Churches, and could thus lull the laity into underestimating the change. How could they denounce popery and call the nation to repentance when popery's rags still hung about them?

The reasons for Elizabeth's unbudgeable stand on the issue are less clear. At no stage did she or her supporters argue that traditional vestments had positive values beyond 'order and comeliness'. Yet this was not merely a matter of the queen's old-fashioned personal tastes. We may speculate that she and her ever-cautious regime hoped that the maintenance of some visible continuity might ease the transition to the new religion. More importantly, however, it became a matter of obedience. The dispute was plainly a proxy for many other battles. If Elizabeth had yielded on vestments, a dozen other demands would have followed. Instead, she took a stand. When the nonconformists cited the concept of *adiaphora* and their own consciences, the regime asserted that, if the question was indifferent, the queen had the right to determine it authoritatively for all her subjects, whereupon they had an absolute duty to obey her.

Characteristically, however, the queen did not fight this battle herself. Rather, she left it to her hapless archbishop of Canterbury, Matthew Parker. Parker himself had no difficulties with vestments, but this was not a fight he would have chosen to pick. Worse, while Elizabeth insisted that he enforce conformity, she refused publicly to involve herself. So Parker – who was not even a member of the queen's Council – was forced to do so as if on his own (limited) authority. In 1565 he issued a set of so-called 'Advertisements' to the clergy, laying down precise rules on vestments; not royal injunctions, nor even episcopal injunctions (which could, at best, have applied only to the province of Canterbury), but orders whose legal status was at best unclear.

First in Parker's sights were Thomas Sampson and Laurence Humphrey, heads of the Oxford colleges of Christ Church and Magdalen respectively. Sampson was a Puritan whose quarrelsome, hair-trigger conscience was exasperating even to his allies, and his loathing for traditional vestments had long been apparent. Parker negotiated with the two dons at gruelling length over the late winter and spring of 1565, finally detaining them at his palace at Lambeth. Sampson and Humphrey had powerful friends. The earl of Leicester, a consistent ally of the Puritans, backed them, and Bishop Grindal of London invited both men to preach at London's prime pulpit, Paul's Cross, at Easter 1565. Magdalen College's statutes, moreover, made Humphrey almost impossible to displace. As so often, due process trumped politics. But Parker was able to muster a range of impressive authorities on his side. Martin Bucer and Peter Martyr Vermigli had both accepted the Edwardian Church's use of vestments. Even more tellingly, when Sampson and Humphrey appealed to Heinrich Bullinger, the chief pastor of Zürich, he not only came down on Parker's side but also sent a copy of his reply to the archbishop. It was a significant victory, for Bullinger was probably the most eminent Reformed Protestant theologian then living. Bullinger knew Sampson, and disliked him: 'The man is never satisfied; he always has some doubt or other to busy himself with.'[9] Sampson, however, would not budge, and was ejected from Christ Church by royal order: the first minister of the reformed Church of England to be deprived for nonconformity. A trickle of other deprivations of vestiarian nonconformists followed over the next few months. The first round had been won by the conformists, but at the cost of a good deal of bitterness.

Puritan hopes were raised again by the failed Northern Rebellion of 1569 and the queen's excommunication in 1570 (see above, pp. 247–8), which hardened the religious battle-lines. It was reasonable to hope that the regime would no longer be so respectful of Catholic sensibilities. In 1570 John Foxe produced a second, much expanded edition of his *Book of Martyrs*, amply supported from within the regime. Where the first edition had simply celebrated Elizabeth's accession, this one paid more attention to what was still undone. Earlier the same year, a young Cambridge theologian named Thomas Cartwright had laid out a manifesto for such reforms. He wanted to replace bishops with a network of elected synods, like the presbyteries that would later emerge in Scotland. Cartwright was driven from office (like his Scots counterpart Melville, he went to Geneva), but when Parliament met in 1571, Puritan hopes were high. The Parliament did indeed enact the Thirty-Nine Articles, but the queen was no more willing to accept radicalism from the Commons in 1571 than she had been from Convocation in 1563. Bills to revise the Prayer Book, and to reintroduce Cranmer's canon law reform, were killed in the Commons by the queen's order (and with much less difficulty than the Puritan articles had been defeated in Convocation). A second attempt to introduce such legislation in 1572 drew a direct rebuke from Elizabeth.

In disarray, Puritans responded in two different ways. Those closest to power bided their time, and resolved in future to persuade and petition their touchy queen rather than peremptorily to demand reform. Foremost among these was Grindal, who in 1570 was made archbishop of York. Less politic and less patient souls chose instead to let off some steam. In 1572 a polemical *Admonition to the Parliament* was printed, the work of two ministers named John Field and Thomas Wilcox. This bitter and immoderate text, which promptly landed its authors in prison, denounced the English Church as still mired in popery. Instead of a Church in which priests of little learning and less godliness parroted the words of the Prayer Book and Homilies, these Puritans wanted a Reformation fired by preaching and built on discipline. And the manner of their protest pushed their cause further from political respectability than ever.

Still the more moderate Puritans could hope. Archbishop Parker, in poor health and ever more withdrawn into his antiquarian studies, died in 1575: Grindal was appointed to succeed him. It looked like the Puritans' moment of opportunity. Instead, it was a disaster. Grindal and other 'advanced' bishops had been attempting to press forward the reformist cause in their dioceses through events which were known as 'prophesyings'. That term suggests – and may have suggested to Elizabeth – something spontaneous and chaotic, but it was and is misleading. Grindal preferred to call them 'exercises'. The name came from the *Prophezei* of the Church in Zürich, on which they were closely modelled. They were, in effect, sober master-classes on Biblical exegesis. Clergy from a wide area would gather in a particular church, to hear a few of their number (pre-selected by the bishop) debate the interpretation of a chosen Biblical text. It was, as Grindal explained, simply a university theology class held in the shires, in order to train clergy to be more effective preachers. Lay people might attend to hear this display of learning, but they were forbidden to take part. The practice had spread rapidly across England during the 1570s. To Grindal (and, it seems, a majority of the other bishops), it was a harmless, cost-free and effective way of building up the Church.

Elizabeth disagreed. Like her father, she feared that public theological debate would inevitably degenerate into idleness, innovation, lay preaching, quarrels, sedition and rebellion. There had indeed been disturbances at some prophesyings, or occasions on which unauthorised ministers had taken part. When she eventually overrode Grindal and ordered the prophesyings suppressed, she denounced them as 'unlawful assemblies of a great number of our people out of their ordinary parishes' for hearing 'new devised opinions'. She even described them as 'invasions',[10] for the fact that people were leaving their own parish churches to attend these events particularly alarmed conformists. Puritans' enthusiasm for sermons regularly led them to travel to hear preachers outside their own parishes. Conformists mocked this as 'sermon-gadding', and feared it as a sign of destabilising and divisive enthusiasm.

Like the vestiarian controversy a decade earlier, the prophesyings were symbolic of a wider cultural divide. This time, Grindal and his Puritan brethren were in no mood to compromise. Rather, they deliberately blew up the prophesyings issue into a full-scale crisis, and tried to use the dangerous international situation to their advantage. The prophesyings were presented as a means not only of building a godly Church but also of stamping out the twin perils of popery and sectarianism. This argument produced, in 1577, the first systematic attempt to count the Catholic recusants in England – a hasty exercise which resulted in only some 1500 of the usual suspects being named, but a harbinger of more systematic efforts to come. The 400-fold increase in recusancy fines in 1581 (see above, p. 248) arose from the same mood. Mirroring this was a sudden assault on a tiny, enigmatic sect known as the Family of Love. The name suggests something profoundly sinister, but they were merely a reclusive group of mystics, originating from the Netherlands but with a presence in Cambridgeshire and some other parts of England. Their secretive practices did cause genuine alarm; and since they conformed outwardly to the established Church, the scale of the sect was unknowable and alarmist assessments of its size impossible to refute. But as recent research has demonstrated, the anti-Familist panic of 1577–81 was not a sober response to a real threat.[11] Rather, it was a replay of the anti-Anabaptist panic of Edward VI's reign (see above, pp. 163–4): conjuring up a largely imaginary sectarian threat in order to bolster the respectability of the Protestant establishment. This time at least, it did not work. Anti-Familist books and sermons were published and preached, some suspected Familists were arrested, and anti-Familist legislation was tabled. But the legislation died in Parliament, and political Puritanism did not see any tangible benefits from its scaremongering.

For despite all this sound and fury, the queen would not yield an inch on the Puritans' substantive demands. In 1577, Archbishop Grindal wrote her a careful but steely letter laying out his own position. With all possible care and humility, he flatly refused to obey Elizabeth's order to suppress the prophesyings. 'Bear with me, I beseech you, Madam, if I choose rather to offend your earthly majesty, than to offend the heavenly majesty of God.' He asked her to leave religious matters to theologians, and not to 'pronounce so resolutely and peremptorily' on them, as if she were the pope.[12] It was, quite consciously, an act of political self-martyrdom. The result of this defiance was six years' virtual house imprisonment at Lambeth Palace. The queen wanted to deprive him of office, too, but Grindal's many friends at court (not least William Cecil) shielded him from the worst consequences of her wrath. During the febrile years of the Anjou match (see above, pp. 234–5), he remained both a prisoner and an archbishop. He was on occasion able to exercise some small influence, and by his simple survival in office he prevented the primacy of England from falling into other hands. But the moderate Puritans' hopes had been cruelly exposed.

The resurgence of conformity

For some time before Grindal finally died in 1583, it was plain who his successor would be. By the early 1580s Elizabeth's religious policy was in the hands of two trusted advisers, and – increasingly – a third, younger man who was their protégé. The duo were the lawyer Sir Christopher Hatton, a confidant of the queen and rumoured to be a crypto-Catholic; and John Whitgift, a Cambridge cleric who had first come to prominence when he wrote a reply to the *Admonition to the Parliament*. Whitgift was made bishop of Worcester in 1577, and in 1583 he succeeded to Canterbury almost as of right. The third man was Hatton's chaplain Richard Bancroft, another Cambridge man, who had already acquired some experience as an episcopal enforcer. When Whitgift eventually died in 1604, it was Bancroft who succeeded him as archbishop. Hatton, Whitgift and Bancroft formed the core of a powerful conformist Protestant phalanx. Hatton's own religious loyalties may have been ambiguous, but Whitgift's were plain: he was an orthodox Reformed Protestant who saw the doctrine of predestination as non-negotiable. However, their doctrinal views mattered less than their (and Elizabeth's) agreement on the urgency of uniformity and good order.

These new conformists were not simply fighting a rearguard action, and their defence of the Elizabethan settlement was driven by more than simple fear of change. While Archbishop Parker had been a uniting figure who shared many aspirations with his Puritan brethren, Whitgift viewed diversity and debate as simple evils. He was as ready as his queen to see Puritanism as presumptuous and seditious, defying divinely ordained authority in the name of impertinent conscience. As such, he took the battle to the Puritan enemy.

Shortly after taking office, Whitgift ordered all clergy (private chaplains and civic preachers as well as parish clergy) to subscribe to articles affirming that the Prayer Book did not contradict the Bible. A substantial group – as many as 400 – refused. Whitgift promptly suspended them from office. The resulting outcry forced the novice archbishop to back down, only to adopt a more subtle method. A series of questions were put to non-compliant clerics, with the intent of separating out the more danger-ous radicals. What made this controversial was that the court overseeing the process – the High Commission, created originally to root out Catholics – could compel clerics to answer the questions and so to incriminate themselves, via a device known as the *ex officio* oath. Refusal was an imprisonable offence. Warning shots had been fired at the Puritans before, but this was a full-scale assault.

Partly in response, a new set of informal Puritan networks started to appear: the bodies known as *classes* (singular *classis*), a name borrowed from an ancient Roman unit of administration. It was a pretentious name for informal gatherings of the godly, but that pretentiousness reflected

some Puritans' hopes that the *classes* would evolve into full-blown presbyteries. The recent development in Scotland, where the 'model' presbyteries
established unilaterally in 1581 had begun to spread across the country,
was an inspiring one. Fired by Whitgift's aggression, and coordinated
through the *classes*, the Puritan movement readied itself for another parliamentary battle. Puritans were now actively trying to be elected to the
House of Commons, and in 1584 and 1586 unprecedented numbers of
them were.

Once there, however, what could they do? Petitions to the queen were
ignored. Detailed bills proposing Presbyterian systems of Church government were introduced in the Commons in 1584 and 1587; on both occasions Hatton, acting as the queen's parliamentary manager, ensured that
the bills were killed stone dead. A few outspoken MPs were given a taste of
imprisonment, parliamentary privilege notwithstanding. Meanwhile, their
tormentor Archbishop Whitgift was raised to the Privy Council in 1586 –
the first Elizabethan bishop to be so promoted. The Presbyterian agitation
succeeded only in provoking a newly forthright defence of episcopacy, led
by Richard Bancroft. Instead of seeing bishops merely as an expedient means
of governing the Church, Bancroft and others began to argue that the office
of bishop was instituted by God's law (*de jure divino*). For those in power,
trying to control unruly Puritanism, episcopacy seemed the only guarantor
of the Church's unity. For those outside, it seemed simply that episcopacy
corrupted, and that *de jure divino* episcopacy corrupted absolutely.

In 1588, Puritan frustration boiled over. Tired of banging their heads
against the queen's stony immovability, a group of conspirators decided to
play the game of popular politics and to attack the bishops from below.
This group organised the clandestine writing, printing and distribution of
a series of scabrous tracts under the pen-name Martin Mar-Prelate. The
identity of the real author, or authors, has never been proved. The outspoken MP Job Throckmorton remains the likeliest candidate, although in
truth 'Martin' was a collective rather than a single individual. The question
matters because these tracts do not read like the work of a committee.
The seven surviving tracts, printed between October 1588 and September
1589, attacked the bishops with vicious directness. They stand out even by
the vitriolic standards of sixteenth-century print. 'Martin', the 'primate
and metropolitan of all the Martins in England', mocked the bishops
mercilessly for their lordliness, self-importance and perceived hypocrisy,
explicitly intending to smash their moral authority so that presbyteries
could fill the vacuum. So the bishops were mere popelings, and Whitgift
the 'Pope of Lambeth'. Indeed, 'friars and monks were not so bad; they

lived in the dark, [but] you shut your eyes, lest you should see the light.'[13] As the presses were spirited from one safe house to another before the fury of Whitgift's and Bancroft's searchers, 'Martin' taunted his pursuers. He also aimed some barbs at the Puritan establishment, whose quiet reasonableness had betrayed the cause. He rightly diagnosed that establishment's fury at his unruly intervention.

For the tracts of 'Martin' mark the point when political Puritanism was finally discredited. Bancroft now had all the excuses he needed to pursue Puritans as seditious, and in 1589–90 he proceeded to roll up their networks. Eventually, in 1593, one of the ringleaders of the Mar-Prelate conspiracy – a young polemicist named John Penry – was hanged for sedition. Two leaders of underground separatist congregations were executed in the same year, under legislation which had been aimed at Catholics. But the regime did not need to make many martyrs. The Martin Mar-Prelate episode was the first of a series of disreputable incidents which helped to take the fight out of mainstream Puritanism. In 1591, a deranged visionary named William Hacket was proclaimed as Messiah by two London Puritans, who for good measure also announced Elizabeth's deposition. He was promptly executed, but he had a long afterlife as a useful bogeyman for conformists to deploy against Puritans. Bancroft, in particular, found wild-eyed Puritan radicals invaluable in his ongoing attempts to discredit the movement. When he became bishop of London in 1597, his chaplain Samuel Harsnett (later archbishop of York) became his enforcer, and was instrumental in exposing a Nottinghamshire Puritan named John Darrell who had built up a thriving business as an exorcist. Darrell was, for Bancroft and his allies, the perfect Puritan: enthusiastic, theologically shaky, and (so Harsnett proved to his own satisfaction) a deliberate fraud. Exorcism was hardly a mainstream Puritan activity, and the episode probably says more about the place of magic in wider English society (see below, pp. 280–2) than it does about Puritanism. But it also helps to explain why it was the prelates who marred the Puritans, not the other way around.

Building Puritanism in the parishes

Puritanism's political ambitions were comprehensively defeated in the late 1580s and were to remain subdued for two generations. But in one sense, these national battles were a distraction. Freedom from traditional vestments, prophesyings, even presbyteries – these were, for most Puritans, means to an end. That end, the real Puritan ambition, was to establish a universal godly preaching ministry, proclaiming the true Word and imposing true discipline on the people. The irony of Elizabethan Puritanism is that while it decisively lost its proxy and symbolic battles, it won some real victories in the quieter but more important battle for the soul of England.

The most unambiguous Puritan defeat was the failure to reform the English Church's polity in any way. English Puritans could only envy the independence from state control, and the pervasive system of discipline, which the Scots enjoyed and endured. Discipline in the English Church was left to the cumbersome and traditional Church courts, whose remit was strictly limited. And bishops remained mitred and rocheted lords of the realm, consecrated to their office and set above their brethren. Yet even here, continuity of form belied a change of substance. Elizabethan bishops were very different animals from their medieval or Henrician predecessors. The prince-bishops and politician-bishops who had attracted so much medieval anticlerical scorn were gone. There were no more Wolseys. Until Whitgift's appointment in 1586, Elizabeth did not even place bishops on her council. She appointed laymen as her Lord Chancellors, a break with ancient custom. She also followed her father's and brother's example by steadily plundering the lands of her bishops. That plunder was hardly driven by reforming ideals, but its effect was to change the nature of episcopacy. Almost all of the bishops lost their London houses, compelling the somewhat impoverished prelates to reside in their dioceses. By medieval standards this was something of a novelty, but most Elizabethan bishops did this willingly. They were, on the whole, conscientious Protestants who were serious about their responsibilities for building the Church in the parishes.

This, indeed, is the real English Reformation, beneath all the political sound and fury. The political changes were an essential prerequisite for change, but from a clergyman's point of view (if not from a politician's) they were merely that. For Protestant believers, Puritan and conformist alike, the ultimate aim of the Reformation was not removing the papacy, reforming the liturgy or refining the Church of England's official doctrines. All of these things were means to a greater end, that of bringing the pure Gospel to England's people, that souls might be saved and that God might be honoured. Ultimately, then, the battles of the English Reformation were won and lost not in set-piece political and theological confrontations, but parish by parish and soul by soul, in a myriad quiet battles and crises which are almost entirely hidden from us. What is clear is that, during Elizabeth's long reign, the steady, unspectacular spread of Protestant ministry and Protestant allegiance amounted to a gradual but decisive tectonic shift.

The great Puritan causes of the reign were all ultimately driven by their fear that the preaching of the Gospel was being stifled. Vestments compromised the new message; prophesyings trained preachers. Yet despite their repeated defeats, the work in the parishes crept forward. Obstructive and traditionalist clergy were slowly driven to the margins; some 300 were deprived of office during the 1560s. A newly educated generation of ministers began to fill their places. The Elizabethan bishops' systematic enforcement of long-established and long-flouted rules helped here: minimum ages for ordination, and the prohibition on holding several benefices simultaneously, began to mean something. A concerted push for better clerical education made itself felt too. The universities, the cradle of Protestantism, now became redoubts of Puritan theology – especially Cambridge, and especially the energetic new college there, Emmanuel College, founded in 1584 explicitly as a Puritan seminary. As committed Protestants were slowly pumped into the bloodstream of the English Church, the preaching ministry for which the Puritans had yearned began to become a reality – slowly, far more slowly than they wished, but relentlessly.

This was a project around which the entire Church could unite. Archbishop Whitgift would brook no challenges to the Church's discipline or authority, but he also took its ministry very seriously. He was particularly concerned by the surviving rump of clergy who were neither graduates nor preachers. He made serious attempts to train those non-graduate clergy who were already in post, promoting the use of the official Homilies and of catechisms. He ordered non-preaching clergy to acquire the Zürich reformer Heinrich Bullinger's daunting sermon cycle, the *Decades*, and to study one of its sermons each week. If Zürich-style prophesyings were being suppressed, Zürich's theology was being aggressively promoted. And even the suppression of the prophesyings was misleading. In their place sprung up 'combination lectures'. These were formal or informal arrangements for pulpit exchanges whereby parishes without a preaching minister had reasonably regular access to sermons, and whereby more sermon-heavy parishes could hear voices other than their own minister's. Although lacking the discursive (and divisive) potential of the prophesyings, combination lectures served many of the same purposes, and they were often organised by the *classes* which had emerged in the 1580s. We know of at least eighty-five such arrangements erected across England.[14] In larger towns, the provision of preaching was better still. Town councils often took it on themselves to appoint a 'lecturer', or preacher, for the town, who was a civic employee rather than an ecclesiastical benefice-holder.

So when Puritans retreated from politics towards a more pastoral and parish-centred focus in the 1590s, it was not simply a bloodied withdrawal. It was a turn towards a battle which they had always held was more important, and which they were already winning. The great Puritan publishing success of the 1590s was William Perkins, one of the very few English writers of the century to be widely read outside his own country. For Perkins, the reformation of liturgy and practice took second place to the reformation of the individual conscience. His theological achievement was to apply the forbidding Calvinist doctrine of predestination to the individual believer's life. That doctrine can lead believers into either despair or conceit; Perkins successfully steered between those two rocks, affirming predestination in the strongest terms while also mapping out how Christians may live (and draw strength from) lives of the highest moral seriousness. His posthumous *Treatise of the Cases of Conscience* became a classic of Protestant devotion. And it had nothing to do with politics.

Others had been treading this path for decades. Richard Greenham was a Cambridge-educated minister who, in 1570, became parson of a small Cambridgeshire village called Dry Drayton. If Greenham was a Puritan at all, he was one of a different stripe, and in Dry Drayton he created a hugely influential model of what godly parish ministry might be. Greenham's principles were Puritan enough, on everything from vestments to predestination, but where men like Sampson sought conflict, Greenham tried to avoid it. His bishop, Richard Cox, had as a Marian exile been a rigorous defender of the Prayer Book (see above, pp. 191–2), but now faced with Greenham's conscientious refusal to wear the prescribed vestments, he turned a blind eye. He was not the only moderate bishop to recognise that he could not afford to lose a hardworking, able, non-confrontational and stoutly anti-Catholic pastor over a technicality. For Greenham's energies went not into political or theological controversy but into pastoral care, and a stream of students from nearby Cambridge came to spend a few weeks or months living with him, learning their trade from an acknowledged master and carefully writing down his pearls of wisdom.

The pattern of ministry which Greenham pioneered, and which spread out across the country with his disciples from the 1580s onwards, began but did not end with preaching. His sermons were not arid or academic affairs, for all his learning: he preached with such passion that his shirt was soaked with sweat, and communicated that passion to his hearers, once provoking a woman to interrupt him by wailing aloud for her damnable sins. Such animated, theatrical performances were again typical of Puritan preachers, who were skilled at their art and who knew that dry, understated monotony gave no honour to God. Greenham's innovation, however, was systematically to bring his message to his people. He would walk out into the fields to talk with his neighbours as they were ploughing. He regularly visited every house in the parish in order to instruct the families (a manageable proposition in a parish of only thirty households). Such one-to-one instruction began with the use of question-and-answer catechisms, but moved on to intensely personal spiritual counselling. Helping believers to apply the doctrine of predestination to their lives, and dealing with the crises of conscience that resulted, was a dominant theme for Greenham, as later for Perkins. Yet his ministry was not solely concerned with matters of high theology. He apparently acted as a kind of informal, one-man kirk session, resolving disputes and quarrels amongst his flock (none of whom took one another to law during the whole course of his ministry in Dry Drayton). His recorded spiritual counsel was also practical and down-to-earth, believing (for example) that a sensible diet was more useful than heroic self-denial for keeping the temptation at bay.

What effect did such painstaking pastoring have? Greenham himself had no great opinion of his achievements at Dry Drayton, claiming that there was 'no good wrought by my ministry on any but one family'.[15] Yet this was too modest. As well as keeping his parishioners out of court, he left one striking record of his work: the names of the babies he baptised. Early modern English people shared a very small pool of Christian names – in the late sixteenth century, more than half of all boys baptised were called William, Thomas or John, and more than half of all girls Elizabeth, Mary or Anne. This was partly because children were traditionally named after one of their godparents, a system which prevented innovation (and sometimes led to identically named siblings). But Puritans, who were uneasy both about godparents and about the use of non-Biblical saints' names, began to give their children new names. Some were Biblical names, in particular from the Old Testament. In Dry Drayton, Greenham baptised children named Daniel, Samuel, Nathaniel, Sarah, Rebecca, Joshua, Moses and Bathsheba – all names which would have sounded alien on English tongues, yet which he evidently persuaded some of his parishioners to adopt. Other Puritans favoured 'grace' names, which turned a baby's name into a one-word sermon: children were named Charity, Grace, Delivery, Tribulation, Ashes, even Preserved. The appearance of a scattering of such new names, solemnly recorded in baptismal registers across the country, is a sign of the insensible spread of Puritan influence.

However, Greenham's self-deprecating comment draws our attention to a point of wider importance. Puritans of the late sixteenth and early seventeenth centuries were consistently gloomy about their impact on the realm. The standards which they expected from their neighbours (and from themselves) were impossibly high. They regularly assumed that the mass of the people – at all levels of society – were slaves to sin, godless and ignorant; and many Puritan clergy readily told their congregations so. The doctrine of predestination, read through a theology which saw the Church as a covenanted people like ancient Israel, made it natural to assume that the English were divided into a godless majority and a small, godly 'remnant'. God would preserve that remnant, but they had realistically to expect to see most of their neighbours damned.

This sense of an unequally divided nation is central to Puritanism. This was a subculture, with its own shared jargon, habits of mind and preoccupations. One historian calls it a 'spiritual freemasonry'.[16] Its self-conscious separateness is a fact of some importance, but it means that we should not take Puritans' estimates of their numerical success or failure at face value. It is true that only a minority of English people were zealous, godly Puritans. However, the wider culture of Puritanism had a much greater impact than many Puritans were inclined to admit. The historian Alexandra Walsham has examined the pivotal Protestant doctrine of providence, which insists both that God is sovereign over all earthly affairs and (therefore) that God's will and purposes can be deduced from worldly events. Walsham's work has demonstrated that the providentialist worldview – so characteristic of Puritanism – was in fact pervasive in English thought by the end of Elizabeth's reign, on the stage and in the gutter press as well as in the pulpit. Neither Puritans nor anti-Puritans liked to admit how mainstream Puritan thought had become, but this conspiracy of silence should not blind us to the fact that, as Walsham puts it, 'zealous Protestantism could . . . be a popular religion'.[17] Puritanism did not take over English culture wholesale, but it did crossbreed with that culture. The process produced some intriguing hybrids.

One notorious example of this crossbreeding is in the field of the supernatural. Medieval Christians, in England as elsewhere, had believed in the existence of witches: that is, of individuals who had access to supernatural powers which they could use to help or to harm their neighbours. Suspected witches were usually (not always) female, and usually (not always) marginal, peculiar or unsettling people. They were regarded with fear, enmity and a measure of respect by the population at large. They were very occasionally prosecuted in the Church courts, but neither Church nor state usually paid them much attention. With the Reformation, this changed. In 1542, Henry VIII made certain kinds of magical acts criminal offences for the first time, although like most of his other penal legislation the Act was repealed in 1547. A new Witchcraft Act was introduced in 1563, following which England had its own nasty little witch-hunt. Our sources for this episode are very incomplete, since we have good records only for the south-east; but we know that there was a spate of witchcraft trials in Elizabethan Essex, in which over fifty suspects were hanged (and nearly five times as many tried). The proportions were the same, but the numbers much smaller, in other south-eastern counties. Prosecutions peaked in the 1580s and tailed off sharply in the new century. This pattern roughly parallels a wider surge in witch-hunting across much of Europe, although the English witch-hunt was relatively subdued: the numbers were small, due process of law was (more or less) followed, and there were no mass panics as occasionally took place in France, central Europe or Scotland. The episode is gruesomely fascinating and continues to be mysterious.

Most Puritans had a clear view of the matter. Magic or witchcraft of any kind was simply wrong: it was either popery or devil-worship. Nor would they accept the use of Christian rituals as countermagic or as defences against witchcraft. But, with a little Biblical backing, they did approve of using the law against magicians of all kinds. The 1563 Act was strongly informed by Protestant loathing of magic, but for many Puritans it was not nearly aggressive enough. Others, however, became uncomfortable with the way the laws were being enforced. Reginald Scot, a Puritan magistrate from Kent, argued in a 1584 tract that witchcraft did not exist and that the panic was itself a popish superstition; however, he was an exceptional and isolated figure. More significant, perhaps, is the Essex minister George Gifford. Gifford's Puritan credentials were excellent (he was suspended for non-subscription by Archbishop Whitgift), but he was uneasy about witch-hunting. The Devil's real instruments, Gifford argued in a 1593 book, were not the desperate old women who were being hanged so regularly in his home county. Rather, they were the white witches and cunning-men who provided magical services to the paying public, for it was they who actually lured good Christians into trafficking with the Devil.

Yet while Puritans consistently argued that white magic and black magic, learned magic and ignorant magic, were all equally diabolical, the wider population heard the message selectively. Puritan strictures helped to legitimise the long-held antipathy towards witchcraft, and they provided a legal route by which 'witches' could be hunted. They did not succeed in turning the population against white magic, nor in discrediting learned magic. Indeed, for all their fulminations, many Protestants were themselves powerfully attracted by ideas which we would now call magical, but which at the time seemed to be at the cutting edge of learning. We cannot simply blame Puritanism, or even Protestantism, for the English witch trials (across Europe, Catholics hunted witches just as enthusiastically as Protestants). We can, however, see this as an example of the acculturation of Puritanism, in which a wider society took the Puritan ideas which it liked and used them for its own ends, while ignoring those that were less congenial. Does this show the limits of Puritanism's achievements, or the extent of its success?

One last, unambiguous Puritan victory deserves to be noted. Throughout the 1540s and 1550s, the most commonly available English Bible was the 1539 'Great Bible' (so called because of its physical size). The translation was widely held to be unsatisfactory, but its replacement was contentious. During Mary's reign, the exiles in Geneva set about preparing a new English translation, which was eventually published in Geneva in 1560. This 'Geneva Bible' was not popular with the new regime. Quite apart from the association with Geneva (never a recommendation in Elizabeth's eyes), the text bristled with marginal notes and annotations which consistently gave an aggressively Protestant slant. No English publisher picked it up, and copies of the Great Bible continued to be produced in London. There was no second edition of the Geneva Bible even in Geneva until 1569. Meanwhile, the regime prepared its own revised version, the so-called 'Bishops' Bible', first published in 1568: this tidied up the Great Bible's translations but did not provide any provocative marginalia. Backed by Archbishop Parker, it rapidly established itself. The Geneva Bible appeared to have sunk like a stone. The reversal of these fortunes was the greatest legacy of Edmund Grindal's primacy. It seems that even before he was translated to Canterbury in 1575, he was promoting the Geneva Bible. The first edition printed in England appeared in 1576. There was another in each of the next two years, four editions in 1579, and twenty-one during the 1580s. It was the authorised Bishops' Bible that fell out of popular use. The Geneva text, its annotations so ready to guide ministers in their preaching and the pious laity in their reading, became the people's Bible. It appeared in every format, for the pocket or for the lectern: a symbol of Puritan ambitions, worming its way relentlessly into private homes and into the verbal landscape of England. It was Shakespeare's Bible, although whatever else Shakespeare was, he was no Puritan. Elizabeth's successor James I tried to fight back with a new, 'Authorised' version in 1611, but that took fifty years to win general acceptance. The Geneva Bible is a symbol of how by 1600 England was, despite itself, permeated by the culture of Puritanism.

Popular religion in Elizabethan England: a group portrait

The questions which we would most like to ask about Elizabethan religion have no answers, and indeed can scarcely be formulated. We have no opinion-poll data, despite some ingenious attempts to conjure it into existence from a range of sources. We might wish to know what the religion of the 'average' English person was, but no such person existed. Nor was a hierarchical age terribly interested in such crudely quantitative questions.

We can make a few sensible generalisations about the changes which those 'average' people saw in their parishes. In the place of Catholic priests, there slowly came to be Protestant ministers. Although in theory the spiritual equals of their flocks, these ministers were as formidably set apart by their learning as their Catholic predecessors had been by their sacramental power. They also took their office and their authority every bit as seriously as those predecessors. However, there were many fewer of them. The number of clergy in England fell by more than half between 1500 and 1600, despite the rising population. A Church of Word rather than sacrament, and one which had rejected the monastic life, had less need of numbers, nor – following the Henrician and Edwardian plunder – could it afford them. If there were fewer clergy in each parish, however, a new figure appeared who in some measure replaced them: the minister's wife, a wholly new creature in English society, and one who was expected actively to model godly family life for the parish. The church buildings themselves changed, too. They became much more like our modern image of a medieval church (see above, pp. 13–14): the walls whitewashed or reduced to bare stone, fixed seating becoming increasingly common, the chaotic kaleidoscope of saints, images and altars gone. Pipe organs, too, were sometimes removed or allowed to fall into disuse. Church buildings themselves commonly fell into some disrepair, caught between Puritan contempt for the material trappings of worship and Catholic sympathisers' reluctance to support the new religion. Church-building, a booming business in the fifteenth century, ceased almost entirely in the sixteenth and seventeenth.

Such generalities, however, miss the most striking feature of Elizabethan religion: its entirely unprecedented diversity. One historian has helpfully suggested that we think of that diversity as a group portrait.[18] We can identify most of the subjects of that portrait; we can place them in relation to one another and make judgements about their character. What we cannot do is make more than a guess at their relative weights.

The outlying characters, standing self-consciously apart from the main group, are the easiest to identify. There is a small band of Catholic recusants. There are the sectarians, tiny groups such as the Family of Love. There is an equally tiny number of Protestant separatists: congregations of embittered Puritans, mostly in London or in the safety of English mercantile communities abroad, whose disillusion with the compromises of the established Church had provoked them into organising their own worshipping life. Such groups appeared as early as 1567, but they always remained marginal. The bishops fretted about 'Brownists' (named sweepingly for Robert Browne, a mercurial separatist of the 1580s), but the threat was more potential than real. For most Puritans, the aspiration to establish a universal godly Church, and the obligation not openly to defy the queen's proceedings, ensured that they would not venture into schism. Some found refuge in the Protestant Church of Ireland, which by the 1590s was both an established Church and a Puritan-friendly minority sect (see below, p. 16). Yet the great majority of English Puritans stood ostentatiously apart from the separatists and sectarians. They are by far the noisiest group on our canvas. They are balanced, however, by a mute group at the other side of the picture: for there, brushing shoulders with the recusants, are the 'church papists' (see above, p. 246), who shade insensibly into the rest of the group.

What of the rest: the silent centre of the Elizabethan Church? Conformity was what the queen demanded of these people, and conformity is what she received. With what mixture of enthusiasm, distaste or bewilderment that conformity was given, we cannot know. Yet a few things can usefully be discerned, or guessed, about these men and women.

First, as the reign wore on, popular Protestantism became increasingly real. The impact of Puritan preaching and pastoring was considerable – even if it did not produce doctrinaire Puritans. The bishops' efforts also had some real effect, not least in the education and vetting of clergy. So too did the regime's official instruments of reform, much as Puritans derided them. The official Homilies were a crude tool of reformation, but not a ridiculous one. Clergy not licensed to preach were supposed to read through the two volumes of the Homilies in a continuous cycle. As we might expect, many clergy and people found this tedious after the second or third iteration, but there were other resources available to fill the gap. Several other approved books were to be found in many parish churches. All parishes were supposed to own Erasmus' expansive *Paraphrase* of the New Testament (in an evangelically slanted English translation). Bishop Jewel's *Apology or Answer in Defence of the Church of England*, Foxe's

Book of Martyrs and – from the 1580s – Heinrich Bullinger's *Decades* were also widely available in churches or parsonages, to say nothing of the Geneva Bible, with its arsenal of marginal comment. Non-preaching clergy who grew weary of the Homilies frequently took to reading to their parishioners from these other texts.

Secondly, if positive Protestantism remains difficult to diagnose with certainty, the same is not true of anti-Catholicism. By the 1570s, this had spread from being a preachers' and politicians' preoccupation to being a widespread popular force. Forty years of anti-papal rhetoric, a xenophobic nationalism, and – after 1570 – genuine outrage against the queen's excommunication and what it meant: all these things helped to make hatred of papists and of popery seem the natural stance for any self-respecting Englishman. The approach of war in the 1580s only sharpened this. In retrospect, the regime's fears of a Catholic 'fifth column' in that war seem excessive. Recent research has shown how far local communities rallied to the cause during the Armada campaign, often putting themselves to considerable expense in defence of queen, Church and country against the Spanish.[19] Importantly, this anti-Catholicism was typically directed at foreign Catholics rather than at local recusants. Respectable Catholic families who were known to be apolitical usually had little to fear from the zeal of their neighbours.

Thirdly, anti-Catholicism was matched by widespread anti-Puritanism. The extent of this is difficult to gauge, since (as with medieval anticlericalism) so much of the evidence is literary. Clearly, however, Puritans were immensely tempting butts for jokes. Sober, earnest, sometimes self-righteous, relentless in their pursuit of godly lives for themselves, noisy in their advocacy of such lives for others – it would have been remarkable if such people were not mocked. And the vision of comprehensive discipline, Scottish-style, which so appealed to Puritans, appalled their more easy-going neighbours in equal measure. Hypocrisy was the easiest and the commonest accusation. Shakespeare was not above the occasional satirical swipe at Puritans, but the sentiment can be found at every level of society. In the 1590s, an obscure Cheshire gentleman wrote an anti-Puritan diatribe which could stand for many. He reviled them as hypocrites, gluttons and troublers of the commonwealth, and as prigs devoid of any real charity. He wished all Puritans might be ducked in the river Mersey, 'to the end they may be replenished with more drops of mercy.' He mocked their style of preaching: 'it is not beating of the breast, flinging of the arms, swaggering in the pulpit, or turning up the white of the eye, but sound doctrine plainly pronounced that edifieth the people of God.' And as that last sentiment suggests, this author was insistent that he was a good Protestant, and no papist – indeed, a 'plain Protestant' as against a 'precise Puritan'. But he admitted, 'I know few papists that are bad, and not one Puritan that is good.'[20] Of course, this is nonsense. We have ample evidence that there were Puritan clergy and laity of heroic virtues and immense pastoral sensitivity. But there was certainly hypocrisy too, and those who find excessive virtue discomforting would naturally prefer to latch onto that. By the end of Elizabeth's reign, this was a common stance: a religion defined by being balanced between two hatreds. Such a religion was, of course, quite capable of being shaped – even shaped decisively – by the influence of the extremes which it rejected.

Fourthly, some positive affection may have been amassing for the peculiar Elizabethan Church in general, and for the Book of Common Prayer in particular. The historian Judith Maltby, who has made this case most forcefully, argues that some of Elizabeth's subjects should be described as Prayer Book Protestants (in contrast to the Puritans' Bible-Protestantism). It is very plausible, although the evidence is indirect. We know that when the Elizabethan settlement was being dismantled during the early 1640s, the Prayer Book was defended with ardour by a surprisingly wide array of people. And we might expect that Cranmer's sonorous prose, whose quality only improves with repetition and which has inspired passionate affection from more recent generations, would have won the heart of sixteenth-century England – unless the very durability of that affection is romanticising our view of the subject. At least, it is plain that the Prayer Book's language was bred in the bone of English-speakers from Elizabeth's reign onwards. Its literary fingerprints are everywhere.[21] We can perhaps also connect this to another mood we have already observed, of the widespread respect and nostalgia for a Reformation along Henry VIII's lines. Such people may have accepted their new identity as Protestants, but, as Puritan preachers worried, they paid much less attention to the rigours of Protestant theology than to older values of communal life and moral obligation. Loyalty to the new religious establishment may have reflected honest Prayer Book Protestantism as much as convenience or inertia. If our Cheshire gentleman did indeed have a religion, this, perhaps, was it.

Or perhaps he belonged to our fifth category: those with little or no religion. When a man from Essex told an ecclesiastical court in 1583 'that it made no matter whether he were a Jew or a Christian, seeing that he do well', was he expressing a commonsense traditional morality, a contempt for all religion, or both?[22] Those who voiced such opinions, along with the common blasphemers and scoffers from whom they are often indistinguishable (see above, p. 23), were liable to be accused of 'atheism', but there were no atheists in the modern sense in Elizabethan England: the intellectual building blocks of a coherent atheist worldview were simply not available. Elizabethan 'atheism', if we can speak of it, was functional rather than philosophical. An 'atheist' was one who lived as if there were no God, regardless of whatever beliefs he or she might formally profess. Hence the Catholic accusation that the Elizabethan regime was 'atheistic' (see above, p. 252). It was a slander, but this much was true. The religious turmoil of the age, and the queen's reluctance to demand more than conformity from her subjects, created an unprecedented space for withdrawal from religious engagement. Such withdrawal is, by nature, invisible and unquantifiable. A few public figures in Elizabethan England had reputations for atheism, giving their names a whiff of brimstone which helped to cement their fame: the conjurer and philosopher John Dee, or the playwright Christopher Marlowe. But more significant are the unknown masses of those who had learned scepticism rather than renewed belief from the Reformation controversies: who sat quietly in church, who on their deaths bequeathed their souls to God in the most cursory terms and who in their lives found that they needed to pay little heed to Him.

Lastly, there was another religious possibility, or set of possibilities, beginning to appear in the later sixteenth century: a cloud no bigger than a man's hand, but worth noticing because of its later importance. This was almost exclusively a clerical movement. It incubated at those traditional ecclesiastical institutions which had managed to survive the successive Tudor culls: the cathedrals, the college chapels of the two universities, and a scattering of idiosyncratic collegiate churches. In particular, it was connected to the strangest church in England, Westminster Abbey, which in Elizabeth's reign became what it has since remained – a cathedral with no bishop, a church with no parish, a free-floating liturgical entity answerable only to the crown. This clerical movement had two strands, theological and ceremonial. Theologically, these men moved on from favouring *de jure divino* episcopacy (see above, p. 274) to trying to reclaim some continuity between the pre- and post-Reformation Churches, and also to questioning the orthodox Calvinist doctrine of predestination. The ceremonial strand – which was the more important – emphasised dignified liturgical worship, traditional church music, and the sacraments, and sought to redress a perceived overemphasis on preaching.

Two names stand out among this group. Lancelot Andrewes was a preacher whose exceptional gifts were widely recognised, but who used the pulpit to advance some daringly novel (or daringly old-fashioned) views about worship. His views chimed with some of the ageing queen's preferences, and she made him dean of Westminster in 1601. Under James I, he would become a bishop and, partly despite himself, the founding father of the Stuart ceremonial revival. The second figure was scarcely noticed at the time. When Richard Hooker died in 1600, he was an obscure theologian whose vast and unfinished treatise *On the Laws of the Ecclesiastical Polity* had been published without making any discernible impact. The book provided some theological underpinning for what Andrewes and others were doing, presenting the medieval Church and even the contemporary Catholic Church as entities of some spiritual worth, and emphasising the value of liturgy and the sacraments. Hooker was a prophet without honour in his own time, and for the historian of the Elizabethan Church, his importance is simply that he demonstrates the range of ideas which were both conceivable and publishable for an idiosyncratic cleric. Yet he would eclipse Andrewes in the end, and his huge book would become a foundation document for that strange religious phenomenon which emerged in the seventeenth century: Anglicanism.

Notes

1 Matthew 18: 15–17 (Geneva Bible).

2 *The forme of prayers and ministration of the sacraments* (1565), p. 19.

3 Margo Todd, *The Culture of Protestantism in Early Modern Scotland* (2002), pp. 263–4.

4 *The forme of prayers and ministration of the sacraments* (1565), pp. 18–19.

5 James Cameron (ed.), *The First Book of Discipline* (1972), p. 173.

6 David Calderwood, *The History of the Kirk of Scotland*, vol. 3 (1842), pp. 546, 551.

7 Robert Pitcairn (ed.), *The Autobiography and Diary of Mr. James Melvill* (1842), p. 370.

8 James Carmichael (?), *Newes from Scotland* (1592?), sig. B4r.

9 Hastings Robinson (ed.), *The Zurich Letters*, vol. II (1845), p. 152.

10 William Nicholson (ed.), *The Remains of Archbishop Grindal* (1843), p. 467.

11 Christopher Carter, 'The Family of Love and its enemies', *Sixteenth Century Journal*, vol. 37 (2006), pp. 651–72.

12 William Nicholson (ed.), *The Remains of Archbishop Grindal* (1843), pp. 387–9.

13 'Martin Mar-Prelate' [ps.], *Oh read ouer D. Iohn Bridges, for it is worthy worke: or an epitome of the fyrste booke* (1588), sig. A2r-v.

14 Patrick Collinson, *Godly People* (1983), appendix.

15 *Oxford Dictionary of National Biography.*

16 Diarmaid MacCulloch, *The Later Reformation in England* (2001), p. 69.

17 Alexandra Walsham, *Providence in Early Modern England* (1999), p. 325.

18 Judith Maltby, *Prayer Book and People in Elizabethan and Early Stuart England* (1998), p. 2.

19 Neil Younger, 'War and the Counties: the Elizabethan Lord Lieutenancy 1585–1603', University of Birmingham PhD thesis (2006), Chapter 2.

20 Folger Shakespeare Library MS V.a.399, ff. 18v–20r.

21 Ramie Targoff, *Common Prayer: the language of public devotion* (2001).

22 Christopher Haigh, *The Plain Man's Pathways to Heaven* (2007), p. 168.

CHAPTER 11

Reformation and Empire

For most of England, and for the lowland areas of Scotland, the Reformation story was, eventually, a story of conversion. For Ireland, Wales, the Scottish Highlands and indeed for some of the upland regions of England, it is first and last a story of conquest. This story's theme is the extension of London's and Edinburgh's power across the islands, culminating in the union of those two crowns in 1603. It is, therefore, a story in which politics leads religion, but in which religion is nevertheless critical. Conversion and conquest were not necessarily incompatible. The process of converting the upland regions to the new religion was slow, but by the end of the sixteenth century was visibly succeeding – except in Ireland, where its failure was almost complete.

Securing peripheries, 1485–1560

The end of independent lordships: Ireland and Wales, 1485–1534

Henry VII and James IV came to their thrones with only limited control over significant parts of their realms. They and their sons set about extending that control and establishing more uniform states. This process was well under way before religious change began to complicate matters in the 1530s. The advent of the Reformation both accelerated the process and changed its nature.

We have already seen how James IV abolished the lordship of the Isles, asserting direct control over the most independent and inaccessible region of his kingdom (see above, pp. 56–7). Henry VII did not attempt anything comparably dramatic. The most drastic change was in Cornwall, the centre of the dangerous rebellion of 1497. The duchy's rights were suspended for eleven years thereafter, and the king's trademark web of financial penalties helped keep this troublesome territory subdued for fifty years. In Ireland and Wales, much less was attempted. Henry was content effectively to subcontract the government of both territories to local magnates, who were given an almost free hand in return for efficiency and loyalty. In Wales, this meant the Gruffydd family in the north and west, and the Dinefwr family in the more populous south. Sir Rhys ap Thomas,[1] head of the latter dynasty, had been one of Henry Tudor's most important supporters in 1485, and he and his affinity helped keep Wales steadily loyal. Between 1504 and 1508, Henry progressively revoked the penal laws imposed on Wales a century before, opening the way for Welsh landowning families to enter royal service and English administration.

Royal control in Ireland was much weaker. The Old English, the descendants of the Anglo-Norman nobles who had conquered the island for England in the twelfth century, fell into two broad factions. The Butler earls of Ormond and Ossory had been the Lancastrian kings' local allies, but from the 1460s they had been eclipsed by the pervasive 'Geraldine' network of affinities constructed by the Fitzgerald earls of Kildare. Gerald Fitzgerald, the eighth earl, was briefly ousted as Lord Deputy during the Perkin Warbeck affair (see above, p. 46), but to govern Ireland against Geraldine opposition would have needed a fight for which Henry VII lacked the stomach. Kildare was restored and, on his death in 1513, was succeeded by his son and namesake, the ninth earl. The Geraldines moved easily through the many worlds of Irish politics. The ninth earl was educated in England and played with the future Henry VIII as a boy; yet he and his allies maintained some dominance over the Gaelic parts of the island, where English lordship meant almost nothing. The extinction of the MacDonald lordship of the Isles in 1493 had created a power vacuum in Ulster, which the O'Donnells and O'Neills strove to fill. The Geraldines and their allies managed to contain this struggle, for the time being. Like Rhys ap Thomas, the Geraldines' achievement was to make it worthwhile for the Tudors to leave them alone.

In the 1520s, these arrangements unravelled in parallel. In Wales, an early sign of trouble was the fall of Edward Stafford, the duke of Buckingham, in 1521 (see above, p. 89). That headstrong scion of royalty was, amongst other things, a Welsh Marcher lord, and it was feared that he might use Wales as a power base for plotting against the king. The Welsh problem became unavoidable in 1525, when Rhys ap Thomas died. The leadership of the family passed to his headstrong grandson Rhys ap

Gruffydd. Cardinal Wolsey, whose administrative vision did not include such powerful magnates, revived a body which had first been created in 1471, the Council in the Marches of Wales. The Council, which sat at Ludlow in Shropshire, assumed executive authority over most matters Welsh. Young Rhys ap Gruffydd was not even given a seat on it. He chafed, and Marcher lords did not chafe quietly. An escalating series of spats between his men and the Council's followed.

Events had taken a similar course on the other side of the Irish Sea. The ninth earl of Kildare had a high opinion of his own authority, which made enemies in both Ireland and England – notably, again, Cardinal Wolsey. He was summoned to England and kept at court (indeed, briefly imprisoned) in 1519–22, with his rival Ormond appointed governor in his place. After a supposed reconciliation in 1524, Kildare was restored to the governorship, but his high-handedness continued. One incident became notorious: when the archdeacon of Leighlin murdered his bishop in 1525, Kildare punished this admittedly heinous crime by having the man crucified. Henry VIII's government wrestled intermittently with the Kildare problem for fifteen years. Kildare's plain belief that he was indispensable to the government of Ireland could have been calculated to rile Henry. The fact that he was indeed indispensable hardly helped.

In the early 1530s, the Kildare and Rhys ap Gruffydd problems became more urgent. This was partly because Wolsey's place in government was now being taken by his former secretary Thomas Cromwell, who took an even dimmer view of such grandees. But it was also because Welsh and Irish affairs, like everything else, were being caught up in the political maelstrom of Henry VIII's Divorce. There was a danger – which the Emperor Charles V did his best to foment – that routine quarrels with the king could mix explosively with opposition to the Divorce. In 1531, Rhys ap Gruffydd was suddenly charged with treason and beheaded. The charges centred on loose talk of prophecies: Rhys supposedly dreamed of claiming a Welsh royal title and of invading England alongside the king of Scots, and had gone so far as to raise money for a trip to Ireland, the Isle of Man and Scotland. Implausible, perhaps, but the regime now had a hair-trigger sensitivity to treason. As importantly, it was said that Anne Boleyn disliked him. Less than a year after his death, she was created marquis of Pembroke, placing a swathe of Rhys's former lands under her control, apparently in an attempt to fill the power vacuum his death had left.

Kildare lasted a little longer, but Cromwell was amassing evidence against him. He was, again, summoned to London in 1533. He stalled – he was gravely ill – but went in early 1534, expecting (correctly) that he would never return. The final crisis was provoked not by him, but by his son Lord Offaly ('Silken Thomas'), who raised a quixotic rebellion in his father's name. This may have been intended merely as a gesture, but if so it went badly wrong, for Henry was confirmed in all his suspicions about Kildare, and the earl died in prison later the same year. Offaly, forced to follow through on his threats, did so with some panache. The rebellion was, briefly, a formidable one. The Geraldines mobilised and Dublin was besieged. Ominously for Henry, Offaly decided – cynically or conscientiously? – to wrap his rebellion in the flag of the old faith. He denounced Henry VIII as a heretic; and he swore fealty to Charles V, who was interested enough to send some armaments and to promise more. This was genuinely alarming. Offaly was breaking an unwritten rule of Tudor rebellion: to make at least a pretence of loyalty to the king.

A Geraldine-led Catholic crusade suddenly seemed plausible. In 1533, one James ap Gruffydd, a cousin of Rhys ap Gruffydd, had travelled in secret to Ireland and then to Scotland. James V welcomed him as a Welsh prince. He sent messengers to allies in Wales and England to canvas support for an invasion. Rumours about him were circulating among the large Welsh contingent in the garrison at Calais; the regime feared that, in the event of a French or Imperial attack on Calais, the Welsh might betray their king. In September 1534, with Lord Offaly's rising at its height, James ap Gruffydd travelled to Ireland to support him. At the same time, the regime was having unexpected difficulties in raising troops in Wales to put down the Irish rising. The Emperor and the king of Scots were waiting in the wings.

In the event, the rebellion was crushed with brutal efficiency. By the end of 1535 Offaly was a prisoner in England, and James ap Gruffydd was in exile on the Continent, where he would remain until 1554. But the danger which Wales and Ireland potentially posed was plain, and the regime now took steps to impose on both territories an authority which they had not felt before.

The Henrician settlements

A new president of the Council in Wales was appointed in 1534: Rowland Lee, the newly minted bishop of Coventry and Lichfield, who was an administrator and enforcer rather than a theologian. Having secured a dispensation from the rule which normally barred bishops from imposing the death penalty, Lee set about trying to impose law, or at least order, on Wales with brutal gusto. 'Stout of nature, ready witted, rough in speech, not affable to any of the Welshry',[2] he saw Wales as a land of lawless impunity, to be reduced to good obedience by exemplary judicial terror. His patron, Thomas Cromwell, supported him with a series of new statutes in 1534–35, all aimed at curtailing the Marcher lords' independence and at introducing English legal norms. The king himself also lent his support. Henry spent much of the summer of 1535 on an extended progress on the Welsh border, throwing the stardust of kingship into some Welsh eyes. Lee preferred to measure his own success more pragmatically, by the number of Welsh criminals he hanged: certainly hundreds, perhaps thousands.

Thomas Cromwell evidently saw this newly assertive Welsh Council as a policy success, for it became one of his models for local government. He seems to have envisaged a series of regional Councils acting as devolved versions of the king's own Privy Council. The Council in the North, a long-standing body, was completely reconstituted in 1537–38, after the Pilgrimage of Grace. It had new powers and was charged with imposing the new settlement in the North of England as forcefully as necessary. In 1539, a Council in the West was established, overseeing Cornwall, Devon, Somerset and Dorset, although this proved ephemeral. By then, however, Cromwell had decided that Wales needed more than mere law-enforcement.

Cromwell had been considering reform of Wales's government since at least 1532. In early 1536, against Lee's advice, Cromwell imposed a new legal structure on parts of Wales, chiefly the Principality (the north-western region which was under direct royal control). These areas were made into counties, on the English model. Whether he always intended more is unclear, but later that year he had the chance, when Anne Boleyn's sudden fall delivered the marquisate of Pembroke, and with it a swathe of the Welsh Marches, into the king's hands. This cleared the way for the 1536 Act for Laws and Justice to be Ministered in Wales. This Act is now commonly known as the Act of Union, but this is misleading, for Wales was already under English rule. It might perhaps be known better as the Act for the Abolition of Wales: for its effect was to turn Wales, for administrative and legal purposes, into a region of England. Wales now acquired counties, sheriffs, magistrates, MPs, and English courts – the latter prohibited from using the Welsh language. Indeed, those who did not speak English were excluded from any role in government. The independent Marcher lordships were extinguished. The loose ends were tidied up in a second, less hurried Act in 1543, which finally snuffed out Welsh law and gave the Welsh Council a statutory basis.

The 1543 Act was drawn up, in part, by the newly arrived contingent of Welsh MPs, who were an early sign of how successful the 'Union' would be. While the new structures rode roughshod over the Welsh-speaking mass of the population, the landed elite whom Henry VII had rehabilitated were now effectively handed control over Wales. This was the outcome Rowland Lee had feared, but events proved him wrong and Cromwell right. The alliance between the English state and the Welsh gentry proved a successful one, keeping Wales peaceful for a century thereafter. The model was sufficiently attractive that Cromwell, again, attempted to use it elsewhere, in a doomed 1536 attempt to reinvent Calais as a normal English borough.

Imposing control on Ireland after the rebellion of 1534–35 was an altogether more daunting task. The defeat of the Geraldines left a dangerous power vacuum, and the regime in London – whose priority, as always, was to avoid giving Ireland any more money or attention than absolutely necessary – had no clear plan for filling it. A new, English-born lord deputy was appointed in 1536. This began a significant pattern: importing Irish government wholesale from England, which led to the arrival of a whole new group in Ireland. The 'New English' distinguished themselves sharply from the old and (they suspected) degenerate Anglo-Irish nobility. The new lord deputy, Lord Leonard Grey, had Old English connections – his sister had married the ninth earl of Kildare – but he had also led the army which had put down the rebellion. He was joined by a new archbishop of Dublin, a Cromwell loyalist named George Browne, to replace the archbishop who had conveniently been killed by the rebels in 1534.

Grey and Browne set out to create a new order in Ireland reflecting that in England and Wales. An Irish parliament met in 1536–37, which recognised Henry VIII as supreme head over the Irish Church. Browne attempted to impose a somewhat watered-down version of the English reforms of the late 1530s, attacking shrines and clerical indiscipline in his province, and even going so far as to marry. The most successful aspect of this programme was his assault on the monasteries: those in the English Pale were dissolved during 1539–40. However, Browne and Grey (who saw his role almost entirely in military terms) fell out badly. Cromwell's fall from power in 1540 weakened both men. Browne remained in post, but renounced his wife, and showed little reforming zeal for the rest of his career. And Grey was replaced by one of the wisest English heads to attempt to rule Ireland in the sixteenth century, Anthony St Leger.

The problems confronting St Leger were formidable. His government had very little revenue, ruled a small part of the island (Dublin, its immediate hinterland and a scattering of other towns) with the restive consent of the Old English establishment, and was almost wholly excluded from the

Gaelic heart of the country. Although perfectly willing to use force, he was a far more political animal than Grey. His most startling innovation – and one which Henry VIII met with some scepticism – was the declaration by an Irish parliament in 1541 that Ireland was no longer merely a lordship but a kingdom in its own right, with Henry VIII as its king. This may seem like gesture politics, but it had some important implications. The English lordship over Ireland had been based, at least in part, on a papal grant to King Henry II, which in the new climate was hardly tenable. More importantly, the creation of the kingdom changed, or aspired to change, the relationship between the king and the Irish lords. St Leger's policy is known to historians as 'surrender and regrant'. The Gaelic lords would renounce their clan titles, formally acknowledge Tudor overlordship, and instead be given noble titles, so maintaining and even strengthening their authority within their own spheres while weaving a nebulous aura of royal sovereignty around them. The extension of English governing structures paralleled what was being done in Wales, but here the outcome was far less certain. The creation of the Irish crown was political sleight of hand, aimed at conjuring up royal authority from almost nothing.

St Leger's cautious implementation of this policy won some real successes. Most spectacularly, he secured the submission of the single most powerful Gaelic chieftain, Conn O'Neill, a Geraldine ally who had been at war with the Dublin regime intermittently since 1534 and who had in 1539 laid claim to the ancient high kingship of Ireland for himself. In 1542 O'Neill negotiated a submission, accepted the royal supremacy, attended Parliament and travelled to England to be made earl of Tyrone. Alongside this and other submissions, St Leger began negotiating the dissolution of the monasteries outside the English Pale, with a few successes, although even then little of the proceeds found their way into his own treasury. And in truth, all of St Leger's achievements were flimsier than they looked. O'Neill and other Gaelic lords were readier to make fine promises and accept splendid titles than they were actually to submit to an English mode of government. But there was certainly no systematic opposition to English rule or to the royal supremacy over the Church during this period. When a trio of Spanish Jesuit missionaries landed in Ulster in Lent 1542, they found little support and were quickly forced to withdraw.

Indeed, one measure of Henry VIII's success in securing his troublesome western realms is that he was able to contemplate using Gaelic lordship as a weapon. For Scotland, too, had a Gaelic problem. The lordship of the Isles had been suppressed in the 1490s, but (like the kingdom of Ireland) this was to some extent a legal fiction, and real royal authority over the Highlands and Islands was at best uneven. The war with England in the 1540s made the Highlands a point of potential vulnerability. This possibility was dramatically conjured into life in 1543 by the escape of Donald Dubh MacDonald, grandson of the last lord of the Isles, who had spent almost his entire life as a prisoner and was now in his fifties. He returned to the Highlands, was acclaimed as chieftain by many of the clans, and by 1544 was claiming to be the true lord of the Isles. The English were interested. In 1545, Henry VIII pledged to restore the lordship in return for Donald Dubh's service. A large-scale attack on Dumbarton Castle, one of Scotland's great strongholds, was planned. Donald Dubh mustered 4000 men in Ulster, under English command. In the event, nothing came of this. The expedition was already in trouble when Donald Dubh suddenly died, and with him the last echo of the old lordship of the Isles. Yet it stands as testimony to how critical control over Britain and Ireland's Celtic regions could be – one way or the other.

Reformation in the uplands

It was one thing to secure minimal consent to the new political and religious dispensation, but another to turn this into a real Reformation of religion. Henry VIII had limited interest in doing so, and Edward VI's regime had neither the time nor the resources to make its undoubted commitment fully felt. This makes the real Protestant achievements of the period all the more remarkable.

The elites of Tudor England assumed that upland peoples would be both barbaric and resistant to religious reform. When the Suffolk-born evangelical activist Thomas Becon was forced to flee London in 1543, he went to the Peak District of Derbyshire: hardly the edge of the world, yet (so he claimed) fellow reformers were asking him, 'Into the Peak? Lord God, what made you there? ... I think you found there very peakish people.' And indeed, the people he found were steadfastly loyal to the old ways. Yet, he was surprised to discover, they were 'reasonable and quiet enough, yea and very conformable to God's truth' when it was preached to them. It helped that some of the gentry, who made it their business to keep up with national affairs, had already acquired evangelical books.[3] So even in the remoter corners of England, there were various routes by which the new religion could spread. Preachers might visit; printed books might be sold; and the local elites might prudently decide to embrace the new orthodoxies, or to be seen to do so.

However, this three-pronged approach – preachers, books and gentry – ran into difficulties beyond the core territory of the English state, for the first two worked easily only amongst English-speaking populations. Where Welsh, Gaelic, Manx, Cornish, French, Norn or even Scots were spoken, matters were more complicated. The obvious solution was translation, and English reformers had at least half an eye on that project from early on, but progress was slow and halting. William Tyndale, the master-translator of the English Reformation, was conscious that his books were written in the English of 'southern men', and he aspired to produce books in the 'old English' spoken in the North and in Scotland: but this remained an aspiration.[4] The first Englishman to act on such ambitions was Bishop Veysey of Exeter, a man without an evangelical bone in his body, but also a former president of the Council in Wales. When Cromwell's injunctions of 1538 required that key parts of the Mass be translated into English and learned by the people – the Lord's Prayer, the Creed and the Ten Commandments at the forefront – Veysey had these English texts supplemented by alternatives in the Cornish language. The next landmark is the work of Sir John Price (the surname is an Anglicisation of the Welsh patronymic 'ap Rhys', and can itself serve as a sign of the assimilation of the Welsh elite). Price was the secretary to the Council in Wales and an antiquarian scholar. In 1546 he published *Yny lhyvyr hwnn y traethir*, a translation of the King's Primer (the authorised book of private prayers published the previous year). It was the first book ever printed in any of the Celtic languages. Price was one of a group of Welsh scholars under the patronage of Sir William Herbert, an Anglicised Welshman who had become prominent at court. Another of Herbert's protégés, Arthur Kelton, published an evangelically tinged poem in praise of the Welsh in the same year. Yet this remained on the level of private enterprise.

Edward VI's regimes took the matter more energetically in hand. A trickle of further books in Welsh followed, and in 1548 a printer named John Oswen was set up in Worcester by the Privy Council, in order to print religious texts for Wales. (It was presumably intended that some of these should be in Welsh, although in the event Oswen published for the more lucrative English market.) Another printer, Humphrey Powell, was established in Dublin with similar privileges, and in 1549 he printed an edition of the first Book of Common Prayer – the first book printed in Ireland, but printed of course in English, the language of the Pale and of the Old English elite. In 1550, the Privy Council in London authorised the production of a translation in Irish Gaelic. This did not materialise, but in 1552 a French edition of the Prayer Book was printed for use in the Channel Islands and Calais.

The slow pace of translation partly reflects the regime's limited resources and attention span, but there were also deeper concerns. To the political and cultural elites in London (and in Edinburgh), the Celtic languages – and even regional variants of English – were marks of degeneracy and barbarism, the tongues of defeated peoples who ought to learn the language of their conquerors. To such people, the self-proclaimed English Empire stood in ancient Rome's place, and English was the new Latin. When the Welsh Acts of Union denied the Welsh language any official status, this was not (or not only) laziness, ignorance and spite, but an attempt to raise the Welsh from barbarism to English civility. An Irish translation of the Prayer Book may have seemed a good wheeze in the Council chamber in London, but the Old English were horrified by the prospect. Lord Deputy St Leger chose instead to have a Latin version of the 1549 Prayer Book circulated for use among the Irish Gaels, which largely defeated the point of the reform. The few Celtic translations that did appear did so alongside a constant drumbeat of English triumphalism.

The extent of the progress of the Welsh and Irish Reformations in this period can be judged from the careers of two English evangelicals who became bishops there: William Barlow and John Bale. Barlow was an outspoken early reformer who became a client of Anne Boleyn's. As marquis of Pembroke, she had him appointed prior of Haverfordwest in 1534; after several other promotions, he became bishop of St David's in 1536. St David's was the most senior and the largest of the four Welsh bishoprics, covering a swathe of the country's south-west. Barlow had grand plans, and a talent for making enemies. He hoped to establish proper Protestant preaching in the diocese, to endow a grammar school, and to move his cathedral from remote St David's to central Carmarthen – a town with a colony of English-speakers. Thus, he hoped, 'the Welsh rudeness would soon be framed to English civility' (he used the phrases 'English civility' and 'Christian civility' interchangeably). On his side was a small coterie of English clergy, many of them supported financially by a network of London evangelicals. He was also supported by his own brothers John and Roger: between them the three Barlows acquired a reputation for high-handed greed which alienated even some evangelicals, and Cromwell gave Barlow only lukewarm support. Meanwhile, the clergy of the diocese – especially at the cathedral which he was trying to abolish – closed ranks against him. Working relationships in the diocese were so bad that when

Barlow was succeeded by one of his protégés, Robert Ferrar, in 1548, the ongoing disputes eventually led to Ferrar's imprisonment and, in due course, to his being handed over to the Marian regime for burning. As such, it is no surprise that the Protestant achievement in the diocese of St David's was limited. Yet Barlow himself was optimistic about the prospects for his flock. He had succeeded in destroying the shrines and relics which had (in his eyes) nourished them in idolatry, and believed that as a result the people were 'seeing the long obscured verity manifestly to display her brightness'.[5] Despite the evidence of his own eyes, and his own utter lack of interest in using the Welsh language, he believed that the foundations of true reformation had been laid.

Compare the situation in Ireland in the early 1550s. In 1551, the regime in London began to pay serious attention to reforming the Irish Church for the first time. Lord Deputy St Leger was not interested. No Irish parliament met under Edward VI; as such the Irish chantries had not been dissolved and the Prayer Book had no statutory force. Archbishop Browne of Dublin had been briefly spurred to another flurry of reforming activity in 1547, but without St Leger's support this quickly fizzled out. In 1551, however, St Leger was replaced by James Croft, one of the Protestant clique running the English regime. At the same time, Archbishop Cranmer set out to recruit Protestants to fill Irish bishoprics. He met with almost total failure. Remote and impoverished postings among barbarians had little attraction for English clerics who felt that the reforming task at home was quite urgent enough. Part of the problem was that Cranmer demanded that his recruits be willing to learn the Irish language. In the end, only two men joined up, Hugh Goodacre and John Bale, and Goodacre was to die shortly after his arrival in Ireland. Bale, however, not only spent some months working in Ireland, but also wrote an account of his experiences shortly afterwards.

Bale had made his name as a viciously anti-Catholic pamphleteer in Henry VIII's reign, a career which he continued with gusto under Edward. He received little official preferment until, in late 1552, he was asked to accept the bishopric of Ossory, a diocese in south-east Ireland, outside the English Pale but with a substantial Old English presence. He accepted, with some unease and with unfortunate timing. He did not make landfall in Ireland until December 1552 and was seriously ill for much of the following spring, giving him only a few months of active ministry before Edward VI's death. Thereafter, Bale escaped via a series of hair-raising adventures in which several of his household staff were murdered and he himself was captured by pirates. This inevitably coloured his recollections of events, but even so it is clear that his ministry had not gone smoothly even before the king's death. The Irish clergy, Bale complained, were sunk in popish superstition. Even Archbishop Browne was a corrupt voluptuary who preached only twice a year (always, Bale claimed, the same two sermons). Bale's attempts to introduce the 1552 Prayer Book were opposed by Irish clergy who claimed (correctly) that the book had no legal status in Ireland. But Bale had no patience with such Irish pretensions. 'If England and Ireland be under one king, they are both bound to the obedience of one law under him' – which was both undiplomatic and plain wrong, but represents a typical English view of Ireland's status. And yet, this cranky, confrontational, lugubrious preacher had some success. He won, or was winning, the battle over the use of the 1552 Prayer Book in his diocese. Preaching in the Old English town of Kilkenny during Lent 1553, he believed that he had won many of the people over to the Protestant Gospel. Most strikingly, once King Edward had died, leaving Bale in a dangerously exposed position, he discovered he had some real friends. After an attempt on his life, the mayor of Kilkenny sent 400 soldiers to escort him back to the town. He marched in their company,

the young men singing psalms and other godly songs all the way, in rejoice of my deliverance. As we were come to the town, the people in great number stood on both sides of the way, both within the gates and without, with candles lit in their hands, shouting out praises to God for delivering me from the hands of those murderers.

It is a tantalising glimpse of what Cranmer's programme for reforming Ireland could have achieved. The Gaels might have been more interested in murdering their upstart bishop than in listening to his English sermons, but the Old English could have been won over. Ireland, unlike Wales, had a fair number of decent-sized towns, the traditional incubators of Reformation sentiment. That moment of popular Irish psalm-singing in 1553 shows us the Irish Reformation as it might have been.[6]

It is worth comparing the career of Bale's Catholic opposite number: Robert Wauchope, a Scotsman who, despite his blindness, became a theologian of international stature. At Reginald Pole's urging, Wauchope was named as archbishop of Armagh and primate of Ireland by Pope Paul III in 1539. The hope, apparently, was to draw the Scots into Irish affairs. However, James V refused to play, and bitterly resented the pope's attempt to grant Wauchope Scottish lands or titles. Caught in such power politics, Wauchope was not able even to set foot in Ireland for more than ten years, finally managing a landing in Ulster in February 1550. He had a distinctly cool reception, not only from the 'other' archbishop of Armagh but also from the Gaelic population of the region, who did not – yet – believe that hostility to men like Bale meant rejecting the English-backed establishment altogether. Wauchope was forced to withdraw to Scotland after only a month, and he died soon afterwards. Next to this fiasco, Bale's adventures seem positively triumphant.

The Celtic Reformations 1560–1603: success and failure

Wales and the Scottish Highlands: the path to Protestantism

At the accession of Queen Elizabeth, there were perhaps only two reasons for Protestants to be optimistic about Wales. The first of these was the beginning of printing in Welsh in 1546, which put Welsh more than twenty years ahead of Scots or Irish Gaelic. Three more Welsh texts appeared during Edward's reign, plus a Welsh–English dictionary. More followed under Elizabeth, notably the Prayer Book and the New Testament in Welsh, both in 1567. Prefaces to these texts argued in stirring terms that the Reformation was a restoration of the true, ancient Celtic Church, so long eclipsed by England's adherence to Rome. A complete Welsh Bible appeared in 1588, and the authorised Homilies in 1606. A total of 23 editions of books in Welsh printed before 1603 survive: a decent trickle, and, compared to printing in Gaelic, a flood.

Yet this was less significant than it appears. Most of the earliest Welsh books were the work of one man, the extraordinarily productive scholar William Salesbury, who has a claim to being the father of the modern Welsh language. However, Salesbury's Welsh was archaic, Latinate and oddly spelt: Welsh for scholars, not for parish clergy. One contemporary claimed that not one Welsh person in ten could understand it. Salesbury has been much criticised for this, but it is hard to see what alternatives he had. Like all the sixteenth-century Celtic languages, Welsh was very diverse. Its classical, bardic form was spoken by a small elite, and was some way from the widely varying (and not always mutually comprehensible) local vernaculars. This problem was to vex every early modern writer in any of the Celtic tongues (although the 1588 Welsh Bible was much closer to vernacular usage). Most clergy who used books in Welsh were compelled to translate them into the local vernacular for their congregation to understand them – which is certainly not to say that such books were useless, but rather to direct our attention instead to the clerical elite through whom the Reformation was mediated.

This was the second and (as it proved) decisive advantage which the Welsh Reformation had secured by 1560: the consent of the elite. Wales's political rehabilitation under Henry VII, and its absorption into the English polity under Henry VIII, had granted its ruling classes access to English structures of power, and so bought their loyalty. The Reformation was a long time bedding down in Welsh parishes, but time and the country's elites were on its side. Critically, this meant that the Church in Wales was not crudely an English colonial import. The majority of the clergy ordained in Elizabethan Wales were themselves Welsh (although there were still plenty of Englishmen, who normally made no effort to learn Welsh). Of sixteen bishops appointed to Welsh dioceses under Elizabeth, thirteen were Welshmen: this was quite unprecedented. The Welsh Church remained grossly under-resourced compared to its English counterpart. Its benefices were poor, and the Welsh-speaking clergy were much less likely to be university-educated than English-speakers appointed to Welsh benefices. Those Welsh clergy who did have university training were concentrated in a few wealthy spots – not least the Welsh-speaking areas of Shropshire, over the now-abolished border with England. One recent scholar has called the Welsh Church of Elizabeth's reign an 'unloved pragmatic compromise'.[7] Wales would not be swept by Protestant passion until the eighteenth century, and it remained a stronghold of Catholic recusancy. And yet, a pragmatic compromise was enough. The Welsh Reformation was secure.

A more intriguing story was unfolding in the Scottish Highlands. The Gaelic peoples of the Highlands were closely linked to the Irish Gaels, and one might have expected them to be equally resistant to religious and political imperialism. James VI's view, that the Highlanders were 'wild savages void of God's fear and our obedience', precisely matches English views of the Irish.[8] But in the Scottish Highlands the Protestant seed fell on fertile ground, and did so, to a remarkable extent, because of one man. Archibald Campbell, earl of Argyll from 1558 to 1573, was one of the leaders of the Protestant revolt of 1559–60. Lacking the political wiliness of some of his contemporaries, Argyll made up for it with his steadfast commitment to the Protestant cause and with raw political power. For as well as holding one of Scotland's premier noble titles, he was also the head of Clan Campbell, the most powerful of the Highland clans. With the power of the MacDonalds broken, he was the closest thing to a lord of the

Isles left in Scotland. Argyll used this unique position to push the Scottish Reformation deep into the Gaelic lands.

His right-hand-man was John Carswell, who had once been his tutor. In 1560, Argyll had Carswell appointed as a superintendent in the new Reformed Church; in 1565 Carswell also became bishop of the Isles. In 1567, he produced and (with Argyll's support) published *Foirm na nurrnuidheadh agas freasdal na sacramuinteadh*, the first book printed in Gaelic. This was a translation of the new Scottish liturgy, accompanied by a Calvinist catechism. The texts were subtly adapted for Highland use. Like Salesbury's Welsh, Carswell's Gaelic was difficult, a mixture of the high, bardic classical Gaelic with some elements of vernacular Gaelic. And the impact of Carswell's book, like Salesbury's, was indirect. What made it effective was that the Highlands' formidably learned orders of bards, who had traditionally supplied many of the clergy for the Highlands, were willing to continue doing so under the new dispensation – given a strong enough steer from Clan Campbell. These bardic clergy were uniquely well equipped to use Carswell's Gaelic texts and mediate them to the people.

The decisive fact of the Highland Reformation, therefore, is the same as that in Wales: the commitment of the social elites. Gaelic Protestant books were in fact produced very slowly. There was no New Testament in classical Gaelic until 1606, and none in the vernacular until 1767. But printed books were a peripheral medium in these societies. Clergy, it seems, used books in classical Gaelic, English or even Latin, and translated off-the-cuff for their people. (Indeed, when attempts were made in the seventeenth century to plug another linguistic gap by producing a Prayer Book in the Manx language, the clergy of the Isle of Man had no interest in it, preferring to translate the text themselves as they went.) And the Campbells pressed the cause relentlessly. Argyll died in 1573, but in 1574 his son and successor embarked on a tour of his lands, ensuring that every church had a minister installed and paid, and a copy of Carswell's *Foirm*. He also sponsored itinerant preachers. Other Highland clans took up the call, notably the MacKenzies, MacLeods and MacLeans. Religious divisions mapped onto pre-existing rivalries: the MacLeods' traditional enemies, the MacDonalds, remained stoutly Catholic. Yet this did not mean that religion was merely a form of tribal identity. In a notorious incident in 1578, a band of MacDonald warriors seeking revenge for an earlier massacre attacked the MacLeods of Waternish, on the Isle of Skye. It was Sunday, and every single one of the local MacLeods was in church hearing the Protestant service. Not even a lookout had been left outside. The

MacDonalds promptly burned the building down, killing all but one of the congregation (before being massacred themselves when another MacLeod raiding party caught them). It is a macabre symbol of how quickly Protestantism had become woven into the structures of Highland life.

Ireland in the balance

Could events in Ireland have taken the same course? The Campbells' sphere of influence stretched across the narrow straits to Ulster, and for one tantalising moment in 1560 it seemed as if their religion might do the same. When Elizabeth's government agreed to intervene in Scotland on behalf of the Protestants in 1560, one of the terms of the treaty was that Argyll would use his influence in Ulster to stabilise Ireland and to further the English interest there. Perhaps naively, Argyll was enthusiastic for this project. Carswell's *Foirm* was aimed explicitly at an Irish as well as a Scottish readership. Classical Gaelic and the bardic orders were common to both countries. Ireland could have had a Gaelic Reformation of its own, quite independent of events in the English Pale.

It did not happen. Elizabeth's regime rapidly cooled towards the idea of Argyll's intervention in Ulster, and the government in Dublin had always been icy towards any Scottish intervention in Ireland. Argyll's enterprises in Ulster during the 1560s were hobbled by obstruction from both London and Dublin. The controversy was about military power, not about religion – indeed, one of Argyll's few serious supporters in Ireland was Adam Loftus, a Puritan-leaning Englishman who was appointed archbishop of Armagh in 1562. Yet in Ireland as in England, Elizabeth would tolerate Reformations only on her own terms. In Ireland, that meant in practice that there would scarcely be a Reformation at all.

The abject (and decisive) failure of the Elizabethan Reformation in Ireland is remarkable, for a number of reasons. As we have seen, in the 1550s the prospects for the Protestant Reformation in Ireland were probably better than in Wales or Highland Scotland. Moreover, during Elizabeth's reign direct English control over the whole of Ireland was imposed to an extent which none of her predecessors had achieved. Yet the victory was to prove a Pyrrhic one, for as she conquered Ireland's territory she also permanently lost its religious allegiance. That loss meant that Ireland would spend three centuries as a conquered and colonised country, shackled unwillingly to its Protestant neighbour: and that it would be the only corner of Europe where the wounds of the Reformation were still bleeding in the twenty-first century.

The reasons for this odd combination of military victory and religious defeat are hotly disputed. Clearly the two are connected. Once Protestantism became the religion of colonisation and Catholicism that of resistance, the Reformation task became dauntingly difficult. Yet it is also clear that a full-scale conquest of Ireland was never Elizabeth's ambition, and that she undertook it in the 1590s only with the greatest reluctance. Nor did she ever intend enforcing a religious revolution there. At the beginning of her reign, the earl of Sussex (a soldierly and unimaginative lord deputy whom she inherited from her sister) briskly ensured that the minimum of necessary changes were made: an Irish parliament in 1560 was coerced into enacting a religious settlement which echoed England's. Yet, following the example of Edward's reign, the Irish Act of Uniformity permitted the use of a Latin Prayer Book in Irish-speaking areas. Sussex regarded this as safer and more fitting than trying to produce a liturgy in the barbarous Irish tongue. In the event, the Latin Prayer Book printed in 1560 was based on the traditionalist 1549 text, not the new 1559 book. It was then widely used, not only among the Gaels, but among the Old English and even in the Pale. Elizabeth was content with this, being even less inclined to assault Catholicism in Ireland than in England.

However, the *laissez-faire* approach to Ireland which almost every English politician would have preferred now seemed impossible. The precarious peace which St Leger had conjured up in the 1540s was unravelling, and the feud between the Butlers and Geraldines was breaking out again. The attempt to repackage Gaelic chieftains as English lords was not working, and the O'Neills of Ulster were aligning themselves with the Geraldines. And Ireland could no longer be left to its quarrels, because of the danger of foreign, Catholic invasion. A degree of English overlordship, of the kind which St Leger had envisaged, was necessary. But this meant compelling the Gaels to recognise the rule of English law, which meant a general 'civilising' and settling project. In many English eyes, such a project implied spreading the Protestant gospel and the English language. It also meant confronting the brutally arbitrary rule of the Gaelic chiefs over their peoples, which English opinion increasingly (and with some reason) saw as bloodthirsty tyranny.

Lord Deputy Sussex was scarcely equipped for such a daunting task. His successor from 1565, Sir Henry Sidney, was an altogether subtler operator. Following the Welsh example, he began the process of creating English-style counties in Ireland. He also planned to establish proper land tenure for peasants, rather than leaving the Gaelic lands in the absolute control of their lords. Yet (inexplicably) the Gaelic lords themselves resisted efforts to civilise them along English lines, and the Dublin regime lacked the resources either to compel them or to buy them off. Always careful with her money, Elizabeth saw Irish projects as bottomless pits. Thus idealistic plans were floated, but not acted on for decades, if at all. An Irish university was proposed in 1570, but Trinity College, Dublin was established only in 1592. In 1564 the English Privy Council proposed translating the New Testament into Irish Gaelic; it was not done until 1607. The Irish Church itself was desperately poor. Only a hundred or so of the entire country's posts were wealthy enough to be able reliably to attract capable preachers. And English officials in Ireland struggling in the face of these difficulties found themselves receiving relentless sniping from London. The lord deputy of Ireland was, by definition, absent from England, and in Elizabethan politics, influence was measured by proximity to the queen. Dublin was a thankless posting, the only consolation being that Irish lords deputy attracted so much criticism that they tended not to hold office for long. If Sidney was unusual, it was in part because he did not regard his appointment as a punishment.

Under these circumstances, there was intense pressure on lords deputy to find quick, cheap and eye-catching solutions. Generally, these were of two kinds. The first was plantation, a scheme whose universal benefits were obvious to almost every English observer. Just as the Romans had civilised barbarians by establishing Roman settlements in their midst, so, it was hoped, colonies of English immigrants in Ireland might spread civility and godliness among the Irish. At the least, they would establish steadings of loyal subjects across the country, helping to break up and contain the Gaelic lordships. The particular appeal of this policy was that it was almost free. The settlers themselves would cover their own costs, in return for grants of land (confiscated from rebellious Gaelic lords). The idea had first been tried on any scale under Mary, and became a staple of English policy thereafter. Settlers were frustratingly slow to come, but significant plantations were established in Munster, in the south-west, under Elizabeth. The great hope was to plant the Gaelic heartland of Ulster, but this was not yet possible. For, of course, plantation created more problems than it solved. The Gaels naturally loathed the intruders. The Old English, too, despised the 'New English' as *arrivistes* and, increasingly, as heretics; and were despised in their turn as deracinated degenerates.

The plantations fed directly into the other policy most readily adopted by the Elizabethan governors of Ireland: war. This was hardly cheap, but it did hold out the elusive possibility of victory. In any case, attacks against plantations, and the regime's inability to distribute significant patronage to either Old English or Gaelic elites, provoked violence whether the regime wanted it or not. Worse, the cheapest way of fighting in Ireland was usually the most brutal – using, as one lord deputy put it, Irish methods. This meant indiscriminate reprisals against whole clans, and the destruction of crops so as to use hunger as a weapon. Since the English had (in extremis) access to larger forces and heavier weapons than any of their Irish opponents, they could usually secure short-term success in such conflicts, and in the 1570s and 1580s successive governors won several such empty victories. Yet their brutal methods hardly settled the country. Nor did the arrival of fresh English plantations in the recently devastated lands. Sir John Perrot, governor in the mid-1580s, tried to break this cycle by introducing permanent garrisons into the interior. Elizabeth vetoed the project as too expensive.

From the point of view of the Protestant hopes, it was the loss of the Old English elites which was most damaging. At mid-century, they – like their Welsh counterparts – were still eminently persuadable, not least because they were deeply committed to English rule. Yet Elizabeth's regime made no systematic attempt to persuade them. They were allowed to continue using a Latin service which was not terribly different from the old Mass, and no attempt was made to enforce the recusancy laws even within the Pale. Cranmer's short-lived effort to place able English preachers in Irish bishoprics was not repeated. What England did send was a new governing elite. The New English marginalised the Old English, trampled what they saw as their rights as Englishmen, and treated their parliament with increasing contempt. If there was a turning point, it was the second rebellion of James Fitzmaurice Fitzgerald, a Geraldine standard-bearer, in 1579. Fitzmaurice (like every Irish rebel from 1534 onwards) wrapped himself in the Catholic cause, but in 1579, for the first time, not only some Old English lords but some of the gentry of the Pale itself rallied to him. The brutal suppression of the rising did not solve the problem. By the mid-1580s some Old English members of the Irish Parliament were openly declaring their allegiance to Rome. Before long Ireland was to become fruitful ground for Jesuits and other Catholic missionaries from the Continent. In 1592, the same year that Trinity College was founded in Dublin, a college for Irish Catholic missionaries was established in Salamanca. Catholic bishops began to reappear alongside the official, Protestant ones. The established Church of Ireland was turning inwards, becoming a Protestant sect most of whose ministers no longer even aspired to convert their Catholic neighbours. With hindsight, the battle for Ireland's soul was already over.

Ireland, England and Essex: the crisis of the 1590s

In the 1590s, the sequence of bloody and inconclusive wars across Ireland reached a perhaps inevitable crescendo. The alienation of the Gaels and (increasingly) the Old English was eased by a newly robust Catholic identity, and given a new importance by the outbreak of war between England and Spain in 1585. When it came, the rebellion centred on Hugh O'Neill, earl of Tyrone but also (in aspiration) *the* O'Neill, restorer of Ulster, and even Ireland's High King. His achievement was to negotiate an alliance with the O'Neills' ancient rivals, the O'Donnells, in 1592, brokered in part by the re-established Catholic bishops. The rebellion gathered pace only slowly. O'Neill carefully played both sides, building his strength while remaining publicly loyal to Elizabeth. The open breach came in 1595, when O'Neill put himself at the head of rebel forces and asked Philip II of Spain to invade Ireland, offering him the Irish crown.

The result was a rising far more comprehensive than any Tudor Ireland had yet seen. New English planters were massacred. Large numbers of the Old English joined the rising. On 14 August 1598, O'Neill won a pitched battle at Yellow Ford in Armagh: Henry Bagenal, the marshal of the English army in Ireland, was killed, and with him nearly half of his army of 4000. English control now scarcely extended beyond the walls of Dublin. The only consolation for England was that Spain had not yet taken serious advantage of the crisis. It was not only the English who tended to forget Ireland until it was too late.

The disaster of 1598, however, pushed Ireland to the top of England's political agenda for the first time in over a century. As such, Ireland became enmeshed in the suddenly turbulent politics of Elizabeth's court. The hard years of the 1590s – war, taxes, plague, poor harvests – had taken their toll on England's political stability. So too had the rise of the extraordinary, mercurial figure of Robert Devereux, earl of Essex. Essex was and remains a magnetic figure, alternately attracting and repelling. Like Edward Seymour half a century earlier, Essex bypassed the normal political channels to appeal to a wider public following – in part because those normal channels were closed to him. The ageing William Cecil, and his increasingly powerful son Robert, dominated the Elizabethan regime, and Essex saw himself and his band of adherents as an opposition to this establishment. Yet at the heart of Essex's power was his influence over the queen. Elizabeth had long built her court life around an elaborate charade that all her courtiers were in love with her, a charade which became increasingly grotesque. Essex was the stepson of the earl of Leicester, to whom the queen had been genuinely close. Yet part of Essex's appeal was that, at times, he refused to play this game and to give Elizabeth the adulation she demanded; while at others, he was her most devoted admirer. She was genuinely drawn to him. Essex, like the ancient nobility of England in whose image he cast himself, was a soldier with a thirst for chivalric honour – in the name of his queen, and if necessary despite her, for in such matters he believed men should not be ruled by women. His relentless advocacy of spectacular military adventures in the Spanish war had set him against the Cecils' caution, although his one sole command – in 1597 – had been a fiasco. When the Irish crisis peaked, and a major military expedition became necessary, it was no surprise that Essex (whose father had once served as lord deputy) should be placed in charge. Yet Essex's power in England was already on the wane. His haughtiness was alienating friends as well as enemies. Even the queen was no longer as susceptible to his charms as once she had been. The Irish expedition therefore became crucial not merely for the future of the Tudor regime but (which weighed more heavily on his mind) for the future of the earl of Essex.

In April 1599, he landed in Dublin with an army some 17,000 strong. He had hoped to crush O'Neill at once in his Ulster heartland, but soon thought better of it – a prudent decision, but coming from such an enthusiastic warmonger it looked like either treachery or cowardice. His numerous English enemies readily whispered such things. He was painfully aware of this, and through the summer the necessity of a swift return to England, by virtually any means necessary, preyed increasingly on him. He even contemplated taking some of his army back with him, to crush his enemies at home by force. Militarily, the summer was not wholly wasted. Essex's forces secured Munster, in the south, so forestalling any threatened invasion from Spain. Yet O'Neill's power-base was untouched, and early skirmishes reinforced Essex's conclusion that he did not have the strength to defeat the rebels. When he finally did march against them, at Elizabeth's direct order, the campaign ended not in a battle but in a parley. Essex and O'Neill met at a ford on the river Lagan, both men riding their horses belly-deep into the water. Their conversation, which no-one overheard, lasted half an hour. A truce was agreed. What the terms were remain unclear, although O'Neill later claimed that Essex had almost agreed to join him in rebellion.

In any case, the agreement secured what Essex now wanted above all: a chance to return to England. He was home three weeks after that meeting, against Elizabeth's explicit instruction that he was to stay in Ireland. It was too late. He met Elizabeth on the day of his return, famously bursting into her chambers before she was fully dressed. They met more decorously a few hours later; but he was promptly imprisoned and never saw her again. Over the following months he was stripped of most of his offices and dignities. The end of his story is a sorry farce. Weighed down by now-unpayable debts, convinced that his political enemies were secretly in the pay of Spain, and still confident of his popularity on the streets of London, he gambled as Edward Seymour had gambled fifty years earlier. He sought help in his planned rebellion against the Cecils from all sides, including James VI of Scotland and O'Neill himself. No help was forthcoming. An attempt to arrest him panicked him and a few hundred followers into action. On 8 February 1601 they marched on the City of London, lightly armed, hoping to rally Londoners to his cause. Instead, the City was held against them. A fraction of them fought their way back to Essex's own London house, and the earl surrendered that evening. He was beheaded less than three weeks later, having made an abject confession of his errors and styled himself to die a model pious death. He was the last victim of the Tudor blood sport of high politics.

Ireland, meanwhile, was in O'Neill's hands. Following Essex's with-drawal, O'Neill offered terms, accepting a vague English overlordship over the island while asserting his own effective control. For a time there seemed little alternative. The Dublin regime was crumbling, and only a rump of Essex's grand army remained. The Catholic missionary effort was giving backbone to the rebellion. In 1600 Pope Clement VIII offered an indulgence to those who fought as crusaders in Ireland. Instead, the English regime now finally committed itself to the grinding, expensive, relentless war which Essex had been unwilling to contemplate. His succes-sor, Lord Mountjoy, a cautious and ruthless soldier, now proceeded sys-tematically to roll the rebels back through 1600 and 1601. The deliberate destruction of crops, on a scale not before seen, was his key weapon.

The decisive confrontation came in 1601, courtesy, ironically enough, of the Spanish. A force of over 3000 Spaniards landed at Kinsale, on the south coast, in September. It was by far the largest Spanish intervention in Ireland, yet almost as far away from O'Neill's base as was possible. Mountjoy besieged the invaders, luring O'Neill to march south to inter-vene. This finally gave Mountjoy a chance to fight a decisive battle on his own terms, at Kinsale on 24 December 1601. O'Neill was routed while the Spaniards remained bottled up. Mountjoy spent 1602 pressing home his advantage mercilessly within Ulster. O'Neill himself finally surrendered in 1603, before he heard the news that Queen Elizabeth had died a week before.

Thus the so-called Nine Years' War ended in genuine English conquest, and devastation, of Gaelic Ireland. Much of Ulster was laid waste, and the ground prepared for systematic plantation by both the English and the Scottish subjects of the new King James: planters who would eventually turn Ulster into Ireland's Protestant heartland. But the conquest also ensured that Catholicism would endure, as the one form of systematic resistance which was still possible, and would become woven into both the Gaelic and the Old English identities.

The failure of the Irish Reformation has been much discussed. Once seen as inevitable in an island whose very soil was Catholic, it now appears a much more contingent and perplexing business. At mid-century, the possibilities for a mass Reformation, or at least for a genuine elite-led Reformation, were real – as Bale's experience with the Old English, and Argyll and Carswell's Gaelic mission, show. In the normal course of events one would have expected the elites, Old English and even Gaelic, to adapt to the new settlement with varying degrees of conviction and enthusiasm. The problem was that, as two recent scholars of the subject put it, 'conquest coincided with religious Reformation and resulted in antagonising virtually all of the local elites, both Gaelic and old English.'[9] Yet it was not a coincidence. It was because of the European Reformation that the English regime had finally roused itself to attempt the military conquest of Ireland, for in the era of the wars of religion the island presented an unprecedented military threat to England. One of the ironies of this episode is that England could secure its immediate safety only by sacrificing its long-term objectives – to say nothing of the lives of tens of thousands of the queen's subjects.

The Irish debacle is more than a sour afterword to the story of the British Reformations. As is often the case with English governments, policy towards Ireland places the whole Elizabethan regime in a different and less flattering light. If the Elizabethan regime's characteristic caution and thrift proved (more or less) successful in England, it was a blood-soaked failure in Ireland. A bolder, more strategic, more imaginative and more generous engagement with the island in the 1560s and 1570s – an engagement which genuinely recognised its different political culture, and tried to work with it – might have secured both a viable Irish state and a viable Irish Protestant Church. Yet such an engagement was never realistically possible. It is not simply that Ireland was, as ever, an afterthought for Elizabeth's regime, a problem to be wished away rather than a responsibility to be shouldered or an opportunity to be grasped. The damp squib of the Irish Reformation, like the faltering progress of the Welsh Reformation, demonstrates that for the English, nationalist prejudices routinely trumped religious ideals. Where religious reform and state-building along Anglocentric lines could go together, they would. Where they appeared to pull in different directions, as in Ireland, the priority was unpleasantly clear. We are forced to conclude that the central story of the Tudor realms was the formation of states, not the Reformation of Churches.

Notes

1 One mark of the distinctiveness of Welsh society was its different pattern of naming, which used patronymics (*ap* meaning 'son of') rather than surnames.

2 J. Gwynfor Jones, *Early Modern Wales* (1994), p. 60.

3 Thomas Becon, *The iewell of ioye* (1550), sigs. B7v, C4v.

4 William Tyndale (ed.), *The examinacion of master William Thorpe* (1530), sig. A2v.

5 British Library, Cotton MS Cleopatra E.iv, ff. 142r, 316r.

6 John Bale, *The vocacyon of Iohan Bale to the bishoprick of Ossorie* (1553), esp. ff. 19r, 28v-29r.

7 Philip Jenkins, 'The Anglican Church and the unity of Britain: the Welsh experience, 1560–1714' in Steven Ellis and Sarah Barber (eds), *Conquest and Union: Fashioning a British State, 1485–1725* (1995), p. 117.

8 Jane Dawson, 'Calvinism and the Gaidhealtachd in Scotland' in Andrew Pettegree et al. (eds), *Calvinism in Europe 1540–1620* (1994), p. 232.

9 Karl S. Bottigheimer and Ute Lotz-Heumann, 'The Irish Reformation in European perspective', *Archiv für Reformationsgeschichte*, vol. 89 (1998), p. 281.

Electing a Monarch, 1603

Elizabeth Tudor died in the early hours of 24 March 1603, after a long and bitterly fought battle with the cabal of illnesses that conspired against her. It was the inevitable crisis for which her subjects had been bracing themselves for more than forty years. The scenario had been imagined constantly, and dozens of plans laid for dealing with it. All of the long reign's discussion of elective monarchy, by both Catholics and Protestants, had led up to this moment.

When it finally came, it turned out that the decision made itself. Elizabeth's successor would be King James VI of Scots, son of the woman whom the entire English political establishment had spent thirty years trying to exclude, and whose death it had at length procured. James was an adult male, he was a Protestant (indeed, a learned one), he was a demonstrably competent ruler and he had a quiverful of children. Along with the legitimacy of his hereditary claim, this was an unbeatable combination. Unlike Henry VII, the last founder of a new English dynasty, James had no need to pretend to owe his throne to 'many' claims. He was Henry VII's most senior living descendant, and that sufficed. The queen was dead; long live the king.

And yet, the new king was 400 miles away. A few hours after Elizabeth's death, a small gathering met at Whitehall: her Privy Council, along with others of the high nobility. These were the men who had governed England and Wales, and conquered Ireland, on the queen's behalf. But in law, her Council no longer existed once her death had dissolved it. The meeting might have been awkward. Some of the councillors did not hold noble titles, and so might be thought to have no natural claim to be the governors of the realm. (This group included Robert Cecil, the principal secretary, whose political dominance had been unchallenged since the earl of Essex's fall.) According to one of those present, these men offered to stand down, giving precedence to the nobility – even to those who had not been members of Elizabeth's Council. The nobility were, after all, the ancient electorate of England's monarchy. The offer was a brief glimpse back into the fifteenth century.

But the noblemen demurred. Elizabeth's councillors, they insisted, should continue to sit in their places, 'in respect of their former authority', and so the Council convened itself as if its dead mistress still lived. If Elizabethan England had mutated from an elective monarchy to a monarchical republic, this was that republic's 'last hurrah'.[1] The Council now solemnly discussed the succession. They heard a report of the queen's dying wishes, discussed the claims of various candidates, and at length concluded that James Stuart was now indeed their king. It was a formality, of course. Cecil had already sent word to Edinburgh. Yet the Canute-like election which took place that morning in Whitehall has its own importance.

When the first Tudor had seized power in 1485, England was a *de facto* elective monarchy. When the last Tudor died, was it one still? The bedrock of James VI's claim to the English throne was inheritance. And the days of rebellions led by proud noblemen were over – the duke of Buckingham's fate in 1521 should have made that plain, and the farce of Essex's rebellion in 1601 sealed the matter for good. But 1603 was not a simple triumph of dynasticism. The new king was able to inherit his crown because the political nation elected to let him do so. Such elections no longer took place on the battlefield, but in the Council chamber. The old nobility who would once have been the king's rivals deferred helplessly to lowborn technocrats such as Cecil. And the election took place outside the chamber, too, in the wider political nation which the Tudors' turmoils had dragged into being: in the House of Commons, among the gentry and the professions, and among the book-reading, sermon-gadding and theatre-going public. The appearance of dynastic stability in 1603 was deceptive. James, sensibly, never entirely believed it. (His son Charles did, with ghastly consequences.)

Why this change? In a word: religion. Henry VII and (initially) Henry VIII did an impressive job of building dynastic stability in England. This collapsed, not principally because Henry VIII lacked an ideal heir, but because he took his kingdom into schism and then insisted on maintaining that schism as a matter of conscience. The unintended consequences of this extraordinary act of will reverberated for the rest of the century, amplified by a series of dynastic accidents: Edward VI's death, Mary's childlessness, and the weirdly parallel careers of Elizabeth Tudor and Mary Stewart. At

each turn, the Tudors' subjects were faced with political choices, opportunities and nightmares which no-one in England had confronted for a
thousand years. As the whole country's religious life came to hang on it,
the succession became too important to abandon to the unpredictable
twists of dynastic fate. Edward VI tried to rig the succession; Mary surely
contemplated doing so; both were overruled by their dead father's rigging,
a scheme which itself owed very little to dynastic legitimacy as such. And
succession-rigging schemes on all sides consumed Elizabethan politics.

By 1603, England had been bent out of dynastic shape for so long
that it had turned into something new. James recognised the most striking
novelty in his own royal style: he would be king of Great Britain, not
of England and Scotland, although that revolution bit much deeper in his
home country. (His third kingdom, Ireland, was yoked unhappily to the
others.) England, like his other realms, had novel, deep and proliferating
religious divisions. It was a country where due process of law had become
one of the few fixed points of politics, even while the law itself changed
as never before. It was a godly commonwealth, a kingdom of heretics,
a monarchical republic. It was simultaneously an ancient realm and a new
polity, abuzz with religious energy and intellectual excitement, fearful,
grasping, murderous, idealistic and very vulnerable. This was what the
short-lived Tudor dynasty had done, despite themselves, to Britain and
Ireland. They would not quickly be forgotten.

Note

1 Patrick Collinson, 'Afterword', in John F. McDiarmid (ed.), *The Monarchical Republic of Early Modern England* (2007), p. 257.

Select Bibliography

Numerous textbooks survey sixteenth-century Britain, although few embrace the whole archipelago. For England, the standard political history remains John Guy, *Tudor England* (1988). A beautifully written recent addition to the canon is Susan Brigden, *New Worlds, Lost Worlds* (2000), which covers England and Ireland. Patrick Collinson (ed.), *The Sixteenth Century* (2002) is an invaluable collection of essays, chiefly but not exclusively on England. Richard Rex, *The Tudors* (2003) provides an engaging set of political biographies.

For Scotland, the new standard is set by Jane Dawson, *Scotland Re-Formed* (2007); Jenny Wormald, *Court, Kirk and Community* (1991) remains excellent, and takes the story up to 1625.

The best survey of the Reformations across both islands is Felicity Heal, *Reformation in Britain and Ireland* (2003). W. Ian P. Hazlett, *The Reformation in Britain and Ireland* (2003) is a stimulating extended essay on the subject.

On the English Reformation, Peter Marshall, *Reformation England 1480–1642* (2003) provides a summary of the vast scholarship. Christopher Haigh, *English Reformations* (1993) is a lively, polemical narrative of events; A. G. Dickens, *The English Reformation* (2nd edition, 1989) is now very dated, but remains valuable. Patrick Collinson's essay 'England', in Bob Scribner, Roy Porter and Mikuláš Teich (eds), *The Reformation in National Context* (1994), is one of the most stimulating short introductions to the topic. Norman Jones, *The English Reformation: Religion and Cultural Adaptation* (2002) is a splendid discussion of what the Reformation meant to those who lived through it. There are also two valuable anthologies of essays: Christopher Haigh (ed.), *The English Reformation Revised* (1987), and Peter Marshall (ed.), *The Impact of the English Reformation* (1997). Anthony Fletcher and Diarmaid MacCulloch, *Tudor Rebellions* (5th edition, 2004) is a much-updated classic introduction to its subject.

For the Scottish Reformation, we are still dependent on two older surveys: Gordon Donaldson, *The Scottish Reformation* (1960), which first tried to break away from Presbyterian triumphalism, and Ian Cowan, *The Scottish Reformation* (1982), which attempts to take full account of local variation. David McRoberts (ed.), *Essays on the Scottish Reformation* (1962) gives a Catholic perspective.

On almost every subject, the *Oxford Dictionary of National Biography* is an invaluable reference.

Chapter 1

On everyday life, see Alison Rowlands, 'The conditions of life for the masses' in Euan Cameron (ed.), *Early Modern Europe* (1999); and C. G. A. Clay, *Economic Expansion and Social Change: England 1500–1700* (1984). On popular culture, see Peter Burke's seminal *Popular Culture in Early Modern Europe* (1978).

The best guide to pre-Reformation English religion is Eamon Duffy's monumental *The Stripping of the Altars* (1992), part I. Robert Swanson, *Church and Society in Late Medieval England* (1989) is a more down-to-earth account. The Scottish dimension is summarised in Alec Ryrie, *The Origins of the Scottish Reformation* (2006), Chapter 1. For particular aspects of pre-Reformation religion, see Susan Wabuda, *Preaching during the English Reformation* (2002); Lee Palmer Wandel, *The Eucharist in the Reformation* (2006); and Clive Burgess, ' "A fond thing vainly invented": an essay on Purgatory and pious motive in late medieval England' in Susan J. Wright (ed.), *Parish, Church and People: Local studies in lay religion 1350–1750* (1988).

On Lollardy, the best study is Anne Hudson, *The Premature Reformation* (1988); Richard Rex, *The Lollards* (2002) is far more sceptical of Lollardy's significance. On anticlericalism, all recent discussion starts from Christopher Haigh, 'Anticlericalism and the English Reformation' in his *The English Reformation Revised* (1987).

Chapter 2

On English political structures, see Steven Gunn, *Early Tudor Government, 1485–1558* (1995). On Scotland, see Jenny Wormald, *Court, Kirk and Community* (1991).

On Henry VII, see S. B. Chrimes, *Henry VII* (1972) and Alexander Grant, *Henry VII* (1985). Michael Bennett, *Lambert Simnel and the Battle of Stoke* (1987) is the best (indeed, only) book-length treatment of its subject; Ann Wroe, *Perkin: a Story of Deception* (2003) is a classy populist account. On Henry's quest for legitimacy, see Sydney Anglo, *Spectacle, Pageantry and Early Tudor Policy* (2nd edition, 1997). On Scotland, Norman MacDougall, *James IV* (1997) dominates the field.

Chapter 3

The literature on the Renaissance is vast and relatively inaccessible. Charles Nauert, *Humanism and the Culture of Renaissance Europe* (1995) is a strong survey. Erasmus' vast corpus is easily approached in John C. Olin (ed.), *Christian Humanism and the Reformation* (1975), which has a valuable introduction. The specifically English context is well addressed in Maria Dowling, *Humanism in the Age of Henry VIII* (1986) and Alastair Fox and John Guy, *Reassessing the Henrician Age: Humanism, Politics and Reform 1500–1550* (1986). For Scotland, see A. A. MacDonald, Michael Lynch and Ian B. Cowan (eds), *The Renaissance in Scotland* (1994), and Carol Edington, *Court and Culture in Renaissance Scotland: Sir David Lindsay of the Mount* (1994). For the supposed link between Renaissance and Reformation, Richard Rex, 'The role of English humanists in the Reformation up to 1559' in N. Scott Amos *et al.* (eds), *The Education of a Christian Society* (1999) is invaluable.

On printing, Elizabeth Eisenstein, *The Printing Press as an Agent of Change* (1979) – or the abridged version, *The Printing Revolution in Early Modern Europe* (1983) – remains the starting point. David D'Avray, 'Printing, mass communication and religious reformation' in Julia Crick and Alexandra Walsham (eds), *The Uses of Script and Print* (2004) downplays print's significance from a medievalist's perspective. Andrew Pettegree, *Reformation and the Culture of Persuasion* (2005) is a *tour de force* which places print in several new contexts.

Chapter 4

Henry VIII's early career is best summarised in two fat biographies: J. J. Scarisbrick, *Henry VIII* (1968) and Peter Gwyn, *The King's Cardinal: the rise and fall of Thomas Wolsey* (1990). On his personal religion, see George W. Bernard, 'The piety of Henry VIII' in N. Scott Amos *et al.* (eds), *The Education of a Christian Society* (1999).

For the early Reformation and its ideas, see – amongst innumerable books – Diarmaid MacCulloch, *Reformation* (2003) and Euan Cameron,

The European Reformation (1991). The early impact of the Reformation in England is discussed in, amongst others, Susan Brigden, *London and the Reformation* (1989); William Clebsch, *England's Earliest Protestants* (1964) – still useful, although much of it has been questioned; Carl R. Trueman, *Luther's Legacy: Salvation and English reformers, 1525–1556* (1994) – which concentrates on theology; and Richard Rex, 'The early impact of Reformation theology at Cambridge University, 1521–1547' in *Reformation and Renaissance Review*, vol. 2 (1999). Robert J. Knecht, 'The early Reformation in England and France: a comparison' in *History*, vol. 57 (1972), pp. 1–16, provides a valuable comparative perspective. Anti-heresy policy is discussed in two key articles by Craig D'Alton: 'The suppression of Lutheran heretics in England, 1526–29' in *Journal of Ecclesiastical History*, vol. 54 (2003), pp. 228–53; and 'Cuthbert Tunstal and heresy in Essex and London, 1528' in *Albion*, vol. 35 (2003), pp. 210–28. On Scotland, see Alec Ryrie, *The Origins of the Scottish Reformation* (2006), Chapter 2; and Jamie Cameron, *James V* (1998).

Chapter 5

The literature on the Henrician Reformation is vast. A few key biographies are, once again, J. J. Scarisbrick, *Henry VIII* (1968); Diarmaid MacCulloch, *Thomas Cranmer: a life* (1996); and Eric Ives, *The Life and Death of Anne Boleyn* (2004). Geoffrey Elton thought that it would be impossible to write a biography of Thomas Cromwell, so no-one has dared try: Elton's own *The Tudor Revolution in Government* (1949), *Reform and Renewal* (1973) and above all his magisterial *Policy and Police* (1971) do the job.

Richard Rex, *Henry VIII and the English Reformation* (2nd edition, 2006) is an excellent analytical introduction. The nature of Henry's policy has been widely disputed: George W. Bernard, *The King's Reformation* (2005) has proved controversial. For more measured views, see Richard Rex, 'The crisis of obedience: God's Word and Henry's Reformation', in *Historical Journal*, vol. 39 (1996), pp. 863–94; Alec Ryrie, 'Divine kingship and royal theology in Henry VIII's Reformation' in *Reformation*, vol. 7 (2002); and Diarmaid MacCulloch, 'Henry VIII and the reform of the Church' in his *The Reign of Henry VIII: Politics, policy and piety* (1995). The foreign-policy dimension of the Reformation is well addressed in Rory McEntegart, *Henry VIII, the League of Schmalkalden and the English Reformation* (2002). The parliamentary side is covered by Stanford Lehmberg's authoritative *The Reformation Parliament* (1970).

Modern study of the impact of Henry's Reformation begins with J. J. Scarisbrick's bleak *The Reformation and the English People* (1984), a view challenged most recently in Ethan Shagan, *Popular Politics and the English Reformation* (2002). Peter Marshall, *Religious Identities in Henry VIII's England* (2006) is an invaluable collection of essays on the subject. Alec Ryrie, 'Counting sheep, counting shepherds: the problem of allegiance in the English Reformation' in Peter Marshall and Alec Ryrie (eds), *The Beginnings of English Protestantism* (2002) assesses the scale of Henrician Protestantism, and Alec Ryrie, *The Gospel and Henry VIII* (2003) examines that movement's nature. Susan Brigden, *London and the Reformation* (1989) is also invaluable.

Chapter 6

The most detailed reference work on Edward VI's reign is W. K. Jordan's now-dated two-volume study: *Edward VI: the Young King* (1968) and *Edward VI: the Threshold of Power* (1970). Jennifer Loach's *Edward VI* (1999) is a more recent biography.

Recent work on the reign is dominated by Diarmaid MacCulloch's *Tudor Church Militant: Edward VI and the Protestant Reformation* (1999: published in North America as *The Boy King*); see also his *Thomas Cranmer: a life* (1996). The reign's politics are analysed in Stephen Alford, *Kingship and Politics in the Reign of Edward VI* (2002). Catharine Davies, *A Religion of the Word: the defence of the reformation in the reign of Edward VI* (2002) surveys Protestant writing from the reign, and Andrew Pettegree, 'Printing and the Reformation: the English exception' in Peter Marshall and Alec Ryrie (eds), *The Beginnings of English Protestantism* (2002) covers print culture. The 1549 rebellions are now examined in an authoritative study by Andy Wood, *The 1549 Rebellions and the Making of Early Modern England* (2007); Seymour's role in them is analysed in Ethan Shagan, 'Protector Somerset and the 1549 rebellions: new sources and new perspectives' in *English Historical Review*, vol. 114 (1999). Shagan also discusses the dilemmas of Edwardian Catholics in 'Confronting compromise: the schism and its legacy in mid-Tudor England' in his *Catholics and the Protestant Nation* (2005). The emergence of the metrical psalms is addressed in a marvellous new study: Beth Quitslund, *The Reformation in Rhyme* (2008).

Chapter 7

Mary's reign has seen a flurry of interest in recent years. Alongside the standard political biography (David Loades, *Mary Tudor* (1989)) and the splendid chapter on Mary in Eamon Duffy, *The Stripping of the Altars* (1992), we now have a very important collection of essays: Eamon Duffy and David Loades (eds), *The Church of Mary Tudor* (2006). William Wizeman, *The Theology and Spirituality of Mary Tudor's Church* (2006) has also moved the discussion on. T. F. Mayer's biography *Reginald Pole: Prince and Prophet* (2000) is comprehensive and controversial. Eamon Duffy, *Fires of Faith: Catholic England under Mary Tudor* (2009) promises to rewrite the subject for us.

Recent studies of Protestantism and persecution are dominated by Thomas S. Freeman. See, in particular, 'Publish and perish: the scribal culture of the Marian martyrs' in Julia Crick and Alexandra Walsham (eds), *The Uses of Script and Print* (2004); 'Dissenters from a dissenting Church: the challenge of the Freewillers 1550–1558' in Peter Marshall and Alec Ryrie (eds), *The Beginnings of English Protestantism* (2002); and his collection, edited with T. F. Mayer, *Martyrs and Martyrdom in England, c. 1400–1700* (2007). Andrew Pettegree, *Marian Protestantism* (1996) remains powerful. Brad Gregory, *Salvation at Stake* (1999) puts the persecution into European context.

Modern accounts of the Elizabethan settlement date from Norman Jones, *Faith by Statute: Parliament and the Settlement of Religion, 1559* (1982), and Winthrop S. Hudson, *The Cambridge Connection and the Elizabethan Settlement of 1559* (1980). Susan Doran, 'Elizabeth I's religion: the evidence of her letters', *Journal of Ecclesiastical History*, vol. 51 (2000), pp. 699–720 is the best recent treatment of this opaque subject. On the regime's policy, see Louise Campbell, 'A diagnosis of religious moderation: Matthew Parker and the 1559 Settlement' in Luc Racaut and Alec Ryrie (eds), *Moderate Voices in the European Reformation* (2005).

Chapter 8

The account of the Scottish Reformation to 1560 given here closely follows that in Alec Ryrie, *The Origins of the Scottish Reformation* (2006). Key recent publications in this relatively thin field include Marcus Merriman, *The Rough Wooings* (2000), a comprehensive study of the wars of the 1540s; Pamela Ritchie, *Mary of Guise in Scotland, 1548–60* (2002), which has rewritten our view of the 1550s; and Jane Dawson, *The Politics of Religion in the Age of Mary, Queen of Scots* (2002), a political biography of the earl of Argyll. Clare Kellar, *Scotland, England and the Reformation 1534–61* (2003) illuminates cross-border issues. Roger Mason (ed.), *John Knox and the British Reformations* (1998) is an invaluable collection. Local studies of the Scottish Reformation are led by Michael Lynch, *Edinburgh and the Reformation* (1981).

On Mary's personal rule, John Guy's *My Heart is My Own: the life of Mary Queen of Scots* (2004) is the most recent scholarly biography. Antonia Fraser, *Mary Queen of Scots* (1969) remains useful. Jenny Wormald, *Mary, Queen of Scots* (1987, 2nd edition, 2001) is a double-barrelled assault on the often-romanticised queen. Gordon Donaldson, *All the Queen's Men* (1983) moves beyond the merely biographical.

Chapter 9

Among the vast literature on Elizabethan politics, my personal selection would include the following. Patrick Collinson's life of Elizabeth in *The Oxford Dictionary of National Biography* is an excellent starting-point. Christopher Haigh, *Elizabeth I* (1988) is an analytical overview. Stephen Alford's *The Early Elizabethan Polity* (1998) has rewritten our understanding of the 1560s, and his new biography *Burghley: William Cecil at the Court of Elizabeth I* (2008) promises to do the same for Cecil's entire period of influence. The nature of the Elizabethan state is discussed in Patrick Collinson's seminal 'The Monarchical Republic of Queen Elizabeth I', *Bulletin of the John Rylands University Library of Manchester*, vol. 69 (1987), pp. 394–424. The debate is now well summed up in a collection of essays on that concept: John F. McDiarmid (ed.), *The Monarchical Republic of Early Modern England: Essays in response to Patrick Collinson* (2007). Natalie Mears, *Queenship and Political Discourse in the Elizabethan Realms* (2005), which concentrates on the Anjou match, has also helped us to iron out some confusions. The question of a 'public sphere' and of participatory politics is dealt with in Peter Lake and Steven Pincus (eds), *The Politics of the Public Sphere in Early Modern England* (2007); see also Lake and Michael Questier's *The Antichrist's Lewd Hat: Protestants, Papists and players in post-Reformation England* (2002) and Lake's ' "The monarchical republic of Elizabeth I" revisited (by its victims) as a conspiracy', in Barry Coward and Julian Swann (eds), *Conspiracies and Conspiracy Theory in Early Modern Europe* (2004). On foreign policy, see Paul Hammer, *Elizabeth's Wars* (2003).

On English Catholicism, see Christopher Haigh, *Reformation and Resistance in Tudor Lancashire* (1975); John Bossy, *The English Catholic*

Community (1975); and Michael Questier, *Conversion, Politics and Religion in England, 1580–1625* (1996). Alexandra Walsham's *Church Papists: Catholicism, conformity and confessional polemic in early modern England* (1993) is authoritative.

Chapter 10

Scottish Reformation studies are now all in debt to Margo Todd's magisterial *The Culture of Protestantism in Early Modern Scotland* (2002). Michael Graham, *The Uses of Reform* (1996) helpfully puts the Scottish material in international context. On the debates over Church government, see Alan R. MacDonald, *The Jacobean Kirk, 1567–1625: Sovereignty, policy and liturgy* (1998) and David Mullan, *Episcopacy in Scotland* (1986). Edinburgh is discussed in detail in Michael Lynch, *Edinburgh and the Reformation* (1981), Perth in Mary Verschuur, *Politics or Religion? The Reformation in Perth 1540–1570* (2006).

The study of English Puritanism is dominated by the work of Patrick Collinson. All of it is worth reading, but note particularly his *The Elizabethan Puritan Movement* (1967), his biography of *Archbishop Grindal* (1980), and two seminal sets of lectures: *The Religion of Protestants* (1982) and *The Birthpangs of Protestant England* (1988). A collection edited by Christopher Durston and Jacqueline Eales, *The Culture of English Puritanism* (1996) is also useful. On Protestant print culture, see Ian Green's *Print and Protestantism in Early Modern England* (2000), and Tessa Watt's *Cheap Print and Popular Piety* (1991). Peter Lake's *Moderate Puritans and the Elizabethan Church* (1982) has helped redefine the field. The problems raised by the concept of *adiaphora* are discussed in Ethan Shagan, 'The battle for indifference in Elizabethan England' in Luc Racaut and Alec Ryrie (eds), *Moderate Voices in the European Reformation* (2005). The impact of martyrology and of John Foxe's work has been much studied in recent years, the best introduction to this work being David Loades (ed.), *John Foxe and the English Reformation* (1997). On Richard Greenham, see Kenneth Parker and Eric Carlson, *'Practical Divinity': the works and life of Richard Greenham* (1998). Naming patterns are discussed in Will Coster, *Baptism and Spiritual Kinship in Early Modern England* (2002), Chapter 6.

For 'popular religion' in the wider sense, Christopher Marsh, *Popular Religion in Sixteenth-Century England* (1998) is an excellent introduction. Christopher Haigh, *The Plain Man's Pathways to Heaven* (2007), provides a subtler and much more detailed 'group portrait' than that sketched out here. The importance of 'Prayer Book Protestantism' is argued in Judith Maltby, *Prayer Book and People in Elizabethan and Early Stuart England* (1998). Alexandra Walsham's *Providence in Early Modern England* (1999) has reshaped the whole field. On witchcraft and magic, see James Sharpe, *Instruments of Darkness* (1996) and Keith Thomas' definitive *Religion and the Decline of Magic* (1971).

Chapter 11

Relations between the various British nations are discussed usefully in Brendan Bradshaw and John Morrill, *The British Problem 1534–1707* (1996). On questions of language and translation, see Felicity Heal, 'Mediating the Word: language and dialects in the British and Irish Reformations', *Journal of Ecclesiastical History*, vol. 56 (2005), pp. 261–86.

Studies of Tudor Wales are dominated by the work of the late Glanmor Williams: see especially his *Wales and the Reformation* (1997) and *Welsh Reformation Essays* (1967). J. Gwynfor Jones, *Early Modern Wales* (1994) is also invaluable.

The only significant work on the Reformation in Gaelic Scotland is that of Jane Dawson, notably her 'Calvinism and the Gaidhealtachd in Scotland' in Andrew Pettegree *et al.* (eds), *Calvinism in Europe 1540–1620* (1994). Her *The Politics of Religion in the Age of Mary, Queen of Scots* (2002) examines the Scottish role in Ireland (on which see also John Durkan, 'Robert Wauchope', *Innes Review*, vol. 1 (1950), pp. 48–65).

Recent debates on the Irish Reformation are well summed up in Karl S. Bottigheimer and Ute Lotz-Heumann, 'The Irish Reformation in European perspective', *Archiv für Reformationsgeschichte*, vol. 89 (1998), pp. 268–309. Steven Ellis, 'Economic problems of the church: Why the Reformation failed in Ireland', *Journal of Ecclesiastical History*, vol. 41 (1990), pp. 239–65 usefully compares the Irish and Welsh examples. Brendan Bradshaw's *The Dissolution of the Religious Orders in Ireland under Henry VIII* (1974) and Alan Ford's *The Protestant Reformation in Ireland 1590–1641* (1997) are key texts which bookend the period. The earl of Essex's career is discussed most recently in Paul Hammer, *The Polarisation of Elizabethan Politics* (1999).

Index